East, West and Centre
Reframing Post-1989 European Cinema

Edited by Michael Gott and Todd Herzog

EDINBURGH
University Press

© editorial matter and organisation Michael Gott and Todd Herzog, 2015, 2017
© the chapters their several authors, 2015, 2017

Edinburgh University Press Ltd
The Tun – Holyrood Road
12 (2f) Jackson's Entry
Edinburgh EH8 8PJ
www.euppublishing.com

First published in hardback by Edinburgh University Press 2015

Typeset in Monotype Ehrhardt by
Servis Filmsetting Ltd, Stockport, Cheshire

A CIP record for this book is available from the British Library

ISBN 978 0 7486 9415 0 (hardback)
ISBN 978 1 4744 2092 1 (paperback)
ISBN 978 0 7486 9416 7 (webready PDF)
ISBN 978 1 4744 2093 8 (epub)

The right of the contributors to be identified as authors of this work has been asserted in accordance with the Copyright, Designs and Patents Act 1988 and the Copyright and Related Rights Regulations 2003 (SI No. 2498).

Contents

List of Figures vi
Notes on Contributors vii
Acknowledgements xiii

    Introduction: East, West and Centre: 'Mapping Post-1989 European Cinema' 1
    Michael Gott and Todd Herzog

Part I Redrawing the Lines: De/Recentring Europe

1. The Berlin Wall Revisited: Reframing Historical Space between East and West in Cynthia Beatts's *Cycling the Frame* (1988), *The Invisible Frame* (2009) and Bartosz Konopka's *Rabbit à la Berlin* (2009) 23
 Jenny Stümer
2. Changing Sides: East/West Travesties in Lionel Baier's *Comme des voleurs (à l'est)* 37
 Kris Van Heuckelom
3. Dubbing and Doubling Over: The Disorientation of France in the Films of Michael Haneke and Krzysztof Kieślowski 51
 Alison Rice
4. Challenging the East–West Divide in Ulrich Seidl's *Import Export* (2007) 65
 Nikhil Sathe
5. Fatih Akın's Filmic Visions of a New Europe: Spatial and Aural Constructions of Europe in *Im Juli / In July* (2000) 79
 Berna Gueneli
6. *Salami Aleikum* – The 'Near East' Meets the 'Middle East' in Europe 95
 Alexandra Ludewig

7	Cinematic Fairy Tales of Female Mobility in Post-Wall Europe: Hanna v. Mona *Aga Skrodzka*	109

Part II Border Spaces, Eastern Margins and Eastern Markets: Belonging and the Road to/from Europe

8	Contemporary Bulgarian Cinema: From Allegorical Expressionism to Declined National Cinema *Temenuga Trifonova*	127
9	The Point of No Return: From Great Expectations to Great Desperation in New Romanian Cinema *Lucian Georgescu*	147
10	'Weirdness', Modernity and the Other Europe in *Attenberg* (2010, Athina Rachel Tsangari) *Jun Okada*	159
11	Lithuania Redirected: New Connections, Businesses and Lifestyles in Cinema since 2000 *Renata Šukaitytė*	175
12	Lessons of Neo-liberalism: Co-productions and the Changing Image of Estonian Cinema *Eva Näripea*	191
13	Decentring Europe from the Fringe: Reimagining Balkan Identities in the Films of the 1990s *Danica Jenkins and Kati Tonkin*	205

Part III Spectres of the East

14	Through the Lens of Black Humour: A Polish Adam in the Post-Wall World *Rimma Garn*	221
15	East Germany Revisited, Reimagined, Repositioned: Representing the GDR in Dominik Graf's *Der rote Kakadu* (2005) and Christian Petzold's *Barbara* (2012) *Nick Hodgin*	237
16	*Barluschke*: Towards an East–West Schizo-history *Kalani Michell*	253
17	The Limits of Nostalgia and (Trans)National Cinema in *Cum mi-am petrecut sfârşitul lumii* (2006) *Mihaela Petrescu*	267
18	The Ideal of Ararat: Friendship, Politics and National Origins in Robert Guédiguian's *Le Voyage en Arménie* *Joseph Mai*	279

Notes 293
Bibliography 311
Index 335

Figures

1.1	Nature *v.* concrete in *Cycling the Frame*	25
2.1	Lionel fantasises about California (and Poland)	40
3.1	*White:* Karol watches mutely as a bank employee destroys his card	58
4.1	Maria watches Olga at work	76
5.1	Daniel and Juli chart a course through Europe	81
6.1	Storytelling in *Salami Aleikum*	100
7.1	Saoirse Ronan in *Hanna*	114
7.2	Orsolya Törö-Illyés in *Bibliothèque Pascal*	122
8.1	*The Island:* Sophie learns that Daneel is from Bulgaria after they arrive there for a beach holiday	141
9.1	Nelu crosses the border in *Morgen*	156
11.1	Gamers taking risks in *Perpetuum Mobile*	181
12.1	*The Snow Queen*	201
13.1	*Underground:* 'drunkenness, madness and monstrosity' at the wedding of Blacky's son Jovan	214
14.1	Adam on the train	229
15.1	Barbara (Nina Hoss) moving forward but often looking backwards in *Barbara*	245
16.1	*Barluschke*, directed by Thomas Heise	263
17.1	An unlikely hero, Lali, makes history, and underscores cinema's fictional nature	274
18.1	Ararat: an ideal and spectral landscape	280

INTRODUCTION

East, West and Centre: 'Mapping Post-1989 European Cinema'

Michael Gott and Todd Herzog

Eastern and Western Europe Twenty-five Years after the Fall of the Wall

The fall of the Berlin Wall and the subsequent expansion of the European Union and creation of the Schengen Zone opened the gates for what have been termed 'new migrations' (Mazierska and Rascaroli, 140). By 1994, an estimated four million people had migrated across the newly opened borders – and this number does not even include the millions who fled war in the former Yugoslavia or the one million Poles who headed west in the three years that followed their nation's 2004 entry into the European Union (Castles and Miller, 116). Though political borders between Eastern and Western Europe have become much more open and fluid, mental borders still divide the continent along the old Cold War lines. Despite their newly gained access to Western Europe, 'Eastern' Europeans have been relegated at times to a second-class status in Western Europe, as the 'Polish Plumber' rhetoric so prevalent during the 2005 French referendum on the EU Constitution demonstrates (Raissiguier, Skrodzka 2011, Gott 2013c). As we approach the twenty-fifth anniversary of the fall of the Berlin Wall and an entire post-Wall generation has entered adulthood, it is an appropriate time to assess the ways in which notions of an Eastern and Western Europe still exist as well as the ways in which a new/old notion of Central Europe has re-entered public discourse and the popular imagination. More recently, factors such as the economic crisis in Europe have underscored increasingly visible north–south fault lines.

To pursue this investigation, this volume turns to European cinema which has been a vibrant space in which to understand and work through notions of and beyond national borders. The fact that a new journal, with the title *Studies in Eastern European Cinema*, was launched in 2010 demonstrates that more than twenty years after the fall of the Berlin Wall, the 'Eastern' label continues to be a valid paradigm. And given that a new journal with the title *Studies in Western European Cinema* would be inconceivable today indicates that the East remains in many ways Western Europe's 'other'. In one line of thinking, Western Europe is Europe, while Eastern Europe finds itself in uncertain ground that is not quite European. The East/West fault line, however, has been exerting enormous pressure on the political, geographical and cultural parameters of Europe and prompting an evaluation of what it means to be 'European'. These pressing questions are being worked out in the political and economic realms but also in the realm of culture. This volume situates itself at these constantly renegotiated borders between East and West, politics and culture, past and present, and asks what is East, what is West and what is Centre a quarter of a century after the (re)opening of the borders between Eastern and Western Europe?

In a special thematic issue of the *Journal of Cultural Geography*, entitled 'Twenty years after the Wall: geographical imaginaries of "Europe" during European Union enlargement', Sellar, Staddon and Young suggest that the term 'New Europe'

> itself highlights the willingness of former Eastern European governments and their publics to embrace a new, 'European' and capitalist identity to overcome the Cold War era distinction between 'East' and 'West' Europe. This gives rise to new cultural geographies emerging alongside the institutional and economic changes brought by EU enlargement. The process of imagining the 'New Europe' is an important rhetorical tool which is being used to sanction a new equilibrium and new power relations within Europe. (255)

The special issue proposes to answer a question based on a provocative premise: how do we define Europe when 'its original historico-geographical origins in the oppositions between East and West, between Capitalist and Communist, between Catholic/Protestant and Orthodox *have been largely if not completely erased*' (Sellar, Staddon and Young 255, our emphasis)? *East, West and Centre* does not aim to argue that the oppositions that date back to the very origins of the idea of Europe and, more recently, politically and geographically ordered the continent's post-World War II, twentieth-century experience have been completely or even largely erased. But they clearly have been altered. While the experience under Communism and the lingering imbalance/inequities within Europe – and European cinema – cannot be ignored, a quarter of a century has passed since the fall of the Iron Curtain and a decade after the first wave of former communist states in the Baltics and Central Europe joined the EU. This is therefore an opportune time to assess what European cinemas on both sides of the old divide have in common. Tim Bergfelder argues that explorations of contemporary European cinema must be predicated on the 'fluidity of identities' and the avoidance of 'containment' (329). This collection arises from the need to examine Europe and European cinema from a new vantage point, one that is outside the traditional parameters of academic discourse that have kept 'West' segregated from 'East' (and 'Central'). One can both acknowledge historical, cultural and economic distinctions within the current parameters of the EU and also explore the points of connection that bind nations and cultures on both sides of the convoluted East/West dividing line. The chapters in this volume attest to the increasingly uncertain and convoluted divisions between East and West, as well as the continuation of historical divisions between East and West.

Étienne Balibar has theorised that European citizenship is a 'citizenship of borders' (2003: 6), of which the old East/West divide is but one. We shall argue in this introduction that cinema is at the forefront of the mapping of the 'new cultural geographies' Sellar, Staddon and Young suggest are appearing in Europe (255). European cinema has increasingly crossed, and otherwise called into question, the borders and vestiges of borders that continue to divide the politics and economics of Europe – before, during and after the Cold War divided Europe politically. Alain Badiou has argued that the fall of the Berlin Wall was supposed to have ushered in a 'single world of freedom and democracy' (Badiou 2008: 38). Instead, he asserts that walls have simply shifted: rather than demarcating the boundary between East and West, walls divide 'the rich capitalist North from the poor and devastated South' (Badiou 2008: 38). Indeed, new fault lines have emerged, marking divisions within Europe and between Europe and the 'East' that lies beyond 'Eastern Europe'. The economic crisis and Eurozone meltdown has also thrust the divisions between southern and northern Europe into sharper relief. Much of the southern portion of 'Western Europe' is now looking, to German eyes in particular, considerably less (Western) European. Greek doubts about their nation's European-ness in the wake of the financial crisis have been theorised to be a driving force behind the films comprising a so-called New Greek Wave (which Jun Okada addresses in Chapter 10 of this volume) that has garnered considerable attention on festival circuits since 2009.

Turning to the divide between Europe and the less-developed world, migrants attempting to reach the continent from the 'Global South' – whether Africa or Asia – have been increasingly visible both in cinema and in public discourse. Eastern and Central European nations have, since 1989, also become destinations for migrants. While encounters between the 'two Easts' – one of Europe and one beyond – are still relatively rare in cinema, they serve to remind us of the relativity of the very notion of 'East' (see Chapter 2, Chapter 9 and, in particular, Chapter 6 by Alexandra Ludewig). Actual and cinematic migrants from Turkey, Iraq and other eastern points also find themselves in Eastern or Central Europe en route to points further west, as is the case in films such as *Výlet / Some Secrets* (Alice Nellis, 2002, Czech Republic/Slovakia), *Nulle part terre promise / Nowhere promised land* (Emanuel Finkiel, 2008, France) and *Kalandorok / Adventurers* (Béla Paczolay, 2008, Hungary). *Spare Parts / Rezervni deli* (Damjan Kozole, 2003, Slovenia) and *Indignados* (Tony Gatlif, 2012, France) place African migrants attempting to cross into Western Europe from the Balkans. The presence of migrants from the global south marks 'New Europe' as both a gateway to Western Europe and a reasonable facsimile of it, as the recurring trope of migrants being dropped off before the destination they paid to reach attests.

Among all the factors under consideration in the following chapters – from co-production practices to market transformations – migration has unquestionably had a singular impact on the 'centre' of Europe and is one of the most visible themes in European cinema since 1989. Berghahn and Sternberg observe that, as a consequence

> of proliferating migrations, European cultures and societies have witnessed a hitherto inconceivable diversification, fragmentation and hybridization. This is reflected in a growing number of films made by migrant and diasporic filmmakers, which challenge a traditional understanding of national identity and what it means to be European. (2)

New understandings and updated mappings of post-Berlin Wall Europe must involve not simply assessments of lateral East/West connections but require a broader, multidirectional analysis of the new borders, orientations, challenges and links that define the fluctuating geography of Europe. Just as the tragedies off the coast of Lampedusa in 2013 have had policy implications for all of the EU, from Italy to nations whose borders do not flank the Mediterranean directly, such as Germany, France – and French cinema – have witnessed a proliferation of clandestine migrants. On one level, this is nothing new. As a nation with a history of immigration on a large scale dating to the nineteenth century, France represents a European exception. The twenty-first century saw waves of immigrants arrive in France from Poland and Armenia as well as from Italy, Spain, Portugal and the former colonial empire. By 1991, one in four people residing in France was an immigrant or had immigrant parents or grandparents (Hargreaves, 6). One updated feature of post-1989 population shifts is the fact that these voyagers often do not intend to stay in France

Acknowledgements

Michael Gott and Todd Herzog would like to thank all the contributors, as well as the staff at Edinburgh University Press, particularly Gillian Leslie and Rebecca Mackenzie. Special thanks to Alexander Weil for editing assistance on several chapters.

Michael Gott and Todd Herzog would like to thank the Charles Phelps Taft Research Center at the University of Cincinnati for its support of a variety of research and scholarly endeavours related to this project. Michael Gott would also like to thank the Centers for European Studies and Russian, East European and Eurasian Studies at the University of Texas at Austin for similar assistance at an earlier stage. Appreciation is also due to Ewa Mazierska, Aga Skrodzka and Hana Pichova for their insight at various stages of this project.

Studies in 1999, is the immediate past Associate Dean (Education), and has also held the position of Academic Director of the faculty's Multimedia Centre. She started university at the RWTH Aachen, holds a PhD from The University of Queensland, a DPhil from LMU München and was awarded her *Venia Legendi* in 2009 [having completed her Habilitation (DPhil habil), the highest German post-doctoral qualification]. Her teaching and research in German Cultural Studies focus on issues of identity and '*Heimat*', and she has published extensively in both German and English on these topics, with her monograph *Screening Nostalgia. 100 Years of German Heimat Film* published in 2011.

Joseph Mai PhD is Associate Professor of French at Clemson University. He is the author of *Jean-Pierre and Luc Dardenne* (Urbana: University of Illinois Press), and of academic articles on Robert Bresson, Milan Kundera, and others. He is currently at work on a monograph devoted to Robert Guédiguian.

Kalani Michell is a PhD candidate in German Studies and Moving Image Studies at the University of Minnesota. Her dissertation, 'Accessibility: Expanding the Cinema of the 1960s/70s to Today', explores how cinema has expanded beyond the traditional space of the theatre, focusing on changing notions of accessibility during this time. She has published on installation art, video art and German cinema, and is currently writing an article about a computer game that restages the wait in line for a Marina Abramović exhibition at MoMA.

Eva Näripea PhD is Director of Film Archives at the National Archives of Estonia and senior researcher at the Estonian Academy of Arts. In 2011 she completed her PhD dissertation 'Estonian Cinescapes: Spaces, Places and Sites in Soviet Estonian Cinema (and Beyond)'. She co-edited *Via Transversa: Lost Cinema of the Former Eastern Bloc* (2008) with Andreas Trossek, and a special issue on Estonian cinema for *Kinokultura: New Russian* Cinema (2010) with Ewa Mazierska and Mari Laaniste. Her most recent co-operation is an edited volume, *Postcolonial Approaches to Eastern European Cinema: Portraying Neighbours on Screen*, with Ewa Mazierska and Lars Kristensen (forthcoming with I. B. Tauris).

Jun Okada PhD teaches film studies in the Department of English at the State University of New York, Geneseo. Having recently achieved tenure, she is completing the writing of her first book, *Making Asian American Film and Video: History, Institutions, Movements*, which is under contract at Rutgers University Press. Okada teaches a broad range of courses on film and issues of race/ethnicity and gender as well as those on transnationality, globalisation, and film theory. She currently lives in Rochester, New York, home of the George Eastman House International Museum of Photography and Film and has published in *Cinema Journal*, *Velvet Light Trap*, *Quarterly Review of Film and Video*, *Film Quarterly* and Journal of Asian American Studies.

Mihaela Petrescu PhD teaches German at the University of Pittsburgh. Her fields of concentration in both her research and teaching are the literature and film of the Weimar Republic, German cinema, and multiculturalism in Germany. Her research on vamps and jazz dancing in Weimar melodramas, male dance instructors during the Weimar Republic, satiric representations of Brigitte Helm and Marlene Dietrich, and pop-feminism and ethnicity in autobiographical writings of Turkish-German female authors has been published in journals such as *Seminar*, *New German Critique* and *Monatshefte* as well as in book chapters. Her most recent project investigates the relationship between gender and post-Communism in the *New Romanian Cinema*.

Alison Rice PhD is Associate Professor of French and Francophone literature and film at the University of Notre Dame. She has published a number of articles, interviews, and translations, as well as two books. *Time Signatures: Contextualizing Contemporary Francophone Autobiographical Writing from the Maghreb* (Lexington Books, 2006) closely examines the writing of Hélène Cixous, Assia Djebar, and Abdelkébir Khatibi. *Polygraphies: Francophone Women Writing Algeria*, recently published by the University of Virginia Press (2012), focuses on Maïssa Bey, Marie Cardinal, Hélène Cixous, Assia Djebar, Malika Mokeddem, Zahia Rahmani and Leïla Sebbar. Her current project, *Francophone Metronomes: Worldwide Women Writers in Paris*, is an in-depth study of women writers of French from around the world, complemented by a series of filmed interviews.

Nikhil Sathe PhD is Associate Professor of German at Ohio University. He has published articles on language pedagogy, German and Austrian literature, and on Austrian cinema since the 1990s, where his primary research focus and publication record has centred on the representation of Eastern Europe and Eastern Europeans in relation to Austria's different post-1989 national identity shifts.

NOTES ON CONTRIBUTORS

Aga Skrodzka PhD is Associate Professor of Film Studies in the English Department at Clemson University. She is the author of *Magic Realist Cinema in East Central Europe* (Edinburgh University Press, 2012). Her research focuses on the notion of European periphery and the alternative aesthetics used in cinema to communicate the sense of peripherality. Her next book-length project, entitled *Kinetic Bodies/Paralyzed Subjects*, addresses the figure of the Eastern European sex slave in recent films about human trafficking, with emphasis on mobility and labour. Both in research and in her teaching, she engages with transnational theory, film theory, feminist theory and critical race theory. She has published articles and book chapters on films by the masters of Polish cinema (Jan Jakub Kolski, Krzysztof Kieślowski, Walerian Borowczyk) but also on Hollywood *auteurs* – John Woo, Martin Scorsese and Michael Mann.

Jenny Stümer was born and raised in Berlin. She is currently a PhD candidate at the Department of Film, TV, and Media Studies at the University of Auckland. Her thesis is entitled *Facing the Wall: Screening through Alienation and Separation* and investigates the way in which political walls, both as metaphorical and material impositions of political conflict, ultimately mediate and thereby interrupt the narrative of the politics of division upon which they rest. Her research interests include visual politics, trauma and affect, as well as critical theory and psychoanalysis.

Renata Šukaitytė PhD is Associate Professor of Film Studies and Creative Industries at the Faculty of Communication, Vilnius University (Vilnius, Lithuania). She has carried out research into institutional and aesthetical discourses of new media art in the Baltic States, while her current research centres on the European film industry and national and transnational dimensions in contemporary Baltic film. She is the author of several articles and editor of Acta Academiae Artium Vilnensis volume entitled *Baltic Cinemas After the 1990's: Shifting (Hi)Stories and (Id) Entities* (2010), and co-editor with Christopher Hales of *The Garden of Digital Delights: Crossmedia Practices in Contemporary Art* (2012).

Kati Tonkin PhD is Associate Professor of German and European Studies at the University of Western Australia where she convenes the European Studies programme and teaches a unit on contemporary European cinema. She is currently preparing for publication articles on a Czech documentary and music in the films of Krzysztof Kieślowski.

Temenuga Trifonova PhD is Associate Professor of Cinema and Media Studies at York University in Toronto. She is the author of *The Image in French Philosophy* (2007) and the edited volume, *European Film Theory* (2008). Her articles have appeared in a number of scholarly, peer-reviewed journals, including *Cinema: Journal of Philosophy* and the *Moving Image, SubStance, Film and Philosophy, Space and Culture, The European Journal of American Culture, Studies in European Cinema, Rivista di Estetica, CTheory: Theory beyond the Codes, Cineaste, Studies in Eastern European Cinema, CineAction, Studies in Comics, Quarterly Journal of Film and Video, The Wallace Stevens Journal, Postmodern Culture, Scope, Kinema, Senses of Cinema, Interdisciplinary Literary Studies*, the *Routledge Encyclopedia of Film Theory*, and in several edited collections.

Kris Van Heuckelom PhD is Assistant Professor of Slavic and East European Studies at the University of Leuven (KU Leuven). He has previously served as Visiting Scholar in the Department of Slavic Languages and Literatures at the University of Chicago. His articles have appeared in *The Slavonic and East European Review, Image and Narrative*, and *Russian Literature*. He is co-editor, with Leen Engelen, of *European Cinema after the Wall* (Rowman and Littlefield, 2013).

on European models of the early Russian novelist, Mikhail Chulkov, and on Pushkin's parodying of Karamzin appeared in *Comparative Literature* and in *The International Journal of the Book*. The collection, *Eighteenth-Century Thing Theory in a Global Context*, with her chapter 'The Battle of the Books in Catherine the Great's Russia', was published in 2013 by Ashgate.

Nick Hodgin PhD is Lecturer in German at the University of Lancaster (United Kingdom). He has published widely on German film and German cultural studies, including *Screening the East. Heimat, Memory and Nostalgia in German Film since 1989* (Berghahn, 2011: 2013) and the co-edited volume on GDR culture, *The GDR Remembered: Representing the East German State since 1989* (Camden House, 2011). His current research includes projects on East German documentary film and international film history.

Lucian Georgescu PhD is Senior Lecturer in Screenwriting at the Romanian Theatre and Film University in Bucharest. He started his professional and academic careers soon after the Romanian Revolution. As a screenwriter, director and critic he has been an active participant in, and commentator on, the celebrated Romanian New Wave cinema movement which has earned accolades around the world. His research focuses on the road movie genre in its American and European iterations. Dr Georgescu is the author of a book on director, Jim Jarmusch, and director of the 2012 film *Tatăl fantomă / The Phantom Father*.

Berna Gueneli PhD is Assistant Professor of German studies at Grinnell College. She received her PhD at the University of Texas at Austin (2011). Her research interests comprise contemporary transnational cinema in a European context, German film history, Weimar and German exile cinema, film sound, and Turkish-German studies. She has published on sexualised ethnic masculinities. Currently, she is working on a monograph on Fatih Akın and contemporary European cinema.

Danica Jenkins is an Honors Graduate in European Studies at the University of Western Australia, and will embark on a PhD in 2014. She has published in the *Australian and New Zealand Journal of European Studies*, and her current research includes projects on modern Russian literature and transnational and Balkan film.

Alexandra Ludewig PhD is Professor of German Studies at the University of Western Australia. She was appointed Convenor of German

Notes on Contributors

The Editors

Michael Gott is Assistant Professor of French at the University of Cincinnati where he teaches courses in European Studies, Film and Media Studies, and French-language culture and cinema. He recently co-edited *Open Roads, Closed Borders: the Contemporary French-Language Road Movie* (Intellect, 2013) and has published articles and book chapters on French, Czech, Belgian and European cinema in journals such as *Studies in Eastern European Cinema*, *Contemporary French Civilization*, and *Transfers: An Interdisciplinary Journal of Mobility Studies*.

Todd Herzog is an Associate Professor, Head of German Studies and Director of the Film and Media Studies Program at the University of Cincinnati. He is co-editor of the *Journal of Austrian Studies*. His books include *Crime Stories* (Berghahn, 2009), *Rebirth of a Culture* (Berghahn, 2008, with Hillary Hope Herzog and Benjamin Lapp), and *A New Germany in a New Europe* (Routledge, 2001, with Sander Gilman). He is currently working on a book about art and surveillance, and editing volumes on German cinema to 1945 (Caboose Books) and German-language detective fiction (Camden House).

Contributors

Rimma Garn PhD is an Assistant Professor/Lecturer in Russian at the University of Utah. She holds an MFA in Fashion Design from Moscow Textile Institute and a PhD in Slavic Languages from UNC–Chapel Hill. Her primary research interests include auteurs, parody and satire, propaganda and censorship as they relate to Eastern European cinema, as well as intertextuality in Russian literature. She has written on Polish and Russian film directors such as Kieślowski and Riazanov. Her publications

INTRODUCTION 5

but are charting a course through Fortress Europe en route to Britain. Such (cinematic) migrants are typically Kurdish, as in *Welcome* (Philippe Lioret, France, 2009), *Eden à l'Ouest/Eden is West* (Costa-Gavras, France/Greece/Italy, 2009), *Inguélézi* (François Dupeyron, France, 2004) and *Bleu, le ciel* (Dominique Boccarossa, France, 2001). More permanent new migrants or immigrants include a Georgian doctor working on a construction site in France which inspired *Depuis qu'Otar est parti/Since Otar Left* (France/Belgium/Georgia, 2003), by Julie Bertuccelli, and a family of Chechens in *Les mains en l'air/Hands in the Air* (Romain Goupil, France, 2010). Switzerland, as discussed in Chapter 2, has a tradition of welcoming refugees, whose stories are told in *Das Fräulein/Fraulein* (Andrea Staka, 2006, Switzerland/Germany) and *Tout un hiver sans feu/A Long Winter without Fire*, by Greg Zglinski (2004, Switzerland/Belgium). In both cases, the immigrants fled war in the former Yugoslavia. Looking beyond the continent's 'centre', even Spain has been affected by East to West migrations. Some 10 per cent of the 191 victims of the March, 2004 Madrid train bombings are from Eastern or Central Europe (most notably from Romania but also Poland and Ukraine). The affected trains originated in Alcalá de Henares, 'home to sizeable Latin American and Eastern European communities made up of predominantly blue collar workers and day labourers who commute to Madrid' (Amago, 11). While Eastern European migration to Spain remains a relatively unexplored theme in Spanish cinema – *Los novios búlgaros/Bulgarian Lovers* (Eloy de la Iglesia, 2003, Spain) representing a notable exception – the topic is addressed in our volume from a Romanian perspective in Chapter 9 (by Lucian Georgescu). The juxtaposition of migrants from the East with workers from the global south has been represented in a growing number of films, from Jean-Pierre and Luc Dardenne's *La promesse/The Promise* (1996, Belgium/France/Luxembourg) to *Lištičky/Foxes* (2009, Ireland/Czech Republic/Slovakia), by Slovakian director Mira Fornay.

Since the onset of the 2008 economic crisis, many Western Europeans are themselves migrating in search of economic opportunity. This suggests that Europe's post-1989 cultural, economic and, indeed, political parameters – as the 2014 events in Ukraine also demonstrate – are still under negotiation. While this volume aims to contest lingering, static East/West dichotomies, it does not present a vision of Europe as a settled and monolithic construction representing a union of pre-1989 East and West. We concur with Mireille Rosello's assessment that, though walls and borders have not disappeared, 'we are in the presence of changing forms of language and artistic visions generated by the fact that territories are now as "uncertain" (Boer 2006) as the way in which we/they are supposed to inhabit them' (7). Such uncertainty is manifested in cinema at times as what our contributors term 'de-centring', at other times by the questioning of one's relationship to (Western) Europe and occasionally by the search for new geographic alignments.

Mapping the New Europe through Cinema

This volume considers the ways in which notions of East and West, national and transnational, central and marginal, are being rethought and reframed in contemporary European cinema. Some of the world's leading scholars in the field assemble in this volume to assess the state of contemporary European cinema, from (co-)production and reception trends to filmic depictions of migration patterns, economic transformations and sociopolitical debates over the past and the present. This volume intentionally looks beyond the handful of national cinemas that receive the most attention in both popular and academic discourse. Contributions address recent films from or about Armenia, Austria, Bulgaria, Estonia, France, Germany, Greece, Lithuania, Poland, Romania, Switzerland and the former Yugoslavia, and the complex and often contradictory notions of East and West that they employ. The volume also looks beyond the dominant linguistic taxonomies of cinema into Germanic, Francophone and Slavic groups. Instead of working within traditional groupings, this volume is divided into three sections which engage with efforts to map Europe in post-Berlin Wall cinema, each organised around an outlook on, or level of, post-Wall European *connectivity*. These mapping endeavours might encompass filmic narratives, production and reception patterns, and commonly include actual maps either as props or symbols. Each of these elements plays a central role in what Klaus Eder terms the 'narrative construction of the boundaries of Europe' (Eder), a process that concerns the evolution of Europe's internal and external borders. Eder's formulation is particularly well suited to be applied to cinema because it relates to the 'stories that people tell each other, thus creating a space of narrative fidelity. Telling stories implies a social relationship and implies a space within which such stories circulate. This symbolic space is bordered by "shared stories"' (Eder, 256).

Films are the stories Europeans tell each other and, in addition to what these shared stories say about the makeup of contemporary Europe, implicit in any notion of cinematic 'narrative construction' is the issue of who is telling these stories to whom and who is producing and financing them. Thus, while the primary focus of this collection is to assess the way Europe is being mapped in these stories, several of our chapters will focus on the production and distribution sides of the equation. The image that adorns the cover of this volume is from *Svetat e golyam i spasenie debne otvsyakade/The World is Big and Salvation Lurks Around the Corner*, by Bulgarian director Stephan Komandarev and co-produced by Bulgaria, Germany, Slovenia and Hungary. Komandarev's film is apt not only because it is discussed in Chapter 8, by Temenuga Trifonova, but also because it represents a multinational co-production that weaves a complex web of cultural identities and affinities. The film stages a return from Germany to Bulgaria by Alexander, whose family left their native land for political reasons when he was young. After a car accident takes the life of his father and mother and leaves Alexander with amnesia, his grandfather, who stayed in Bulgaria, comes to Germany to take his grandson on a return trip. The hope is that retracing the steps involved in the family's earlier migration, including an internment camp for refugees in Austria, will allow Alexander to reconstruct his memories and rediscover his identity. While he does eventually 'remember' his Bulgarian self, the film avoids essentialising ethnic and cultural roots by also painting the young man as a transnational European citizen. When, en route to Bulgaria, Alexander meets his future girlfriend at a coastal campsite in Slovenia, they introduce themselves in English before switching to German after they learn that, while they are from other places (Hungary in her case), they both live in Germany. The films analysed in the following chapters represent these new mappings of Europe narratively, linguistically, culturally, sometimes musically, and, in many cases, in their production, distribution and reception. Despite the breadth of this volume, a certain number of films which are not covered in the subsequent chapters merit mention here as they are particularly representative of the ways that cinema – in productive and narrative terms – has been ahead of the curve in new mappings of Europe. These examples underscore the increasingly uncontainable, uncertain nature of contemporary European cinema. A common thread in an ever-expanding list of films is the way in which conceptions of East and West are relativised. These films engage with 'borders' within Europe which, in a variety of different ways, have been displaced from the continent's margins to various points within. As Balibar argues, it is at these very borders, the putative frontiers, where the very central task of forging European citizenship is undertaken. It is the border areas that are 'at the centre' of the building of a European public sphere (Balibar 2003: 1–2).

The stalled post-communist road movie *Bolse vita* (Ibolya Fekete, 1995, Hungary) is a European 'mapping' film of reference, in which the director credits the events of 1989 as a 'sudden flash' that opened her eyes to new possibilities which transcended what was seen as the choice for

Hungarian directors at the time: to embrace the national at the expense of an international audience or vice versa (Waller, 21–2). Fekete's film, which has the distinction of being a Hungarian production with almost no Hungarian characters and virtually without dialogue in the Hungarian language (Waller, 26), would foretell a new direction taken in European cinema. *Bolse vita* posits that Budapest, situated between a collapsing USSR, a West eager to seek out new markets, and a Yugoslavia on the verge of breaking apart at the seams, might be the middle of sorts of a newly realigned Europe, if only for a fleeting moment. The characters include Russians, who start the film on Russia's east coast, pointing out that they could go in either direction to get to the 'West'. They eventually make their way west to Budapest where their paths cross with a Welsh woman and a Texan who have headed 'East' in search of adventure and opportunity. The babble of languages and pell-mell adoption of capitalism represent a compelling vignette of life on the border zone in a continent where everything has come apart. If the film does not seem to be able to propose a coherent and clear path to putting things back together, it does serve as a memorable precursor to subsequent films that stage continental crossings or narrate the previously unthinkable comings together which result from those displacements. Several chapters, including 7 and 9, will discuss films set in or traversing the Hungarian–Romanian borderlands. Chief among those films is *Im Juli/In Juli* (Fatih Akin, 2000, Germany), the subject of Chapter 5 by Berna Gueneli and a road movie that, unlike *Bolse vita*, follows its protagonists across the continent while also positioning Budapest at the middle of a Europe defined by shifting borders and linguistic chaos. No fewer than six languages – from East and West – are spoken in *In July* but films need not display linguistic profusion to be representative of shifting parameters of European cinema.

Mirek n'est pas parti (Bojena Horackova, 1996, Czech Republic/France) is set in Paris and made by a Paris-based Czech director but features only Czech actors, primarily speaking Czech. *Morgen* (Mirian Crisan, 2010, Romania/France/Hungary), a film discussed in Chapter 9, follows a Turkish migrant attempting to cross the Hungarian–Romanian border. Despite the German title, there is no German dialogue to speak of beside that word, uttered as a promise of a crossing that may never come. The director of *Marussia* (Eva Pervolovici, 2013, France/Russia) is a Romanian based in Paris who studied cinema in Edinburgh, and its producer a Croatian who set up shop in the French capital. The two protagonists and virtually all the secondary characters are Russian. Indeed, as in *Mirek n'est pas parti*, despite the setting in the French capital, the film contains almost no French dialogue. *Une Estonienne à Paris/A Lady in Paris* (2012, France/Belgium/Estonia), by Estonian director Ilmar Raag, departs from this template. The French cinema icon Jeanne Moreau plays an elderly Estonian living in Paris who has entirely lost touch with her Estonian side and speaks exclusively French even within a coterie of fellow exiles and with a newly arrived Estonian woman who was brought to care for her. A different twist on a lingua franca is audible in *Transylvania* (Tony Gatlif, 2006, France), a French film set exclusively in Romania and featuring primarily dialogue in English, the language used in the exchanges between the two stars: German-Turkish actor Birol Ünel and Italian actress Asia Argento. Gatlif compensates for the loss of linguistic particularity by revelling in the traditional music of Transylvania that drives the film forward (Gott 2013c: 13). Despite its official status as a solely French production, Gatlif's film troubles the very notions of national cinema and national identity. Contemporary European cinema's resistance to compartmentalisation is on display in a multiplicity of East/West cinematic encounters narrated in English in films such as *Prag/Prague* (Ole Christian Madsen, 2006, Denmark), *2 Sunny Days* (Ognjen Svilicic, 2010, Croatia/France), *Dvojina/Dual* (Nejc Gazvoda, 2013, Slovenia/Croatia/Denmark) and the aforementioned *The World is Big and Salvation Lurks Around the Corner*.

Transylvania also reminds us that the new map of Europe (and of European cinemas) is not simply the result of an East to West movement, a '(re)joining' of the continent's Eastern borderlands with its Western 'centre'. 'Western' European directors with Central European origins or orientations have highlighted the fact that the ground is shifting in 'Old Europe' creating increasingly disoriented subjects for whom mobility is equated not with liberty but with loss, as is the case in films such as *Code inconnu/Code Unknown* (Michael Haneke, 2000, France/Germany/Romania), which is under discussion in Chapter 3, and Finkiel's *Nowhere Promised Land*. The latter also reminds viewers in France, a nation that tended to see East to West migrations framed in terms of 'invasion' in political discourse, that there are other trajectories in post-1989 Europe. Ewa Mazierska and Laura Rascaroli read *Code Unknown* as a film that calls into question the very notion of 'home'; whether Romanian or French, the protagonists are unmoored and lack a permanent hub (Mazierska and Rascaroli, 142).

While this is but a small sample of films that are undertaking a remapping of post-1989 European space, our list would seem to suffice as a demonstration of the transnational and boundary-crossing tendencies of contemporary European cinema. Even beyond the well-documented practice of multinational co-productions, contemporary European cinema is weaving an interconnected web that calls into question not only the category of national cinema but also the compartmentalisation of films within discrete East and West frameworks.

Film is an inherently collaborative medium. This volume is also highly collaborative; it assembles a diverse set of scholars from points all around the globe to assess the state of European cinema and the stories it tells about Europe today. The eighteen chapters contained here are divided into three main topical sections, each of which combines discussions of films from various places united under common themes. The first section looks at the blurred lines between Eastern and Western Europe in the twenty-first century. The second section examines threshold spaces and marginal spaces, especially as they apply to transnational markets. The third section examines the lingering spectres of the East that continue to haunt Europe through the lens of both sides of the former East/West divide.

Redrawing the Lines

During the Cold War, the dividing line between Eastern and Western Europe ran through the city of Berlin. The breaching of that division on the night of 9 November 1989 remains the symbolic end of that division, even as the political process of (re)integrating Europe continues to this day. Because of the centrality of Berlin to Europe – East, West, and Central; Old and New – the first section of this volume, 'Redrawing the Lines: De/Recentring Europe', takes Berlin as its geographic and thematic starting point. Chapter 1, Jenny Stümer's 'The Berlin Wall revisited: Reframing historical space between East and West in Cynthia Beatts's *Cycling the Frame* (1988), *The Invisible Frame* (2009) and Bartosz Konopka's *Rabbit à la Berlin* (2009)' explores the meaning of the Berlin Wall as an imaginary and as a concrete space at the heart of 'New Europe' in three documentary films. Subsequent chapters in the opening section remain conscious of how the 'wall in the head' continues to inform views of Europe while examining films that trouble East/West divisions by narrating connections and voyages made possible by the new alignments on the continent. The chapters and the films they discuss present a vision of a remapped and recentred – or decentred, from a Western European perspective – Europe from a variety of vantage points on the East, West and Centre spectrum. This section questions the common notion of a 'road to Europe' and the ensuing discourse that implies an East to West trajectory. Rather, it paints a picture of a 'New Europe' that is not defined as such simply owing to expansion on its Eastern frontier. Each chapter analyses cinematic voyages from and to points that could arguably be considered the cultural, economic and geographic centres of Europe: France, Germany, Austria, Switzerland, Hungary and Poland.

Examined together, these films 'queer' the cultural and geographic parameters of 'central' Europe in the broadest sense of the term, understood by Daniela Berghahn as fundamentally about resisting containment within clearly demarcated spaces and categories: '[q]ueerness therefore implies transgression, subversion and dissent, and is often conceived of as a state of "in-between-ness"' (Berghahn 2011: 133). Kris Van Heuckelom's chapter 'Changing Sides: East/West Travesties in Lionel Baier's *Comme des voleurs (à l'est)*' opens the door to this reading through its discussion of a film in which the 'return' to distant origins by a gay Swiss protagonist quite literally presents a queer vision of Switzerland and the Swiss 'fortress' at the heart of Europe, and by extension subjects the idea of being (Western) European to the same process of radical reassessment. Where Van Heuckelom approaches a Swiss film from the perspective of a scholar of Poland and Polish cinema, Alison Rice's Chapter 3, 'Dubbing and Doubling Over: The Disorientation of France in the Films of Michael Haneke and Krzysztof Kieślowski', considers very similar questions from the angle of a specialist of Francophone cultures. Rice argues that the portrayal of migration and exile in films by Haneke and Kieślowski stimulates seemingly contradictory reactions in viewers. 'Doubling over' refers to both the pain and the laughter that inspired and is documented by these transnational directors' work. Rice's essay examines how these films 'resituate and reorient' France and Western Europe in relation to the East.

Nikhil Sathe turns to the resurgent and famously bleak world of New Austrian Film in Chapter 4, 'Redirecting the Gaze: Western Perceptions of Eastern Europe in Ulrich Seidl's *Import Export* (2007)'. His close examination of the act of looking in Ulrich Seidl's *Import Export* reveals a clear power division between East and West that is reflected in sexual and gender constellations. By foregrounding the act of looking, he argues, Seidl forces viewers to recognise and reflect upon power hierarchies and the ways in which they are manifested through the gaze. Berna Gueneli argues in Chapter 5, 'Fatih Akın's Filmic Visions of a New Europe: Spatial and Aural Constructions of Europe in *Im Juli/In July* (2000, Germany)', that the celebrated Turkish-German director also implicitly addresses contemporary sociopolitical issues and, through his use of spatial and aural cues, imagines an open and cosmopolitan Europe that can transcend social, geographic and political divisions.

Iranian-German director Ali Samadi Ahadi's broad comedy *Salami Aleikum* is stylistically a long way from Seidl's neo-neorealist film. But, in

Chapter 6, '*Salami Aleikum* – The "Near East" meets the "Middle East" in Central Europe', Alexandra Ludewig demonstrates that this seemingly unambitious comic strip-style film harbours a profound metapoetical reflection on feelings of loss, and comments on the mythologies through which people build a sense of home and community in the diaspora.

Together these contributions paint a picture of a 'New Europe' in which barriers have fallen and in which mobility has become the norm, as Ewa Mazierska and Laura Rascaroli suggest in their study of European road films (Mazierska and Rascaroli, 1). The final chapter of the section, however, Aga Skrodzka's 'Cinematic Fairy Tales of Mobility in Post-Wall Europe: Hanna *v*. Mona', furnishes a warning against overly euphoric readings of mobility as an inherently liberatory process. Skrodzka's assessment of two films which represent female itineraries across contemporary Europe – one moving from North to South, the other from East to West – emphasises the notion that travel and trafficking are two sides of the same coin in 'borderless' Europe. Both films employ fantasy and, in turn, romanticise and exoticise their protagonists, and, when considered together, Skrodzka contends that they 'provide an accurate and quite realistic depiction of the bifurcated nature of transnational mobility in the unifying Europe'. Given the 'traditional pejorative link between femininity and mobility' (Mazierska and Rascaroli, 186), it is not by chance that films about females travelling through New Europe offer the best opportunity to problematise the reading of post-Wall mobility as synonymous with progress. Nor, Skrodzka argues, should female migration on East/West or South/North axes be unquestioningly and exclusively linked to received notions of trafficking and exploitation.

The Road to and from Europe

Though many of the films covered in this volume narrate literal travel, the symbolic 'road to Europe' (Mazierska 2013: 151) discourse that gained currency after 1989 encompasses a variety of issues that are also considered here. For our purposes, the 'road to Europe' is a multidirectional process that involves literal and economic mobility, political and cultural shifts and the production and distribution of films which were highlighted above. The post-communist transition has typically been framed as a movement 'towards' Europe. Without so much as leaving their home, residents of some places of the former 'Eastern Europe' were to become 'Central Europeans' and then 'New Europeans' (Iordanova 2005: 237).

Building on the complex trajectories and problematic female mobility addressed in Skrodzka's chapter, the second section paints a more muddled picture of a decentred Europe by focusing on the 'other' Europe(s). The films in this section could be seen as examples of what has been theorised as 'the cinema of small nations' (Hjort and Petrie) or as 'cinema at the periphery' (Iordanova, Martin-Jones and Vidal). While the geographically – and commonly culturally and economically – marginal spaces addressed by our contributors have generally been either overlooked or geographically segregated in English-language scholarship, they are central to this collection. The contributions which make up 'Border Spaces, Eastern Margins and Eastern Markets: Belonging and the "Road to/from Europe"' widen our lens to include the (Eastern) geographic perimeters of the continent, though by taking an approach which transcends the commonplace geopolitically derived West/East binary. From the Balkans to the Baltics, these chapters home in on some arguably successful examples of transition in societies and inter-European co-operation in film industries, with a focus on the lingering legacy of the 'wall in the mind' and economic and cultural imbalances that remain. Nonetheless, these chapters underline just as many points of contact and European continuity as they do inequities, as signalled by the success of the Romanian post-communist film industry on the European festival circuit starting in the first decade of the twenty-first century, the casting of French actors to play the roles of 'marginal' Balkan Europeans in two films under consideration (in chapters by Jun Okada and Danica Jenkins and Kati Tonkin), and the growing practice of co-production between Baltic and 'Western' European industries. Add to this the success in the 'West' of co-productions by directors such as Šarūnas Bartas of Lithuania, whose films are addressed in Šukaitytė's chapter, and a picture emerges of European cinema as a conduit for East/West rapprochement or at least collaboration.

The casting of French actors in the roles of European 'others' represents a thread linking this section to chapters by Van Heuckelom, Jun Okada and Alison Rice in the previous section and by Joseph Mai in the final section. While the casting of (Western) foreign actors sometimes is done for marketing purposes, in the films analysed in this collection, this casting gesture always brings to bear an ideological agenda. The potentially 'hidden' otherness of Western European actors serves as a reminder that East/West points of contact are not new; France, in particular, has a long tradition of intellectual and working-class immigration from points across Europe. 'Return' films are addressed in each section. This prevalent category of contemporary European cinema engages directly with the post-1989 parameters of the continent, retracing voyages by (often young) people to the place of their birth or to the site of family roots that go back a generation or more. Frequently travelling across East/West demarcation lines, these films use the trope of individual or family identity exploration actively to reconfigure the parameters of Europe by simultaneously crossing newly opened 'hard borders' and by engaging with new 'soft borders' (Eder).

Chapter 8, 'Contemporary Bulgarian Cinema: From Allegorical Expressionism to Declined National Cinema', by Temenuga Trifonova, opens this discussion with an exploration of Bulgaria's cinematic ambivalence between inward-looking 'allegorical expressionism' and outward-oriented 'declined national cinema' (Rivi). Trifonova offers an overview of immigration and internal migration in Bulgarian communist and post-communist cinema in order to examine the gradual post-1989 evolution in the ways by which Bulgaria films demarcate the border separating the self from 'the Other.' As a director who also teaches screenwriting and cinema theory in Bucharest, the author of Chapter 9, Lucian Georgescu, writes from a perspective within Romanian cinema. His contention is that cinema provides a privileged vantage point to explore issues of identity in post-communist Romania. Like the previous chapter, 'The Point of No Return: From Great Expectations to Great Desperation in New Romanian Cinema', also explores a variety of films depicting immigration or attempts to emigrate. Georgescu suggests that the New Romanian Cinema, which emerged on the global stage in 2005, paints a rather bleak portrait of life in contemporary Romania, where disillusioned citizens are heading towards Western Europe en masse. The cinematic productions under discussion, however, demonstrate that Romanian cinema has successfully reached a broad European and, indeed, global audience. The Romanian film industry represents a global success story both in reception terms and through its engagement with 'effective co-production circuits, involving German, French or Swiss financing sources' (Nasta 155, 202). The next chapter, by Jun Okada, '"Weirdness", Modernity and the Other Europe in *Attenberg* (2010, Athina Rachel Tsangari)', also draws on the context of a cinematic 'wave' to examine the question of how a Balkan nation sees itself in relation to Europe. The Greek 'weird wave' has been theorised as a response to that nation's financial crisis but, as Okada suggests, this is just the latest episode in which Greece's problematic inclusion in (Western) Europe has been called into question.

Chapters 11 and 12 shift to the Baltics, another region characterised by East/West 'geographic in-betweenness' (Mazierka, et al., 10). Renata Šukaitytė's chapter, 'Lithuania Redirected: New Connections, Businesses and Lifestyles in Cinema since 2000', explores the shifting economic and social landscape of Lithuania through the optic of (cinematic) characters she labels 'adventurists'. Offering an examination of communist and early post-communist films before homing in on contemporary case studies, Šukaitytė suggests that a picture emerges in post-Soviet Lithuanian cinema of an uneasy period of transition between East and West, with transnational exchanges becoming commonplace but often involving the black market or otherwise 'mysterious' transnational networks. Where Chapter 11 explores Lithuanian's transition from 'East' to 'West' through the optic of characters who have adapted to the new neo-liberal system by becoming 'adventurists' or transnational gangsters, Eva Näripea's chapter, 'Lessons of Neoliberalism: Co-productions and the Changing Image of Estonian Cinema', explores the practice of co-production between Estonia and the 'West'. In both cases, through links to Scandinavia, 'North' emerges as a potential new social, economic and production framework for Baltic cinemas. Näripea's case studies point to a profound 'sense of "liminality" in the collective Estonian psyche, which is torn between a desire to belong to the "advanced North" (in global as well as regional terms) and a persistent spectre of historical "Eastern" subjugation'.

Chapter 13, 'Decentring Europe from the Fringe: Reimagining Balkan Identities in the Films of the 1990s', returns to the Balkans to assess how the spectre of past subjugation and of contemporary war has affected cinematic relationships between the states comprising the former Socialist Federal Republic of Yugoslavia and Western Europe. Through a comparative analysis of transnational projects by Balkan-born directors, locally produced films and a UK production, Danica Jenkins and Katie Tonkin explore how the Western gaze viewed late twentieth-century Balkan conflict through the prism of orientalism. They argue that, while the films under consideration narrate a causal trajectory of historical Balkan violence against which Western progress and civilisation could be affirmed, by replicating and subverting aspects of these narratives, these films successfully foreground them as ideological constructions and actively participate in their reimaging.

Spectres of the East

Whereas the first two sections have sought to avoid containment, the final section engages the most directly with the lingering legacies of Communism in Eastern Europe. 'Spectres of the East', while emphasising points of contact across the East/West divide, brings together chapters that acknowledge the different historical experiences that mark Europe's East and West, all the while seeking ways to transcend the burden of history and assess how the once taboo past has become a rich source for cinematic inspiration. In this section, chapters by Rimma Garn, Mihaela Petrescu and Nick Hodgin explore cinematic strains of Polish, Romanian and German *Ostalgie*, with an eye on the role played by communist-era heritage in the cinema industries of those nations. Kalani Michell's chapter takes a different tack, considering what a documentary film about an East German spy reveals about how the heritage of the 'East', and of East–West crossings, is representative of the cinematic climate of post-Wall Germany. In Chapter 14, 'Through the Lens of Black Humour: A Polish Adam in the Post-Wall World', Rimma Garn compares two of the films that make up an octology by Marek Koterski on the Polish experience since 1985. Koterski, who directs comedies, has received limited attention in English-language critical circles despite having been championed as Poland's 'new national director' by Ewa Mazierska (2013: 159). Garn argues that Koterski's post-1989 work suggests that a sense of black humour forged in the tribulations of the past is the ideal approach to the trials of Poland's post-communist transition. Nick Hodgin argues in Chapter 15, 'East Germany Revisited, Reimagined, Repositioned: Representing the GDR in Dominik Graf's *Der rote Kakadu* (2005) and Christian Petzold's *Barbara* (2012)' that these two twenty-first century films mark an important shift in representations of the German Democratic Republic. Unlike films of the 1990s (such as *Das Versprechen/The Promise*, Margarethe von Trotta, 1995, Germany), which cast their protagonists as victims of history, both Dominik Graf and Christian Petzold place their characters in a position in which they must choose whether to stay in or leave the GDR. This, in fact, connects them to GDR-era films such as *Der Geteilte Himmel/Divided Sky* (Konrad Wolf, 1964, GDR). As different as they are from each other, these two films allow for a higher degree of differentiation between representations of the GDR than had previously been the case.

The innovative documentary *Barluschke*, about a historical secret agent whose story initially seems more like a work of fiction, also takes a markedly different retrospective look at the GDR, as Kalani Michell demonstrates in Chapter 16, '*Barluschke*: Towards an East–West Schizo-History'. Recognising that an 'objective' presentation of the history of East and West during the Cold War cannot possibly be achieved, *Barluschke* instead offers an ultimately inscrutable take on that history which reads it within the context of a schizofrantic family history that parallels the equally schizofrantic East–West history. Mihaela Petrescu's Chapter 17, 'The Limits of Nostalgia and (Trans)National Cinema in *Cum mi-am petrecut sfârşitul lumii* (2006)', builds on Georgescu's chapter on migration in Romanian cinema. Petrescu discusses a film that also addresses indirectly the themes of migration and escape but focuses on the lives of those who stayed in Romania during the final years of the Ceauşescu regime. Analysing Cătălin Mitulescu's feature film *Cum mi-am petrecut sfârşitul lumii/ The Way I Spent the End of the World* (2006), Petrescu contrasts the sometimes nostalgic portrait of youth in communist Romania to the more wistful and less critical German brand of *Ostalgie*. At the same time, this film's depiction of characters faced with a perplexing decision between staying and leaving brings it very much in line with the retrospective takes on the GDR that Hodgin analyses in his chapter.

Mobility and, by extension, mapping remain essential to this portion of the collection. Petruscu's chapter presents an example of a recent trend in cinema to address attempts to migrate to the West during the communist period. Joseph Mai's closing chapter, 'The Ideal of Ararat: Friendship, Politics and National Origins in Robert Guédiguian's *Le voyage en Arménie/Armenia*', continues with both the travel and nostalgia threads, albeit from a very different geographic perspective. His analysis of *Voyage en Arménie/Armenia* (2006) aptly completes the volume by tying back together the Eastern and Western perspectives. Mai argues that the cinematic 'return' narrated in the film by French director Robert Guédiguian, whose grandparents migrated to France during the period of the Armenian genocide, not only invites viewers to reassess the place of France in Europe but also expresses a lingering tension about communist ideology in Europe. The film's protagonist is herself a former communist activist, and Mai's chapter examines how the film approaches the conflicting discourses on solidarity, friendship and communist legacy in a post-1989 European landscape. In the process of introducing the protagonist – and the viewers – to post-communist Armenia, the film also represents a challenge to exclusionary strains of French identity politics by revealing a long-standing heritage of Eastern 'otherness' at the heart of contemporary French identity.

Parameters and Definitions

The geographic terms that we have employed in this introduction and that will reappear throughout this volume are not fixed, are often relative, and occasionally overlap. For this reason, our aim here is not to settle on uniform parameters but to sketch out some precedents that should be kept in mind while reading this collection. Western Europe, despite the recent North/South cleavages discussed above, has generally been a relatively uncontroversial term. It is also one that has outlived its use, except when it is used as a point of comparison to demarcate something to the East as somewhere which is not 'West', or perhaps for guidebooks, which must draw geographic lines somewhere. 'Eastern Europe', on the other hand, remains a thornier topic. Anikó Imre contends, not without reservation, that there is nothing more accurate than 'Eastern European', a classification that avoids the erasure of 'common regional histories'. Nonetheless, she insists that the region's 'shifting boundaries, internal differences and constructed identities' must be taken into account (Imre, xvii). Other scholars define 'Eastern Europe' as the countries that made up, between the solidification of communist rule and the fall of communist regimes in 1989, the Warsaw Pact and the Federal Republic of Yugoslavia which are today 'labelled as postcommunist' (Mazierska, et al., 1). This comprises nations such as Hungary, Poland and the Czech Republic that tend to see themselves, and are often theorised by scholars as, Central European. For some, 'Eastern Europe' begins only at Poland's former eastern border with the Soviet Union (Hames and Portuges, 1). Yet we cannot look to the erstwhile boundaries of the USSR for a definitive solution, for the Baltic states that were annexed by the Soviets in 1940 have 'perceived themselves natural parts of the West' (Mazierska, et al., 10). As this volume's two chapters on Baltic cinema suggest, that region has since 1990 been looking towards the North to forge alignments that transcend East/West dichotomies. A final contentious classification engaged with in the follow pages is the Balkans. Misnamed for a mountain range in the 1800s, it was not until 1878, when Bulgaria, Romania and Serbia gained their independence, that the term 'Balkan' became commonplace (Mazower, xxviii). Historian Mark Mazower writes that '[f]rom the very start, the Balkans was more than a geographical concept', one that evoked a series of stereotypes associated with the 'the wild and lawless countries between the Adriatic and Black Seas' (Mazower, xxviii). Since 1989, when some of the 'former Eastern Europeans became Central Europeans' and later transformed again into 'new Europeans', the Balkans have again been relegated to the periphery (Iordanova 2005: 237). Yet, as Dina Iordanova points out, within this problematically European space, often described as 'Europe's doorstep' (see Chapter 13), 'real exchanges' have been fostered after the end of communism, resulting in a 'vibrant and viable cultural space that includes Greece and Turkey as well as the former communist states' (Iordanova 2005: 238). Thus, despite the fact that the term 'Balkan' often designated a space relegated to Europe's periphery engrained with negative connotations of 'violence, savagery, primitivism' (Mazower, xxviii), it also demarcates a vibrant and variable cultural zone that transcends East/West dichotomies. The use of the above terms will vary in the chapters that follow, as we have elected to allow the authors of each essay to employ the geographic signifiers of their choice.

One final necessary clarification relates the scope of the geographic parameters of this volume. The films under consideration cover European spaces from Spain in the West to Armenia in the East.[1] Those nations, however, are on the fringes of this volume's scope and we arrived there in only an itinerant fashion, via voyages narrated in a French and in a Romanian film. Our attention is primarily focused on the centre of the continent – a grouping that encompasses nations on both sides of the Cold War divide – and the 'East'. For the purposes of this volume, our Eastern boundary corresponds to the border of the European Union. As with any endeavour of this nature, it was impossible to include everything we would have liked to, and certain nations were left out.[2]

Part I

Redrawing the Lines: De/Recentring Europe

CHAPTER 1

The Berlin Wall Revisited: Reframing Historical Space between East and West in Cynthia Beatts's *Cycling the Frame* (1988), *The Invisible Frame* (2009) and Bartosz Konopka's *Rabbit à la Berlin* (2009)

Jenny Stümer (University of Auckland)

With the fall of the Berlin Wall in 1989 marking the end of the Cold War, twentieth-century history had officially come to an endpoint. When in 2009, however, the twentieth anniversary of this event was marked by (among other things) various filmic contemplations of the walled past, it became clear that history had never ended but, instead, continued to be rewritten through the present. The past was repeatedly rewound, edited and projected, revealing that the Wall's demise had not resulted in a single unified narrative but had brought about various, and often ambivalent, ways of apprehending, rethinking and reframing history through the numerous biographies and memories it encapsulated. This exposed a radical gap in the post-communist experience, an in-between space shifting between East and West, past and future, us and them. Without the Wall to give shape to these trajectories, the past was thus simultaneously opened up and rendered inaccessible; it remains available only, as Hayden White has argued, through the faculty of the imaginary and its mediation (White 1987: 57). In this way Berlin, the historic city of the twentieth century, a modern palimpsest and traumatic *Wunderblock*, according to Huyssen (1997: 60), does not simply function as a historical text but also serves the setting for an imaginary space through which to (re-)examine its own historical remake through cinematic reconstruction. The Berlin Wall persists at the centre of this text, just as it sat at the centre of the city, ironically decentring the coherent whole of both city and history through an empty space or defining absence at its core. The absolute in-betweenness marked by history's death strip offers a point from which to work through the present-day imaginaries precisely because the aesthetic of absence was crucial to the concrete Wall's operation as a political imposition from the outset. This core absence adhered to an invisible structure of meaning that maintained (and perhaps evoked) the Wall, securing its psychological effectivity. In this context Berliners often speak about a 'mental' Wall which has outlived the demise of the actual Wall, leaving an invisible structure that persists and through which the concrete imposition of the past is still maintained. The Wall thus functions as both a projection screen and mirror, an intertextual phenomenon, mediating the past's traumatic imposition and expressing the past as a form of continuous absence.

Cynthia Beatts's *The Invisible Frame* (2009, Germany) as well as Bartosz Konopka's *Rabbit à la Berlin/ Królik po berlińsku* (2009, Poland/ Germany) engage with the Berlin Wall as an imaginary and a concrete space, providing a setting for historical ambivalence that reflects on the shifting trajectories of an experience of the past. Both Beatts and Konopka explore the physical and psychological space provided by the Berlin Wall as a means of investigating a specific perspective on and about the East, tangible in the visible and invisible remainders of this monument. In this way they debate historical perception and invite reflection on the larger political parameters of a (post-)communist world. *The Invisible Frame* beckons questions about the ambiguous relationship between past and present, following Tilda Swinton on a philosophical bike ride along the absent Wall in an impossible attempt to access the 'other side' of history. The haunting invisibility of the monument comments on the obstacles of understanding the past from the point of view of the present and evokes a sense of retrospective separation and introspective alienation. Similarly, Konopka's allegorical reimagining of the past through his documentary about the rabbits inhabiting the former death strip, defamiliarises the Wall's meaning and simultaneously projects its totalitarian effectiveness, reminding the viewer of the ambivalence of historical mediation. In this way both films complicate the accessibility of the past, particularly the East's past, and thereby reconsider processes of historical othering, and perhaps wilful forgetting against the backdrop of the Berlin Wall.

The Invisible Frame

Investigating the interplay between outward and inward perspective within historical space, Beatts's *The Invisible Frame* (2009) resonates with her earlier attempt to mediate the Wall through a bike ride in *Cycling the Frame* (1988, West Germany). Both films show Tilda Swinton cycling along the Wall's 160-kilometre route through Berlin and Brandenburg as she contemplates her experience of the space through inner monologues. Though the two films are meant to stand

Figure 1.1 Nature v. concrete in *Cycling the Frame*.

independently, according to the director, both journeys communicate different 'underlying layers of consciousness' (Beatts cited in Petrowskaja 2009) across the historical space and thereby articulate the Wall as a physical, metaphorical and also psychological demarcation across time. In this sense, both films provide 'psychogeographic, philosophical mediations', as Anke Westphal (2009) points out and invite an exploration of expressed and repressed history. Utilising the 'outsider' as the catalyst of inward and outward perspective, the films both negotiate identity in a landscape that is maintained by the ambivalent appearance and disappearance of Cold War history, yet enable an engagement with the Wall leading beyond its physical imposition. The first film, *Cycling the Frame* (1988) was produced by non-Germans for a television series called *Looking from the Outside* and presents the physical imposition of the Wall as an internalised sense of frustrating finality. This also cements perspective, however, and positions the outsider always in relation to the Wall as an artificial margin and thus perhaps also in relation to a philosophical endpoint. Kristensen explains that this immovable viewpoint allows Swinton's character to achieve increasing assurance in response to the concrete obstruction (Kristensen, 2). In this way, Swinton is directed by the Wall, and her perspective towards the physical and psychological imposition is unequivocal: She hates the Wall and she wants to shoot a hole in it. Twenty-one years later, on the other hand, the Wall, if not completely gone, is absent and thereby disrupts the indisputability of the experience. The introspection enabled by the Wall in 1988 is now replaced by the search for new frames twenty-one years later (Kristensen 3). Swinton's 2009 journey reveals an impossible desire to understand the other side of this space, a return to the excluded perspective in search of what has emerged from it, only to reveal that the East's perspective is still walled off.

With the object of the Wall gone, the engagement with the past in *The Invisible Frame* is experienced as increasingly contentious, leading to a nostalgic search for definite frames of encounter. As Swinton sets out on her journey, she passes the various memorials across Berlin that seek to preserve a sense of what the now absent Wall was like. It seems that Swinton does not gain any insight from these cues, as her inner monologue is silenced. Rather than accessing the past, the monuments echo Mila Ganeva's (266) criticism of the city's continuous effort to 'bring the past back to surface, of course in a neat, clean, attractive form', as this sense of 'clean' history ignores the significance of absence as a form of horror vacui accompanying the Wall. Swinton expresses a wish to complete her experience of the historical space in a way that is no longer limited by the physical obstruction of the Wall. 'I want to know what the wall was like from the other side,' (Beatts 2009) she states as she leaves the tourist attractions behind to follow the invisible frame. Her impossible journey to the other side of history is disrupted, however, by a sense of permanent disorientation. She gets lost repeatedly, encountering haphazard pathways and graffiti-covered road maps. The encounter with the Wall is complicated by the loss of its physicality, leading Swinton to seek it through other objects such as fences and hedges, always searching for direction and a way back. Kristensen (3) remarks that, with the 'wall as something that gave shape to history' gone, her perspective is no longer anchored as 'there is no "outerland" where the self can be reflected and space internalised' (Skoller, cited in Kristensen, 3). This also reinstates the Wall, however, as a potential mirror and projection screen for historical identities as much as spatial arrangements. If, as Étienne Balibar (2009: 193) outlines, the notions of partition and walling are a means to 'maintain oneself as unified', then the disappearance of the barrier creates the loss of unity in the physical and psychological senses, ironically leading to a nostalgic projection of all kinds of borders, fences and partitions, such as can be seen in the numerous *Kleingärten* or garden allotments that can be found all over Berlin and Brandenburg. In this way *The Invisible Frame* also articulates nostalgia for a lost object of history, a sense of direction and the possibility of 'definite' knowledge. Though such definite knowledge is, of course, illusionary, this notion of a 'self-evident and definite' (Kristensen, 3) framework is not simply sentimental but also functions as a reminder of the Wall's own pervasiveness which led people to believe that it would simply always be there.

Through her own ideological dislocation, Swinton discovers the mechanisms of the Wall's psychological work which are sustained precisely by systematically evoking a sense of ignorance and erasure still tangible in the historical space that was once governed by this dynamic. In this regard, it is essential to point out that a wall does not simply work to erase the other side but, ultimately, invites the viewer to forget the sight of the wall itself. This is reflected in the blank screens that famously marked the Eastern side of the partition but it is also observed by Swinton in 1988 when she explains that 'West Berliners seem to be so studiously ignoring the Wall' (*Cycling the Frame* 1988). Whereas Swinton initially contrasted this phenomenon with the 'enormous attention given to the Wall by the men in the towers from the East' (*Cycling the Frame* 1988), twenty-one years later the whole space seems to be submerged in a sense of wilful amnesia and historical forgetting. In her study of *Post-wall German cinema and National History*, Mary Elisabeth O'Brien remarks that such wilful amnesia is symptomatic for the filmic engagement with events of German reunification, or *die Wende*, and that this phenomenon attests to an effort 'towards unanimity by erasing all evidence of conflict' (O'Brien 2012: 23). In 'digging under the surface of reunification' (cited in Petrowskaja 2009), however, Beatts articulates this persistent erasure by focusing Swinton's attention to the Wall's absence, thereby questioning and challenging the prerequisite to ignore it, and thus opening up the possibility of deconstructing the Wall's logic. As Swinton puts it, 'When this Wall, this ex-Wall, this manifestation of a ghost-Wall was here it felt so much more invisible than it is now. It has my attention in a way it never did before' (*The Invisible Frame* 2009). Thus, it is only through the Wall's absence that she comes to understand the Wall's brutal pervasiveness – a brutality she identifies as 'translated into some kind of stoic acceptance' (*The Invisible Frame* 2009) and now wilfully forgotten in the landscape of the present. This notion of amnesia aligns the Wall's pervasiveness with the loss of memory evoked by a traumatic injury as the need to forget 'what has become useless, or too difficult to accommodate'(O'Brien 2012: 26), and thereby suggests that a traumatic walled past still exerts pressure on the present.

Because the Wall's invisible structure is internalised by those who live with it and/or outlive it, the Wall becomes a means of a traumatic encounter that evokes post-communism's radical in-betweenness, manifesting itself within the shifting trajectories between us and them, here and there, now and then. The internal Wall thereby also serves the means of trauma precisely because trauma occurs 'on the threshold between remembering and forgetting, seeing and not seeing, transparency and occlusion, experience and its absence', as Huyssen (2003: 16) puts it. Similarly, the Wall draws on these dialectics to exercise its psychological effectiveness. The efficiency of absence in this context conceptualises the Wall as that which can never be adequately represented but persists as an internal conflict. For Swinton, the wish to bring the two sides together through some kind of knowledge of 'what the Wall was like from the East' (*The Invisible Frame* 2009) remains unfulfilled and yet her impossible desire acknowledges this traumatic wound and its uncanny resonance with the present. We see her zigzagging the line of cobblestones that marks the Wall's former route, 'as if sewing the two sides together' (Beatts, cited in Petrowskaja 2009). This expresses the desire to heal the troubled past and the haunted present through 'instinctive ghostwork', as Beatts describes the journey in an interview (Petrowskaja 2009). It is the articulation of this traumatic impossibility, however, that summons the meaning of Swinton's excursion. Quoting Russian poet Anna Akhmatova, Swinton frames her last kilometres as an acknowledgement of loss when she addresses the historical other, stating,

> I bear equally with you the black permanent separation.
> Why are you crying?
> Rather give me your hand, promise to come again in a dream.
> You and I are a mountain of grief. (*The Invisible Frame* 2009)

It is this impossibility of closure and yet continuous entanglement of past and present that suggests that historical space can never be adequately read; rather, it must be permanently rewritten.

Of course, the rewriting of historical space is always twofold in the sense that it is as revelatory as evasive. In the case of German reunification, it was made clear instantly that there was no intention to preserve GDR (German Democratic Republic) history. As the then minister of the interior, CDU (Christian Democratic Union) politician, Wolfgang Schäuble, put it in 1990,

> my dear citizens, what is taking place here is the accession of the GDR to the Federal Republic, and not the other way around (. . .) We are not seeing here the unification of two equal states. We are not starting again from the beginning, from the position of equal rights. (cited in Cooke, 3)

The historical space of the East was literally rewritten in the light of the West, most evidently reflected in the obsessive renaming of streets after unification. Swinton encounters examples of this as the signposts of a rewritten history. She passes streets called *Einheit, Freiheit* or *Kuckucksruf* (Unity, Freedom or the Cuckoo Call).[1] The houses are restored and polished, making room for new generations that have no active memory of the Wall. The long shots of graceful house facades are underlined with sounds of children that remain absent from the image, as if the future was haunting a present that cannot deal with its own past. 'Acres of shame and rewritten history' (*The Invisible Frame* 2009) prevent Swinton from gaining a perspective of the East, often leading her to lose her orientation or to question whether she is in the East or the West. On the other hand, the past erupts unexpectedly in ruins that attest to the East's decaying presence. Swinton utilises these moments to put herself into the shoes of the other, taking the perspective of a border guard from a watchtower and reciting a to-do list while cycling around the remainder of a monument in the shape of a Soviet star. Yet, none of this provides retrospective meaning; despite, and because of, everything being open, the historical space is, instead, layered with new experiences across time.

Though Swinton never accesses the past, her journey attests to the non-linearity of historical time. In this regard, Richard Terdiman (132) points out that 'human temporality, (. . .) is always underlain and rewritten by other times' and thus we cannot assume the past's persistence (and thereby liberate ourselves from it). Instead, we have to engage it through a continuous 'confirmation, as the form the past takes now'. Swinton expresses this notion when she muses 'now you see it, now you don't. It's like a trick of the light and then you come around a corner and something is completely unchanged' (*The Invisible Frame* 2009). As the Wall flickers between past and present, it becomes impossible to write it into a map (or to find it solely according to its former route) precisely because it is also a temporal phenomenon attesting to the circularity of historical occurrences. Swinton often fails to locate the Wall on the map she is using, finally leading her to the conclusion that 'maps are very fake things. They tell you that time has stopped but it hasn't. It's going on, remaking itself all the time' (*The Invisible Frame* 2009). This is reflected in Swinton's literal circling, singing a repetition of 'round and round and round and round' and her constant encounter with, and musing about, 'new walls'. In this way, the historical space of the Wall is shown to circulate and itself to be associated with cycles of history and nature.

The image of nature is utilised to evoke the circularity of history but also provides a sense of metaphoric estrangement, allowing for commentary on the politics of space. Beatts continuously evokes nature to ironise the politics associated with the Wall. The poppy fields that have taken over the space of the Wall, for example, evoke former chancellor Helmut Kohl's often quoted (and much criticised) promise of blossoming landscapes in the East (Cooke, 3) while also attesting to a naturalisation of the Wall's absence. This is interesting because the earlier *Cycling the Frame* utilises the image of nature to contrast the Wall and to reinstate the monument's monstrous and artificial disruption of ordinary life. The bullet Swinton wants to shoot into the Wall serves the purpose of creating a hole to save a little bee, amplifying the point. In *The Invisible Frame*, however, the space has been taken back by nature and thus the Wall itself, in its 'absent' presence, has been rendered natural. Despite Swinton's best efforts to become part of this naturalised landscape by disappearing in a bush or lying in a field waving her hands with the rhythm of the wind blowing through the grass, she thus does not ultimately emerge in the historical landscape. Despite nature's best efforts, the Wall still cuts through space as signified in the image of a dead snake lying on the concrete. This comments on a historical space in which the past is still active, yet overtly ignored, and thereby imprisons the present. Swinton thus concludes that real freedom is not achieved through getting over the past but through a fearless engagement with it – fearless precisely because such engagement does not accept the silent walls of the present.

Rabbit à la Berlin

Konopka's 'natural documentary' *Rabbit à la Berlin* (2009) explores the space in between the no-man's-land of the two Berlin Walls (erected to the East and the West). The film draws on the story of an expanding rabbit population that lived in the walled-off pasture and retells the history of the GDR from the rabbits' point of view. In this version of history the Wall was erected to protect the rabbits, providing plenty of food and equal access to underground caving within its 120-kilometre parameters. Konopka creates an allegory for the troubled comfort of totalitarian imprisonment and civil apathy, investigating the rabbit's microcosm analogously to East German life, but also enabling more general reflections on the fine line between security and surveillance. Approaching history like an exercise in zoology, Konopka's 'fairy-tale allegory docu-genre' (Konopka, cited in White 2009) posits the Wall as unnatural by producing a denaturalisation of the rabbits on the walled-off death strip. As in *The Invisible Frame*, such denaturalisation enables 'a visible metaphor' (Rosolowski, cited in Rezková 2009) about the Wall, debating the conflicting interpretations of the past. Just as the East is remembered both nostalgically and critically, the film traces a continuum based on cosy appeasement from 'natural' struggle to the evocation of a lethal prison. On the other hand, nostalgia does not necessarily oppose critical engagement, as Daphne Berdahl, among others, has pointed out (Berdahl 1999). Thus, the satirical tone that accompanies the film's allegorical form and ironic distance addresses history through defamiliarisation and reveals a crisis of accessing the irretrievable past. The abstract experience of the East is estranged through the rabbit perspective, putting pressure on historical truths and challenging dominant forms of storytelling. Human truths are reframed as bizarre, mirroring the way in which the East has been made strange (to) itself.

With the GDR gone, the past is projected as a means to make sense of the present. This often leads to discussions that characterise the East as either a callous dictatorship or a caring homeland. Engaging this dichotomy through the perspective of the death strip utilises spatial in-betweenness to show how the mechanisms of Utopia and dystopia play out concurrently. The Eastern experience is positioned within the complex two-foldness of being simultaneously a victim and a pillar of the regime. This is reflected in the archival footage of people happily waving their flags at a parade juxtaposed with images of increased fortification and surveillance, leading to an even more peaceful existence for the rabbits on the death strip. *Rabbit à la Berlin* thus alludes to media depictions of the GDR as 'a noble experiment gone wrong' (O'Brien 2012: 4) but turns this notion on its head by depicting the unwarranted aggression of the regime against its own citizens through images of lethal crop spraying in an attempt to control the expanding rabbit population. The traumatic implication of such routinised cruelty is addressed through the defamiliarising tactic of using animal imagery as a stand-in for communal human traits, as has been done in works such as Art Spiegelman's *Maus* or John Marsden's *The Rabbits*. This is most hauntingly demonstrated in a former guard's assurance that no one shot the rabbits placed alongside contrasting gun sounds and images of dead or injured humans being carried from the death strip. The juxtaposition satirises the infamous commentary of a western journalist about escapees from the East being shot like rabbits, while it lays ground for the numerous scenes in which the rabbits are repeatedly shot as a way to articulate visually the traumatic enforcement of the shoot-to-kill policy on the death strip. The walled-off pasture becomes a microcosm on to which the ambiguities of the Eastern experience are projected. The utopian moment is reframed as a nightmarish awakening, evoking an East German paralysis that outlives the Wall's physical demise. After the Wall has fallen, we see an elderly couple standing in a hole in the Wall looking disoriented, as if they did not dare to cross the line. The Eastern self remains confined to the death strip of a walled past, alluding to Mitchell's idea of landscape 'as a cultural practice', (Mitchell 2002: 5) and a visual field which does not merely signify the structures of political power but also functions as an agent of its ideology.

The landscape of the death strip exemplifies the inherent spatiality of politics and rearticulates the politics of the walled state from the forgotten no-man's-land at its margin. The Wall, as both limit and condition of Eastern life, condenses the meaning of politics in the GDR and provides insight into the mechanisms of oppression. Carl Schmitt (2003: 70) points out that political and social orders become visible through 'the initial measure and division of pastureland' in an act of order and orientation that produces an 'enclosure' or 'spatially concrete unity' by which the law of its politics, or *nomos*, is established. *Nomos*, 'quite literally a wall' according to Hannah Arendt (1958: 63–4) spatially evokes 'a kind of no man's land between the public and private' which enables a political community in which the Wall secures political life on one side and shelters the biological life of the family on the other. Following this logic, it becomes possible to read the political within the enclosure. Thus, by situating the biological life of the rabbits on the pasture between the GDR's wall(s), Konopka allegorises the political order of the GDR as a totalitarian entity precisely because the spatial organisation in which the rabbit life takes place collapses the notion of home and homeland. This becomes visible in the spatial negotiation of the death strip as a nature reserve but also alludes to an Eastern life in which the sanctuary of the home was permanently subject to arbitrary state surveillance and intrusion. As Arendt explains further, 'to have no private place of one's own . . . meant to be no longer human', (1958: 64) and, one may add, in the logic of Konopka, perhaps to be a rabbit.

The Wall creates a political order alongside psychological imperatives and thereby creates a particular identity reflecting both on East and West. The 'rabbit identity' is documented as a 'species' promoting critical commentary and historical othering alike. Community is established in relation to the Wall and, as Silberman (2011: 3) points out, 'grounded not on solidarity but on disavowal and exclusion'. Silberman further suggests that, for the majority of GDR citizen's, identity 'existed only because of the Wall' and the images it prevented and simultaneously created, thus reinstating the Wall as a psychological projection screen. For Konopka, this particular identity is reflected in the notion of the rabbit or 'the rabbit's people of the world (. . .) those people who want to have a simple life and want to have at least some area of fresh grass' (Interview Bartek Konopka 2009). This rabbit-identity, however, is also associated with the notion of fear and ignorance. The German terms *Angsthase* (literally 'scared rabbit', a reference to a coward) and *Versuchskaninchen* (literally a 'test rabbit', and the equivalent to the English 'guinea pig') both comment on the psychology of the GDR's 'niche society' (Gaus, cited in Betts 2010: 10) as evasive and passive. The notion of *Angsthase* is evoked in the first minutes of the film, introducing the species as 'naturally fearful' and as 'hiding in caves' when feeling threatened (*Rabbit à la Berlin* 2009). The notion of *Versuchskaninchen* further alludes to the idea of the GDR as a social experiment which treated its citizens as dispensable. Whereas such ideas comment on East German civil debility, they may also satirise the common view of East Germans as a simple species that tends to portray 'the East as a quainter more natural Germany', as Hodgin (2011: 67) explains, a portrayal through which the FRG (Federal Republic of Germany) could affirm its superior credentials, as suggested by Paul Cooke (2005: 12). *Rabbit à la Berlin* takes this idea as its modus operandi and thereby also draws attention to the way in which such a view is naturalised within a discourse of truth. This view is literally exemplified in the notion of the death strip as a well-maintained 'zoo' where visitors could watch the rabbits from purpose-built viewing platforms, a spectacle outdone only by its bizarre reality during the era of the Wall.

The reinterpretation of the historical image enables multiple perspectives and alludes to the fact that the possibilities of history are largely evoked and remembered through media. The rabbit perspective on history renders the past absurd and bizarre through the eyes of the rabbit on the one hand and through our own looking at the rabbits as the centre of historical events on the other. The two perspectives oscillate in the film, reimagining the facticity of the archival footage and diverting it from established meanings. Such a 'naive' history allows for an examination of history outside itself, in the form of 'the strange behaviour of humans' (*Rabbit à la Berlin* 2009). By focusing on the banality of historical detail in order to access the larger truths, Konopka opens up questions of representation and about the ambivalence of historical mediation. Similar to the numerous (filmic) rewritings of GDR history, the past in *Rabbit à la Berlin* is easily twisted with the help of media images and archival footage, some of which were taken from foreign archives and various YouTube videos. This comments on the representation of the twentieth century through media, particularly with regard to the media's active role in the fall of the Berlin Wall, which was arguably a media event even while it happened. Such history-in-the-making functions as a reminder that all history is essentially mediated and that the power of ideological framing emerges from the centre and its associated perspectives. *Rabbit à la Berlin* highlights this in the depiction of the numerous high-ranking visitors on both sides of the Wall who use the obstruction as a projection screen for their own politics, an effort which is, in turn, easily reframed from the perspective of the rabbits as being all about them. While such a reframing never seems to stray far from its underwritten histories, it establishes the allegorised image on screen 'both as a site of vanguard political analysis and as a space of aesthetic alterity', (Trumpener 2001: 115) in which 'old signs lose their original meaning when looked at from a new perspective' (Xavier 349). What remains unsaid or unseen also colours the historic imagination. Konopka's depiction of the GDR is thus not simply a study of its political immobility decentring the facts; it simultaneously encapsulates the notion of resistance through a slight twist of the focal lens.

It is precisely the image of the rabbit that delineates a history of the resistance that was already in the picture. Whereas the film positions the rabbits as naively engaging with the Wall that falls as inexplicably and suddenly as it had appeared, the interviews with Thierry Noir, Peter Unsicker and Manfred Butzmann reinstate the rabbit as a symbol of political struggle. All three artists have focused their work on a criticism of the Wall, using it as a screen for political commentary and utilising the rabbit as a symbol of freedom, precisely because it was the only creature capable of occupying the pastureland. Thierry Noir created a rabbit homage through graffiti on the surface of the western side of the Wall, as did Butzmann from the East when the border was opened, while Unsicker designed an Easter postcard depicting a giant rabbit breaking through the obstruction. In the context of art, the rabbit, of course, also evokes the late Joseph Beuys to whom the rabbit represented an element of movement and action (rather than passivity and fear), and thus could be used as a sign of transformation. Most notably, however, the very notion of a 'rabbit film' evokes a reference to East German filmic resistance. Kurt Mätzig's 1965 reformative film *Das Kaninchen bin ich* (*The Rabbit is Me*), though different in form, also addressed the problem of political disengagement as support for the structures of totalitarianism and (constructively) criticised the lawmaking of the GDR system as having fatal social implications. The film was singled out by the state and withheld from release, paving the way for a wave of film bans in the same year. These films persisted as underground legends and are still collectively known as the *Kaninchenfilme*[2] (rabbit films) (Trumpener 2001: 116). Barton Byg explains that, because of their belated circulation after the fall of the Wall, these films now ironically attest to the regime's failing rather than contributing to the reform anticipated by their creators (79). The meaning of the rabbit is thus layered and carries multiple truths underneath the surface, similarly to the workings of the political allegory itself, reminding us that human truths are transcribed and projected, evoking different readings in different contexts.

Conclusion: Human Nature

In their attempt to negotiate and perhaps transgress the historical meaning of space, both *The Invisible Frame* and *Rabbit à la Berlin* shift the view to what is invisible about (or behind) the Berlin Wall. The irretrievable past is engaged as a perspective, decentred from its former fixed positions and relegated to a perpetual in-betweenness. In this way the concretisation of history and its spatial organisation, as exemplified in the Berlin Wall, give way to contemporary contemplations about ongoing political compartmentalisation and limitation, intimating that the Wall is a naturalised human obsession. *Wer Mauern baut, hat es nötig* (*Those Who Build Walls, Need Them*) states an iconic graffiti from the final days of the Berlin Wall, accentuating that the logic of the Wall carries across a variety of past and present contexts. Alain Badiou claims that 'twenty years later it is clear that the world's wall has merely shifted' and that 'new walls are being built all over the world' leading him to the conclusion that 'the "unified" world of globalisation is a sham' (2008: 38). Swinton's fascination with 'new walls' in *The Invisible Frame* further emphasises this idea and reminds the viewer that the Wall's traumatic remainders erupt all over the world, an idea most obviously highlighted by the film's dedication to the people of Palestine. Imagining the past from the point of view of the present thus also becomes a means to imagine the future precisely because the Wall can be projected and shifted at will and thereby never completely banished. The Wall functions as a screen of personal and political identities and mirrors the particularities from which it emerges while projecting itself on the world. In this context, Balibar explains that partitions are always local and global, providing 'a regime of meaning and power under which the world is represented as a "unity" of different "parts"' (2009: 201). Thus, walls are subject to transnationalisation and always work as projections of a political order and disorder that seek to unify themselves through modes of exclusion. The last image of *Rabbit à la Berlin* shows a 'contemporary' rabbit held captive in a box with his fearful eyes peeking out through a slim opening. This image springs the analysis from its historical enclosure, suggesting to the viewer that we cannot free ourselves from our past and that the possibility of imprisonment is as pervasive today as it was then. It also aligns the notion of the Wall yet again with the notion of fear, and sends a final warning about the continuum that links security with imprisonment. Similarly, Swinton explains towards the end of her bike ride that 'It's a fearful heart that builds a wall and a fearless heart that can live without it' (*The Invisible Frame* 2009). Both films thus cannot provide an adequate reading of the historical past but they enable a reading of the self in relation to the historical space. They thus contemplate what the past means (or could mean) now. Konopka warns us about the fatal compromises of ignorance and inner retreat, as Swinton demonstrates not just the spatialisation but also the internalisation of the political. Ultimately, both films encourage an engagement with, and a fearless rejection of, a totalising world in which the walls of the present (re)appear as the bitter requirements of a 'unified' world.

CHAPTER 2

Changing Sides:
East/West Travesties in Lionel Baier's
Comme des voleurs (à l'est)

Kris Van Heuckelom (KU Leuven)

Following the collapse of the Iron Curtain and the subsequent enlargement of the European Union, immigrants from the former Eastern bloc have received increasing cinematic representation across the European continent. Concurrently, the past two decades have seen a considerable – albeit quantitatively less significant – proliferation of road movies which focus on the opposite (West–East) trajectory, creating a diverse body of films that only recently has become the object of scholarly research. Though both categories of films have their own characteristics and can be juxtaposed in a variety of ways – 'negative' versus 'positive' voyages (Gott and Schilt 2013), 'trafficking' (Brown, Iordanova and Torchin 2010) versus 'travelling' (Mazierska and Rascaroli 2006) – most of these films share a strong involvement with the increasing impact of transnational mobility on the continent's sociocultural space in the aftermath of the Cold War.[1]

This chapter examines the francophone Swiss production *Comme des voleurs (à l'est)/Stealth* (2006), the second feature film of the Lausanne-based film-maker Lionel Baier.[2] For a variety of reasons, *Stealth* is rather atypical in its engagement with the shifting East/West divide after 1989. First of all, Baier combines within a single narrative various aspects of both 'travelling' and 'trafficking' along the East/West axis: while the first part of the film largely revolves around the encounters between the Swiss main character (Lionel Baier, played by the director himself) and an undocumented Polish au pair (Ewa), the second part of the film shifts focus to a turbulent road trip from Lausanne to Warsaw undertaken by the protagonist and his older sister Lucie. What is more, though both portions of the film – at least at first sight – would seem to be aligned with the bulk of European films dealing with post-1989 migration and transnational mobility, Baier's authorial approach adds a particular twist to various narrative tropes and cinematic conventions that typify the on-screen treatment of East/West encounters.

One of its most significant examples relates to the narrative thread of inter-ethnic coupling which plays a prominent role in both parts of the film. As I have argued elsewhere (Van Heuckelom 2011, 2013), many films dealing with post-Wall westbound (especially Polish) labour migration tend to combine images of a troubled host society with the portrayal of vigorous newcomers from the East who possess the physical and mental potential to rejuvenate the Old Continent and restore its disintegrating social and moral frameworks. More often than not, these filmic fantasies of transnational redemption go hand in hand with the deployment of (heterosexual) inter-ethnic romances. At first sight, Baier's film seems to be informed by a similar agenda: a West European protagonist at odds with himself discovers 'a new set of options' (Kopp 2010: 301) in the arms of an attractive immigrant of East European extraction who is in search of legal and material stability in the West. What is more, the main character's sudden enthusiastic engagement with all things Polish seems to go along with 'a nostalgic restoration' of 'healthy masculinity' (Rydzewska, 218) which finds apt expression in his forced efforts to free himself from his homosexual orientation. Significantly, however, while the first part of the film closes with Lionel's announcement of his (paper) marriage with his East European 'love interest' – another common thread in contemporary European films about migration – the voyage portion of the film shifts focus to Lionel's re(dis)covery of his (sexual) identity which reaches a climax in his idyllic romance with the Polish film student Stanisław. As I will argue in my discussion of *Stealth*, these significant reversals and plot twists do not only point to Baier's rather idiosyncratic and unconventional approach to film-making but are part of a larger attempt to build a narrative universe that serves a twofold purpose: not only does it aim to reconfigure the relationship between Eastern and Western Europe, and to reposition the former as a centre in its own right, but it also helps Baier to root his native Switzerland more firmly in the continent's past and present.

Appropriating the American Frontier Myth

To a certain extent, *Stealth* draws its particular atmosphere from the fact that Baier – apart from being the director and co-scriptwriter of the film – plays the part of the main protagonist and creates an on-screen persona loosely inspired by his own biography.[3] Opening in Lausanne on Christmas Eve of 2004, the film brings into view two francophone Swiss siblings (Lionel and his sister Lucie), each of whom is going through a crisis in their personal life. While Lucie struggles with an unexpected pregnancy and fears the prospect of raising a child with a partner whom she does not really love, her brother seems to be fed up with the well-regulated life he leads with his long-time partner Serge and fantasises about escaping from everyday routine. Yet, in spite of the personal dilemmas both siblings are faced with, they differ strongly from each other in terms of character and behaviour. As a social worker responsible for guiding asylum seekers, Lucie is deeply immersed in 'real life', while her homosexual brother – a cultural commentator for the francophone Swiss radio – is portrayed as a creative and romantic soul, a writer who repeatedly loses himself in daydreaming and fantasies (Legast, 113).

From the very outset of the film, the main protagonist's seemingly unrestrained imagination is fostered by his readings of a copy of Blaise Cendrars's 1925 novel *L'or* (*Sutter's Gold*), a book that figures as one of the most significant props in the film. Based on the life story of Johann August Sutter (1803–80), Cendrars's acclaimed prose debut offers a fictionalised account of the rise and fall of the Swiss-born adventurer and pioneer Sutter who, after founding a large estate in the coastal area of Upper California, falls victim to the gold rush and the sudden influx of gold diggers and squatters. As a director, Baier deploys a particular editing technique to visualise the role of 'Sutteresque' fantasies in the personal life of his on-screen alter ego: at several points in the first part of the film, he replaces the original background of a Lausanne-set scene set with an 'exotic' background. This device is used for the first time in the very beginning of *Stealth* when the protagonist spends a spare moment in his car glancing through *Sutter's Gold*. While we hear Baier's off-screen voice reading a fragment from Cendrars's novel, the background is filled with the image of a wide-open landscape of a (Californian) desert and a rugged chain of mountains.[4] If the quote from *Sutter's Gold* functions as an incitement for Lionel to break with the normalcy and routine of his Lausanne life and embark on a personal conquest for 'gold', then the imaginative power of the novel sets in motion a series of events that ultimately lead up to the Baier siblings' road trip from Switzerland to Poland.

Significantly, though Lionel's fantasies initially have a rather vague object (Sutter's 'gold'), the discovery of his Polish roots suddenly provides his quest with a more specified set of spatial signifiers which is exemplified by another instance of fantasising. While the dreamy journalist Baier drifts off in thought during a boring editorial meeting, his off-screen voice reads another fragment from *Sutter's Gold* (which exposes the Swiss pioneer's obsessive desire to explore 'a land further to the West').[5] Simultaneously, another wide-open Californian landscape fills the background of the screen, followed by a blowing Polish flag appearing in the front.

Figure 2.1 Lionel fantasises about California (and Poland).

The subsequent Lausanne-set episodes highlight the impact of Sutter's story on Baier's on-screen persona, who now obsessively immerses himself in Polish language, culture and history. One more scene makes the imaginary substitution of Sutter's California with Baier's Poland complete: in yet another moment of absent-mindedness triggered by his readings, Baier's pensive and dreamy facial expression in front of the camera is accompanied in the background by the image of a snow-covered plain and the sound of a bleak rustling wind.

Strikingly, while the very word 'East' is never used in the film and appears only in the subtitle, references to the 'West' occur much more often (not least in quotes from *Sutter's Gold*). Inspired by his readings of the novel, Baier's protagonist relocates the American frontier myth to the European continent, in the mean time replacing the mythical Far West with an equally mystified Eastern Europe inhabited by mysterious, slant-eyed Slavs. Importantly, however, although in both cases the continental periphery is perceived as the edge of civilisation, distant from the centre, there is a significant difference in approach. Inasmuch as the widespread romanticisation of the Wild West relies on the idealisation of the western territories as a space of unlimited opportunity and liberty (an idea that continues to live on in the American Dream), the East/West divide in Europe has been constructed through a discursive process of otherisation, setting the civilised West apart from the alleged backwardness and cultural deficiencies of the barbaric East European other (Wolff). In the mean time, by adopting the American frontier myth in his approach of the newly 'opened' East European territories and exposing the region's exotic appeal as an uncharted land of opportunity, Baier at least partly transgresses the traditional orientalist paradigm.

Throughout the first part of the film, Baier's on-screen alter ego puts much effort into aligning himself with the East European (or Slavic) other, both in physical and in behavioural terms. Following his forced attempts to offer proof of his typical Slavic, semi-oriental physical hallmarks, Baier starts to renegotiate and reconfigure his sexual identity, much to the surprise (and growing dissatisfaction) of his immediate circle, in particular his partner Serge and his sister Lucie. Lionel's gradual transition from 'soft masculinity' – of which his homosexuality is the most prominent element – to a 'harder' form of masculinity is heralded by his sudden patriotically inspired engagement with a typically macho-dominated sport such as football (the rules of which he does not seem to understand).[6]

Subsequently, after his Polish friend Ewa moves in with them, Lionel imposes upon his gay partner Serge a series of measures that mark his eagerness to cover up their homosexual relationship and everything else that might offend Ewa's – Polish – feelings and mentality: hand shaking instead of cheek kissing, sleeping in separate bedrooms, and no more queer-themed pictures on the wall. In an agitated conversation with her mother, Lucie aptly describes her brother's rapprochement towards Ewa as a form of 'switching sides' ('Il a viré de bord'). The culmination of Lionel's performative 'heterosexualisation' takes place during an idyllic family picnic, at which he informs his parents and his sister about his upcoming marriage with his Polish partner. At this point, one more significant physical change lends visual prominence to Lionel's personal transformation, namely the disappearance of his bleached hairdo (which Ewa had called 'funny, just like straw') in favour of ordinary brown hair.

It is tempting to approach this remarkable turnover from a broader perspective and relate it to a widespread narrative trope in post-1989 European cinema dealing with East/West encounters. As Kristin Kopp has aptly remarked with respect to the function of Polish immigrants in recent German film, Polish characters are often 'introduced into German space as agents of personal rescue' and offer a 'new set of options' to local protagonists who are at odds with themselves and their immediate environment (Kopp, 301). As such, instead of representing a site of civilisational backwardness and barbarity, the East comes to serve here as an imaginary repository of more traditional traits and values that the affluent, but degenerated and increasingly dysfunctional, West seems to have lost.

Such an interpretation of Baier's cinematic engagement with Polishness gains additional resonance if we take into account another film in which the Polish actress Alicja Bachleda-Curuś (who plays Ewa in *Stealth*) is cast in the role of a Polish au pair, namely the German film *Herz im Kopf / Heart over Head* (2001, directed by Michael Gutmann). Focusing on the romance between a Polish immigrant (Wanda) and an erratic German teenager who has just lost his mother, the film shares a series of plot details with *Stealth*. While exposing the exploitation of the girl by her German employers (who treat her badly and make her live in the basement which recalls Ewa's situation as described by Lionel), the narrative foregrounds the girl's potential to restore balance in the emotional life of her German love interest with whom she eventually moves in.

In the meantime, however, thinking retrospectively of Bachleda-Curuś's role in *Heart over Head* helps to lay bare the undeniably parodistic twist which Baier gives to his main character's quest for self-discovery. More often than not, Baier pushes the narrative thread of a troubled local longing for emotional and physical transformation to the extreme and puts his on-screen alter ego in rather implausible situations which often – as Alain Boillat has indicated – 'border on the burlesque' (2008: 149). Quite ludicrous, for instance, are Lionel's repeated attempts to enforce an essentialist view of ethnic identity, most notably when he tries to convince his partner Serge of his inherently Slavic looks. Therefore, rather than creating another conventional fantasy of transnational redemption within the framework of a 'negative voyage' narrative, Baier seems to shift focus to the very mechanism of fantasy and foregrounds the way in which the stories and narrative patterns we consume (through film, literature, television . . .) guide and drive our actions and emotions.

Navigating between John Sutter and Wilhelm Tell

Baier's interest in the figure of John Sutter (as fictionalised in Cendrars's *Sutter's Gold*) does not only bear relevance with respect to the main protagonist's fantasy-driven behaviour and his appropriation of the American frontier myth but should also be related to the Swiss setting of the film. As Lionel indicates in one of his arguments with his sister Lucie, the discovery of his Polish roots acts as a relief for him: it means that 'the lake-dwelling Swiss' are not their ancestors which, in turn, implies that 'everything we learned in school does not concern us'. Interestingly, during their agitated discussion about Swiss identity and how it has been imposed on them by the Swiss educational system, both Lucie and Lionel deploy the French word '*Helvète*' (Helvetian). Given the historical resonance of the term – derived from the antique (Roman) name for Switzerland (Helvetia) and still used in the country's Neo-Latin name Confederatio Helvetica – it is difficult to avoid thinking here of one of the alleged founding fathers of the Helvetian confederation of cantons, the legendary mountain peasant Wilhelm Tell.[7] While Tell has come to function as the cornerstone of Swiss national mythology and embodies a collective selfhood which is defensive, protective and humanitarian, the nineteenth-century pioneer, John Sutter – the founder of a 'New Helvetia' on American soil – may be seen as a transgressive figure who, unlike his legendary compatriot, defies boundaries and intrepidly charts new territory.

Interestingly, however, though Sutter serves as the spiritual patron of Lionel's obsessive engagement with his East European roots, the exploration of his Polishness takes place within the safe confines of his Swiss home town and its immediate surroundings (which gains additional visual expression through the car of his employer with which he usually drives through Lausanne). Initially, hence, the journey of self-discovery on which Lionel embarks is rather more spiritual than geographical in nature. Along the same lines, it is quite striking that the first part of the film strongly exposes Switzerland's reputation as a popular immigration destination. This is related, first of all, to the magnet function of Switzerland as a First World state with a highly advanced economy and elevated living standards but is also in line with the country's 'strong tradition of humanitarian aid and open frontiers for refugees' (Sciarini, Hug and Dupont, 70). Baier's protagonist occasionally aligns himself with this tradition when he classifies his help to Ewa as an act of hospitality and humanitarian concern. Apart from the Polish au pair, immigrants make their on-screen appearance in various configurations (notably an African immigrant attending the annual Christmas dinner of the Baier family and asylum seekers at Lucie's workplace). A more subtle historical reference to Switzerland's status as an immigrant-receiving country emerges when Lionel shows his audio recorder to Ewa and mentions in passing the name of its inventor, the Oscar-winning audio engineer Stefan Kudelski.[8]

In cinematic terms, the image of Switzerland as a safe and protective haven for the weak and oppressed finds expression in the idyllic picnic scene during which Lionel announces his marriage with Ewa. The rustic setting of a meadow near a lake surrounded by hills brings to mind what Maria Tortajada has called the Swiss 'landscape of national spiritual defense', a landscape designed to envision 'an idyllic mythology around the idea of "armed neutrality", of "Switzerland as a *terre d'accueil*", the soul of the countryside and of rural life' (115). Significantly, however, while Lionel's traditionalist parents enthusiastically welcome his marital plans, the visual cosiness of the picnic scene is cut short by a sharp exchange of words ignited by Lucie who sees through the falseness of her younger brother's transformation. Paradoxically, it is Lucie who suddenly jumps into Lionel's car and 'kidnaps' her brother, in order to take him on a real 'Sutteresque' journey to the East and confront him with the stupidity of his Polish fantasies. As such, the backward glance which Lionel casts from inside the car towards the picnic party epitomises the end of his fantasy-driven engagement with Ewa (and all things Polish) within the safe and protective confines of his Swiss home country.

What follows then might be called a 'return road movie' (Gott 2013b, 2013c) in which two siblings of distant Polish heritage undertake an eastward journey to settle the question of their East European roots. Insofar as their motor trip through Germany, the Czech Republic and Slovakia is set before the enlargement of the Schengen Area, the ease with which they cross the subsequent national borders (which are usually shown in travelling shots) underlines their status as privileged tourists from the West. In the meantime, their journey receives a certain outlaw dimension through the fact that they drive a 'stolen' car belonging to Lionel's employer.[9] Another nod to the road movie genre is given by the transformative and therapeutic effect of the journey. After they cross the Czech–Slovak border, Baier decides to step out of his self-delusion and unravels the phantasmic character of his engagement with Ewa and his 'heterosexualisation'. This confession is followed by another – physically more painful – reality check during a short stopover in Slovakia where Lionel and Lucie come to the aid of a Slovak woman beaten up by her male partner. The consequences of their well-intended but unwelcome intervention are sore. Lionel's confrontation with 'hard' Slovak masculinity begins with his face being smashed against the hood of the car and ends with a crazy car chase in the Slovak–Polish border region. Apart from being indicative of Baier's generic eclecticism as a film-maker, this 'noirish' turnabout serves to make the protagonist feel the 'reality' of the East and urge him to traverse his fantasy which is epitomised by the physical damage caused to his Swiss 'bodies' (a bruised nose, a blood-stained shirt and a broken car boot). A similar sobering effect is generated by the first Poland-set episode. The morning after the car chase, the Baier siblings wake up in their vehicle which turns out to be parked in the town of Oświęcim (Auschwitz). The combination of a shrill and tinny extradiegetic sound with a slow-paced travelling shot (showing images of smoke going up in the air and columns of people walking next to a wired fence) cannot but evoke reminiscences of World War II and the Holocaust. In what seems to be another ironic twist, the Oświęcim sequence also includes a shot of the letterings 'Twój dom' ('Your Home') on the signboard of a local shop. Subsequently, we see Lionel hastily grabbing and bolting food in a Polish supermarket, after which he declares to Lucie that 'it is time to go home now'.

In the toilet of the supermarket, however, a deus ex machina appears in the person of the Polish film student Stan. Insofar as he helps to cure the injuries caused to Lionel's 'bodies' – cleaning and treating his nose, washing his shirt, getting the car repaired – the young man seems to act as the epitome of 'soft' and 'caring' Slavic masculinity. What is more, the idyllically located family cabin into which he invites the two siblings and the sincere romance that unfolds between him and Lionel may be said to serve as a counterbalance to the prematurely aborted pastoral scene in Switzerland during which Lionel announced his marriage with Ewa. Along the same lines, Stan's easy-going attitude and open-mindedness turn out to be instrumental in melting down the troubled relationship between Lionel and his sister. Quite significant in this respect is the particular setting in which Lucie eventually decides to confide her innermost feelings to her brother and share with him the secret of her pregnancy: while she joins the two lovers in their too narrow single bed in the cabin, Stan (who holds Lionel in his arms) becomes partly invisible and constitutes a physical and symbolic bridge between the two siblings. Though afterwards, the ways of Lionel, Lucie and Stan part, the fact that the goodbye scene is concluded with a symbolic economic transaction – Lionel exchanging his Swiss shirt for Stan's Polish sweater – epitomises the sense of (East/West) equality which characterises their relationship (as opposed to the relation of economic dependency which existed between Ewa and Lionel).

The idyllic stopover in southern Poland is then followed by the second portion of their road trip (to Warsaw) which takes on the form of a detective-like quest for the Polish pedigree of the Baier family. Seemingly in accord with the prominent role of Sutter's westward peregrinations in the first part of *Stealth*, visual and verbal references to the American frontier myth keep returning in the road movie section of the film and lay bare the similar but inverted character of the siblings' quest (West Europeans exploring the continent's East). As another symbolic tribute and narrative follow-up to Cendrars's novel, the eastward trip of the Baiers finds material expression in the notes and drawings Lionel makes on the blank pages and margins of his Polish copy of *Sutter's Gold*.

Throughout the road movie section, the Swiss (and, by extension, West European) identity of the co-travellers is epitomised by several close ups of the letterings on the sides of the driving vehicle. While the inscription 'Radio Suisse Romande' points to the car as the property of a Swiss stateowned institution and turns it into a driving micro-piece of Switzerland on foreign territory, the ordinal number, which figures prominently on both sides of the car ('la 1ère'), may be said to epitomise the travellers' First World status. In the meantime, however, though some travelling shots taken from inside the car may evoke a sense of East European primitivism and economic backwardness (albeit not in the vein of Sacha Baron Cohen's *Borat*), the Poland-set portion of *Stealth* portrays the East of Europe in a rather balanced way, that is to say as a blend of traditionalism and modernity caught in a process of socio-economic transformation: decent roads alternate with small rural roads used by Polish Fiats and local peasants in their horse-drawn buggies, while pictures of the industrial wasteland of Silesia are combined with images of modern industries, foreign investments and new commerce.

Centring Warsaw, Decentring Lausanne

While the trip to Warsaw initially goes smoothly and harmoniously (as suggested, for instance, by images of the car zigzagging over the Polish highway under the tones of Maurice Ravel's *La Valse*), the co-travellers' situation changes when a Swiss hitchhiker drives off with their vehicle and strips them of all their belongings, including money and documents. This episode does not only mark the shift from a car-centred road trip to a less motorised form of mobility (hiking and hitchhiking), it also heralds the two siblings' gradual transformation from mobile Swiss tourists into undocumented, stateless immigrants. This significant reversal of status reaches its culmination after they arrive in Warsaw (on foot) and try to find their way in the Polish capital. Quite symbolically, whereas the Swiss part of the film largely revolves around Lionel's and Lucie's efforts to assist illegal immigrants and asylum seekers (out of, respectively, personal and professional concerns), the siblings now come to occupy the position of the people they used to help. What is more, while Lucie considers the possibility of turning herself in to the Swiss embassy and asking for repatriation, Lionel prefers to stick to his disenfranchised status and persuades his sister to continue their joint adventure (if need be with the help of 'someone who looks after *sans-papiers*'). To obtain forged Polish papers, the siblings then resort to survival strategies typically used by undocumented immigrants. Using the terminology proposed by Gott and Schilt (2013), one may say that their initially 'positive' voyage starts to assume some of the hallmarks of a 'negative' one.

In terms of setting, it is undoubtedly significant that some of these Warsaw episodes take place in the immediate surroundings of the so called Tenth Anniversary Stadium, for many decades one of the most prestigious Warsaw venues for communist festivities and propaganda meetings. In the 1980s, a lack of maintenance and financial resources led to a rapid dilapidation of the entire complex, after which immigrants from the East (mainly the former Soviet Union and Vietnam) turned it into a huge open-air marketplace (usually referred to as 'the Russian market'). While the sequences set at the stadium point, first of all, to some of the socio-economic side effects of the post-1989 transition from communism to capitalism, they also foreground the Polish capital's growing reputation as an immigrant-receiving metropolis in its own right. On the premises of the former stadium, we see Lionel and Lucie bargaining with other (mainly Asian) 'immigrants' to whom they sell their last Swiss belongings (their designer clothes) and from whom they eventually receive false Polish documents.

Lionel's obtaining of a forged Polish identity card (in the name of his Polish great grandfather Adam Baier) has both symbolic and practical implications. Apart from offering him an alternative, pseudo-official way to reclaim his Polish selfhood, it also allows him entry into the Polish National Archives to reconstruct the Polish pedigree of the Baier family. In what transpires as another deus ex machina, the archival searches of the Baier siblings bring them in touch with a distant Polish relative, Henryk Baier, who invites them to his house and helps them to resolve the mystery surrounding the fate of their Polish–Swiss ancestor Adam Baier. In combination with the changing status of the Swiss siblings during their journey to the Polish capital, the concluding Warsaw-set sequences reinforce the idea that the Poland-set part of the film should be seen as a cinematic reversal of the initial portion set in Lausanne. While *Stealth* opens with atmospheric images of lit-up Lausanne during Christmas time, it closes with very similar shots of the Polish capital taken during end-of-year celebrations, some twelve months later. In both cases, the viewer receives close-ups of the hustle and bustle in vibrant European metropolises which – in spite of their different geographical location and historical background – seem to be highly interchangeable.[10] Within the span of one year, the story has come full circle, whereas its main protagonists have successfully 'switched sides'.

Along similar lines, it is undoubtedly significant that the life story of Lucie's and Lionel's great grandfather Adam Baier – who married a Swiss girl working as an au pair in interwar Warsaw – reads as an inverted prequel to the Lausanne story of Lionel and the Polish au pair Ewa. By means of these various narrative reversals, Baier's *Stealth* highlights the relativity of the centre–periphery opposition, both in the present and in the past, and underscores the arbitrariness and fluidity of geopolitical signifiers such as East and West.

Narrating Familial and Transnational Stories

If the road trip to Poland functions as a transformative experience for both siblings and brings them closer to each other, then it also leads to reconciliation on a more general level. Lucie's initial scepticism about her brother's obsessive interest in fiction and his fantasy-driven behaviour gradually gives way to an awareness of the beneficial and catalysing influence stories and storytelling may have on interpersonal relations. This thread links up with one of the most prominent motifs running through the dialogues of *Stealth*: the inability and/or unwillingness of close relatives to communicate with each other and share their stories. As it transpires, the issue of sharing stories bears particular relevance to the Polish portion of the film. Through their close encounters with the Polish branch of the Baier family, Lionel and Lucie help their Polish relatives to complete the missing links in the story of their family, and vice versa. Perhaps not coincidentally, these narrative gaps largely revolve around the further story of their great grandfather Adam Baier after he divorced his Swiss spouse and went back to Poland in the early 1930s. In filmic terms, Lionel's and Lucie's premonition about what happened to their great grandfather during the war finds expression in three inserted underwater sequences which repeatedly interrupt the film's linear structure. If these hazy images of a drowning soldier and his horse have been lingering in the subconscious of the two Swiss siblings, then Henryk Baier provides confirmation for their suspicions and informs them that their great grandfather indeed perished during World War II (as a member of the Polish cavalry fighting against German tanks).

Though it might seem a broad interpretive stretch, the unwillingness of Lionel's Swiss family to talk about the fate of the Poland-born great grandfather can be seen as an allegorical reminder of the rather delicate position which both the war and the Holocaust occupy in Swiss collective consciousness. In spite of the country's neutrality throughout World War II and its successful resistance against Germany, Switzerland has faced repeated attacks for its shady dealings and silent collaboration with the Nazis and, more recently, for the illegal appropriation of dormant accounts of Holocaust victims by Swiss banks. Therefore, as if it were to confront his Swiss audience with the 'other' side of the World War

II experience, Baier repeatedly grants memorial sites related to the war and the Holocaust a prominent place in the Polish trajectory of his protagonists.[11]

From a more contemporary perspective, Baier's transnational cinematic endeavours may be seen as an attempt to align his native Switzerland more visibly and palpably with the geopolitical and sociocultural changes taking place in post-Wall Europe. Often referred to as 'die Sonderfall Schweiz' ('the special case Switzerland'), the Swiss Confederation is perhaps the only West European state that has remained relatively unaffected by the European integration process that started in the early 1950s. Even today, in spite of the far-reaching economic integration with other European countries (mainly realised through bilateral agreements), the lack of institutional integration with the European Union continues to sustain widespread stereotypes such as Switzerland 'the landlocked island' and 'an anomaly at the centre of Europe' (Bewes, 7). The central role of familial and transnational storytelling in Baier's film can be further clarified if we take into account Klaus Eder's considerations about the narrative construction of Europe as an 'identitarian space'. As Eder claims,

> The people in Europe share not only particular histories of their particular past but they also share a common past as soon as they start to define a common space of communication of these histories. Who participates in such communication then becomes part of Europe in a cultural sense. To turn the boundaries of such a communicative space, i.e. its 'soft borders', into hard borders of Europe is a political project. But the cultural basis of such borders is contingent upon the readiness to share one's own history with the history of the others around her/him. (268–9)

In *Stealth*, Baier may be said to set up such a communicative space within which shared stories – especially those about the past – are able to circulate. Rather than engaging in a politically oriented project of integration, he sets up a bottom-up identity project at the heart of which lies the need to create intimate narrative bonds between relatives, families, communities and nations. Significantly, in what seems to be the ultimate example of Baier's penchant for deploying reflexive tropes, one of the final scenes of *Stealth* reveals to the viewer the actual meaning of the protagonist's – and the director's – Polish surname. '*Bajerować* in Polish means to tell stories', we hear Henryk Baier's wife confide to Lionel when he parts from his Warsaw relatives and his sister Lucie at Warsaw Central Station.

Finally, by way of a coda, it is undoubtedly worth adding that Baier's cinematic engagement with the East/West divide in *Stealth* marks only the beginning of a long-term artistic project, namely a cinematic tetralogy themed around the four cardinal points. At the 2013 edition of the Locarno

International Film Festival, Baier presented his most recent feature film, *Les Grandes Ondes (à l'ouest)/Longwave* (Switzerland/France/Portugal), a historic comedy about two Swiss radio journalists who accidentally find themselves in Lisbon during the Carnation Revolution. Though the film stands on its own in terms of plot and characters, the subtitle, *à l'ouest* (*to the west*), and the narrative focus on the foreign peregrinations of Lausanne-based journalists point to the fact that *Longwave* – not unlike its eastwardly oriented forerunner – takes the city of Lausanne as the geographical focal point from which the continent's cardinal directions are measured and explored. Though it is, obviously, too early to assess Baier's project in its entirety – provided that he will manage to complete the two remaining parts of the cycle – *Stealth* exposes the paradoxical character of Baier's engagement with Europe's shifting landscape: by embarking on a cinematic road trip through the continent, he literally displaces his native Switzerland from the centre of attention, while simultaneously trying to save it from its narrative isolation.

CHAPTER 3

Dubbing and Doubling Over: The Disorientation of France in the Films of Michael Haneke and Krzysztof Kieślowski

Alison Rice (University of Notre Dame)

In an early scene from Krzysztof Kieślowski's *Blanc/White* (1993, Poland/France/Switzerland) a Polish immigrant struggles to defend himself in a Parisian courtroom despite his lack of competence in French. Karol Karol speaks hastily to the judge, imploring him to listen to his side of the story before granting his wife a divorce: 'Where is equality? Is my not speaking French a reason for the court to refuse to hear my case?' His translator renders these comments in French but Karol's wife declares that she no longer loves him and the unconsummated marriage is annulled.

It hardly seems surprising that a film by a Polish director whose opening scenes take place in France should explicitly evoke the question of language. What Kieślowski succeeds in doing so brilliantly in this film, as in others, is engage with more than one tongue. French may be the language of the courtroom at the outset but it is not the language that dominates throughout the script. Kieślowski creates a complex text in which Polish is also portrayed as a language of law and power, thanks to the transnational, cross-cultural movements of Karol and the two other principal protagonists, his French ex-wife Dominique and his countryman Mikolaj. It is thanks to the latter that a dejected and destitute Karol is able to leave Paris and rebuild his life in a post-1989 Poland. The bilingual nature of this cinematic production means that, unless the protagonists are proficient in both French and Polish, a certain form of translation is necessary. The various characters in the film are not entirely autonomous, therefore, because they must often rely on others to communicate for them, like Karol Karol before the judge.

In an earlier film by Kieślowski, *La Double vie de Véronique/The Double Life of Véronique* (1991, Poland/France), relying on another to speak on one's behalf is necessary in a very literal sense, not simply for the advancement of the plot. The actress Irène Jacob plays two roles in this movie, that of the eponymous French music teacher and that of a Polish soprano whose name is the same in translation, Weronika. Since the actress is not fluent in the two languages, her voice must be dubbed into Polish for the film to work. Critic Jonathan Romney notes the shortcomings of this process: 'Although there are moments when Weronika/Véronique seems prone to a cloying chirpiness – arising partly from Weronika's dubbing into Polish – Jacob displays a vibrancy and a sustained alertness that energize the screen' (2006: 13). These comments remind us of a linguistic barrier that is an integral part of transnational European film-making, a barrier that dubbing cannot always effectively overcome, even when the performances of talented actors compensate for some of what is lost in translation.

In Michael Haneke's multilingual *Code inconnu*/*Code Unknown* (2000, France/Germany/Romania), the challenges of communicating effectively from one tongue to another are brought to the forefront in a variety of fragmented scenes. Much of the action takes place in Paris, the metropolis that has drawn immigrants from multiple locations ranging from Mali to Romania. The scenes that give insight into the story of Maria, a wife, mother, and grandmother who has left her home to provide for her family, paint a rather bleak portrait of the experience of an Eastern European immigrant in the West. This displaced individual finds herself without a voice, not only in France where she is reduced to begging in silence, but also in her homeland when she is deported and where others brag of their success in finding employment in Dublin, for instance. *Code Unknown* is a film that contains a portrayal of the actual process of dubbing and that, therefore, is especially attuned to the difficulty of providing a voice for oneself (even when one is proficient in the language of expression), let alone attempting to speak on behalf of someone else.

Like the Austrian Haneke, Kieślowski established a reputation as a film-maker in his native country of Poland before bringing his talent to bear on films produced and shot (at least partially, if not entirely) on French soil. Each in his own way, these directors have contributed new perspectives to film-making in Europe. As Colin MacCabe asserts in his analysis of Kieślowski's *Three Colors* trilogy of which *White* is the second instalment, 'what he had achieved in these films marked a cross-fertilization of the two great postwar European cinemas that could never be surpassed' (13).[1] In the paragraphs that follow, I focus on the way in which three films made in the 1990s, Kieślowski's *The Double Life of Véronique* and *White* and Haneke's *Code Unknown*, shed light on crucial themes at a pivotal time in European history. These three cinematic creations from this momentous decade depict complex interactions between Eastern European protagonists and their French counterparts prior to the expansion of the European Union in 2004, when Poland became a member, and 2007, when

Romania joined. It is my belief that these filmic texts provide invaluable insight into complicated cultural questions – with economic, linguistic, political and religious implications – that many still pose today about what should constitute Europe and what it means to be European.[2]

Critics Niven Kumar and Lucyna Swiatek construct a convincing argument about the workings of Haneke's films: 'Ironically, Haneke shows that the "civilizing process", which the west imposes on the Orientalized Other, is the self-same process it imposes upon itself' (319). They maintain that, in two films in particular, 'the presence of that which is the other is never quite the other, but is always and already part of the inside'. In my view, what is significant about films like Kieślowski's *The Double Life of Véronique* and *White* and Haneke's *Code Unknown* is that they provide such compelling insight into the experience of 'European others'. While these others are certainly not the 'Orientalized Other' evoked in postcolonial conversations, there are nonetheless parallels between the experiences of these various others in their relationship to France. The Eastern European figure in these films is often ostensibly ostracised, rejected and even ejected in flagrant ways but the violence of the French reaction to this image of the Other – who has penetrated the hexagonal borders of this Western European country – only thinly veils the recognition of these others and of their place within France. Haneke and Kieślowski succeed in turning inside out the conceptions of 'centre', of 'that which is "outside of culture"', as Kumar and Swiatek express it, thereby disrupting 'binary oppositions' through their film-making (319). While France figures prominently in these works, it is not the only focus of the films, and it is certainly not the sole centre of interest or unique location of culture. Instead, France is placed in context with respect to other national entities, such as Poland and Romania, in meaningful ways.[3] When they highlight the potential for personal transformation – among Western and Eastern Europeans alike – brought about by travel and immigration, and when they underscore the possibilities for economic improvement and language acquisition on either side of national borders within the larger space of Europe, these films portend a change in the allure and the aura of France, and presage a conversion of its status, at the dawn of the twenty-first century.

Doubling Up:
Musical Strains and Serendipitous Solidarities

For the Polish Weronika, a rising soprano, and for the French Véronique, a music teacher, music is much more than a profession; it is a way of being.

The very lives of these two characters in Kieślowski's *The Double Life of Véronique* are musical. Their sensitive, trained ears make them especially attentive to the sounds that surround them. Their haunting singing voices seem to have an immediate and profound effect on all who hear them. Weronika makes experts marvel and exclaim about the uniqueness of her vocal instrument. Likewise, Véronique inspires a great sigh of dismay from her instructor when she stops taking voice lessons. She opts to stop singing because of a tremendous, inexplicable sense of grief that suddenly comes upon her. Afterwards, she is on a quest to fill a void, to find what is missing. A man named Alexandre then enters her life.

When Véronique receives a cassette tape of a sound collage in an anonymous package, she is intrigued. She plays the tape over and over, actively listening to every sound it contains to work it out: 'Playing detective, Véronique traces the tape to Paris's Gare Saint-Lazare, where she finds Alexandre waiting for her' (Romney, 12). She is disconcerted when this puppeteer, whom she first met at the school where she teaches, indicates that the collage was part of an experiment for a novel he plans to write. She suddenly takes off, running down a busy street, with Alexandre on her heels. The chase is interesting but what is noteworthy about this scene is how it seems to prolong the intense listening exercise that Véronique has engaged in thus far, to find the particular café at the precise railway station where the sounds had initially been recorded. As she flees Alexandre, Véronique continues to listen carefully, and spectators are focused on the protagonist's aural environment as well. She takes refuge in the entry-way of an apartment building, watching from the windows of the doors and, as always, listening intently. Alexandre slows his footsteps right in front of this building, looking disappointed but not giving up. Then, he pulls out a handkerchief and blows his nose. The door that separates him from Véronique muffles the sound of Alexandre's blowing, and something about this softened noise seems to touch her. Her musical ear is evidently attuned to the multiple meanings of sounds, and the physiological needs of her pursuer have made him more human in her eyes – and ears. This tender moment of listening to, and feeling for, another provides a foretaste of the two protagonists' physical and emotional reunion shortly thereafter when Alexandre and Véronique become lovers.

Véronique and Alexandre later connect through conversation as she opens up to him and allows him to discover the contents of her large handbag. When Alexandre comes across photographs Véronique took during her travels to Eastern Europe, she starts to unravel the mystery of her deep sense of grief. 'Where is this?' Alexandre asks, immediately discerning that the photos are not from nearby: 'It's not in France.' She responds, 'That was on a trip to Czechoslovakia, Hungary and Poland. That must be in Krakow.' He studies the images and, focusing on one in particular, states, 'That's a beautiful picture. And you in that big coat.' Because she knows that she took the pictures rather than posing for them, Véronique looks disconcerted: 'That's not me.' But Alexandre insists, 'Sure it's you,' and hands it to her. She examines the picture of this female figure staring with such intensity and inquisitiveness. She says that the woman's coat is not hers but, as she touches the photo, her breathing falters. Then she lets out a sob and collapses on to the bed.

Véronique's new lover quickly comes to her and embraces her, kissing her face, drying her eyes with his fingers, feeling her pain and covering her with affection. In this powerful scene of shared emotion, Véronique's Polish double has brought her closer than ever to another human being, has precipitated their lovemaking and now is observing it, seemingly, as the image continues to look on. Véronique's cries of pain turn into gasps of pleasure, of sensual engagement, of climax, and then of relief, and she finally recovers from the intensity of this moment, looking again upon the image that returns her gaze.

The melody that runs throughout *The Double Life of Véronique*, the song Weronika was singing when she died, picks up in the next scene as Véronique wanders the halls of an apartment. Weronika's death was precipitated by a heart condition first revealed in the film just after Véronique took a picture of her. These two individuals, leading such similar yet such different lives, came so close to each other at a serendipitous moment in a large square in Poland. Véronique was visiting Krakow on a guided tour with a French group when the police arrived to quell the violence of a political demonstration. As the young Frenchwoman rushed to board the bus along with the other tourists, Weronika spots her and remains riveted, fixing her eyes on Véronique without any concern for what is happening around her. Motionless, Weronika stares at the bus as it moves in the opposite direction, then turns, and everything in the scene seems to be circling around in a dizzying motion, until the bus speeds away. During this time, Véronique is snapping pictures, including the shot of Weronika whose eyes never truly caught those of the object of her gaze, this individual who is also dressed in red and black, this woman who resembles her down to the last detail, this Western equivalent of herself. Shortly after this overwhelming moment, Weronika collapses in the street, falling into the leaves, clutching her heart.

The morning after their discovery of the photo containing Véronique's lookalike, Alexandre presents his lover with a new puppet he has created. He responds to her question, 'Is that me?' with 'Of course it's you,' in an echo of the discussion of the night before. When she finds that he has made a second puppet she asks, seemingly troubled, 'Why two?' He asserts that he handles them a great deal and therefore needs duplicates. Véronique holds and manipulates one of the puppets while the other one remains inert, and Alexandre reads his story of two girls who are born in different countries but who resemble each other down to the last detail. He speaks of how one has learned the lessons of the other, how the pain of one has allowed the other to escape from danger:

> That day, at 3:00 in the morning, they were both born, each in a different city, on a different continent. They both had dark hair and brownish-green eyes. At two years old, when both knew how to walk, one of them burned her hand on a stove. A few days later, the other one reached out to touch a stove but pulled back just in time. Yet she couldn't have known she was about to burn herself.

Véronique listens with great feeling, her eyes filled with tears, then lifts her hand to her face as he pronounces the final words in a gesture that is filled with inexplicable pain. She maintains composure but, when asked if she likes it, remains silent. He says, 'I think I'll call it *The Double Life of* . . . I haven't decided what to name them.' She does not answer; she turns and leaves. She seems emptied, as she slowly and deliberately takes each step that leads her away from this room, this narrative. We have to wonder if the incident Alexandre describes, of the one who suffered and the other who learned from the suffering of her double, might not have multiple implications. Perhaps vocal performances might have led the French protagonist to a demise reminiscent of that of her Polish double, and the fact that she suddenly felt compelled to quit might serve as a parallel to the movement away from the stove that saved the child from getting burned.

In an interview, Kieślowski denies that the death of the Polish protagonist in *The Double Life of Véronique* has any meaning that can be applied to his own trajectory.

> Working with French co-production money, he devised a story about a girl who dies in Poland and her double who goes on living in France. Clearly his symbolic farewell to Poland? 'It wasn't my intention for it to be a symbol of anything. A girl dies in Poland, that's all'. (Romney, 1993)

When, in the final scene, Véronique reaches out her hand and touches a tree with an open palm, however, this resolute gesture seems to indicate that some meaning can be made from the meeting of these two individuals on a square in Poland in the middle of the tumultuous political scene that surrounds them. Whereas Weronika fell down, collapsing into the leaves following their chance encounter, Véronique has in the end come to embrace the trunk of a tree, drawing strength from the knowledge that someone resembling her down to the smallest feature has existed in another place. Unlike Alexandre's statement, this individual did not grow up on another continent but, prior to 1989, it might have seemed as though this were the case. The fact that the two came so close to each other but didn't touch does not mean that both lives were not touched in other ways by this relative proximity and the realisations that it ultimately brought about. The knowledge and experience of Weronika have perhaps contributed to the strength of Véronique in the end, and the 'doubling up' of their talents might have positive consequences that are as unexpected as their moment of meeting. On a deep level, the recording devices that surround us (including cameras of all sorts) and that are ever more a part of our technologically oriented world, might make unforeseen solidarities possible not only across geographical but also across temporal barriers.[4] As Weronika declares with such passion and conviction, 'I feel like I'm not alone . . . like I'm not alone in the world.' The musical strains that speak to individuals across linguistic divides might also serve to unite those whose ears are open to the beauty of new rhythms and tonalities.

Doubling Back:
Economic Refrains and Romantic Retributions

Upon leaving the Palais de Justice after his marriage is annulled in Kieślowski's *White*, the foreigner sees his ex-wife unloading a big red suitcase that contains all of his belongings. Later that evening, he discovers that he is no longer able to withdraw money and when he visits a bank, a gentleman off-screen declares that it is not only his marital status that has changed: 'Karol Karol. Your account has been frozen. It is no longer valid. It's invalidated. Cancelled.' All these synonyms seem to be offered to help this man from elsewhere understand what dire economic straits he is in. Karol attempts to grab his card, clumsily saying the word 'carte' in French but the bank employee insists that he cannot return it to him and cuts it up in front of him. Then Karol laments his monetary loss in clear French: 'Mon argent'.

Given this early sequence of events, it might seem counterintuitive that, in a review for the *New York Times*, Caryn James refers to *White* as 'witty', a 'rich, light-handed marvel', and declares that it is 'laughable on purpose'. Part of what makes this film easier to laugh about, I would argue, is the 'doubling back' that marks its movement. We learn that their lovemaking was passionate when Dominique and Karol were on Polish soil, prior to their wedding in France. Despite the fact that, in a heated

Figure 3.1 *White*: Karol watches mutely as a bank employee destroys his card.

scene where she discovers him in their Parisian hair salon the morning after the divorce was pronounced, the Frenchwoman declares that she will never come with her husband to Poland, she does follow him to Poland in the end. In the salon scene, however, she claims the upper hand, exploding after Karol loses an erection yet again and then asks for forgiveness: 'I'll win every trial. The divorce, the property settlement, everything. Because you never understood anything.' Dominique declares, 'If I say I love you, you don't understand. And if I say I hate you, you still don't understand. You don't even understand that I want you, that I need you. You understand? You understand? No.' She sets fire to the curtains and lets him know that she will inform the police that he came to the salon to get revenge. He is forced to flee, leaving everything behind. But she has foretold the future: he will exact revenge when he is back on his turf, thanks in large part to the generosity of his newfound friend, Mikolaj.

Karol and Mikolaj first meet in the hallways of the metro, a highly symbolic location for those who are penniless in Paris. Karol is attempting to make a little money with a tune, playing a Polish tango on a makeshift instrument, a comb with a handkerchief folded over it. It is therefore music that draws Mikolaj to Karol; the former recognises the strains that fill the station and immediately addresses the latter in their native tongue. The diplomas sticking out of the open suitcase beside Karol bear witness to his past as an award-winning, well-travelled hairdresser who had successfully practised his art in cities such as Sophia, Budapest, Warsaw, and even Paris. It was in Budapest that we first saw his French wife-to-be, and the very sight of her was empowering and inspiring: 'I won the competition'. Karol wants to show the object of his affection to his new friend and they emerge from the underground station to see two figures, that of Dominique and that of her new lover, silhouetted in her window. Karol is devastated and immediately descends into the metro station to call his former wife on the phone, only to find himself obliged to listen to the sounds of her orgasm. He declares his love for her and hangs up in anguish. To add insult to injury, the payphone swallows the two francs that remain. But Karol won't stand for this injustice. He approaches the metro agent and insists, in French, that he return his change. When he receives the two-franc coin, when he recovers what is rightfully his, things seem to turn around for Karol. Getting back that money is symbolic of the 'getting back' of his life that will happen once he returns to Poland, as well as the 'getting back' at Dominique through his plot of revenge that ultimately, though arguably, leads to getting her back.

Doubling back to Poland in the case of Karol Karol means starting over in a setting that allows for economic growth at a rapid pace. No longer content with hairstyling, Karol gets in on schemes that make his money grow quickly, in a country where neon signs are now aglow, as on the front of his brother's store. This is a location which his brother insists has changed during Karol's absence: 'This is Europe now'. All is not positive here, however, especially for Mikolaj who seeks to end his suffering. Karol agrees to put an anonymous individual out of his misery when Mikolaj proposes that he do so in exchange for a consequential sum of money. Then, when they meet in the dark, Karol goes ahead with the act but shoots a blank into his friend's chest. Mikolaj doubles over, expecting an imminent demise, but discovers that he is still alive and decides he doesn't wish to die after all. A relieved Karol tells his friend, 'We all know pain'. His friend answers, 'Sure . . . but I wanted less of it.' Then they smile, even laugh, and, in the next scene, the two men are sliding across the ice on a white wintry morning, having fun. Mikolaj declares, 'I feel like a kid again', and follows this joyful news with the optimistic words, 'Everything's possible'. In this intense sequence, a set of actions has the liberating effect of bringing these two men back to their childhoods and enabling them to see their lives anew.

Karol is deeply invested in re-establishing himself and creating a successful, lucrative life on his native soil. But he never loses sight of his ex-wife who has effectively become synonymous with her country. A white bust of a woman, which he brought all the way from France, sits in his room. Four men had broken this treasured object upon his arrival in Poland but he immediately put it back together and contemplates it regularly. It can be seen to represent Dominique but it is also a bust of Madeleine, a symbol for the French Republic. As in *The Double Life of Véronique*, a cassette tape plays a meaningful role in *White*, for Karol is seen listening carefully to the oral conjugation of French verbs. He repeats these verbs in the past subjunctive in a scene that closes with the pronunciation of the words 'que je plusse', a phrase that hints that, if he only had pleased his wife, things would have turned out differently for Karol in France. He utters these words as he kisses the lips of the white bust. Just like the two-franc coin that he tries to throw into the river but that sticks to the palm of his hand, Karol is connected to France through the person of Dominique.

It is crucial to the storyline of *White* that Karol Karol masters French over time and subsequently seduces his ex-wife; his command of the language allows him to avoid the pitfalls of translation, to take matters into his own hands and 'dub himself', so to speak. In the added final scene of the film, there is a reconciliation of sorts between Dominique, who has been imprisoned in Poland, and Karol who has found a way into the prison grounds to see the woman he made love with just before her arrest. He observes her through binoculars, as he did at the cemetery when she attended his graveside funeral service after he faked his death in order to lure her to Poland. She makes hand gestures, her own invented movements that exist outside the national tongues that they have both had to stutter in when they were in the other's country, and communicates her desire to marry him again, a declaration of love that makes tears stream down Karol's face. Though they are separated for the moment, they have come full circle in their relationship and now share the promise of a future together, once again.

Doubling Over: Sensible Silences and Outstretched Hands

If an improvised sign language manages to communicate a meaningful message at the close of Kieślowski's *White*, it is a more formal sign language that serves as a framing device for Haneke's *Code Unknown: Incomplete Tales of Several Journeys*. At the outset of the film, a group of deaf children engage in a game of charades and make sense of their acting not by shouting their guesses but by signing to each other. The final scene of the film is similar, for the camera reveals a child enacting an emotion that the others are unable to put their finger on with an appropriate hand motion. The kids are attempting to find a point of connection, of understanding, but they remain in the dark, as the scene disappears without a solution, without any resolution.

In the remarkably long, seamlessly shot second scene from Haneke's *Code Unknown*, a young Frenchman who has come to Paris from his father's farm hastily throws his rubbish on the lap of a Romanian woman before moving along on the crowded street. Outraged by this disrespectful gesture, a protagonist of African descent defends the woman by insisting that the young man apologise to her. The two young men end up fighting, and it is the individual whose family hails from Mali who ends up suffering as a result of his attempt to intervene on the Romanian woman's behalf. We learn from his mother's words, pronounced in her native tongue, that Amadou was hit and humiliated at the police station. As for the woman, whose name we later learn is Maria, her suffering is arguably greater. The unfortunate, unintended outcome of Amadou's attempt to lend her a hand was that police apprehended Maria and discovered that she was an undocumented immigrant. In a later scene, we see people boarding an aeroplane one by one until, finally, we recognise Maria who is escorted by policemen to the door of the aircraft. Then she is placed in the custody of the flight attendants and her handcuffs are removed. Not a single intelligible word is spoken in this scene. We hear muffled conversations but no distinguishable message is conveyed. What is happening does not need to be articulated; it is clear that Maria is being deported.

In her homeland, Maria visits a house that is being built with the fruits of her efforts in Paris. She declares, 'It's beautiful. Very good', and appears truly pleased with the progress that has been made in the construction of the abode. But her daughter indicates that her fiancé's place is 'bigger, better, and lots more besides'. A disheartened Maria questions her daughter, 'You don't like this one?' And her daughter replies, 'Yes I do!' Maria seeks to know the fiancé's opinion, 'But Sorin doesn't?' Again, her daughter replies affirmatively, 'Yes, he does. It's not finished, that's all.' If the house is unfinished, then Maria's work in France is also unfinished, and she reluctantly agrees to take advantage of what her daughter terms 'a good opportunity' and travel in hiding in a truck back to the French capital. During her stay in Romania, Maria attends a wedding and the music at this festive event is echoed when Maria finds herself squatting once again in a dark Parisian building with her countrymen and women. She leaves the flute and the clapping behind to take refuge in a hallway after learning some bad news. She had hoped to find gainful employment this time selling newspapers in Paris, and a friend had promised her that she could have her licence. But now this is not possible, and she is faced with the prospect of begging on the streets again.

In the dismal hallway, Maria breaks down and cries as she confides in a fellow Romanian woman. 'One day, in Certeze, I gave some money to a gypsy beggar. She was so dirty, I ran to wash my hands to avoid catching a disease. She simply disgusted me.' Her interlocutor replies, 'So?' Maria continues, 'Last winter, on Boulevard St Germain, a well-dressed man was about to give me 20 francs. But when he saw my outstretched hand, he threw the bill into my lap as if I nauseated him.' She continues her narrative, emphasising the physical impact the Frenchman's disgust had on her: 'I rushed back here and hid myself in the attic. I cried my eyes out all day. It was so embarrassing. Do you see?' She continues to speak but her words are not translated. The result on the spectator is one of gratitude for the words that have been rendered sensible through the use of subtitles in the multilingual cinematic text that is *Code Unknown*. These spoken words are made available to the viewer who now has the impression of having taken a useful glimpse into the inaccessible experience of this Eastern European woman whose lack of proficiency in French makes her doubly outcast in the city where she precariously resides.

While Haneke's film certainly could not be called funny, there is a moment of unusual, inexplicable comic relief to be found when an actress, Anne, and a fellow actor are in the process of dubbing their own voices. They are standing in front of microphones, watching a large screen showing a silent film in which they are fooling around in a swimming pool. The scene itself is light-hearted, at least at first, but the work of dubbing their own voices, of supplying the official sound at this stage of the production, seems to have struck a unique chord within Anne, played by Juliette Binoche. She is doubled over with laughter, unable to control herself, and the actor by her side seems to be wavering in an in-between state, tempted to let himself go and laugh with her but compelled to listen to the voice of the director who instructs him to pull himself together and regain composure. The hilarity of this scene stands out in contrast to the apparent gravity of so many of the other scenes in this film.

In the penultimate scene, Maria is wandering the same street that marked her disgrace at the film's opening. She is seeking a place to sit with an outstretched hand, a place to beg for money. The extradiegetic drums that provide the rhythm for this sequence belong to the group of deaf children who regularly create a collective beat out of the silence that characterises their lives. This chorus of co-ordinated drums appears to move along with Maria as she seeks a spot to sit. She finally plops down, ever so gently, and doesn't occupy much space, but a gentleman and a young teenager come along and talk with her, appearing to convince her that this location is not for her. We cannot hear their words. We do not even know in what language these interlocutors are speaking but Maria grabs her things, appearing intimidated, as the two male figures watch her go off. We cannot help but remember the kind intentions of Amadou in the earlier scene and wonder what compelled him to act. In the meantime, we have learned that he knows sign language, that he has a younger sibling who is deaf. This sensitivity to silence, to the inability to make oneself properly heard in a society filled with noise, may have been what prompted him to speak up on behalf of Maria. Though her deportation was far from a positive outcome, Amadou's gesture did enable Maria to reunite with her family, and this trip back to her homeland might have been beneficial on some levels. It certainly didn't discourage her from returning to France to try to reach other hearts with her outstretched hand. On a different level, Haneke's inclusion of Maria's travels in his film might successfully touch viewers by making them aware of the stories of many who share her plight. It also might inspire them to view Paris through a different, less Francocentric lens.

Conclusion

The movements that characters from Eastern European countries manage to make in films by both Haneke and Kieślowski are remarkable in the way they resituate and reorient France in particular, but Western Europe in general, placing it in relation to the East, in a constant motion that precludes seeing this location as the sole goal of Eastern European individuals. Instead, the way that Romanian and Polish protagonists go back and forth between their native countries and France, both literally and figuratively, and even temporally, means that they are sensitised to the multiple vantage points from which Europe can be viewed and understood, and the various points of contact that can be developed between different cultures and countries. The provocative, probing cinematic work of Haneke and Kieślowski stimulates two seemingly contradictory reactions in viewers, and the term 'doubling over' refers to both the pain and the laughter that these films inspire. These intense feelings bring about a change in perspective, disorienting preconceptions about the fixity of France and convincingly replacing them with a new comprehension of the oft-overlooked fluidity of its relationship with the rest of Europe.

CHAPTER 4

Challenging the East–West Divide in Ulrich Seidl's *Import Export* (2007)

Nikhil Sathe (Ohio University)

Ulrich Seidl's *Import Export* (2007, Austria/France/Germany) opens with an older man trying to start an antique motorcycle while standing in a snowy landscape with a white prefabricated slab building in the background. With no apparent road into this field, the scene's blocking, along with its symmetrical framing and the man's direct gaze at the camera, reveal the film's deliberate staging and attempt to awaken our awareness as viewers of this film. Without any geographical context, such as the location intertitles that appear later in the film, the viewer is further invited to draw assumptions about the location on the screen. The Socialist-era style architecture, the older vehicle, the man's fur hat, and the frigid landscape suggest somewhere in Eastern Europe or the former Soviet Union but, devoid of any context, viewers can only assume this by activating preconceptions regarding East and West. This short sequence, indeed, remains extraneous from the film's narratives, sharing with them only the presence of snow. This opening scene encapsulates two aspects that are central to an understanding of Seidl's film: first, the film's critical reflection on the power dynamics inherent to the act of looking – both, in general and as a cinematic self-reflection – and second, the film's challenge to prevailing conceptions of East and West in a post-1989 Europe. After locating *Import Export* in the context of Austrian cinema and within Seidl's controversial film-making, this chapter will examine key sequences to show how the film visualises the power hierarchies – which here involve East–West relations – that are established through the gaze by calling attention to the act of looking and of being watched. From this reading, it will become clear that the film's narrative conflicts and use of graphic imagery enact a critique of Western perceptions and prejudices that ultimately aims to enable a new way of looking at Eastern Europe and Eastern Europeans.

Looking at Eastern Europe in the Cinema of Ulrich Seidl

A contender for the top prize at Cannes in 2007, Seidl's *Import Export* is one of the most discussed works of recent Austrian, cinema which has enjoyed a critical renaissance since the 1990s. This cinema, which has been described as the 'New Austrian Cinema', is characterised by its formal integrity and its sober, unflinching portrayals of the malaise of Austrian society and the larger post-industrial Western Europe as it both integrates and clashes with the former East and the global South (Dassanowsky 2008: 31). A central focus of Austrian cinema's examination has been the problematic of Eastern Europe.[1] This focus is a response to the continental shifts of 1989 that transformed the East–West division of Europe and prompted Austria's shifting self-definitions, which are reflected in post-1989 musings on a central European identity, Austria's 1995 entry into the European Union, and the rise and prominence of the radical right in Austrian politics from the late 1980s into the 2000s (Boyer 1989: 312–14, Judt 1990: 42–3). Particularly regarding the entry of Eastern European countries into the European Union, this Austrian reconfiguration has unveiled ambivalent or contradictory positions on Eastern Europe which is imagined both as a special relative and a promising economic opportunity, yet also as a backward, chaotic, or criminal other that threatens an imagined Austrian centre.[2]

This backdrop is reflected in depictions of Eastern European figures in Austrian cinema. Film-makers have laid bare Austrian arrogance, condescension, aversion and anxieties, yet also an exoticised attraction and romantic idealisation of Eastern European simplicity, innocence or otherness that seems to promise the Austrian figures completeness and identity. In the majority of Austrian films, the East–West relationship has been drawn along gender divisions, echoing common Western European ascriptions of feminine elements to Eastern Europe in opposition to an ostensibly masculine West (Goddard, 87). A representative film illustrating these trends is Barbara Gräftner's *Mein Russland/My Russia* (2002, Austria) in which the wedding of a Ukrainian woman and an Austrian man is threatened when the disapproving Austrian matriarch reveals to her family the bride's past as a nude dancer. Foregrounding the matriarch's aversion to, yet simultaneous infatuation with, the bride's uncle, *Mein Russland* satirises conflicting Austrian perspectives. The film further deconstructs how socio-economic conditions confine the Ukrainian bride to illicit milieu and how she is burdened by unmastered legacies entwined with her past which is embodied in her fatherless child who remains in the East, a recurring motif in Austrian cinema.

Import Export presents the viewer with a range of Eastern European locales. The film features a female Ukrainian, Olga, who leaves her infant behind to find work in Vienna, but, as the title implies, also contains a parallel narrative in which an Austrian man, Pauli, accompanies his stepfather on a business venture to Slovakia and then to Ukraine where he, too, will eventually look for work. Eastern Europe is not a new setting for Seidl: his documentary, *Mit Verlust ist zu rechnen/Loss is to be Expected* (1992, Austria), contrasted a village in the Czech Republic with one on the Austrian side of the border. As Martin Brady and Helen Hughes argue, that film clearly painted the Eastern side in a more sympathetic, if romanticised, light (216). About that film's setting, Seidl has noted: 'The East has always interested me. I find so much there that is interesting and good and exciting. I always feel comfortable there and cannot join the choir of those who demonise the "backwardness" of the East' (Grissemann, 115).[3] In the early scenes of *Import Export*, however, Seidl's film, while not exactly demonising an Eastern backwardness, omits any traces of modern life in his images of Ukraine and seems to meet Western expectations of Eastern European backwardness. If the cinematography's tight symmetry and meticulous *mise en scène* may create striking imagery, the film adheres to a 'compendium of conventional images of Eastern Europe' (Goddard, 88). Seidl's Ukraine remains a world of nuclear reactors looming in the background, Soviet era monuments, crumbling architecture and antiquated infrastructure, apartments with broken lifts and no heating or hot water, destitute state workers, and massive industrial facilities that now appear as ruins. To be sure, such imagery is not gratuitous and serves the clear dramaturgical function of justifying Olga's motivation to seek work elsewhere but it bears more than a touch of nostalgia and Western romanticisation of a quirky splendour, such as in the scene in which Olga celebrates the news of her trip to Vienna in a former miners' social hall by dancing the tango to a sentimental 1930s Russian song.[4] In the second half, however, the film's representation of Eastern Europe and the region's inhabitants shifts to highlight the Westerner's gaze. In the earlier scenes, which consist predominantly of long- to medium-range shots, the camera aims solely on Olga, as it observes her daily routines and struggles. In the later scenes, however, the camera interrupts its viewpoint by foregrounding constellations in which a Westerner is watching Eastern Europeans: in Vienna, we namely watch how Olga's employers observe her, and in Slovakia and Ukraine, it is Pauli and his stepfather watching various locals. As we will see, this shift in perspective allows the film to call attention to its representation of Eastern Europe and to elicit our self-reflection on the power of our roles as spectators of the film and the at times graphic images on the screen.

If Seidl's films have not always foregrounded the dynamics of the gaze, a direct, often visceral confrontation with the viewer has been a major impulse throughout his *oeuvre*. His films have been criticised for their extreme imagery and subject matter which Matthias Heine dubs a 'pornography of misery' (2007a). Seidl's many documentary works, which zero in on the banal absurdities of life across social classes, have been charged with exploitation, manipulation and ridicule of their subjects. His first narrative film, *Hundstage/Dog Days* (2001, Austria), was equally criticised for its graphic portrayals of sex, abuse and rituals of humiliation. Though *Import Export* was well received, such criticism persists in the reactions to the film and its portrayal of pornography, poverty, prostitution and the startling conditions in the Viennese geriatric ward where Olga finds work. When asked about the dangers of depicting shocking material, Seidl responded: 'For me, the greater danger would be not to show it' (Heine 2007b).[5] In a later interview, Seidl again asserts the humanistic thrust of his cinema:

> With my films, I attempt to cast an unvarnished look at life, at a specific societal reality or to penetrate into private spaces, ... which we, however, gladly repress, because it is uncomfortable to look at them. I attempt to lure the viewer into looking at a reality and to confront it, because I believe that this is something that ultimately concerns us all ... (Grissemann, 34)[6]

But, in showing and demanding that viewers engage with imagery that we would rather avoid, Seidl risks gratuitous sensationalism and the ethical breaches of exploiting his often non-professional actors.

Seidl's controversial techniques and subjects have led a number of critics to locate the director at the forefront of a 'New Extremism' in European art cinema since the 2000s. Asbjørn Grønstad theorises this cinema, including works by Seidl, as being 'unwatchable' on multiple levels: they are not only emotionally or viscerally unpleasant and depict what has previously been presumed unrepresentable but also attempt to 'trounce visual pleasure and shake the spectators into a deeper awareness of things of a political, ethical, cultural, aesthetic or epistemological nature' and ultimately to draw forth a 'different modality of looking' (10). In her reading of *Import Export*, Catherine Wheatley stresses that it is specifically the indeterminacy whether this extreme imagery constitutes staged, fictional moments or whether it bears real traces of violence that afford them their profoundly disturbing nature which ultimately incites viewers to recognise their own predicament in the suffering, humiliation or exploitation they see on-screen (100–1). By demonstrating how Seidl's film and others like it bear an appeal to the viewer to adopt a new way of seeing, Grønstad and Wheatley provide us with a useful insight into the film's disturbing passages as well as its reflection on the representation of Eastern Europeans. In the aforementioned constellations, in which the film not only portrays something extreme but also another figure watching, we must note the metacritical level that is aimed as well at the viewer's reflection on the act of looking itself. In *Import Export* there is a further political dimension in that these scenes of looking are directed almost exclusively by Westerners at Eastern Europeans. As the following readings of a number of key scenes will show, the film's constellations of watching, which are indeed inherent to the narrative as well, allow *Import Export* to interrogate the very manner in which the West views and discursively constructs Eastern Europe.

Export: Western Europeans Looking at Eastern Europeans

Within the 'export' narrative, the dynamic between power and looking is central to the protagonist Pauli's conflicts and is developed well before his arrival in Eastern Europe.[7] Pauli's narrative may revolve around his unemployment and attempt to become independent but it is driven by a crisis of masculinity as he is shown contending with the ideals of a hypermasculinity based on physical strength, exploitation and dominance over others. In an exercise sequence shot in Pauli's room, the link between the gaze and power becomes clear as the *mise en scène* underlines the masculinity he emulates: amid sundry sports equipment, Pauli shadow-boxes before a mirror, all under the watching eyes of a Bruce Lee poster. Not only is Pauli being, figuratively, watched by a paragon of virulent masculinity, he is also gazing on and literally fighting his own reflection, intimating his struggle with his ideals. Pauli's failure at his new job further illustrates his conflict and reinforces the power attributed to the gaze. After conducting training as a security guard, Pauli becomes a nightwatchman at a shopping centre where he is shown commanding power observing security cameras and later sealing entrances. When he must confront a group of Turkish-Austrian youths, however, they easily overcome Pauli and proceed to taunt him – stripping and whipping him, dousing him with beer, and finally dancing around him singing in Turkish. These intruders into the mall have now become the observers as they each stare at this watchman during their dance. The humiliation, exposed body and sexual overtones in this sequence become particularly significant through its placement after a sequence featuring Olga performing at an Internet pornography studio where other figures take virtual control of her body. This juxtaposition creates a parallel between the two protagonists: Pauli not only fails to fulfil his ideal masculinity but also becomes more like Eastern European women who, in the film's economy, will be shown to be contained and exploited by Western figures with greater power.

The principle exploiter in Pauli's narrative strand is his stepfather, Michael. This figure's aggressive and dominating masculinity becomes synonymous with his role as an agent of Western economic exploitation of Eastern Europe. Michael is first shown joining Pauli shadow-boxing and later appears alone narcissistically gazing at himself before aggressively slapping flabby parts of his physique. The film underscores Michael's domineering masculinity by visually associating him with the figure of the cowboy: Michael is placed alongside paintings of Native Americans and Wild West landscapes in his apartment and always appears in plaid shirts, jeans and cowboy boots. If Michael is outfitted as a tamer of uncharted territory, his job suggests the frontier mentality of the Wild West: venturing to the outer reaches of the market frontier of Eastern Europe, Michael is a distributor for a company that is placing outdated electronic casino games and gumball machines into depressed and provincial spaces in Eastern Europe. These machines aim to exploit others whom Michael deems inferior, and he pointedly refers to Eastern Europeans with the derogatory '*Russentschuschen*.'[8] To pay back his debts to Michael, Pauli must accompany him on a delivery during which Michael taunts Pauli with his sexual bravado and challenges him to feats of masculinity. These challenges all aim at some form of domination over an Eastern European figure which becomes enforced through acts of looking.

The power of the gaze becomes particularly significant in the controversial sequence shot at the notorious Luník IX housing project for Romany in Košice, Slovakia. With this locale, Seidl might earn the aforementioned accusation of creating a 'pornography of misery', as the cameras are turned on the extreme deprivation at this site where there is nearly 100 per cent unemployment, and which has been ethnically segregated from the non-Romany population (Huber, 27). The Westerner's disbelief and arrogance are highlighted to the viewer by reaction shots of Michael's disgusted gaze as he drives into the complex and by his mocking dismissal that this will never be a profitable site.[9] Highlighting imagery of the site's decrepit infrastructure and destitute residents, the film cannot succeed here in undermining Western perceptions of Eastern European backwardness and otherness. The sequence at this site, however, does call into question Michael's presumption of superiority, in that the narrative significance of the sequence turns on Pauli's refusal to assume a position of power. Arriving at the complex, Michael challenges Pauli's manhood by daring him to venture inside. Annoyed, but unwilling to decline, Pauli enters a building where two men presume he must be looking for a prostitute. Pauli has no such intention, and does not merely reject the men's offers, but recognises the power ascribed to his presence and refuses to accept this role which Seidl's film conveys by foregrounding the act of looking. Before the men take Pauli to the woman, they make him wait in a family's living room. In a frontal, medium shot, a young girl stares at the camera curiously yet disdainfully and then looks away as Pauli, in reverse shot, nervously returns her gaze. When the men then take him to the sex worker, Pauli, unwilling to assume the role they expect of him, repeatedly looks away as they attempt to direct his gaze at her. Unlike his uncertain attempt to meet the young girl's glances, Pauli now seems to acknowledge the position of dominance implicit in his gaze and thus refuses to employ it with this woman. This sequence not only marks a stage towards Pauli's later rejection of Michael but also underscores how a privileged position of looking, be it the one that the Romany figures expect of the Western visitor or that of the cinematic apparatus itself, enacts a position of dominance over the object of the gaze. Just as the film presents us with scenes that could easily confirm the worst Western stereotypes of the East, Pauli's actions seem to demand not that we look away but that we look with a heightened awareness of the power and consequences inherent to our gaze.

The observer's power becomes subverted in Pauli's confrontation with Michael. This occurs in perhaps the film's most controversial sequence which features a Ukrainian sex worker with Michael who demands that Pauli watch him. The figure constellation in this sequence is established in two earlier scenes where Pauli grudgingly acquiesces to remain present while Michael tries to seduce Eastern European women. In the first, Michael attempts to entice a Slovakian woman with smarmy adulation but, when Pauli refuses to help him by offering Russian translations, Michael dismisses Pauli as a failure, stating that his flirting is simply an accepted part of his job that Pauli should emulate.[10] In the second scene, Michael bets that he can seduce a random woman in a Ukrainian bar but he instead delights in making obscene remarks to her in German that she cannot understand. In both instances, Pauli must watch Michael's ridiculous attempts to assert his potency which, particularly in the latter case, he can do only by taking advantage of an unequal partner.

In the culminating sequence with the sex worker, the centrality of the gaze becomes crucial to the repudiation of Michael's attempts to dominate Eastern European figures. When Pauli goes to the hotel room to collect money for the bar bill, he finds Michael staring at the sex worker's exposed genitalia. Instead of giving Pauli the money, Michael makes him wait, promising that he will now show him the true power of money. He then proceeds to make the naked woman perform humiliating acts, such as pretending to be a barking dog that he pulls around, laughing on command, or repeating vulgarities in German that she cannot understand. Many reviewers have criticised how Seidl's camera in this excruciating scene too readily becomes synonymous with the Michael's voyeuristic gaze on to the naked body of the woman who, as reviews and interviews with the director note, is a non-professional actor who in reality is a sex worker (Wheatley, 99). Helga Druxes, for example, writes that, by disturbing the viewer with an abjected female body, 'A predictable outcome of this scene may well be viewer disgust and a refusal to engage with the rest of the film' (398). While we can certainly take issue with the sequence's gender representations and its underlying ethical quandary, we must not overlook the constellation that predominates in the sequence and that has been prefigured throughout the film: Seidl is framing foremost not the uncomfortable scene of human exploitation but, rather, a scene of one person not wanting to, even refusing to, watch it. For much of the sequence, Pauli is in the foreground and is shown looking away or shaking his head in disgust while Michael continually prompts him 'Look at me'.[11] Finally, Pauli, frustrated with the wait and Michael's bravado, not only does look directly at Michael but also pulls off Michael's clothes while the sex worker attempts to fellate him. It is now Pauli challenging Michael's masculinity, telling him that if he intends to have intercourse, he should do it and end his 'perverted games'.[12] Michael, who has no erection throughout the sequence, puts his pants back on, seemingly realising that he has now been exposed. He blames Pauli's nagging for his impotence, to which Pauli counters: 'You did tell me that I should watch you'.[13] With Pauli's actions, the film metacinematically compels the viewer to question its own graphic nature: it stages someone watching extreme imagery but also someone else refusing to do so who eventually brings it to an end. The viewer's rejection that Druxes hypothesises is thus inscribed on the screen itself. Pauli, however, does not refuse to engage but, instead, while not undoing this misogynistic representation, does unmask and reject the exploitative nature of Michael's gaze.

Resolving Pauli's conflict with Michael, this sequence encapsulates Seidl's critique of Western perceptions of Eastern Europeans. By directing his eyes at Michael, Pauli not only undoes Michael's bluster about his sexual prowess, and empties the facade of his aggressive masculinity, but also emancipates himself from Michael, leaving him the following morning for the open road. Pauli's interruption of Michael's interaction with the sex worker resonates on a geopolitical level. Michael's presumptions of special connections that he attributes to his charm and business savvy are dispelled as exploitation and coercion through his economic advantage, a clear parallel to the unequal balance of power between Eastern and Western Europe that is often obscured by flowery rhetoric of community and partnership. Pauli's unwillingness to watch and refusal to participate in Michael's humiliation of the woman may not release her from this exploitation but rejects the dominance and superiority that Michael intended to enforce. The centrality of the act of looking in this sequence thus invites the viewer's reflections on the representation of Eastern Europeans as well as the perspectives from which they are viewed by the West which becomes especially significant in the film's parallel narrative.

Import: An Eastern European being Watched in the West

With Olga, the film's thematisation of the power of the gaze shifts from a questioning of the Westerner's privileged position to an emphasis on the Eastern European's experience of being observed and determined. The protagonist experiences domineering and exploitative gazes by Westerners even before she arrives in Austria. While in Ukraine, Olga briefly works at a pornography studio, where women perform for Western clients via webcam. The sequence at this site bears numerous similarities to the one with Michael and the sex worker. Both are introduced to startle the viewer: like Pauli, Olga walks along innocuous corridors and doorways before entering one where she is suddenly confronted with a woman exposing her genitalia. Both also script a sense of unease by showing each protagonist's unwillingness to watch. The film not only shows Olga observing other performers before her debut but, indeed, overloads the frame with multiple levels of observation. This is evident in the scene shot from behind a performer at work. Her body appears at the bottom of the frame, and in the centre are the computer screens on which she is looking at the website and the genital close-up that the customer sees. Behind the monitors in the background, Olga can be seen observing, but continually looking away, perhaps anxious about her debut or embarrassed by her trespassing into the performer's space as she exposes herself in this manner.

For the portrayal of Olga's performance, Seidl calls attention to the power dynamics inherent to the gaze – both that of the customer and of the film viewer. The framing of this sequence indeed refuses to make such a distinction, making what the viewer sees identical to what Olga's customer sees. Using a frontal, medium shot that is filmed with a single, static long take, the composition seems to offer no diversion from Olga's nude body. The sound in this sequence, however, forges a distance between the viewer and the customer. Its long duration places the viewer inside Olga's diegetic space where both silence and ambient sounds are audible, such as the rustle of the bed and, of course, the instructions by the customer whose disembodied voice and transmission static are coming from computers inside the room. In this quiet aural environment, the German-speaking customer's loud, nasal voice intensifies the virtual infraction that is being made into Olga's space. This becomes all the more pronounced as his commands become more aggressive as Olga refuses or fails, given her poor German and English skills, to perform the actions he demands. This sense of intrusion is heightened through the stark contrast with the immediately preceding sequence which follows Olga at home as she heats water to prepare for her standing bath. This sequence documents the physical difficulties and labour needed to care for her body, rather than its pure display. This strategy aims to stifle the viewer's identification with the voyeuristic male client's gaze. Regardless of the effectiveness of this strategy, the sequence at the studio remains a disturbing experience, in which the film most directly links the act of looking to coercion and control: Olga must literally perform what the snarling client wants to see. It is particularly significant that the client curses Olga for showing her face instead of her genitalia, indicating his intolerance of any dissonance from his subjective fantasy image. That these demands, with which she fails or refuses to comply, are ordered by a German speaker reiterates the film's critique of Western preconceptions of Eastern Europeans and foreshadows Olga's fate in Vienna.

In Austria, Olga remains repeatedly the object of the policing, controlling gazes of authority figures. Olga, whose legal status as a migrant remains unclear, finds employment doing cleaning work. In one absurd scene at a private home filled with mounted animal heads, Olga attempts to clean a stuffed fox's teeth while the homeowner watches disapprovingly, only to complete the task herself to demonstrate the proper method. Olga works briefly as an au pair for a dysfunctional Viennese family. She is shown being spied on by the matriarch, who peers at Olga through drawn blinds or the clouded glass of Olga's door. As Goddard points out, the domestic work Olga performs in this home depends on her physical presence and labour, in particular, the cleaning and polishing we are shown, but the end product of her work – cleanliness and care – demands her absence and invisibility (2011: 90). When Olga is perceived as intruding and becoming more visible, namely when the matriarch sees her children playing happily with Olga, she loses her job. That news is delivered to

Olga in a sequence in which the homeowner is shown rifling through and sniffing Olga's belongings, making gestures of disgust that echo Michael's reaction shots at the Romany complex. The matriarch then picks up a picture of Olga's child but, when Olga demands its return, she does not acquiesce immediately and then terminates Olga's employment without offering a reason. By withholding the picture of Olga's child and then sacking her, the matriarch asserts her Western presumption of privilege to determine and to look at Eastern Europeans as she pleases.

When Olga begins working in a geriatric ward in Vienna, she remains subject to monitoring gazes but also, to a certain extent, assumes the role of a viewer too.[14] At this public nursing home, Olga receives work performing janitorial services but begins, even though it is forbidden, interacting with the elderly patients. Unlike the many instances in the film in which Olga is the object of an authority figure's gaze, it is now Olga, standing next to the supine patients, who directs her gaze on to others, as she helps or simply accompanies them. The actions in these scenes appear as gestures of kindness and human connection for the isolated patients. Whereas the real nurses take an artificially friendly, infantilising, impatient or even aggressive tone with the patients, Olga is often shown listening or talking to the patients, holding a patient's hand or combing another's hair.[15] Through these scenes of Olga and different patients, the film reinforces the association between power and the act of looking, only now stressing a benevolent nature.

Olga's forbidden interaction with the patients, however, triggers her conflict with the head nurse, Maria, which the film employs to illustrate how Olga becomes determined by Western preconceptions. Maria's more powerful position entitles her to observe her staff and the cleaning crew. When she spies Olga combing a patient's hair, Maria berates Olga who protests that she was a trained nurse in Ukraine. When Maria retorts that, 'Here, you are a cleaning woman', her words constitute a performative that literally defines who Olga is.[16] Olga's conflict, however, is not limited to this territorial matter and the rules of the nursing home but, again, revolves around Maria's prejudices. Maria namely accuses Olga of taking the job solely to convince a patient to marry her to secure her legal status in Austria which, as an earlier scene suggests, is what Olga's friend and co-worker Natascha has done. While Olga does not seem to be searching for such a union, it becomes a possibility when Erich, a patient for whom Olga smuggles in chocolates, announces that he would like to help her by marrying her, but later dies.[17] The framing when Maria makes her accusation stresses the authority of her gaze: it features a medium shot of a tiny room in which Olga stands on the left sorting dirty laundry.

Figure 4.1 Maria watches Olga at work.

Maria, apparently on a cigarette break, enters from behind her to the right of the frame and watches her from behind as Olga works, her eyes never veering from Olga. This blocking not only conveys the imbalance of power but also a revealing dissonance: Maria is watching Olga literally do the dirty work but makes allegations of her deceptive, ulterior motives, intimating how Maria views her not through Olga's actions but through her own preconceived expectations, as if Eastern Europeans can be viewed from only one perspective.

While Maria defines Olga as a fraud and as a threat to the territorial order of her workplace, this extends to a personal level when she perceives Olga to be a sexual competitor. This perception again illustrates how her preconceived notions determine her view of Olga as a highly sexualised Eastern European woman which, as Anca Parvulescu notes, is commonplace in Western prejudices regarding the East (2012: 851–2). The concluding sequence of their conflict again foregrounds the act of watching. During a carnival party, in which the patients and staff have painted faces and costumes, reaction shots of Maria show her laughing and admiring the antics of Andi, a Viennese male nurse. The viewer has already seen Andi watching and flirting with Olga earlier but Maria first sees this at the party when Andi histrionically insists that Olga dance with him. After the hand-held camera follows them past the onlooking patients, it then breaks to close in on Maria, whose face is now transformed by rage.[16] As in the laundry room scene, Maria is then shown watching and following Olga from behind. She then attacks Olga in an empty corridor, only finally to be

CHALLENGING THE EAST–WEST DIVIDE 77

subdued by Olga. Like Olga's pornography client, Maria is enraged by the sight of Olga's face. She continues to strike at it, relenting only when Olga manages to hold Maria's face to the floor where she can no longer see it. The use of language is marshalled to underscore Olga's overpowering of Maria. If Maria earlier corrected Olga's proficiency in German when she made her allegations, Olga now significantly speaks entirely in Ukrainian when she restrains Maria. With this brief act of resistance, Olga's narrative is resolved. She may not ultimately have released herself from Maria's authority but she has succeeded in challenging it and reasserting her own agency in defining herself.

Conclusion

If the conclusions of both narratives turn on acts of defiance against dominating figures, their final images suggest different outcomes for the protagonists. Olga appears with her Eastern European co-workers as they laugh together, presumably about the incident with Maria. Pauli, after failing to find work as a labourer at a vegetable market, is then shown attempting to hitchhike along a rural road. The static long shot of Olga and her companions contrasts with the tracking shot that briefly follows Pauli but then stops as he walks into the horizon of the open road, suggesting stasis for Olga and an indefinite, yet greater mobility for Pauli. As Helga Druxes reminds us, this difference leaves unchallenged gender stereotypes that envision the male as mobile and the female as restricted and limited (516). Anca Parvulescu extends this gendered distinction to the geopolitical level, arguing that the privileged level of mobility projected on to the male Western European and not the female Eastern European illustrates what she calls Europe's 'new wall', which combines '. . . the international sexual division of labor, as well as the new racial, ethnic, and citizenship-based European stratifications . . .' (857).

Seen within the context of the film's reflection on the perception and representation of Eastern Europeans and its emphasis on the act of the looking, however, the final images of these narratives are significant as markers of the protagonists' transitions. Olga's placement in that confined space foregrounds her predicament yet reflects her minor triumph over Maria. As nearly all her interactions with Westerners show, Olga's defiance will probably not bring substantial liberation from the controlling gazes that have defined and even attempted to control her throughout the film. In the final image, though, as Olga and her co-workers sit around the table laughing, their gazes fixed on each other, this community of Eastern European women is free, however temporarily, to view themselves on their own. Similarly, Pauli's departure at the close of his narrative illustrates his liberation but also the uncertainty of his trajectory. Pauli can proceed into the Ukrainian horizon towards which he walks but, as the cessation of the tracking camera's motion implies, his future prospects in it are risky and doubtful at best. He has, however, freed himself from his overbearing stepfather, Michael. This is clearly reflected in Pauli's placement with his back towards the camera. Looking out into the open space before him, Pauli can view the East without Michael's domineering perspectives.

Through these two narratives which traverse the changing landscape of a continent whose unification is expanding, yet remains divided, and through the film's careful foregrounding of the act of looking, Seidl's *Import Export* implicitly impels us to recognise how the power hierarchies it depicts are manifested through the gaze. As the examples of Michael and any of the Western European figures who assert their authority over Olga show, the imbalance of power and capital that remains between East and West is reflected in these figures' presumption of dominance, superiority, and especially of an entitlement to view Eastern Europeans as they choose. Of the many Austrian films that reflect on Eastern Europe and Eastern Europeans in Austria, then, *Import Export* occupies a unique position in that it turns its cameras on to these places and peoples while simultaneously forcing us to consider, to look at, the very dynamics of the manner in which we see them.

CHAPTER 5

Fatih Akın's Filmic Visions of a New Europe: Spatial and Aural Constructions of Europe in *Im Juli / In July* (2000)

Berna Gueneli (Grinnell College)

'Europe as such does not exist,' states sociologist Gerard Delanty in his article 'What does it mean to be a European?' (11, 19). It is a discursive construction (Elsaesser, 48; Hudson, 409). Various disciplines, organisations, and interest groups such as the European Union, political parties, and academic disciplines have repeatedly (re)constructed and (re)defined Europe and things European. The recent building ban on minarets in Switzerland and the outlawing of the hijab (veil) in French schools warrant once again the revaluation of the changing sights and sounds of Europe. Cinema provides one way of imagining concepts of Europe (Sieg, 2, 62). The films of Turkish-German director Fatih Akın offer current, popular examples for cinematic evaluations of Europe and Europeanness. Turkey's role in this new Europe becomes relevant, especially considering the recent protests (starting in the summer of 2013) in Turkey against socially conservative prime minister Recep Tayyip Erdoğan and the solidarity that was shown across Europe, including a YouTube video by Akın, for the protesters.

In this chapter, I analyse two audio-visual aspects of Akın's *In July*: space and sound. The first part discusses the spatial conceptions of Europe (city and landscapes) and the second, the sounds of Europe (music and languages). Both of which, ultimately, construct Akın's cinematic visions of a diverse and connected Europe. Akın, the recipient of the European Parliament's first Cinema Lux Prize in 2007 for *Auf der anderen Seite / The Edge of Heaven* (Germany/Turkey/Italy) is arguably one of the most prominent directors in Germany and Europe today, whose films challenge solidified binaries such as East/West and centre/margin. According to the 2007 president of the European Parliament, Hans Gert Pöttering, the EP awards *'annually a film that raises attention to current social questions that affect our continent and highlights European Integration especially'*. Furthermore, the film should 'highlight the richness of linguistic diversity within the European Union'. Akın's filmic Europe is a diverse, interconnected space, in which multi-ethnicity and multilingualism are prominent in a variety of regions that have often been seen as historically and politically distinct.

In the field of cultural geography, Doreen Massey conceptualises space as a perpetually changing entity which comes into being through multiple interconnections of people, places and things material (Massey 2005: 9, 13). Following Massey, I perceive Europe as a changing entity with various dynamic interconnections. Hence, European space is not a clear-cut, organised entity with centres and margins that can be firmly defined. Akın's cinematic imagination of Europe subtly echoes the shifts and fluxes of a connected and expanding European space with blurring boundaries. This interconnectedness of a formerly divided European North/South and East/West is reflected through the general aesthetics of Akın's films which I call his aesthetics of heterogeneity. This cinematic space often depicts interrelational, heterogeneous local sights and sounds across Europe. For example, by juxtaposing the sounds of global electronic music with local Black Sea music from north-eastern Turkey or Hamburg-based Brazilian-German reggae bands with voices of Islamic religious prayers in his films, Akın's soundscapes reflect a vast and complex polyphony which is often excluded from conventional depictions of Europe (Gueneli 2014). Languages, dialects, and accents, such as English, Turkish and Serbo-Croatian, as well as *Hamburgisch*, Bavarian, and Black Sea dialects further enrich the new sonic heterogeneity of Europe. Akın's films become a projection screen for new networks of European city-, land- and soundscapes that are informed by links to places in Turkey, Eastern and Western Europe, and South America. It is precisely these transnational connections in Akın's cinematic Europe, I argue, that challenge existing geopolitical, national European borders. In developing this argument, I look at the specificities of *mise en scène* (spaces) and sound in *In July*. First, I will introduce *In July* and its themes of space and borders.

This light-hearted road movie is different (in terms of genre, plot and style) from Akın's more recent, critically acclaimed feature films, such as *Gegen die Wand/Head-On* (2004, Germany), *The Edge of Heaven*, and *Soul Kitchen* (2009, Germany). Yet, *In July*'s visions of Europe are very similar to the more recent films. These films offer a coherent narrative of a connected and polyphonic cinematic Europe (Gueneli 2014).[1] A central feature of this European space is its reliance on movement. This is foregrounded by various modes of transport, the movement of the characters and the mobile narrative structure. The travels of the characters link local places and help create the filmic space of Europe.

Similar to Massey's space concept, Akın's cinematic imaginations of Europe seem to be reflected in the interrelations of the people, places and entities in his films. Massey proposes a progressive and 'global sense of place'. She suggests that a place comes into existence through the multiple connections it has to other places; it consists of networks of social relations which are constantly in flux (Massey 2008: 262, 263). Through these networks, the specificities of places are perpetually reinvented. The connections in Akın's films are shown through landscapes that continue seamlessly across borders, parallel city spaces and cosmopolitan travellers. They are also exemplified through music/sound that is not bound to a particular place and which creates a link between geographically distant places.

European places figure prominently in *In July*. The beginning of the film immediately highlights the setting: 'somewhere in Bulgaria'. The narrative begins with a young, dark-haired, mysterious-looking man, Isa (Mehmet Kurtuluş), getting out of his Mercedes which has a Berlin licence plate in pre-EU Eastern Europe. This opening sequence introduces the audience to the main character Daniel (Moritz Bleibtreu) who, in travel-torn clothes, tries to get a ride from Isa. After Daniel explains that he is on the way to find his love interest Melek (Idil Üner), the story continues with Daniel's flashback narrative. The flashback explains why the teacher in training came from Hamburg to Bulgaria and is on his way to Istanbul. Starting in Hamburg and moving further south-east, Daniel

Figure 5.1 Daniel and Juli chart a course through Europe.

travels through a Bavarian town, Vienna and various Eastern European locations.

Eventually, the frame narrative continues with Daniel and Isa at the Bulgarian-Turkish border. From here, the last sequences portray Daniel on his way to a desired meeting point in Ortaköy-Istanbul where he hopes to meet Melek. Instead, he meets his travel companion Juli (Christiane Paul) and both confirm their mutual love. The film ends with the continuation of their travel into the 'shitty-south'.

Beginning 'somewhere in Bulgaria' and ending on the way to the 'shitty-south', *In July* is both a European road movie and a politically conscious film that makes deliberate choices to underscore the porousness of borders. The spatial continuity among the city- and landscapes replaces previously established and commonly accepted geopolitical concepts of Europe (through ritualised, politicised acts of border crossings). This continuity is best symbolised through various travellers throughout post-1989 Europe. Akın connects classic European cities, such as Hamburg and Budapest, but also Istanbul. At the same time, rural landscapes throughout Central/Eastern Europe are linked, exposing a fluid continuity. These connected spaces are interrupted and opposed by man-made borders. While thematising the connectedness of European space, the film explicitly addresses the theme of borders which play a key role as complicated, metaphorical antagonists to the continuity of landscapes, as I shall discuss below. The director invites the viewers to reflect on national borders by casting himself as a Romanian border official (Göktürk, 153, 154). The following section on European spaces, and later on sound, will give insights about Akın's audio-visual conception of a connected Europe.

European Spaces: Borders, Landscapes and City Spaces

The Hungarian–Romanian border sequence shows Daniel in the midst of his trans-European travel. He arrives with a stolen car at the stylised, though primitive, border. The setting is an open, sunny space, seemingly in a Mediterranean climate, which is occupied in the centre by a building which is divided in half, one half being the Hungarian border office building and the other the Romanian. The border is marked by a simple pole, the uniforms of the two officers, their automatic weapons, and the large national flags. Daniel explains to the Romanian officer (Akın) that his documents were stolen. The officer calmly eats sunflower seeds and plays a game of *tavla* (backgammon) with his Hungarian counterpart at the symmetrical centre of the border which coincides with the centre of the frame. He does not allow Daniel to enter Romania: 'No passport, no Romania!' Disheartened, Daniel stares into the endless road and fields which continue seamlessly on the other side of the border. He then sees Juli on the Romanian side. For Daniel to cross the border, they agree to perform a ritual of marriage. The Romanian officer witnesses the wedding ritual and allows Daniel to enter Romania but not without asking for his vehicle as a 'wedding present'. The neutralisation of the border through this fake wedding unmasks the border as arbitrary and constructed.

This sequence relies especially on the opposition of stylised versus non-stylised formal details to make suggestions about borders. While the landscape is open and continuous, the stylised border breaks the centre of the frame. It symbolises an artificial divide of the otherwise seamlessly continuous rural space. The setting (border props) emerges as almost stage-like. The overall design of the border is exaggeratedly symmetrical which, in addition to the comedic acting of Akın, further questions the highly conventionalised ritual of border crossings. Through the staged wedding at the equally staged border, the film reminds the audience of the constructedness of national borders. The unofficially wed groom crosses a previously impermeable border without his passport. The barriers that seem momentarily to inhibit movement are exposed as artificial, physically constructed and, ultimately, obsolete. As randomly as they seem to have been established, they are abolished. The comic treatment of border crossing further diminishes the meaning of borders. Nationality is a fading academic concept in twenty-first-century Europe and increasingly has been replaced by a focus on regionality (Hudson, 406). This is visualised in the film with a focus on regional continuities of European rural and urban spaces. While the countryside connects various rural spaces throughout Europe, the vivid and cosmopolitan cities seem to connect European urban spaces, as I will analyse further below.

The relevance of the countryside in *In July* is two-fold. As discussed above, by continuing across borders, it shows a unity and connectedness of regions. The European landscape functions as *locus amoenus*. In literature, a *locus amoenus* is a place outside the city, away from people, buildings and technology. Michael Squires describes the 'lovely place' as 'a natural site, both shaded and beautiful, whose basic ingredients are trees, a meadow, and a spring or brook' (Squires, 670, 671). Juli and Daniel are depicted in such contemporary, European *loci amoeni*: the Danube river, the heath and the forests in Romania. The film combines these settings of 'river', 'heath' and 'forest', turning the landscapes of Central and Eastern Europe into a large *locus amoenus*. At the same time, this *locus amoenus* is located close to rundown petrol stations, rusty ships or narrow, unpaved roads. By being edgier and rougher, these settings are an ironic reversal of classic European ideas about what constitutes a *locus amoenus*.

The Danube river, originating in the German Black Forest and passing through Central and Eastern European capitals, empties into the Black Sea and, as such, connects the regions and nation states in Central and Eastern Europe. Floating on the river as stowaways on a small East European cargo ship, Juli and Daniel smoke cannabis, sing a classic American love song ['Blue Moon Revisited (Song for Elvis)', performed by the Cowboy Junkies] and compose the poetic love vows to be used on Melek. While the couple travels on the ship, the background depicts, first, city lights which resemble shining stars, and later, forest silhouettes in the dark. This *locus amoenus* does not exclude the rusty transport vehicle which Daniel and Juli boarded illegally.

A similar bonding moment between the two is set in the Romanian heath. Sitting on the grass, picking flowers, Juli and Daniel contemplate how to proceed with their travel. The heath continues beyond the camera frame to suggest an open, infinite landscape. A counter shot reveals their closeness to a rundown petrol station. Instead of resulting in a moment of disillusionment, the scenery is incorporated into this alternate *locus amoenus* which allows for these sights of decay. Deciding to steal a car in Bonny and Clyde fashion, Juli and Daniel become petty criminal lovers in Eastern Europe. Ultimately, these settings are romanticised landscapes that function as edgy *loci amoeni* which include the stereotypical harsher realities of Eastern Europe (rusty boats, decrepit filling stations and criminal activities). Eastern Europe provides a seemingly uninterrupted *locus amoenus*. At the same time, the landscapes also provide a direct opposition to the city spaces which present another layer of *In July*'s connected European space.

The three major European cities in *In July* are Hamburg, Budapest and Istanbul. Though these cities are marked by their differences because of their individual histories, geographies and economies, they are revealed as connected. Ethnically diverse characters, musical mixtures, and local landmarks predominantly mark Akın's cityscapes. They offer an audiovisual experience of classic European cities which become the backdrop for the filmic love story. My discussion is primarily focused on the city by night and the city during the day. By specifically emphasising entertainment venues and marketplaces in Hamburg and Budapest, the film grounds the similarities that connect these West/Central European cities.

The nightlife sequence in Hamburg begins with a close-up of the lead singer of the local band Niños con Bombas, beginning the Spanish song

'*Velocidad*' with a loud scream straight into the camera. The camera zooms out showing the open-air stage of the band and then cuts to Daniel. Accompanied by the rhythmic, upbeat song, the camera adopts Daniel's perspective and slowly moves into the vibrant entertainment venue. People dancing, drinking and talking are positioned on either side of the frame. Daniel moves timidly through the young partygoers. Meanwhile, the band, which is now shown with a case of the local 'Astra' beer underneath its bass, has introduced the next song. The singer says that 'Ramona' is a 'love song' that goes beyond borders. Shortly thereafter, Daniel meets Melek outside the bar.

The opening shot of the Hamburg nightlife sequence introduces major components of Akın's visions about the (European) city. The nocturnal city becomes a site of musical entertainment. The vibrant music becomes a part of the city and the young metropolitan audience. The Hamburg-based band features members from Chile, Brazil and Germany but, at the same time, represents the local music scene. The lyrics are in Spanish, true to the band's habit of presenting musically and lyrically mixed forms. The band often also incorporates English and French in their songs, which are ska, jazz, punk, and cabaret influenced. Through the opening scene, Akın establishes the major components of the city: ethnic diversity, cultural multiplicity and dynamic interrelations of the people and places that ultimately create the local city space of Hamburg (Gueneli, 2014; Hillman and Silvey).

These components of the city are reiterated during Daniel's trek across Hamburg-Altona. Daniel and Melek walk through iconic places in Altona. These are all marked as ethnically diverse and represent today's European 'global city' in which ethnicity becomes an important component.[2] They visit a Turkish restaurant which has an oriental decor depicting the Bosporus Bridge in Istanbul. The diegetic sound of Turkish classical music (featuring the instruments *saz* and *ud* which are central to Turkish musical traditions)[3] accompanies the couple's conversation. Later, they walk to the 'Elbstrand' (the Elbe river beachfront between Blankenese and Altona). Here, the couple receives a bottle of Astra from a man with a presumably East European accent and Melek sings a song in Turkish. Hamburg allows for sonic mixes to create a polyphonic city space, which offers varied sensual, aural and visual experiences.

Through these interrelations, the city becomes a cosmopolitan venue.[4] Cosmopolitanism in *In July* emerges, among other things, with the experience of ethnic difference. Thereby, the film connects to a larger discourse. Mica Nava and Mike Savage et al. discuss the rapid emergence of the discourse on cosmopolitanism in the social sciences and in the humanities within the last decade. Savage et al. see cosmopolitanism as intrinsically linked to globalisation. It is reflected in a 'willingness to engage with the other' and to have a global awareness in general (Savage et al., 181). Nava identifies cosmopolitanism as a mainstream phenomenon in today's global cities. It signifies openness to the world (Nava, 3, 4). This kind of global openness is prominent in *In July*'s local places which are the product of local/global networks. It should be stressed, however, that Akın's cinematic cosmopolitanism is not blind to violence, deportation of migrants, manslaughter or terrorism. While Akın's cosmopolitanism connotes openness to the world, it also exhibits aspects of the, at times, harsh realities of the characters' lives, such as the difficulties of legal bureaucratic or illegal border crossings. These are exemplified in more depth in *Head-On* and *The Edge of Heaven*.

The night scene in Budapest is similarly cosmopolitan. The scene, set in an underground dance club, is infused with dance music, drugs and petty criminality. The sequence begins with Daniel and Luna (Daniel's interim travel companion played by Branka Katić) navigating through twisted paths into a glossy Hungarian club, filled with punks and other guests. The ethnically ambiguous Luna and the bartender (Birol Ünel) provide Daniel's dinner. Shortly after, a close-up of Luna's hand shows her pouring narcotics into Daniel's drink. The sequence continues depicting the scenery in slow motion, suggesting Daniel's narcotised perception of the place. Daniel joins the people on the dance floor to the tunes of 'Suicide Swing' performed by J*Let featuring Nero Gato. It is unclear whether this eclectic song is diegetic or non-diegetic, reflecting Daniel's intoxicated condition. The sequence ends with Daniel being thrown out of Luna's car after she seduces him and steals his ring.

Like the open-air club in Hamburg, the Hungarian club offers a pulsating entertainment venue. Lured by Luna's sexuality, Budapest at night becomes a place for Daniel's sensual encounter. Some of the characters seem edgier, wearing flamboyant outfits and hairstyles. Luna, who seems to be a vagabond from former Yugoslavia, the bartender, and a street vendor represent segments of the mixed population in the Balkans. The casting of Serbian-born Katić, Hungarian-born Gábor Salinger, and Turkish-born Ünel is a way of visualising the diversity of Central/Eastern Europe in Budapest. The languages spoken include Serbo-Croatian, Hungarian, German and English, suggesting a cosmopolitan environment.

While the cities at night are depicted as entertainment venues, the cities during the day offer a glimpse of architectural sights. The marketplace, symbolic of meeting places for different demographic populations since the early modern period (Fenske), features prominently in both cities. In Hamburg, the colourful flea market is in a plaza at an intersection between historic buildings and contemporary bars. It is here, that Juli, a street vendor, encourages Daniel to buy a ring with a Mayan sun symbol. Finally, Juli hands Daniel a Spanish flyer to join an event. After the lively market interlude, the scene continues with Daniel's walk through Hamburg-Ottensen.

The scene introduces the viewers to the architecture of nineteenth-century apartment buildings in Ottensen. Daniel lives in such a house. On the stairs, Daniel meets his Afro-German neighbour Kodjo (Ernest Herrmann). Kodjo is dressed in a Jamaican sports jersey, has hair spotted with dye, smokes a bong, and talks in a fake Jamaican-English accent about his travels to Jamaica. Asking Daniel to house-sit, however, he quickly switches to his native Hamburg dialect, showing his playful code switching. The interior of the building, coloured in orange and blue paint, relativises the illusion of the nineteenth-century atmosphere created through the facade of the buildings. It allows for a contemporary portrayal of the place. The house, which is reminiscent of historic Ottensen through its architecture, is portrayed as a place for contemporary, ethnically diverse Hamburg citizens.

In Budapest, the market scene is similarly colourful. Daniel witnesses how Luna sells his ring to a Hungarian street vendor. After Daniel forcefully retrieves his ring, the action extends from the market scene into the city. A car race scene through the historic old town of Budapest leads the audience through Hungary's eighteenth-/nineteenth-century architecture. This includes a long shot of the famous *lánchíd* (Chain Bridge) crossing the Danube river. The bridge is a nineteenth-century construction which links the city's two historic parts, Buda/West and Pest/East.

Ultimately, both cities depict the market as a starting point for architecturally unique sights. The scenes in Hamburg are short and represent only the beginning of the travel narrative, yet Akın manages to portray an ethnically, musically and architecturally diverse and vibrant city which also coincides with its northern characteristics (for example, at the Elbstrand). The same is true for Budapest which is a Central European stop in the midst of Daniel's travel. These cities both become representatives of classical European cities with old towns, marketplaces, historic buildings and a river along their cityscapes, as well as places for cultural, linguistic and musical diversity in which locality is emphasised.

Massey's discussions about space and place relate to *In July*'s filmic projection of European local city spaces. In arguing for a progressive and global idea of locality/place, Massey states that:

[i]nstead ... of thinking of places as areas with boundaries around, they can be imagined as articulated moments in networks of social relations and understandings, but where a large proportion of those relations, experiences and understandings are constructed on a far larger scale than what we happen to define for that moment as the place itself, whether that be a street, or a region or even a continent. (2008: 262)

The idea of a place does not need to be reactionary and require boundaries (Massey 2008: 260, 261). Massey opts for a 'progressive sense of place', allowing for a multiplicity of networks within a place: 'If it is now recognized that people have multiple identities then the same point can be made in relation to places' (2008: 261). She further stresses that the geography of social relations is transforming and that 'such relations are increasingly stretched out over space': '[W]hat gives a place its specificity is not some long internalized history but the fact that it is constructed out of a particular constellation of social relations, meeting and weaving together at a particular locus' (2008: 262).

In *In July*, European cities are portrayed as distinctly vibrant places that are connected through their vivid cosmopolitanism. Though many of the characteristics described above could be seen as part of any metropolitan cityscape, these are nonetheless constructed as distinctly European through the specific composition of languages, streets and architecture. These cities are explicitly marked as Hamburg and Budapest, as a part of a larger European history, culture and lifestyle, but also as places in flux with blurring boundaries which do not exclude interactions and exchanges with places beyond a geopolitical Europe. These cinematic cities are momentary constructs as suggested by Massey. Budapest thus refrains from being an Eastern 'margin' to the 'central' position of Hamburg in Europe and becomes an equally desirable and cosmopolitan European urban space.

Furthermore, the cities are constructed as spaces for love. Metropolitan settings, such as Paris and Berlin, have prominently denoted sexuality and carnal desires in literary works (Gerstenberger, 24–6). Akın decentralises these traditional spaces of desire by choosing Hamburg, Budapest and Istanbul equally to represent such sites for love/desire.[5] The final sequence in the film portrays daytime scenes in Istanbul that highlight this further.

Daniel arrives at a bus terminal in Harem on the Asian side of Istanbul. He walks through the crowded city, along the Bosporus passing the *kız kulesi* ('maiden tower') in historic Üsküdar. The scene then cuts to the European side of Istanbul. Daniel walks through the plaza in the historic district of Ortaköy. Ortaköy was already a cosmopolitan neighbourhood during the time of the Ottoman Empire with diverse religions and ethnicities living together. Here, Daniel meets Juli and declares his love. Encircled by the waters of the Bosporus, the first Bosporus bridge, the Ottoman neo-baroque-style Ortaköy mosque and the people standing around them at the plaza, Daniel and Juli kiss. The camera, showing close-ups of the kissing couple, grounds the circular construction of the frame by moving around Daniel and Juli. Istanbul, like Hamburg and Budapest – contoured with diversity and multi-ethnicity, historical landmarks and contemporary musical mixtures in the non-diegetic sound – becomes a space for love.

European Sounds

Like the land- and cityscapes, the soundscapes in *In July* are instrumental for Akın in constructing his visions of a diverse and decentralised Europe. As sound designer Randy Thom puts it: '[m]ovies are about making connections between things (. . .) Sound is one of the best ways to make those connections (. . .) between characters and places and ideas and experiences (Thom and Brophy, 10). Such connections take centre stage in Akın's films. The interwoven connections of people, places and things material are achieved through the *mise en scène* and through language/music in the soundtrack. Turkish pop music, Spanish-language songs from Hamburg, Canadian pop songs on the Danube and German psychedelic music in Hungary portray the aural diversity of the film and highlight a cosmopolitan aural space. Furthermore, Turkish, English, and East European languages and the different accents of the protagonists emphasise linguistic diversity. Linguistic variations become 'the aural norm' and 'replace the idea that "strange" sounds' and languages are limited to the '"other" immigrant in the Western city' (Gueneli 2014: 349; Tonkiss, 303).[6] The film provides an acoustic potpourri of languages and music.

As is typical for Akın's films, the music in *In July* is polyphonic.[7] The opening sequence in Bulgaria, for example, ends with the diegetic music of Turkish musician Sezen Aksu. Here, Aksu's tape is a hint at multidirectionality of migration.[8] Before moving south-east with Isa, the tape travelled from Turkey to Germany (a reference to cultural transfers between the two nations). Aksu's song has become a part of a new European sound. In the 1970s and 1980s, Turkish greengrocers in German cities had started to import Turkish cultural goods.[9] Today, many foreign media are readily available in private and public spheres in Germany (Europe). Turkish media commodities in Germany are often discussed critically. As Andreas Goldberg states, Turkish music, video, or television broadcast have often been read as a 'retreat from society', as an act of self-isolation from German society (420). Calling the Turkish media consumption in Germany a 'medial ghettoization', Goldberg further states that the function of the media recalled fears about immigrant integration (420). There were 'anxieties, that the strong dedication to (Turkish) mother tongue media would gradually lead to a social exclusion of the foreign population from German communication structures' (434). In *In July*, these 'anxieties' are replaced by an inclusiveness of the media. Turkish music does not feature as an exotic commodity nor as an alien element that alludes to foreignness. The Turkish pop song becomes one alternative which exists simultaneously alongside other (pop) songs.

Aksu's song becomes a part in the European soundtrack of *In July* next to music by the New York-based, multi-ethnic band Brooklyn Funk Essentials, an 'acid-jazz, funk and hip hop collective, featuring musicians and poets from different cultures' (anon., n.d.). They feature songs with Turkish folk music rhythms, instruments, and artists such as Laço Tayfa. Aurally, this results in a 'musical heteroglossia', a dialogic creation of music, which blends styles, traditions and instruments. Generally, in Akın's films, music as diverse as American funk bands, Turkish pop or classic *Yeşilçam* music,[10] folklore or modern dub versions of Eastern European songs, become commonplace in the creation of the soundscapes of Europe.

Rob Burns states that '[l]ike geographical borders, linguistic and musical boundaries are constantly crossed or dissolved in Akın's films, all of which, with the exception of *Solino* (2002), are polyglot' (2007: 13). In addressing the last song of *In July*, Burns stresses the fusion quality of the music, which 'provides a perfect complement to the film's broader vision: a fusion of musical styles and voices that blend together jazz, reggae and folk and sets off English lyrics against clarinet, an instrument beloved in Turkish folk music' (Burns 2009: 23). Ultimately, regions starting in Hamburg and going through Central/Eastern Europe and Turkey are linked through a diverse European soundscape. These connections help to lift binaries between centre and margins.

In Akın's films, Europe's polyphony is further enriched through languages (Gramling 2010).[11] The languages – like the music and travellers – are not bound to a specific region. For example, to begin *In July* in Bulgaria with two German-speaking characters suggests a blurring of language borders: the editing disconnects language and country/place. Similarly, the sequence in Budapest, where Slavic languages, English, and German are spoken, normalises linguistic diversity in the European soundtrack, disconnecting language from a particular geopolitical space. This invites an interpretation of culture and place as suggested by

FATIH AKIN'S FILMIC VISIONS OF A NEW EUROPE   91

anthropologists Aghil Gupta and James Ferguson (66). The scholars discuss the assumption of many disciplines that certain cultures live in fixed geographical locations. This seems particularly inadequate in today's globalised world with its moving cultures/peoples. They criticise that '[t]he distinctiveness of societies, nations, and cultures is predicated on a seemingly unproblematic division of space, on the fact that they occupy "naturally" discontinuous spaces'. The display of 'people, tribes and cultures' on maps depicting an 'inherently fragmented space' is inadequate (Gupta and Ferguson, 61). Cultures and people 'cease to be plausibly identifiable as spots on a map' (Gupta and Ferguson, 64). Certain fields still present people and places as 'solid, commonsensical [sic], and agreed on', when they are, in fact, 'contested, uncertain and in flux'. They argue that mainly national elites and states construct and maintain reified and naturalised national representations (Gupta and Ferguson, 64). Gupta and Ferguson suggest moving 'beyond naturalized conceptions of spatialized "cultures" and to explore instead the production of difference within common, shared, and connected space' (66).

In *In July*, diverse characters in geographically different settings speak numerous languages. The speakers travel with their languages and create acoustic connections between the spaces. The protagonists' dialects and accents are heard from Hamburg to Istanbul. This sonic diversity recalls Hamid Naficy's conception of 'accented cinema' – an aesthetic category that is organised around exilic, diasporic and ethnic film-making (Naficy, 10, 11, 23–5). Naficy argues that the protagonists' accents – a relevant alteration of sound – make the 'other' audible and force the 'dominant cinema to speak in a minoritarian language' (25). In other words, 'it is impossible to speak without an accent' (Naficy, 23). Yet, it is only with Akın that a democratisation of accented language takes place (Gueneli 2014: 350). Akın's protagonists, from all cultural backgrounds, speak with 'accents'. For example, German characters speak foreign languages with German accents. The soundtrack displays the diversity of European sounds and creates a multisonic Europe.

Moreover, Akın's linguistic diversity adds more languages to the European soundtrack, as established, for example, by Wim Wenders's 1994 European road film *Lisbon Story*. Ewa Mazierska and Laura Rascaroli point out that Wenders excluded certain marginal languages (for example, Turkish, Irish or Serbo-Croatian) from *Lisbon Story*, favouring languages associated with Western Europe, such as German, French, Spanish, Portuguese and English (204). Akın adds previously marginalised languages to the acoustics of post-1989 Europe. This polyphonic sound is in dialogue with the landscapes. It reiterates on an acoustic level the film's visions of a diverse and multi-ethnic Europe creating a new aural experience of Europe, refraining from setting boundaries or conceptualising centres/margins.

Conclusion: Decentralised Europe?

In July imagines Europe as a cosmopolitan, decentralised space that is promoted as open and traversable. It includes 'other' European spaces, such as Eastern Europe and Turkey. Europeanness becomes an attitude, a mobile, cosmopolitan lifestyle. To be European, as Delanty puts it, 'is ... to recognize that one lives in a world that does not belong to a specific people' (19). Daniel's quest furnishes an example of the progress of cosmopolitanism. In the course of a voyage across Europe, a seemingly bourgeois, uptight and naive teacher turns into an open-minded cosmopolitan. His educational journey (*Bildungsreise*) does not take place along the traditional route of German classicism (to/through Italy; a route he initially suggests) but along an unconventional route through a still largely unknown post-1989 Eastern Europe which Juli prefers and which is, in fact, used by Turkish-Germans travelling between Turkey and Germany. This journey suggests a desire for new explorations. Turkey as a destination might be as educational as Italy was imagined to be for Goethe. By negotiating with the people and places on his travel, Daniel becomes a more balanced person, whose *Bildung* consists of the acquisition of a cosmopolitan identity, a value the European Union likes to endorse.

The EU has recognised and accordingly utilised cinema as a tool for projections of European values and lifestyles. Katrin Sieg argues that

> [t]hrough substantial cultural funding programs it [the EU] has sought to foster positive popular identification with European identity and values. The EU's cultural policy has stimulated the visual, narrative and theatrical imagining of European community as cosmopolitan, tolerant, and diverse (2).

Furthermore, 'Cinema contributes to the popular, ideological project of imagining Europe by asking what kind of transnational community is desirable and possible' (Sieg, 62). Daniel's metamorphosis turns him into a – to use Sieg's words – 'cosmopolitan, tolerant, and diverse' European subject traversing Eastern Europe. Daniel's and his companion's desires and movements are represented as 'non-stylized' (acting and costume) and understandable (empathy) as opposed to the stylised depiction of borders. The film thus appeals to a wider European audience that envisions a cosmopolitan, traversable Europe. Generally speaking, this could be a vision of Europe that might be compatible with the cultural agenda of the European Union. Akın's Europe, however, includes spaces beyond the margins of geopolitical EU borders (for example, Turkey) and subtly refers to the limitations of movement to/from such places.

Akın's film seems to project both a vision of a cosmopolitan subjectivity, which allows for multiple affiliations, and – through a variety of transnational connections – a 'hybrid and decentralized' Europe. Luisa Rivi talks about a 'hybrid and decentralized' make-up of contemporary Europe in her discussion of films by prominent European directors, such as Michael Haneke, Gianni Amelio and Luc and Jean-Pierre Dardenne. Akın might be part of a larger project/trend in which contemporary directors envision a decentralised Europe. Yet, Akın's visions, which normalise heterogeneity/polyphony and promote a 'mobile sense of place', have not been accepted in all European realities. The Swiss minaret ban, the German public discourse on the sound of muezzins, and the French/Belgian ban on the full-face hijab stand opposed 'to the aestheticized sights and sounds in Akın's films' (Gueneli 2014: 352) that do not discriminate between the 'centres' and 'margins' of Europe. That Akın is a spokesperson for an open-minded Europe has been exemplified through his response to the 2009 Swiss ban of minaret buildings. Akın states that, as the child of Muslim parents for whom minarets represent an 'architectural completeness' of religious buildings – and not a politicised Islam – he was personally offended by the xenophobic referendum. He would subsequently cancel his appearance at the *Soul Kitchen* premiere in Switzerland (anon. 2009).

It remains a matter of interpretation if and how much artistic productions such as films adequately represent or comment on geopolitical, social or historical changes. The boundaries between Akın, the director/public figure, and his work are often blurred as he frequently, and deliberately, connects the two by commenting on current sociopolitical events as in the examples above. In addition, his award-winning films often have a distinctly European casting, setting and soundtrack and, as well, reference European issues all of which seem to invite an interpretation of his work within a European framework. As I have argued here, I believe that Akın's films, in fact, do comment on sociopolitical situations in Germany/Europe by displaying a particular cinematic imagination of a new Europe, a Europe that aspires to be cosmopolitan, open-minded and connected, without ignoring the existing geopolitical impediments.

CHAPTER 6

Salami Aleikum – The 'Near East' Meets the 'Middle East' in Europe

Alexandra Ludewig (The University of Western Australia)

Intro/Easts

This chapter will analyse the feature film *Salami Aleikum* (2009, Germany) by the Iranian-born German director, Ali Samadi Ahadi, as a postcolonial commentary on the reinvention of the 'near' and 'middle' east in mainstream German society. Ahadi plays with the idea that present-day Germany has two political entities that can be referred to as 'der Nahe Osten' (literally the 'near east'; in English the 'Middle East'). In this romantic comedy, images of many 'easts' serve to complicate further the German-centric East/West divide by referencing a confluence of stereotypes and homogenisations that conflate Arab and Persian cultures, the Far and the Middle East, as well as the much closer, but seemingly no less estranged, regions within and beyond Germany's 'east', that is, Poland and the former communist GDR (German Democratic Republic). In doing so, this seemingly broad and unambitious comedy reveals itself to be a self-reflexive metapoetic commentary on narrative, identity and myth-making.

Postcolonial Discourse

In *Salami Aleikum* the encounter between East Germans and Persian immigrants serves as a vehicle to expose stereotypes and xenophobia, colonial attitudes, and the willing exploitation of exoticism at play in many societies. Rather than problematising alterity, however, similarities between these East Germans and Persians are uncovered after the initial clash of the two representatives from very different 'easts', as they come to understand that each has lost their respective homeland (*Heimat*). They bond by allowing one another to reinvent themselves as an exotic 'other'.

The stereotypical families used to exemplify this rapprochement are the East German Bergheims with their adult daughter, Ana, and the Persian migrants to West Germany, the Taheris, whose son, Mohsen, is in his late twenties. It is the offspring of both families who instigate the departure from a diasporic mentality which feeds off the invention of a glorified past. Ana's and Mohsen's emancipation – achieved by refusing to adopt this old-style mentality – serves as a vehicle for change and thus breaks the vicious circle their parents have manoeuvred themselves into by clamouring for their lost past and therefore living in, and surrounded by, relics of that past.

Both families have lost their homelands and have found it hard to adjust to the new realities in the unified Germany. The Bergheims lost their jobs and their dignity when the state-owned textile company for which both parents worked ceased to exist in 1989, and their athlete daughter, who had been competing at an international level as a shot-putter, was exposed in a doping scandal. The Taheris left Persia for exile in the capitalist West Germany (FRG/Federal Republic of Germany) when the transition from the Shah's autocratic monarchy to the Ayatollah's Islamic republic took place in 1979, transforming the monarchy into a religious dictatorship. Their new life in West Germany began in Cologne where the Taheris opened a butcher's shop. When, after nearly two decades, their business comes under threat in the form of the local health authorities, their second *Heimat* forces them into further exile. Their son's naive business venture with a shady Pole brings the family to the East German provinces where anyone is more popular than West Germans, especially if they promise to invest in the region. Predictably, Ana Bergheim and Mohsen Taheri fall in love; however, before the happy union between the next generation goes on to cure the older representatives of the two very different Easts and thus fulfil the film's genre-specific happy ending, each particular 'other' is constructed, deconstructed and reconstructed in a gradual reversal process which mocks colonialism.

Dreaming up Utopias

The film's opening sets a fairy-tale mood. A female narrator speaks in a soft voice about how some people find their calling in life by following in their ancestors' footsteps while others have no plan whatsoever. The voice-over is accompanied by a panning shot of a quirky cobblestone street, albeit clearly located in 'Köln'. It is here that the Taheris opened a butcher's shop when they fled from Iran, and it is their adult son Mohsen – whom viewers see sitting in the window and knitting – who is identified by the narrator as someone who has not yet found his calling in life. As the camera pans to the first floor of the apartment building where the family lives directly above their shop, several flags become visible. Three different curtains adorn the facade and entrance of their butcher's shop: an Iranian and a German flag, as well as the red and white emblem of the local soccer club '1. FC Köln', with its mascot animal, a billy goat. This evidence of the migrant family's integration into their new society is given further credence when their business, which sells sheep's and goat's meat, is shown to have a loyal and extremely multicultural customer base. The people queuing to be served are visibly of different ethnicities; among them a black African, a Muslim and an Indian. While contemporary West Germany is depicted as a multicultural setting, the interior of the Taheris' flat has all the hallmarks of life in the diaspora. Like a simulacrum, it is decorated with an abundance of trinkets which Mohsen must carefully negotiate when making his way through, trying to avoid low-hanging lamps and other decorations – as well as his father.

The problematic father–son relationship identifies the difficulty in overcoming the past as a generational issue, with the younger generation rejecting the ways of its elders. In this case, Mohsen's father, Abdul Taheri, is trying to cut corners to raise his profit margin by forcing his son to butcher without a licence and illegally to dispose of their waste, especially offal, in the neighbourhood rubbish bins. On the whole, Mohsen is shown to clash with his overbearing, authoritarian father who, as a Persian man in exile, is more 'Persian' than anyone in Persia could possibly be. His pride knows no bounds when he recalls his family's forebears ('all of them heroes', before explaining more prosaically, 'well, engineers, politicians and scientists', at least until Mohsen arrived), and his adoration of Persian culture (which he boasts is the fount of civilisation: 'medicine, philosophy, mathematics and alcohol, all from Persia') makes him appear as a caricature.

By way of dealing with his father's personality, and the fact that he is a failure in his father's eyes as he is a sensitive young man who does not like the family business and cannot stand the sight of blood, Mohsen knits which also underlines his feminine qualities. In a metapoetical reference, the audience first sees him sitting by the open window in their Cologne apartment while knitting, taking in the sights and sounds of the street which is deliberately depicted as a fantastic dream-like setting. Butterflies dance in the sunshine, an old-fashioned circus poster shows animals moving under water and a rickshaw driver pedals past old men smoking water pipes and drinking Turkish tea, thus setting a peaceful scene reminiscent of exotic holiday destinations rather than contemporary Cologne. This *mise en scène* seems to bring Mohsen's daydreaming alive, and is another of his coping strategies. He travels into his fantasy and his seemingly endless knitted scarf tells in its design, colour combinations, patterns and craftsmanship of tumultuous and harmonic periods in Mohsen's life, and is thus also a metapoetical reference to the patchwork of episodes and styles within the film itself.

Shifting Ground

When Mohsen's father suffers a stress-induced heart attack, Mohsen must rise to the challenge of managing the butcher's shop. Wanting to impress his father, Mohsen invests in a new business model, in which he will only have to import fattened sheep, supposed 'Musterschafski' (exemplary 'sheepski'), from Poland which will not be slaughtered in-house but rather by a Polish business partner. Mohsen hands over everything in the till to the gold-chain-wearing, suit-clad Polish underworld figure, whose greeting 'Salami Aleikum' also gives the film its name and starts Mohsen on his rite of passage.

Mohsen's trip due east brings him into the territory of the Bergheims when his car breaks down halfway between Cologne and Poland, and he is stranded near the fictitious village of Oberniederwalde. Cinematographically, his arrival quotes visual and acoustic elements of the horror genre (the obligatory dark, rainy night, with thunder and lightning, an owl screeching and a wolf howling) as well as the American western genre (the lone star walking past deserted houses along an empty village street with the sense that a showdown is imminent). Lost, cold and afraid, Mohsen ambles past the gates and fences of those houses, with the camera filming him from behind their railings; he clearly does not belong here and is set apart from the rest of the scene. This further raises the sense of doom and fear, estrangement and alienation.

Indeed, the place where Mohsen has become stuck is no paradise; Oberniederwalde in Saxony has definitely seen better times. During the GDR period it was an industrial centre famous for its textile factory which was run, among others, by the Bergheims. When the Berlin Wall fell and the GDR ceased to exist, so did the unprofitable company. With its closure, the Bergheims and many other villagers lost their jobs and many have since left this impoverished place of no work and no hope. The swastika sprayed on to the town sign hints at the values which have filled the void. Meanwhile, the Bergheims have tried to establish themselves as innkeepers in this rather rundown and increasingly deserted East German backwater but clearly struggle as they sublet part of the pub to a local woman offering hairdressing services.

Their reinvention has been just as radical as their daughter's. In the 1980s, the teenage Ana was an extremely promising shot-putter in love with her young trainer and aspiring to compete for the GDR at the

Olympics. After unification, however, a doping commission disqualified her, her trainer left for the west and Ana was forced to start afresh. She has since become a mechanic and guards her emotions, appearing rough and tomboyish.

Visually, the encounter between the tall, athletic and strong mechanic, Ana, and the very petite, effeminate, knitting Mohsen is another constellation akin to a caricature. Exaggeration seems the stylistic feature of choice; when Ana stands in front of Mohsen, tall and illuminated from behind by the sun, seemingly glowing and elevated, 'with hair like a cap of gold', she appears to Mohsen like an angel and his saviour. In turn, he is keen to impress her and to appeal to her by embellishing the truth. He claims to be a vegetarian, just like Ana, and, rather than purchasing Polish sheep for their meat, he declares that he is interested in their wool as he and his family are in the textile industry. His scarf and the wool he is knitting with seem to confirm this claim, and Mohsen thus continues to spin stories and lies while his scarf – in parallel with the film's plot and reflecting the fact that he is in love – likewise takes on magical patterns and magnificent designs in a metapoetic reference to the magic of storytelling.

Memories of Lost Father(lands)

Mohsen Taheri, the twenty-eight-year-old son of a Persian Cologne butcher, and Ana Bergheim, the thirty-year-old daughter of factory workers-cum-innkeepers in Oberniederwalde, thus become the vehicle for the rapprochement of the two 'easts', which are each dominated by the mindset of the strong father figures. And it is the fathers who must undergo the biggest mental shift to achieve mutual understanding. Both men have had to deal with a fall from positions of minor importance: Abdul Taheri as a low-ranking military officer under the Shah's regime in the Iranian region of Baluchestan, and Hans Bergheim as a foreman and brigade leader in a GDR factory considered one of the best performers in the eastern bloc. For the Bergheims the good old days are exemplified by the export history of their textiles, the world of communism and job security. Mr Bergheim proudly shows off the machinery in the now deserted production hall. The equipment is falling apart as he touches it, however. When the state-owned enterprise was wound up during the process of German unification, Hans Bergheim felt hurt and lost: 'They took a part of my life away back then. All I had left was hope,' but after twenty years of futile correspondence with potential investors, most importantly the Chinese, he has also lost his hope.

Like the Taheris' simulacrum, the Bergheims have created a diasporic space for themselves and the local community in both their private residence and the pub which are adorned with photos recalling the apparently golden days of the GDR whose glory is also recalled by the Bergheims as they watch video recordings of old soccer matches in which their favourite team won. The end of the respective regimes under which they lived and worked forced both men from greatness to insignificance. With every retelling the past has taken on more mythical features, becoming grander and more impressive, whereas real life has grown increasingly dismal.

Both father figures have cultivated diasporic identities, glorifying their past, their personal achievements, their worth and importance, and their respective cultures' international standing. For Abdul Taheri the reference points are mythical Persia, his studies, his military rank in the army, the old monarchy (Shah of Persia) and his heroic family. Glimpses of the truth shine through, however, when Mohsen's mother, upon seeing dirty sheep on the factory site, is reminded of Baluchestan, their home region in Iran, an impoverished mountain region on the border between Pakistan und Iran. Likewise, his wife corrects Taheri's boastful claim that he had been a general (maybe just an officer or even just an 'NCO') and that he supposedly studied many subjects at university ('five subjects, or was it only four, or perhaps just three?'). Taheri's pride is contrasted starkly with his reduced circumstances which have seen him earning a living as the untrained and inept owner of a butcher's shop. As the film director explains: 'I would like to use the Persians' pride to make caricatures', and

Figure 6.1 Storytelling in *Salami Aleikum*. Courtesy of Dreamer Joint Venture.

he uses the butcher's shop to show the 'loss of meaning/relevance the family has suffered since their emigration' (Ahadi qtd in Kamalzadeh).

He feels this to be a common trait of many Persians in exile whom, he claims, constantly lament: 'My god, what we used to be when the Shah was still in power . . . what houses we used to have!' (Ahadi qtd in Kamalzadeh). According to Ahadi, once in Germany, nostalgia and/or paranoia have become typical responses to emigration and the discontent it has resulted in for many of them. In the Taheris' and the Bergheims' cases, nostalgia is indeed combined with paranoia.

Overcoming Deep-set Fears

Representative of a trained and educated lower middle class in their respective homelands, both families display mentalities and biases stereotypical of their respective society's dominant outlooks and ideologies. With its focus on borders between cultures, regions and ideologies, the film exemplifies their prejudices. The 'other' is problematised as a general mindset in the stand-off scenes between the families but also, more generally, by imagined divisions: the border guards securing European Union territory from what lies to the East, and the East Germans defending their values against those from the West. As such, the fault lines between friend and foe in the microcosm of Oberniederwalde are representative of the general state of mind: fear of the unknown and of the 'other'. Mohsen's encounter with the German East is marked by apprehension and fear, just as the Bergheims' response to him initially mirrors the phobic projections of a distinctly white Christian/Western imaginary world, as identified by Said (1978), and referencing the proponent of the Muslim Orient as the ultimate 'other' – to be feared and taunted. Mohsen is initially viewed with suspicion and rejection. In a deliberate act intended to humiliate this stranger and put him in his place, he is served fried pig's kidneys.

The film's director employs intentional exaggerations to make his point. He quotes common prejudices and stereotypes: Ana is tall, strong, blond, blue eyed and compared to a German oak. Abdul Taheri proudly explains: 'We're not foreigners, we are Persians'; Hans Bergheim insists 'we don't have anything against foreigners' (only against West Germans/'Wessis'!), while the film references Arabs and terrorism, the GDR and doping in sport and the Chinese as investors in the West. Bar the two lovers, every character in the film spouts slanderous, racist slogans: Ana's one-time love interest warns against migrants ('Foreigners always bring over the entire clan and then it will be Little Asia here . . .'), bemoans the fact that 'the wogs are stealing the chicks' and claims to know that 'all orientals are essentially phoneys and big-mouths'. His suspicion about others, whether 'Chinks' or 'Mullahs', are forgotten, however, when he falls in love with a Persian woman. Indeed, it is love that seems to have the power to transcend differences, initially in the form of mail-order brides from catalogues perused by some of the men. Without seeing the absurdity of the situation, one of them wonders how long Mai Ling from Nomkai, twenty-five years old and with no formal education, would take before she would feel at home in Oberniederwalde – especially as East Germany is depicted as the hotbed of neo-Nazism. The town's adolescent males sport shaved heads, Iron Cross tattoos, jackboots, army-surplus trousers and leather jackets. They walk around holding beer cans and spitting continuously. The swastika graffiti around the place make this connection clear.

Just as the Bergheims and their fellow villagers have definite ideas about the dangers posed by West Germans, and foreigners in general (especially those from further east), the Taheris have a stereotypical image of the east of Germany and have internalised West German prejudices regarding Eastern Europe ('Every Persian knows you don't do business with a Polack'); they even remember to pack a baseball bat when travelling east.

Ironically, however, both families think of themselves as progressive. The Bergheims regard their knowledge of Karl May's imagined Red Indian Winnetou (a figment of the imagination of the author who never visited America himself) and their love of Austria (as tourists they have ventured no further than the Kitzbühler Alps) as evidence of their openness towards other cultures – thus only showcasing their provincial limitations. Mohsen, initially addressed as 'Moses', conjures up images of terrorism (the Caliph of Köln, backyard mosques, 'Mullah' alarm) and backwardness (camel drivers), before images of modern Iran emerge more clearly. Yet, even then, that nation conjures up images of 'nuclear programs, reactor encasements and radiation suits', and remains a threat.

The film plays with the notion that the stereotypical Muslim in German cinema is 'either a victim or a social problem' (Berghahn 2009: 55) before debunking it by showing Mohsen to be just as fallible and human, and therefore just as likely to be a perpetrator and agent of racist ideas as any other person in the film. This realisation slowly comes to all of the characters. A rapprochement takes place which also plays on the stereotypical multicultural ideas of many Germans: the first contact is culinary and sees Oberniederwalde embracing exotic foods.

The entente continues to be marked by prejudices about the 'Orient' as a homogeneous form of the 'other'. The villagers think that Mohsen and Abdul Taheri are rich and famous men, conflating them with Saudi oil sheiks and incorrectly inferring that 'over there [they] are all influential and famous people' who have come to the former GDR 'because of our very special competence'. Both families are deluded about each other's financial position.

When the Bergheims see that the 'other' can be of benefit to them and their community, they attempt to respect Islamic tradition; in an inept gesture, Mr Bergheim offers his toilet mat to Mohsen as a prayer rug and shows him which way east, that is, Mecca, lies. Their customarily drab menu, featuring mashed potato with sauerkraut, goulash, or tomato soup and fried pig's kidneys, suddenly offers oriental dishes, such as lamb kebab, kofteh (Persian meatballs) and fessenjan (Persian chicken casserole with walnut sauce). Indeed, one patron remarks: 'Finally [. . .] something edible.' The lure of the new and exotic also stimulates the men's fantasies, with one of them inquiring of Mohsen: 'Is it true that Persia has such pretty woman? How could I meet one?' By now Mohsen knows how to save the lost souls around him and responds: 'In Persia we have a saying, do not look around the corner, if you can look straight ahead; and diamonds are often concealed in rags.'

In their monocultures, both families, as representatives of their respective groups in society, have ignored basic human instincts, such as curiosity and the desire for diversity. They have unwittingly suppressed renewal and are only now allowing themselves to crave something new: irrespective of whether this is exotic women, food, sayings or wisdom.

Ultimately, the people in Oberniederwalde, a part of the former GDR left behind by the structural renewal elsewhere, and the Persian emigrants recognise their own fate in each other's situation. As director Ahadi explains in the promotional material accompanying the DVD release in 2011: 'Both come from a world which no longer exists. [. . .] Both families invoke a homeland which is no longer. When they meet, they lead each other to believe that they are rich. That is another thing they have in common' (Ahadi 2009) And both admit to deceiving themselves as much as they have deceived each other.

Abdul Taheri explains his charade by confessing to Hans Bergheim: 'Maybe Mohsen is right, and I am just a ridiculous show-off [*lächerlicher Angeber*],' but justifies his behaviour as follows:

> We didn't have it easy when we came to Germany. We had nothing. My wife actually wanted to open a restaurant. I'd never slaughtered an animal in my life. All I had was my imagination and my stories, which she still enjoyed back then, and my uniform.

While his tall tales now bore his wife, to the Bergheims and the other villagers, they are new and exciting, as they speak of hope. Hans, in return, also confesses to the lies of a lifetime, admitting that he has always hated textiles. The Taheris can relate to the fate of these one-time party loyalists who are lost in the capitalist world. They come to understand that the richness of each other's history and culture is their biggest capital, and worthy of further exploration.

Blossoming Landscapes Due to Syncretism

Abdul Taheri's über-Persian demeanour, which in the past has led to tensions in his family, becomes a central feature of their business venture and the source for a message of hope for everyone. His language is full of exotic imagery and his values have taught his son to believe in love and miracles, money and fairy tales. Mohsen's tenderness dazzles Ana, and his romantic traits suspend reality with the gentle exaggerations of a make-believe world. Having grown up with his father's boasts, and seemingly influenced by his own renditions of Persian fairy tales, Mohsen truly believes both in love and in good fortune. The goodnight tale that Mohsen's father recites and reinterprets in one of many flash-back scenes tells of a prince who can win over his princess only when he acquires riches. Abdul queries: 'What is the use of being brave and proud, and of having a big heart?' His personal interpretation of the story is that you cannot transform deserts into blossoming landscapes without money. Accordingly Mohsen believes: 'We will buy the factory, everything will be fine.'

In turn, Hans Bergheim realises that the Persian overhaul of his restaurant's menu and decoration, that is, all that 'Persian charade', has been extremely popular with his guests and has netted a princely sum. This sparks his business idea, a celebration of exoticism, in which the drab factory building is transformed into something resembling a Persian bazaar. Using textiles from the former GDR, the old factory is transformed and reality is covered up and blocked from view, and the Orient is recreated as a bazaar from Aladdin's magical and lyrical fantasy world. To fill the imaginary space with magic, Hans Bergheim intuitively knows that this venture can achieve only a semblance of authenticity with the help of the Taheris: 'We can only do this together'. In the empty halls of the fabric factory and with the remaining pieces of cloth, they decorate the bare walls and fixtures, transforming the space into a bazaar and a large hammam, containing a sauna, a day spa and a 'fountain of youth'. Thus, the best of seven thousand years of Persian high culture and the remnants of forty years of East German socialism are combined to create a blossoming landscape of a very different calibre. In a play on inter-ethnic relations, the bazaar comes proudly to showcase ethnic alterity at the interstices of two 'eastern' cultures. Like many contemporary shopping centres, casinos and 'wellness temples', this artificial world thrives on performance of clichés, referencing internationally recognisable masks and roles, among them self-ironically colonial fantasies.

Ultimately, the Taheris' and Bergheims' dreams can be accommodated in the bazaar and are allowed to occupy a distinct space in the German *Heimat*. Capitalising on the expectations of locals and of tourists of the Orient, with cloth woven in the GDR decorating and masking the defunct factory site, the world constructed by the Bergheims and the Taheris conforms with the prejudices and exotic dreams of Westerners ignorant of the others' cultures and thus mimics the workings of 'Ostalgie', a nostalgic reinvention of the GDR's culture in contemporary memory which has netted huge profits when commercialised in *Ampelmännchen* memorabilia and other items of GDR consumer culture. The film's essence, however, not wanting to repeat the shortcomings of postcolonial theory (or, indeed, of Ostalgie) by falling back on distinct and separate cultures, advocates a multicultural hybridity and is not afraid of colonial mimicry (cf. Bhabha, 85–94). Defying their sense of loss of identity and deflated self-importance, the Bergheims and the Taheris are allowed to resurrect beloved aspects of their ethnicity and their past in a playful and tongue-in-cheek witticism on reality and history, authenticity, purity and syncretism. They thereby, selectively re- and decolonise themselves, turning their fortunes around. The bazaar and the wedding ceremony between Mohsen and Ana serve as the materialisation of their most colourful dreams and illustrate one of Abdul Taheri's fairy tales: 'Animals came to the prince and each had a flower with it, a rose, a carnation, etc. and soon the entire desert had transformed into a blossoming garden and when the princess woke up and saw the flowers she feels in love with him . . .'

The blossoming landscapes promised to East Germans in the early 1990s by West German reformers and politicians, which for so long seemed to have materialised only in the cemeteries of the former GDR, now finally do exist. Within the film's logic the saviours come from the East rather than the West, and they do not invest money but instead humanity, warmth and a sympathetic attitude. The new business venture actually embodies the derelict factory's former motto: 'Socialism, that is humanity in word and deed'.

Narrating Cultures

The skilful veiling of the factory site and its masquerading as a bazaar and oriental oasis form a deliberate reference to the capitalist sell-out which took place in the period of 'Kohlonisation', a popular pun – Helmut Kohl was then the German chancellor – referring to the early 1990s in Germany when the West 'colonised' the former East Germany and its old culture(s) and achievements were devalued.

By deliberately displaying their past in a museum-like set-up, distance is created along with intimacy. The locals deliberately imitate/perform/ showcase aspects of their culture (their expertise with textiles resurrects the best aspects of the GDR company; the village demonstrates its solidarity and the sense that everyone is in the same boat and is working towards society's betterment) while also allowing the Taheris to do what they are best at: spinning a yarn and weaving a rich oriental tapestry of stories and feel-good hospitality.

The new narrative transforms their environment and themselves: the hairdresser Gisela now paints people's hands with henna, and her love interest, Rudolf, has become a pasha. Even the former neo-Nazis are suddenly found lounging around the pools, having discovered youth and beauty and shaken off their fascist ideology. Abdul's and Hans's hanging moustaches are transformed, along with their personal situations and their surroundings, with their whiskers turning upwards in unison with their upbeat co-operation. The butterflies from the opening sequence make another appearance, this time in the make-believe Persian oasis in which Bergheim acts as tour guide and Abdul Taheri is the star attraction. As the cultural attaché of the Shah of Persia he rejoices: 'it really can't get more authentic than this'.

The oasis thus serves as the creation of myths as narratives capable of explaining the world, with grand narratives that generate meaning and can be directed towards both the past and the future, thereby aiding the individual. This film and its depiction of the possibility of overcoming crises and capitalising on difference reveal much about the workings of myths in general. Myths often reflect on and respond to things about ourselves which discomfit us, about latent collective wishes, reservations and reprimands. According to Hans-Christoph Blumenberg, myth-making may be seen as an attempt to counter the 'Absolutismus der Wirklichkeit' [absolutism of reality] (Blumenberg, 9), as a response to a seemingly predominant arbitrariness, and as a means of endowing life with meaning through art and interpreting it with telos.

The oasis in the middle of the East German provinces is a myth-making factory which aids orientation, thereby making the complexity of socio-economic processes more manageable for the people from the two 'easts'. Their combined myth-making exercise aims at positive self-assurance and constructive interpretations of the past for the present and the future. It also allows the people from two very different cultures to access one another's stories, whereby people like the Bergheims and the Taheris have access to one another's constructions and fictions relating to their respective pasts. By allowing the other 'side' insight into the most intimate spheres of one's psychological make-up, understanding can be fostered. Through the process of reactivating one's own memory, thus preventing it from being forgotten, as well as by acknowledging differences, these diverging narratives form the basis for a common future. Their fused oasis, the bazaar populated by both families and their stories, thus fulfils individual and societal functions, as a core for cohesion and as an aid for mutual understanding. At the same time, it revives two pasts, though more in the form of a readable (rather than a liveable) alternative to the present. Their myths thus become the foundation for a common future narrative, a basis for the self-confident embrace of different histories to prepare for a harmonic reality. As with all myths, this is not an attempt at revision, or to present truths and factual matters. By foregrounding the element of construction and fictitious invention, it is evident that only a spiritual, psychological and symbolic truth can be achieved. Nevertheless, it is a truth that is essential for a positive experience of *Heimat* [homeland] and an unproblematic coexistence. This confident and creative handling of the two families' pasts, as well as the sharing of memories, myths and misgivings, has coincided with, or prepared the ground for, a new relationship with storytelling and film/cinema.

Alterity and Hybridity

Fusing various cinematic traditions from extravagantly theatrical to comic-strip, animation to picture-postcard settings, and caricature to complete suspension of reality, Ali Samadi Ahadi's film demonstrates creative responses to crisis management. He was inspired as much by Bollywood as by 1970s Iranian films (in which actors suddenly turn and face the camera to address the audience and start singing) and the works of Michel Gondry (such as *Eternal Sunshine of the Spotless Mind*, 2004, USA) and Jean-Pierre Jeunet (*Le fabuleux destin d'Amélie Poulain*, 2001, France), resulting in this especially fantastic romantic comedy. The director explains the reasons behind this rich mixture of styles:

> We tried to get close to the dreams of our protagonists and to render their imaginations visible. [. . .] Sequences in which we let ourselves be inspired by fairy tale movies like The Story of Little Muck, Ali Baba and the Forty Thieves, and animated films like Dumbo or The Sandman [. . .]. Right from the beginning we wanted to mix as many styles as possible, from classic hand-drawn pictures to the

most up-to-date 3D technology [...] virtual sets, set extensions, stop motion, 2D and 3D animations, special effects, character animation. (Ahadi 2013)

The film's title *Salami Aleikum*, first used as a pun greeting by the Polish gangster figure, and later repeated by father Bergheim in an attempt to acquire some basic Persian greetings, plays on the salami-like garlic sausages the Taheris produced in their butcher's shop, as much as on the syncretism of different cultural ingredients. 'Salaam aleikum' (peace be with you) as well as other polite sayings are mangled when the Bergheims try to appeal to their visitors from the far East. It is not just the pleasantries that appear strange and semi-authentic, however; his actors suddenly fall out of their roles and address the audience directly (breaking the fourth wall), and a lamb is used as the story's narrator. In doing so, the film applies alienation effects as well as, at times, a decidedly 'Eastern' perspective, cites fairy tales, references myths and thus arrives stylistically at a world viewed from a Persian perspective. With this hybrid aesthetic strategy, the film appeals to a transnational audience who can recognise aspects of their own cultures. This also applies to the film music which fuses oriental sounds generated by the *tablas*, *darabukka*, *oud*, *toubak*, *daf* and vocal neigh with Western orchestral instruments including the harp, violin, viola, clarinet, saxophone and double bass.

As such, this romantic comedy is a metapoetical commentary on myth-making and home-making. The underlying message is that any strong society requires positive foundation myths to build strong communities for the future.

Conclusion

The film exemplifies common reactions to the feeling of loss, whether it is of one's homeland, job, family members or standing. A flight into a reinvented past furnishes a diaspora that thrives on mythologising. *Salami Aleikum* uses this existential constellation as a starting point for a politically incorrect and extremely funny exploration of issues of home/land, exile and diaspora, nostalgia and escapism, and alienation and homecoming – all narrated from the perspective of a German-Polish lamb. Fusing various cinematic traditions from Bollywood to comic-strip, animation to picture-postcard settings, and caricature to complete suspension of reality, Ali Samadi Ahadi's film demonstrates creative responses to crisis management by championing the arts as an antidote to reality, as well as the idea that history should not be allowed to get in the way of good storytelling, not only in cinema in general but also in Ahadi's overlapping 'easts'.

CHAPTER 7

Cinematic Fairy Tales of Female Mobility in Post-Wall Europe: Hanna v. Mona

Aga Skrodzka (Clemson University)

In the ensuing narrative I bring together Szabolcs Hajdu's *Bibliothèque Pascal* (2010, Hungary/Germany/UK/Romania) and Joe Wright's *Hanna* (2011, UK/Germany/USA), two recent European films, directed by a Hungarian and a British director respectively, that foreground the act of female mobility and the perceived feminisation of European (and global) migration in divergent, yet complementary, ways. The pairing of these two cinematic texts is motivated by their strategic use of fantasy as both a narrative trope and a coping mechanism for their female protagonists. This fantastic element, I argue, points to the continued unease with regard to female mobility, as such, and the complications that arise in the process of representing that mobility. While both films employ elements of the fantastic (Wright's film incorporates the Brothers Grimm fairy tale 'Snow White', and Hajdu's film engages magic realism as a storytelling strategy), and unabashedly engage in romanticising and exoticising their protagonists, when considered together, they provide an accurate and quite realistic depiction of the bifurcated nature of transnational mobility in the unifying Europe. In telling ways, both films racialise the female on the move and frame her within the economy of loss. By doing so, the films perform what Ewa Mazierska and Laura Rascaroli define in their seminal study of the European road movie as the 'traditional pejorative link between femininity and mobility' (2006: 186). Ultimately, my analysis showcases how the pre-Wall divisions between the First and the Second Worlds and the historical inheritance of Nazism and Communism seem to linger on in the New Europe, determining the possibilities and potentialities of women on the move. These new inflections of the old divisions put in question the grand idea of the post-war European community as one that had been successfully reconstituted strictly in opposition to the violence precipitated by the Marxist and Fascist ideologies.

In his 1998 book *Globalization: the Human Consequences*, Zygmunt Bauman diagnoses the disconcerting bifurcation in the modes of global mobility when he identifies the split between those who travel today as 'tourists', and whose experience of mobility is desirable, and those who move with the stigma of being forever a 'vagabond', who move 'because they have no other bearable choice' (93). As with any binary pair, Bauman explains, the two depend on each other: 'There are no tourists without the vagabonds, and the tourists cannot be left free without tying down the vagabonds.' There is an economy to this relationship, and this economy resembles the many exploitative contracts that characterise the labour relations in the late capitalist economy. Arguably, Hajdu's and Wright's films, when viewed side by side, replicate the relationship and bring into focus the incommensurability of the European 'tourist' and the 'vagabond'. It is then no surprise that the independent Hungarian film tells the story of the 'vagabond', Bauman's metaphor for the migrant subject, and the extravagant British-German action thriller showcases the story of the 'tourist', a figure that stands in for the member of the exterritorial, supranational corporate elites. Hajdu's vagabond is Mona Paparu (Orsolya Törö-Illyés), a single mother living in Romania, whose very unspectacular journey takes her across Europe to Liverpool where she ends up working as a prostitute in an upmarket brothel. Wright's embodiment of the European tourist turns out to be Hanna Heller (Saoirse Ronan), a German adolescent girl who has been trained to be an assassin, and whose assigned expedition is a dazzling and frenetic replay of the empowering mobility of Tom Tykwer's Lola in *Run Lola Run* (1998, Germany). Mona and Hanna never cross paths; diegetic worlds apart, they obviously cannot meet. Their generic difference, one being a protagonist in a whimsical magic realist tale about the 'mundane problems of making ends meet' (Bori 2010: 166), the other a heroine in a thriller that boasts a 'command of the visual poetry of action' (Ebert 2011), speaks of an actual socio-economic difference that keeps the real-life Monas and Hannas, the Second and the First World, apart in contemporary trans-European voyages. The two characters are the polar opposites in how they experience the celebrated freedom of movement (of labour, capital, resources, etc.) that is the hallmark value of the European unification project. The two women traverse the same roads and cross the same 'open' borders within Europe, yet they do not meet, because, as Bauman would argue, the late capitalist 'tourists' and 'vagabonds' never meet in Fortress Europe. They might occupy the same spaces, often in very intimate proximity, yet their economic and political status ensures their symbolic distance. When comparing the cinematographic treatment of space in the two films, that symbolic distance becomes evident. Hanna's Europe is constructed through numerous long shots of open vistas, often presented in their natural light. As she darts and leaps through a variety of different landscapes, the space seems to shrink concentrically around Hanna, who dominates it. Mona's Europe, especially once she embarks on her westward journey, is shot in cropped shots at night. Claustrophobically, her space closes in on her. Obstructions proliferate and contain her movement.

So what do Hanna and Mona tell us about the journeys undertaken by women in the post-Wall Europe? The answer is complex because both films engage the fantastic and simultaneously avoid, though to a different degree, the critical approach employed by transnational cinema that typically frames issues of female mobility within the narrative conventions of the 'social problem' film such as Pawel Pawlikowski's *Last Resort* (2000, UK), Ulrich Seidl's *Import/Export* (2007, Austria/France/Germany), or the Dardenne brothers' *Le silence de Lorna/Lorna's Silence* (2008, Belgium/France/Italy/Germany). One way to decode the politics of the two texts is by bringing into focus the treatment of the mobile female body offered by the two film-makers and the way in which that body is discursively racialised.

White Power as Girl Power in *Hanna*

In a less than subtle way, Wright's film uses a forced, faux-feminist agenda to revive the myth of the white European, promoting a veiled message of white supremacy, and therefore it resonates with (perhaps contributes to) the rising popularity of the white power and neo-Nazi discourses in Europe (evidenced by the institutionalisation of the far-right parties in European party politics), a surge in hate crimes (such as the 2011 massacre in Norway perpetrated by the neo-Nazi extremist Anders Breivik), the prevalent negative sentiments directed against asylum seekers and the widespread populist critiques of any comprehensive pro-immigration policy. Relying on a dubious intertext that combines the Brothers Grimm fairy tale 'Snow White', the Cold War spy stories, and the history of governmentally sanctioned experiments on humans, the film constructs an image of white agency that is as blatantly retrograde as it is politically correct because it takes the form of a frail adolescent girl who wraps her enemies around her finger. In a gesture reminiscent of classic blaxploitation cinema, where the spectacularised black female is endowed with agency that stands for Black Power as in the fighting heroines in Jack Starrett's *Cleopatra Jones* (1973) and Jack Hill's *Coffy* (1973) and *Foxy Brown* (1974), Wright's film uses a spectacularised white female to speak of White Power. In contrast to the blaxploitation genre where femininity is endowed, mature and fertile, here the White Power materialises as atrophied femininity. The film takes the sixteen-year-old Hanna – a German by birth and an *Über*-human by experiment – on a journey across continents and national borders, where soulful ethnic subjects provide foil for this ideal of a New European citizen, aptly described by Ginette Verstraete as 'someone with a thin connection to any single place – a rootless, flexible, highly educated and well-travelled cosmopolitan, capable of maintaining long-distance and virtual relations without looking to the nation-state for protection' (2010: 8). Hanna's whiteness is championed through her innocent (defeminised) and intensely mobile body. On the other hand, the film makes it evident that Hanna's supreme agency is due to her genetically induced preference for primal and animalistic behaviour which the film inadvertently links back to femininity. Arguably, the film champions white agency as a privilege of the European female while exorcising all femininity from the female body. Luminescent, at times almost translucent, weightless, speaking languages of many cultures, yet belonging to none, Hanna is the white European whose palatable and politically acceptable whiteness displaces the brown body on route to the European marketplace.

Hanna is not a film about trafficking or sex slavery though it is a film about a clandestine transnational voyage and exploitation of the female body. Much like any of the numerous recent films about trafficking of the Eastern European flesh for the purposes of sex industry, this film frames whiteness as highly fetishised/reified category linked specifically to the female body. *Hanna's* film-maker, Joe Wright, is a British director who is known for his very popular contributions to the ongoing British heritage cinema trend. His very stylised adaptations of literary classics have quickly become a sought-after commercial product. Wright directed *Pride & Prejudice* in 2005, *Atonement* in 2007, and *Anna Karenina* in 2012. *Hanna* is not a heritage film per se (unless one considers the Grimms' fairy tale to be its heritage source text), it is an action film. Yet, it is important for my analysis of *Hanna* to note that its film-maker enthusiastically partakes in peddling heritage nostalgia that glorifies life under the imperial rule and frames European history well within the heroic paradigm.

Set in contemporary post-Wall Europe, *Hanna* tells the story of Hanna Heller, a sixteen-year-old German girl, who lives in the remote Arctic wilderness (Finland to be specific) with her father Eric Heller (Eric Bana), an former CIA Cold War operative who went into hiding to keep a secret which the CIA would not want him to disclose. The secret has much to do with who Hanna is: a super soldier, whose DNA make-up has been engineered in a highly classified programme that recruited pregnant women from abortion clinics across East Central Europe to produce a cohort of superior fighters by altering their genetic profiles. Eric Heller was directly involved in managing the programme at the facility based in rural Poland. Eventually the programme was terminated and all involved liquidated with it, with the exception of Eric and Hanna. Out of sympathy for newborn Hanna and her mother Johanna Zadek, Eric tries to save the woman and her child. Their escape is not wholly successful: the mother Johanna is shot dead by Marissa Wiegler (Cate Blanchett), another CIA agent who becomes Hanna's nemesis later in the film. Eric does save the child and himself and decides to go into hiding and raise the girl to be the super-assassin that she was born and engineered to be. In the harsh Arctic conditions, he trains Hanna in the art of combat and survival. Away from civilisation, Hanna grows up not knowing what music sounds like or what art feels like (as we find out, her emotions have been suppressed to enhance her combat skills). Eric teaches her a number of languages and forces her to memorise endless encyclopedic facts about nature, culture, geography and the history of the world. Hanna's education is designed to turn her into a worldly person, a global citizen, who can conceive of her identity outside of any national belonging (or any community, for that matter). The father's education prepares the girl to exist in a world without technology or where technology became defunct. The physical drills that Hanna practises with stolid determination are meant to harness her full bio-engineered potential. After long days of rehearsing the elaborate survivalist protocol, we see Eric read Brothers Grimm fairy tales to Hanna as the only tender exchange between father and daughter. Knowing that Hanna will one day want to come out of hiding, and when that happens she will once again become a target for the CIA, Eric ensures that Hanna is ready for confrontation with Marissa Wiegler. When Hanna makes her decision to leave, Eric activates an old radio transmitter which immediately alerts Wiegler to the Hellers' location. A bizarre *deus ex machina* detail, the transmitter seems to exist solely to facilitate a single action in the film, that of bringing Marissa and Hanna together, in what becomes a race to kill. The remaining two-thirds of the film stage this spectacular race as a thrilling adventure in extreme globetrotting. Frequent narrative and visual cues posit the confrontation between Marissa and Hanna as that of the evil stepmother and the Snow White from the Grimms' fairy tale, therefore marking the race as a female competition to win the title of 'the fairest of them all'. While some viewers might not immediately see Hanna as the Snow White, most viewers cannot help but see her as very white.

Aesthetically, the film emphasises Hanna's whiteness in ways that cannot be overlooked. Unlike Richard Dyer's concept of invisible whiteness (Dyer 1988), Wright's staging of whiteness is pronounced and

Figure 7.1 Saoirse Ronan in *Hanna*.

carefully revealed. Played by the Irish American actress, Saoirse Ronan, Hanna embodies the white Aryan ideal.

For this role, Ronan's hair and eyebrows were bleached and she is frequently photographed in the luminescent style of the classic Hollywood period, when the use of intensely lit, radiant close-up of the female star's face punctuated the narrative with an image of glamorised whiteness. Famously, in his 1946 film *Gilda* (USA), Charles Vidor photographs Rita Hayworth in the luminescent manner described above, in the midst of the modernist, all-white interior which mimics and reinforces Hayworth's carefully constructed 'white goddess' demeanour. At this point of her career, Hayworth, formerly Margarita Carmen Cansino, had her Latina appearance rid of its ethnic characteristics through extensive bleaching and years of electrolysis (McLean, 43). In *Hanna*, the classic Hollywood set is replaced by the equally glamorised natural environment shot on location in the Finnish region of Kuusamo, one of the most snow-secure places in Europe. Here Hanna's staged whiteness is paired with the natural whiteness of the Arctic landscape, therefore framing whiteness as a natural attribute, a biological fact rather than a constructed category. Apart from race, the location hints at the new global North/South divide that has replaced the East/West geometry of the Cold War.

The film opens with a lengthy scene of Hanna stalking and hunting a caribou in the pristine, snowy landscape of the European North, which provides the Aryan-looking hunter with a perfect cover. At one with her environment, Hanna moves gracefully and quietly. She attempts to kill the animal with an arrow but, having missed the heart, she has to shoot it down with a pistol. She proceeds to disembowel her prey. The bloody guts, in a grotesque vignette, spill over the immaculate environment, punctuating the spectacle of whiteness with a splash of dramatic colour, therefore making the viewer suddenly conscious of the colour white – the previously undetected, yet expansive aspect of the scene. I find these opening images of white on white to be illustrative of what Sarah Ahmed calls the 'phenomenology of whiteness'. Ahmed engages Husserl's philosophy to show whiteness as 'a way of exploring how whiteness is "real", material and lived' (Ahmed, 150). She argues that, although whiteness as race is obviously not a biological fact, it does, however, exist as a 'background to experience' (Ahmed, 150). In certain spaces, under certain circumstances, white bodies dominate their surroundings and make them white. In those situations the bodies and the surroundings gravitate towards each other, forming a kind of unison, with shared attributes, a likeness, making those who are *not* white immediately different and deviant. Ahmed explains that when white bodies become 'habitual' in certain surroundings, then whiteness becomes that which 'lags behind', unnoticed: 'When bodies "lag behind", then they extend their reach' (Ahmed, 156). The white bodies flow beyond their physical limits within the space, taking up more space. Ahmed describes this as a 'sinking' feeling, linked to comfort:

> Comfort is about an encounter between more than one body, which is the promise of a 'sinking' feeling. To be comfortable is to be so at ease with one's environment that it is hard to distinguish where one's body ends and the world begins . . . White bodies are comfortable *as they inhabit spaces that extend their shape* . . . In other words, whiteness may function as a form of public comfort *by allowing bodies to extend into spaces that have already taken their shape*. (158, author's emphasis)

Ahmed is talking about institutional space and how that space is white, as it functions for whites, existing in a symbiotic relationship with the bodies that occupy it, but I find her theory useful in my attempt to understand the racial dynamics in *Hanna* where natural space, the Arctic wilderness – here also shorthand for the global North – becomes coded as white and for whites. The opening scene of the film, in no uncertain terms, visualises what Ahmed argues is a uniquely white privilege of being, in her words, 'so comfortable and so infinitely at ease with one's environment that it is hard to distinguish where one's body ends and the world begins'.

In a sense, then, that first scene of Wright's film champions whiteness as an attribute of the natural world. The film suggests that, before any human, civilising manipulations ever take place, the world is white. This message becomes clear when we consider the fact that Hanna is presented in contrast to technology which, in the film, is an attribute and the realm of the ethnic other. At one point the action of the film takes us to Morocco where Hanna for the first time in her life witnesses television and electricity. These encounters are depicted as exciting to Hanna on some level but mostly disturbing and painful to her uncontaminated cognitive interfaces. By framing the ethnic other as the technological threat to the white subject, the film echoes some of the paranoid theories that circulate in the nativist circles of the European far-right political organisations.

It would be too simple, however, to dismiss Hanna as one toxic, racist anachronism. Both the film and the character become more complex when the narrative divulges Hanna's peculiar genesis, her birth as a bio-engineered human. The CIA programme that Hanna's mother – who was looking to abort her pregnancy – is a part of, evokes in a clumsy way the infamous Nazi *Lebensborn* ('Wellspring of Life') programme. Launched in 1935, the *Lebensborn* project was a concerted effort on the part of the Nazi government to offset the unprecedentedly high abortion rates in the interwar Germany and the rapidly decreasing birth rate. Clinics were set up across Germany and the neighbouring Nordic countries (including north-eastern European countries) to promote breeding and raising of the Aryan children under optimal conditions. During the war, with the staggeringly high war casualties on the part of the German army, the demand for Aryan offspring became so desperate that the racial purity rules were relaxed, and almost any woman and child with blond hair and blue eyes willing to participate would be admitted to the programme. Additionally, a high number of blue-haired and blue-eyed Scandinavian, but also Slavic, children were kidnapped and transported to Germany for Germanisation and acculturation into the Aryan regime. This happened despite the fact that the racial purity laws determined the Slavs as an inferior race. The *Lebensborn* programme and the massive kidnapping campaigns across Eastern Europe, both well-kept secrets during their implementation, disclose not only the highly constructed aspects of the Nazi racial policy but also the frantic efforts to keep the unsustainable Aryan ideal alive. Wright's film intentionally gestures towards the history of *Lebensborn* but quite uncritically restages it as a Cold War project developed by the Western forces to fight their 'good' battle against the Soviet Block. The racist rationale that fuelled the *Lebensborn* initiative is thus replaced here by the much more wholesome American motivation to eradicate the communist regime. The fact that race remains the ideological category in this conflict, as it remained an unspoken term of the Cold War rhetoric, is carefully eclipsed through the narrative choices.

Wright begins his film by offering to the viewer the spectacle of the Aryan ideal. As he continues telling Hanna's story, this ideal is revealed to have been engineered by the American scientists, perhaps a nod to the

American origins of eugenics.[1] One would hope that, along with this staged disclosure of Hanna as artifice, Wright would deconstruct Hanna as a white fetish. Unfortunately, the film scrupulously avoids this gesture. Instead, something more perverse is offered to the viewer. Displacing Hanna's whiteness, her retarded femininity valorises and contemporises her anachronistic and nostalgic appeal. Through her youthful, innocent omnipotence, the character of Hanna consecrates white race via the empowering ideals of girl power. The close-up of the blond, blue-eyed girl's face, intensely focused on executing precise action that propels the narrative along, is an image that dominates Wright's film, and functions as the revised signifier for palatable and politically acceptable whiteness. Importantly, the film's hierarchy of ideology situates feminism – here a cartoonish version of politically disengaged post-feminism, a direct descendant of Naomi Wolf's 'power feminism' – in the service of white supremacy. In her 1993 book, *Fire with Fire*, Wolf advocates a renewed feminist discourse, different from the previous feminist discourses that, in her opinion, situate women as victims, that would be invested in female strength and empowered agency.[2] Her emblematic figure for the new feminist is an American female soldier fighting the Gulf War. Much like that soldier, Hanna represents the dangerous collusion of Western feminism with neo-(liberal) colonialism.

When I analyse *Hanna*, on some level a narrative about mobility within the European context, side by side with the films that feature Eastern European women engaging in immigrant passages, trafficking transports and illegal border crossings, it becomes immediately clear that Hanna's journey is not their journey. And this is not solely due to the contrast in the direction of her movement. Significantly, she moves from North to South and then from West to East, unlike the women in most traffic films, and unlike Mona in *Bibliothèque Pascal*, who tend to move from South to North and from East to West. Largely, due to its investment in the action/fantasy genre, Hanna's story is removed from social reality and, as such, it resists any form of critique that would centre on capitalism and race/class privilege, the kind of critique that would bring Hanna's journey in dialogue with some of the recent criticisms of globalisation and neoliberalisation (for example, Bauman 1998, Golumbia 2009, Harvey 2005a). Yet, as I have tried to argue, the film evokes many of the tensions and conflicts that are representative of the troubling divisions within the New Europe. As a character in a commercial film product, and framed within the limits of the depoliticised discourse of girl power,[3] Hanna cannot be considered apart from the interests of global corporate capitalism, whose neocolonial dynamic replicates the old patterns of colonial expansion.

Journey of the Ethic Body in *Bibliothèque Pascal*

Much like Wright's film, *Bibliothèque Pascal* uses fantasy to construct a myth about European women and their movement across borders. It may be argued that Hajdu's intensely self-conscious, yet somewhat utopian, act of cinematic myth-making, which features a woman as a storyteller who narrates her experience of being trafficked and exploited as a fanciful literary adventure, is an act of rhetorical resistance. Along with the other 'Third Generation' film-makers, such as Ferenc Török, György Pálfi, Kornél Mundruczó and Benedek Fliegauf, Szabolcs Hajdu belongs to the post-1989 Hungarian New Cinema movement. This movement is invested in the experimental and auteur traditions, and shaped by the radical experiences of mobility brought about by the transition from communist past to capitalist future. In Flora Talasi's words:

> Born in the late 1970s, these filmmakers passed through the kindergartens and schools of the late-communist era – or at least came into contact with such typically Eastern European patterns of socialization. As teenagers they experienced the dissolution of the Eastern Bloc and the short period of political awakening at the beginning of the 1990s. It was a generation who saw a new world opening up around them, and for whom the experience of individual and cultural mobility became formative. As young adults, they found themselves in a free, but disillusioned and highly polarized society in Eastern Central Europe. (2014)

In *Bibliothèque*, Hajdu focuses on the challenges posed by the post-communist proliferation of mobility. Specifically, he confronts the undesirable mobility of the Eastern European immigrant (Bauman's vagabond) by wresting the uncomfortable movement away from home in a story that returns some symbolic agency to the displaced and dispossessed immigrant subject. The mode of fantasy employed in *Bibliothèque* differs in a number of important ways from the fairy-tale element used in *Hanna*. The Hungarian director uses magic realism, with its long and well-theorised tradition of political critique (Skrodzka 2012, D'haen 1995), to offer an intervention and to comment on the reality of female mobility in the post-communist Europe. He constructs his narrative from the perspective of a Hungarian-Romanian woman who is saddled with the legacy of the political, economic and moral bankruptcy of the communist system. Unlike Wright's fairy tale, Hajdu's narrative is hyperconscious of its own fictitious status as it is simultaneously attuned to the social reality in which it unfolds. As fanciful as it gets, the imaginary tale devised by Mona functions as a mechanism to reinsert her into the normative fabric of her society.

The film opens with the scene that takes place in a Romanian child welfare services office where an official is interviewing a mother (Mona) whose child is now under the state's care. The mother is petitioning to regain the custody of her child. The male official wants the mother to explain why she had left her daughter (a girl named Viorica) in the care of an incompetent relative (who ends up exploiting the child's paranormal abilities for financial gain) and left the country. Specifically, he wants to know what Mona was doing while living abroad. Mona tells her story which constitutes the narrative proper of the film and, in the end, wins back the custody of her child. It is not, however, because her story makes the official sympathetic to her plea. Indeed, the official doubts every detail of Mona's colourful tale and forces her to change her account for the benefit of his official report.

The story that Mona chooses to tell is not the story that the official wants to hear. The experience that is being narrated is the experience that many Eastern European women have shared since 1989 when, in dire economic circumstances, they decide to leave their families behind and seek employment abroad as sex workers, nannies, maids and live-in nurses, hoping for the maximum income earned relatively quickly (Crisan 2012; OECD 2001). In most cases, similarly to the experience of the majority of bonded labourers in other sectors of the global economy, the women soon find out that their employment engagement involves exploitation at best (and slavery at worst), the worker's rights are non-existent and the income they hoped for barely pays the bills. Their journey to a foreign country, often the first journey undertaken in the woman's life, may end in confinement and complete prohibition of mobility, both physical and economic. The official discourses (both the governmental discourse of social control and the philanthropic anti-trafficking discourse) insist on framing the migrant experience connected to sex-affective labour well within the vocabulary of criminality and modern-day slavery, completely removing agency from the women involved, often portraying them as victims to international organised crime syndicates. Laura Agustín, one of the few feminist scholars who question the medicalisation and criminalisation of sex-work migration, points out that the official discourses remove all agency from 'the poorer women of the world' and frame the migrant sex workers, who often carefully plan out their migrant journeys, 'as though migrants were naive women who only yesterday were carrying water on their heads in some remote countryside' (Agustín, 68). Recent mainstream cinema contributes to this sensationalised and trivialised account of migrant sex work by producing films that deploy scenes that can be best characterised as semi-pornographic spectacles filled with shackled, brutalised female bodies confined to the ubiquitous sperm- and blood-stained mattress. Here, examples might include Luc Besson's *Taken* (2008, France/USA/UK), Olivier Megaton's *Taken 2* (2012, France), Marco Kreuzpaintner's *Trade* (2007, Germany/USA), Larysa Kondracki's *The Whistleblower* (2010, Germany/Canada/USA), or Christopher Bessette's *Trade of Innocents* (2012, USA/Thailand). In *Bibliothèque*, to a limited degree, Mona resists both the official discourse that pathologises sex-work migration, as well as the spectacularised version of that experience imagined in cinema, by confabulating a story that portrays her as more of an agent than a victim.

In the course of Mona's story, which is told in a distinctly picaresque tone, the viewer finds out how Mona becomes a mother as a result of a one-night stand with a stranger on a beach, how subsequently the stranger is apprehended and killed by the police, how Mona raises her daughter as a single mother, eking out a living as a puppeteer, and how eventually her own father precipitates her passage to an upper-class brothel in Liverpool, the eponymous Bibliothèque Pascal, which caters to clients whose tastes in sexual fantasy are literary, and where different rooms are devoted to different works of literature, including *Lolita* and *The Adventures of Pinocchio*. Mona delivers sexual services as Joan of Arc from George Bernard Shaw's play *Saint Joan*. Though she is confined to one room, the space of her confinement in no way resembles the dark and dirty dungeon staged in so many of the recent films that attempt to address the phenomenon of sex trafficking. As she narrates her experience of working abroad to the childcare official, and by extension to the film viewer, Mona neither occludes nor dwells on the negative aspects of her migrant experience. There are scenes that document Mona being smuggled across borders in a cargo container, being sold from the trafficker to the brothel owner, being drugged and beaten into compliance at the brothel. Throughout her ordeal, and in the scenes just mentioned, Mona is shown to be composed, observant and in control of her fate. She takes in the new surroundings and never panics. When eventually she is brutalised, she questions her pimp and devises ways to protect herself. As the narrator of her own story, she scrupulously protects her dignity in the midst of very undignifying circumstances. When she prefers to take recourse to fantasy, the viewer gladly respects her choice.

Thus the film refuses to participate in what Agustín refers to as the 'discourses of pity and helping' projected on to those involved in the sex industry (2005: 68). Neither does the film resort to images that would open up the woman's experience to voyeuristic consumption, aestheticisation and ultimate trivialisation which, according to Ann Kaplan and Ban Wang, are the real dangers involved in trauma representation (2004:

11–12). In the end, the viewer envisions, with the help of the images provided, only the magic realist version of Mona's escape from the brothel. According to that version, Mona is saved by the Balkan brass band which has marched all the way from the Romanian periphery to England, after having been projected via her daughter's dream. Both the viewer and the childcare official may doubt this resolution and suspect that Mona was victimised much more severely than she is willing to contemplate but the film cleverly denies visual representation to what might have actually happened and what the official insists Mona verbalises for his sake. On the other hand, the film does not volunteer a narrative of histrionic empowerment on a par with Hanna's story. This might be because 'power feminism' is rarely in the vocabulary of Eastern European women, including those who are feminist minded. But neither is 'victim feminism', as Mona's tale suggests.[4] When the official convinces Mona to provide him with a more 'realistic', that is, disempowered, version of her experience, so that he can issue a positive decision in Viorica's custody case, Mona reluctantly agrees to change her story. In the process of retelling it, she is reduced to tears and retraumatised. Therefore the film may be suggesting that this 'realistic' interpretation of her experience is a result of the compulsory 'regime of truth', as Foucault would have it. This more 'plausible' version situates Mona as an absolute victim of sex trafficking, a woman of virtue who would never consider sex work as a viable means of supporting herself, and even less so consider narrating her experience of engaging in sex work as a picaresque tale of bizarre adventures. Fortunately, the latter version does not materialise on screen, leaving Mona's initial version, recorded in the cinematic register, as the authoritative one.

In his effort to comment on the vicissitudes of sex-work migration in the New Europe, and specifically the experience of women who travel to the West from the impoverished Other Europe, Hajdu constructs a number of heavy-handed visual tropes that mimic the stereotypes which are employed in the populist discourses that address migrant mobility linked to the sex industry, and illegal migration in general. One of those stereotypes is the figure of the naive, uneducated woman who 'only yesterday was carrying water on her head in some remote countryside'. Another is that of the gypsy who, unattached to any given nation, cunningly crosses the borders to cheat, rob and 'steal your daughter'. Finally, there is the stereotype of the racial other. When the viewer first meets Mona, as a character in her own tale, she is vaguely exoticised and racialised as non-white or not sufficiently white. Her Eastern European whiteness has a shade to it, which forces it down the hierarchy of racial purity.[5] Valorised by her excessive affect, Mona is racialised in the same way that the Balkan

Figure 7.2 Orsolya Törö-Illyés in *Bibliothèque Pascal*.

Europeans were racialised as barbaric, irrational and inherently violent by the Western media reporting on the Balkan Wars. She is wearing ethnic jewellery and a hairstyle reminiscent of the Middle Eastern and/or Romany fashion. Orsolya Törö-Illyés's brunette features are emphasised through make-up and costume.

She is surrounded by the intoxicated (and intoxicating) Balkan collective straight from the cinematic world of Emir Kusturica, dancing, fist fighting, brass band and mud included. The *mise en scène* filled with colourful yet overstatedly shabby buildings, costumes and objects creates a sense of 'third worldness', despite and in contrast to the diegetic European space in which the story is supposedly unfolding.

Like many Eastern European film directors before him, Hajdu employs extremely broad strokes to paint the Eastern European periphery in an act of ironic self-deprecation, whose aim is to confront the West's idea of the East and, as I argue elsewhere, 'to subvert the very real postcolonial legacy between Western Europe and its adjacent peripheries' (Skrodzka 2012: 14). Certain scenes tap into the established iconography of the periphery and frame the major characters in the film as smugglers (Mona's father is the villainised 'Gypsy' who absurdly steals his own daughter and sells her to the traffickers), fortune tellers (aunt Rodica who serves alcohol to a child in order to project her dreams and sell them to the public), fairground performers (Mona as a puppeteer and Pascal as a unicycle circus acrobat), and petty criminals (the homophobic gangster Viorel). In one of the early scenes, we see Mona riding in a gypsy-style covered wagon. This choice of vehicle deepens the way in which Mona's journey is coded as belonging to nomadic mobility which, both romanticised and maligned, is popularly thought of in the European context as the rite of the freewheeling Romanies. The film's visuals push the intentionally sloppy, often grotesque, gypsy associations which, not surprisingly, were quickly picked up on by the Western film critics who wrote favourably of the film's 'gypsy ebullience' (DeWitte 2011), and 'Gypsy traditions' (O'Connor 2011), or praised it as 'a gypsy ramble' (MacEwan 2010). Despite the fact that the narrative details clearly suggest that Mona is a Hungarian-Romanian, who speaks both languages and who is not related to the Romany people, the forced ethnic trappings seduce the viewer, only to dupe her/him into stereotypical optics. In the end the ethnic markers dissipate into thin air, perhaps to visualise the ephemerality of the symbolic register through which they acquire all of their meaning.

I see this strategy as Hajdu's effort to poke fun at the commodification of Eastern Europe as an exotic culture for consumption. In *Strange Encounters*, Sara Ahmed theorises this kind of cultural commodification in terms of 'stranger fetishism' and cultural racism (2000: 114–17). According to her argument, the Western subject consumes the exotic other, the ethnic/racial stranger, in order to consume the world symbolically. The stranger becomes the commodity fetish, an empty, yet heavily ontologised category 'assumed to have a nature' (5). Ahmed argues that 'the act of welcoming "the stranger" as the origin of difference produces the very figure of "the stranger" as the one who can be taken in' (97). Accordingly, Mona and, by extension, every Eastern European become the stranger who can be taken in, only after her strangeness has become her identity. What is so refreshing in Hajdu's film is the humour and cleverness with which the film participates in ontologising Mona as a 'stranger fetish', only to de-ontologise that fetish through the use of yet another global commodity: the Balkan brass band.

In her essay entitled 'European Kinship: Eastern European Women Go to Market', Anca Parvulescu discusses the role of Eastern European women in the export of the 'immaterial affective labour' and argues that women like Mona who leave their own children behind to go West,

> can reproduce white children in a Europe worried about the birth rate among its 'native' population. They raise these children dutifully, disseminating the motherly love that, it is argued, has become scant in the Western world in the wake of second-wave feminism. Eastern Europe is a fresh reservoir of love. (2011: 206)

This 'immaterial affective labour', which often requires physical stamina, is quickly becoming the domain of the ethnically and racially othered body and therefore a category easily subsumed into the ontologised figure of the stranger that Ahmed insists becomes 'a means of defining "who" we are' (Ahmed 2000: 113). It is the love of the racial/ethnic stranger that the Western subject consumes today as a commodity in the face of the 'slow atrophy of the capacity to live emotionally' which, in 1930, Ethel Mannin famously anticipated to become the 'the ultimate decadence of the white civilized people' (qtd in Dyer 1988: 56).

Conclusion: Carelessly Mobile and Mobile Care

For the sake of my comparison it is important to note that, unlike Mona, who is very much configured within her experience of sex work as well as her maternal skills and affective ability (which is being questioned by the childcare official), Wright's Hanna is a woman whose empathy has been completely suppressed. She does not engage in sex-affective labour, not only because of her immature femininity but because she has been specifically born and raised not to feel in order to be able to perform her work as a super soldier. Furthermore, Hanna's mobility is enhanced by her ability not to feel/care while Mona's mobility is a function of her willingness and ability to feel/care for strangers and for her own family. Ultimately, the characters of Hanna and Mona speak to the tension between different models of European feminism and different experiences of femininity. This tension is a direct result of the market mechanisms involved in '"emotional imperialism", whereby emotional resources are extracted from poor countries' (Arlie Russell Hochschild qtd in Parvulescu 2011: 208). Parvulescu is quick to point out the irony behind some of the root causes of emotional imperialism which arguably implicate Western women who have outsourced the work of pleasing their men and children to their Eastern neighbours. While viewing Hajdu's and Wright's film concurrently, one becomes aware of the complexities that characterise the new labour relations in Europe. Whether it is a grand myth of empowerment or a dark tale of clandestine exploitation, the cinematic fantasy of female mobility speaks of the new economy that problematises the European unification and integration efforts. While arguably mobility in borderless Europe has been extended to an unprecedented number of its residents, the experience may not always conform to the ideal of mobility as a liberatory practice. In the process of visualisation on-screen, the abstraction of the global flow predictably disintegrates and gives way to diverse fantasies that wrestle with local particularities.

Part II

Border Spaces, Eastern Margins and Eastern Markets: Belonging and the Road to/from Europe

CHAPTER 8

Contemporary Bulgarian Cinema: From Allegorical Expressionism to Declined National Cinema

Temenuga Trifonova (York University)

The increased mobility of people within Europe has shaken up the sociogeographical fixity of a continent of nation states, creating new modes of transnational culture and becoming a recurrent subject in what Luisa Rivi calls 'declined national cinema' (Rivi). Rivi appropriates Gianni Vattimo's notion of 'weak' or 'declined' thought – *pensiero debole* – and transfers it to the debate on national cinema. The notion of *pensiero debole* refers to the exhaustion – but not the vanishing – of the project of modernity (the belief in reason, progress, history, the nation state, etc.). In *The End of Modernity: Nihilism and Hermeneutics in Postmodern Culture*, Vattimo argues that the postmodern is 'not only [...] something new in relation to the modern, but also [...] a dissolution of the category of the new – in other words [...] an experience of "the end of history" rather than ... the appearance of a different stage of history' (4). Vattimo does not read the postmodern dehistoricisation of experience nostalgically or pessimistically. Rather, he argues that the ideas of Nietzsche and Heidegger

> offer us the chance to pass from a purely critical and negative description of the postmodern condition, typical of early twentieth-century Kulturkritik and its more recent offshoots, to an approach that treats it as a positive possibility and opportunity. Nietzsche mentions all of this [...] in his theory of a possibly active or positive (accomplished) nihilism. Heidegger alludes to the same thing with his idea of a Verwindung of metaphysics which is not a critical overcoming in the 'modern' sense of the term. (11)

Heidegger's term *Verwindung* seeks to describe the overcoming of modernity and metaphysics, 'a going-beyond that is both an acceptance and a deepening' (Vattimo, 172). Analysing the etymology of the term *Verwindung*, Vattimo underscores the connotation of 'convalescence' (to be healed, cured of an illness), also linked to resignation, and the connotation of distortion (to turn, to twist). One is cured of an illness and, at the same time, resigned to a pain or loss:

> Metaphysics is not something we can put aside like an opinion. Nor can it be left behind us like a doctrine in which we no longer believe; rather, it is something which stays in us as do the traces of an illness or a kind of pain to which we are resigned. It is neither a critical overcoming nor an acceptance that recovers and prolongs it. (Vattimo, 175)

Following Heidegger and Nietzsche, Vattimo insists that post-*histoire* (weakened history) is not yet another discourse that tries to legitimate itself on the grounds that it is more up to date and thus more valid or more authentic than the bankrupt discourse of modernity.

In her book *European Cinema after 1989* Rivi relies on Vattimo's notion of *pensiero debole* to describe the exhaustion – but not the vanishing – of national cinema. For Rivi, the decline of Europe's master narratives does not mark their end; instead, these narratives are realised in declined ways, 'through the introduction and acceptance of concepts of plurality, alterity, difference, opaqueness, and heterogeneity' (32). This process involves Europe acknowledging its past myths and master narratives and, instead of trying to overcome the past or recover it nostalgically, rethinking its master narratives to make them reflect the new social, political and economic realities. Thus, Rivi argues that, rather than discarding the concept of national cinema in favour of 'post-national cinema', we should approach post-1989 European cinema as 'weak' or 'declined' national cinema, one that acknowledges the different ways in which transnational forces and supranational bodies are altering the notion of national identity and national cinema. 'Declined' national cinema dramatises the dissolution of national identity without, however, erecting another type of identity in its place that tries to legitimise itself as 'more authentic' because, as Vattimo reminds us, authenticity, 'understood as what is "proper"', has itself vanished (25).

In what follows I examine a number of recent Bulgarian films about internal migration, immigration before and after 1989, and post-communist spiritual homelessness in order to expose the first cracks in the monolithic body of Bulgarian national cinema. Though the geopolitical transformations that have been reshaping the actual and metaphorical borders of the new Europe have given rise to new genres and styles in Bulgarian cinema, there is still considerable continuity, both in terms of style and subject matter, between pre- and post-1989 films, as evidenced, for instance, by the persistence of allegorical expressionism as the dominant mode of representation in Bulgarian cinema which is challenged only occasionally by less provincial styles of film-making.

Allegorical Expressionism and Provincialism

Val Todorov's study, 'Bulgarian Cinema: Constants and Variables', provides a helpful starting point for exploring the shifting relationship between cinematic style and national identity. Todorov identifies several persistent stylistic features of Bulgarian cinema, among them theatricality and allegorical expressionism. Theatricality refers to the subordination of visual expression to narrative which can be attributed to the fact that the Bulgarian film industry was built upon an already established theatrical tradition (Todorov 1999–2013). Inasmuch as under communism film production was controlled by the state, emphasis was placed not on cinematic language but on the script which was expected to carry a film's ideological message. Recent films exhibit a greater concern with the visual language of film, a reflection of Bulgarian film-makers' increased exposure to other filmic traditions, including non-European ones (for example, Iranian cinema). With the exception of the 'poetic realist' cinema of the 1960s and 1970s, the prevailing stance of Bulgarian cinema has always been allegorical expressionism, exemplified by philosophical and moral parables and allegories. The fact that allegorical expressionism did not disappear from Bulgarian films after the fall of communism suggests that it was not simply a strategy of resistance to totalitarian censorship. Rather, allegorical expressionism originates in Bulgaria's ethnopsychology and folklore, and in its Eastern Orthodox and pagan past. Referencing Liehm and Liehm's 1981 study, *The Most Important Art: Soviet and Eastern European Film after 1945*, Todorov reads allegorical expressionism – schematism – as a manifestation of the peculiarities of Bulgarian ethnicity, specifically Bulgaria's historical sense of isolation and provincialism.

The tendency to schematism or allegorical expressionism stands for a literal approach to story, conflict and characterisation on analogy with parables or fairy tales which always have a clear message or moral conveyed in an allegorical manner. As a literary device, allegory is characterised by its transparency and simplicity. The terms that make up an allegory refer to each other in a straightforward manner: something concrete stands for an abstract concept or idea in a relationship of correspondence or reference that is clearly marked. Though indirectly expressed, allegorical meaning is finite and unambiguous. Significantly, for Liehm and Liehm, schematism is synonymous with autocensorship where censorship is not (or not necessarily) political censorship but rather a self-imposed limit on the meaning one wants to convey and the means one believes are necessary (or sufficient) to convey it. In short, autocensorship refers not to Bulgarian film-makers' experience of being forced by outside powers to delimit/disguise the meaning(s) they want to convey but rather to the limited nature of the meaning they want to convey in the first place, to a certain deficiency of expression, which Liehm and Liehm view as a result (or evidence) of Bulgarians' historical sense of provincialism.

This decoupling of censorship from its usual association with politics (communism = censorship), and its coupling instead with ethnicity and history, are particularly illuminating in the present moment when discussions of national and supranational identity, national and transnational cinema, provincialism and globalism, dominate European cinema scholarship. One important question that emerges from such considerations is whether transformations in cinematic styles – for instance, a movement away from allegorical expressionism towards other, more complex or ambiguous tropes –follow (or accompany) geopolitical and ethnic transformations, such as the transition from national to transnational Europe/cinema. In other words, we could view the persistence of allegorical expressionism in Bulgarian cinema as evidence of a persisting sense of national provincialism grounded in an obsolete notion of a unified national identity impervious to transnational flows. Conversely, the appearance of a number of films that refuse to function as extended allegories or parables might be seen as a sign that the certainties associated with that style – the schematic notion of national identity as constructed by stable referents that remain in a stable, one-to-one relationship with each other – are gradually giving way to a polycentric and fluid notion of Bulgarian identity constructed by constantly migrating referents that never freeze in a one-to-one correspondence but continue circulating, on analogy with the new Europe's migrating bodies and minds. This way of looking at cinematic style is consistent with a poststructuralist understanding of how identity is constituted in the first place. The idea that Bulgarian film-makers used allegorical expressionism to fight political censorship captures only in the most schematic way the relationship between film-makers and historical reality, as if film-makers carry around a toolbox with different styles from which they choose the most appropriate tool (style) to fit their purpose. The fact that certain cinematic styles persist beyond their 'expiry date' suggests that style is not merely a tool existing independently of the idea a film-maker wants to convey but, rather, emerges organically from a film-maker's sense of his/her own place in historical reality.

What is then the relationship between allegorical expressionism and provincialism?[1] Understanding an allegory depends on one's familiarity with *both* terms that make up the allegory: both the surface meaning and the real/hidden meaning. Allegory depends on a precise knowledge of the local, hidden meaning which is always already given rather than constructed in the course of viewing the film. Reading an allegory – whether literary or cinematic – does not depend on the viewers' reading skills but on their prior knowledge of the hidden/local meaning. No matter how experienced viewers might be in reading a film's visual language, the meaning of the allegory will escape them because it is not found in the purely visual language of the film which is never fully codifiable. In allegorical expressionism, then, meaning is always found on the level of narrative, not on the level of the visual. Inasmuch as allegory relies on an insider's knowledge of the specific historical, social and political context in which the allegory operates, allegorical expressionism is not a transnational-friendly style.

Internal Migration, the Trauma of Immigration and Spiritual Homelessness

Significantly, the majority of films Todorov gives as examples of Bulgarian cinema's allegorical expressionism, hence of its provincialism – the 1970s (internal) migration cycle that includes *Momcheto si otiva/A Boy Becomes a Man* (Lyudmil Kirkov, 1972), *Mazhe bez rabota/Men without Work* (Ivan Terziev, 1973), *Darvo bez koren/A Tree without Roots* (Christo Christov, 1974), *Selyaninat s koleloto/A Peasant on a Bicycle* (Lyudmil Kirkov, 1974) and *Wilna zona/Villa Zone* (Eduard Zachariev, 1975)[2] – explore the narrative trajectory (migration) and the deep structure of feeling (homelessness) central to contemporary European, including Bulgarian, cinema. Like Todorov, Violetta Petrova also sees the trope of the journey (physical and/or imaginary) and what she calls 'the synecdoches of glocalisation' in recent Bulgarian films as reinterpreting key moments in Bulgarian cinematic history: 1. the internal migration explored in the 1970s migration cycle; 2. the formation of national myths of identity (the internalised Other); and 3. the young generation's existential angst in anticipation of Eastern Europe's velvet revolutions (Petrova 2006).

While the migration cycle explored migration within the nation – village–city migration – recent Bulgarian films treat the subject of migration on a transnational scale.[3] Does this necessarily mean that they manage to break free from the provincialism of the 1970s films? To understand the allegory of 'a tree without roots' played out in the films of the migration cycle one needs to be familiar with Bulgarian national psychology. The eroticised mythopoetic imagery of Mother Earth that permeates the films of the migration cycle points

> to a central dichotomy in the cultural history of Bulgaria – rural and urban – and registers a colossal social movement: the exodus from village to big city as a result of the process of a fast and at times brutal modernization and industrialization. (Petrova)[4]

Scholars usually read the migration cycle as resisting the unifying, optimistic ideology of socialist realism. This is precisely what makes it provincial: to understand the allegory of the divided self, viewers have to be familiar with the peculiarities of socialism in Bulgaria. At the same time, however, the divided self in these films has another, transnational aspect insofar as it dramatises a more general conflict, that between tradition and modernity. In this respect, the allegory of exile in the migration cycle prefigures more recent explorations of exile in transnational terms.

Though recent Bulgarian films explore the theme of migration and homelessness in transnational, rather than national, terms they continue to invoke the old city versus village dichotomy, positing the village as a morally and spiritually privileged realm, a source of 'authentic national identity', and contrasting it with the post-communist city as a place of exile, moral decrepitude and inauthenticity. *Pismo do Amerika / Letter to America* (Iglika Triffonova, 2001, Bulgaria/Netherlands/Hungary), *Mila ot Mars / Mila from Mars* (Zornitsa Sophia, 2004), *Shivachki / Seamstresses* (Lyudmil Todorov, 2007), and *Svetat e golyam i spasenie debne otvsyakade / The World Is Big and Salvation Lurks around the Corner* (Stephan Komadarev, 2008, Bulgaria/Germany/Slovenia/Hungary) demonstrate that post-communist Bulgarian cinema is still dominated by a conservative nationalistic discourse based on a perennialist notion of national identity rooted in the nation's ethnoscape, ethnohistory and ethnomemory, and allegedly 'corrupted' by post-communist developments, such as immigration and globalisation. *Letter to America* tells the story of two friends: Kamen, a theatre director who emigrates to the United States, and Ivan, a writer who remains in Bulgaria. Kamen's emigration is treated as a pretext to explore another kind of movement, the reversal of the village–city migration in the migration cycle, namely the return of the disaffected city intellectual (Ivan) to his roots. The film constructs both village–city migration and emigration as two forms of spiritual sickness which can be cured only by a return to the roots of Bulgarian identity, the village. *Mila from Mars* tells the story of a sixteen-year-old orphan, Mila who is sold to Alex, a successful businessman, and, later, her pimp. The pregnant Mila escapes from Alex and hitches a ride to a village near the border which is all but abandoned except for a group of peasants involved in marijuana trafficking. The villagers adopt Mila as a sort of a surrogate communal granddaughter. The film is an extended *allegory* for the nation's continuous attempts to reconcile its communist past and agrarian roots with its nouveau riche present and uncertain future. Here the past, implicitly identified with traditional folk life, is positioned as a pure *Heimat* in danger of being polluted or profaned by the present that is the foreign amorality and capitalist greed of free-market mobsters which the film constructs as perversions of Bulgarian national character. *Seamstresses*, which tells the story of three young girls moving to the capital in search of employment, examines the loss of ideals in the movement from village to city. Ruled by the evil forces of capitalism, the corrupt post-communist city is positioned as alien to Bulgarian identity and sensibility of which the three small-town girls are, allegedly, the embodiment. In *The World is Big and Salvation Lurks around the Corner*, too, the only cure for national amnesia is a road trip from the host country back to the lost homeland. Alexander, a young Bulgarian man who emigrated with his parents to Germany in the early 1980s, suffers a car crash as a result of which he loses his memory. It is then up to his grandfather, who travels from Bulgaria to Germany, to restore his grandson's memory. To emigrate, the film suggests, is to condemn oneself to a life of alienation and loneliness. In Germany Alexander is stuck in an unrewarding job, translating vacuum cleaner manuals, living alone in an apartment full of empty boxes: Germany for him remains an address, not a home. These films continue to subscribe to a view of emigration as an inherently schizophrenic experience resulting in a pathological state (split identity or amnesia). While the communist regime exaggerated its appreciation for folk culture in order to naturalise communism and conceal its ideological character, post-communist films revive the fascination with village life, and the sentimental/organic notion of the nation on which it is based, as a convenient antidote to bleak post-communist reality, thereby perpetuating the long outdated 'sleeping beauty view' of national identity as 'the awakening of something extant, which had merely been dormant' (J. Hall 1995: 11).

The second moment in Bulgarian cinematic history which, according to Petrova, prefigured the more recent reconfiguration of Bulgarian identity as 'multiple, broken, quivering, shattered, virtual', includes the series of 1980s historical epics exploring key moments in the formation of the nation. Petrova reads the most important one – *Vreme na nasilie/Time of Violence* (Lyudmil Staikov, 1988), which deals with the violent conversion of Bulgarian Christians to Muslims during the period of Ottoman domination – as illustrating 'the drama of the internalized other' (2006). By making Karaibrahim, the cruellest of the Ottomans – who is, significantly, of Bulgarian origin – the protagonist, the film 'redirects the attention from inter-ethnic to intra-ethnic tension', with the result that 'the narrative oscillates between the notions of internalized other and a plural self'. The film, Petrova claims, 'implicitly promotes a sense of belonging to the larger Balkan community, which shares similar historical sentiments and concerns'. The 1980s historical epic's construction of Balkan identity as always already 'doubly occupied', to use Elsaesser's term (Elsaesser, 48), anticipates more recent engagements with this issue, such as Zornitsa Sophia's *Prognoza/Forecast* (2008), in which a group of friends from different Balkan countries go surfing on an isolated Turkish island. Early in the film Sophia strategically plants seemingly harmless comments expressing deep nationalistic sentiments to prepare us for the full-blown Balkan conflict that will erupt later. The nationalistic comments are, however, offset by scenes emphasising the fundamental similarities (language, sense of humour, machismo) between Balkan nations. Indeed, the film suggests that the Balkan conflict is, to a large extent, the result of trading an inside/ Balkan/shared worldview for an outside/detached/Western worldview which exaggerates the differences between Balkan nations.

The third point in Bulgarian cinematic history that anticipated the reformulation of Bulgarian identity as multiple and hybrid was the period between the late 1980s and the early 1990s which saw the arrival of a new generation of film-makers – later known as 'the lost generation' – interested in exploring not key moments in the nation's history but the existential problems of disillusioned young people. Krassimir Kroumov's trilogy, *Ekzitus/Exitus* (1989), *Malchanieto/Silence* (1991), and *Zabraneniat plod/ The Forbidden Fruit* (1994), is representative of this cycle of films which announced the arrival of a new, post-communist, morally ambiguous subject and anticipated the fragmented subject of post-2000 films. Kamen Kalev's *Iztochni piesi/Eastern Plays* (2009, Bulgaria/Sweden), Iglika Triffonova's *Razsledvane/The Investigation* (2006, Bulgaria/Germany/ Netherlands), and Ivan Tscherkelov's *Raci/Crayfish* (2009) continue the legacy of 'the lost generation', returning to its major preoccupations: existential angst, crime, violence, moral ambiguity, feelings of displacement and homelessness. Kalev and Triffonova are not interested in the economic and political transformations taking place during Bulgaria's never-ending transition period but in the spiritual and moral after-effects of the geopolitical shocks to the system. Though their films explore the experience of homelessness, they do so neither through the subject of internal (village–city) migration nor through the trauma of emigration. In *Eastern Plays* homelessness is not associated with emigration; instead, the film looks for the roots of the spiritual and moral homelessness experienced by those who did not emigrate. Rather than locating Bulgarian national identity in its idealised agrarian past and contrasting it with the 'evils' of emigration or capitalist exploitation, Kalev paints a complex picture of the amoral, opportunistic culture of post-communist Bulgaria without offering a cure for this spiritual malaise.

Investigation treads similar territory but does so – in a radical departure from the films of 'the lost generation' – through the eyes of a female protagonist, the sole female detective on the Sofia police force, a married woman who feels morally and spiritually homeless. This existential psychological drama runs counter to Western expectations of Eastern European and Balkan film-makers to make explicitly antinationalist films in order to be considered cinematic and worthy of festival exhibition. Triffonova's film is a Cain-and-Abel crime drama based on material she gathered while working on an earlier documentary (*Razkazi za ubiystva/ Murder Stories*, 1993). Detective Alexandra Yakimova attempts to crack a perplexing case of a man who has vanished without a trace. Though she has no solid evidence, she suspects that the man's brother, Plamen, might have killed him and buried the parts of his severed body somewhere. Conventional detective methods prove useless in solving the case. It is only when Alexandra finally 'cracks' emotionally, when she learns to love – first the criminal she is investigating and then her own family, from which she feels alienated – that Plamen confesses to the murder. The murder investigation thus serves as an occasion for Alexandra's self-investigation as she comes to realise that the Other – embodied by the person with whom she is least likely to identify, a murderer – is not merely an abstraction positioned somewhere on 'the outskirts' of her own self; rather, her private self is always already in a state of 'semantic occupation' by the Other.[5]

Investigation picks up the idea of the always already occupied self, treated in the 1980s historical epics in ethnic, religious and national terms, and reinterprets it in ethical or existential terms. The question of nation-building gives way to the care of the self and the ethics of the self. Once Plamen senses that Alexandra understands him – that she understands his motive for murdering his own brother not through means of deduction but through empathising with him – he readily confesses to the crime. The film is more interested in exploring the basis for establishing a community of fellow human beings than in a top-down approach to nationhood or citizenship. The first step in challenging the ideology of the nation is not to ask how national borders are drawn – as Étienne Balibar does in *We, the People of Europe?: Reflections on Transnational*

Citizenship (2003) where he argues that, as an institution, the nation rests upon the formulation of a rule of exclusion, of visible and invisible borders materialised in laws and practices – but rather to ask how the self draws the border separating her from 'the Other'. The separation between self and other, between the innocent and the guilty, between the detective and the criminal, is the basis for all other divisions, including those at the level of the nation: the unspoken and unwritten law of personal human relationships is the foundation of the Law. Alexandra begins the investigation using traditional methods which render the criminal an 'object of study': she observes him in the prison yard through a pair of binoculars; she looks at pictures from the scene of the crime; she jots down notes on sticky note slips; but it is only when she identifies with Plamen as a human being, instead of seeing him as an 'Other', that he confesses to the crime. Significantly, the film ends with Alexandra attending a production of Shakespeare's *Twelfth Night*, a play about mistaken identities that drives home the point that 'mistaken identity' is a contradiction in terms. Identities cannot be 'mistaken' because identity is never singular: the Other is constitutive of the Self.

While Triffonova explores homelessness in existential terms, Cherkelov's *Crayfish* focuses on the political and socio-economic roots of the spiritual homelessness of its protagonists, two small-town, working-class drifters, and presents us with two different responses to the ongoing socio-economic-existential crisis in which the 1989 generation remains trapped: cynicism (Doca) and passive acceptance (Bonzo). Doka and Bonzo are hired by two rival business partners to earn some quick money but eventually find themselves on opposite sides and, without suspecting it, one of them kills the other. Though they are both in their thirties Doca and Bonzo still live like the teenagers they were in 1989. The film effectively conveys the debilitating sense of stagnation that permeates all relationships in contemporary Bulgaria: between friends, lovers, parents and their children, co-workers, politicians and citizens. The Communist Party is no longer in power but the new leaders of the home-grown brand of neo-liberalism continue its legacy of total control and ruthless manipulation. The film cuts back and forth between Bonzo and Doca's mundane existence, the secret machinations of Bulgaria's nouveau riche class (parvenu 'businessmen'), and an assortment of vestiges of the communist regime (an ex-cop, former members of the Communist Party throwing patriotic orgies in abandoned party hotels, the head of the Bulgarian army driving around aimlessly in his refurbished Russian car). After 1989 communist apparatchiks 'reinvented' themselves as leaders of the neo-liberal order, the businessmen, aka mafia kingpins, who now exploit the country economically rather than politically. The setting of an important conversation between one of the rival businessmen and his personal adviser is emblematic of the way in which business is conducted in Bulgaria: not through official, legal channels but from a random hotel room, the back of a car, or a bathroom. The other businessman seems to operate from a 'real' office, wearing a suit and surrounded by other men dressed in suits, while a secretary dutifully takes calls behind the glass door. And yet, his office, empty except for the table covered with laptops and junk food, seems ready to be folded up the minute someone suspects the business transactions carried out in it are illegal.

In another emblematic scene, Bonzo's mother goes shopping with Bonzo's pregnant wife in what used to be the capital's biggest shopping centre, now a mall. 'Nothing will ever change in this country!' she tells her daughter-in-law. 'They made a shiny, expensive store but the people working in it are the same stupid, uncultured *tekezesari*.' She uses the word *tekezesari*, whose original meaning is 'members of the Communist Labour Co-operative', as a derogatory term to refer to people whose way of thinking has not changed post-1989. While in earlier films, as we have seen, the village was depicted as the last stronghold of Bulgarian national identity, here the word '*tekezesar*', or 'peasant', is used to signify the illusory nature of the transition period and the regression to old, communist, 'pre-European' attitudes. The film presents former communist leaders' reinvention of themselves as successful businessmen as a regression to non-European attitudes identified with communism. 'These same *tekezesari* with their stupid, leering faces will bury us,' Bonzo's mother says scornfully, helplessly. As if to confirm her statement, the director cuts to a long shot of half-naked old men and women, drinking themselves into a stupor, singing the Bulgarian national anthem and waving the national flag in an abandoned Communist Party hotel while, outside, a former commander-in-chief in the Bulgarian army drives around in circles and shoots randomly at a fat pig rolling around in the mud, 'guarding' the national flag. This image, which encapsulates Bulgarians' view of their country's leadership, is, as is often the case in Bulgarian cinema, sexually inflected, presenting the former communist leaders' neglect of the country in terms of sexual abandon and promiscuity, and depicting Bulgaria's current state in terms of sexual perversion.

A 'Declined' Bulgarian Cinema?

As I suggested earlier, there are signs that Bulgarian cinema is finally entering the stage of 'declined cinema' in at least two ways. First, recent films revisit a familiar subject – forced emigration under communism – in a new light: *Zad kadar/Voice-over* (Svetoslav Ovtcharov, 2010) and *Stapki v pyasaka/Footsteps in the Sand* (Ivaylo Hristov, 2010) depart from the self-congratulatory, democratising discourse of 1990s films, which were preoccupied with exposing 'the truth' about totalitarianism, and replace the pathos of revealing secrets and assigning guilt with an exploration of emigration in personal, rather than political (allegorical), terms. Second, a couple of recent films – *Misiya London/Mission London* (Dimitar Mitovski, 2010, Bulgaria/Hungary/UK/Macedonia/Sweden) and *The Island* (Kamen Kalev, 2011, Bulgaria/Sweden) – suggest that Bulgarian cinema is finally learning to play postmodern games with national identity.

Voice-over begins in a self-referential manner with a film crew getting ready to shoot the film we are about to see, an autobiographical story in which the director of the film (Anton) is also the protagonist, a cinematographer separated from his family in the late 1970s when his wife and son leave for West Berlin to get the best possible treatment for the boy's bronchitis. Though they don't leave with the intention of emigrating, a year later Anton's wife informs him they are not coming back. Anton is not a poor struggling artist but a respected film professional whose work is supported by those in power. The film does not portray him merely as a victim of the system. Indeed, from the very beginning, his ethical position is left ambiguous. When the director of the film he is working on is fired for failing to follow party directives Anton assures him that he will also leave the film in solidarity. When the party assigns a new director to the project, however, Anton continues working on the film, breaking his promise to his friend. Anton's betrayal motivates the film's first director to seek an appointment with Senior Lieutenant Angelov of the Bureau for National Security and report to him – in exchange for two glasses of *airyan* and a croissant! – that Anton is a potential enemy of the state (because of his connections with the West). Based on this 'testimony', and under the pretext that it would be a pity for Bulgarian socialist culture to lose such a talented cinematographer at the height of his artistic career, Angelov places Anton under surveillance.

The banality of Angelov's methods of surveillance and the matching banality of the 'reports' (that is, gossip) he collects, underscore the extent to which surveillance is integrated into people's everyday life. One of Anton's neighbours shares all too willingly her observations of Anton and his family, painting them as dangerous traitors. They prefer the West's 'casual lifestyle' to the hardworking communist lifestyle. Anton is, allegedly, condescending towards the neighbour, a woman from the countryside who is obviously not part of Sofia's 'cultural elite': under the communist regime, class distinctions, particularly divisions along educational and city/village lines, persisted despite the pretence of a classless society. Anton travels too often to West Berlin and appears to be extremely well paid while the neighbour's own husband, a war veteran and a member of the Communist Party, barely makes ends meet. Finally, Anton's wife is known to 'entertain Arabs at home', although, as Angelov reminds the neighbour, Arabs are from the (good) East, not from the (evil) West, a comment that exposes another well-disguised feature of communist society, its underlying racism. The banality of surveillance is dramatised in a scene in which Anton's neighbour opens his postbox, using her knitting needles, and read his wife's letter to him.

Angelov and his admiring female protégé (a recent graduate of the Bureau for National Security) finally get their hands on some 'hard evidence' when Anton and his wife begin sending each other gifts and letters through a German family who travel to Bulgaria for a holiday. Angelov suspects the Germans are in charge of a secret 'underground railroad' for smuggling Bulgarians to the West. Therefore, he intercepts any attempts on Anton's part to travel to Berlin or of his wife to return to Bulgaria. Anton's career as a cinematographer is threatened when the next film he is hired to work on is stopped for political reasons and he learns of plans for the publication of an incriminating article about the film's director (Karlo) that paints him as 'a dangerous formalist' and a homosexual involved in a secret relationship with Anton. Eventually Angelov reaches the conclusion that Anton is not a traitor (though his wife is), promising Anton to help him finish Karlo's film but demanding in return that Anton file for divorce.

The film complicates the usual victim–victimiser relationship by refusing to treat Anton purely as a victim and Angelov as a mindless apparatchik following orders. Indeed, the film suggests that Angelov himself does not believe in the communist rhetoric he is supposed to stand up for. At one point he tells his assistant: '"Doubt everything!" says . . .?' She completes his thought, responding 'Marx!' in an attempt to impress him with her knowledge of communist literature, to which he replies jokingly 'Groucho or Chico?', mocking her for taking the communist reference seriously. As Anton's marriage disintegrates, partly because of his blind dedication to his work and his unwillingness to sacrifice his job for his family, Angelov and his female assistant develop a romantic relationship which humanises them to some extent. *Voice-over* draws attention to the political promiscuity characteristic of recent Bulgarian history: people and parties may change their names but what appear to be the faces of 'new Bulgaria' are the same old Communist apparatchiks. In the last scene we see Anton, a lot older, behind the camera, shooting the film we have just seen, surrounded by the same people who separated him from his family years ago (Angelov's former assistant is now Anton's First Assistant on set).

Like *Voice-over*, *Footsteps in the Sand* explores emigration in personal rather than political terms. Slavi returns to Bulgaria for the first time in twenty years and recounts his story to a group of customs officers at Sofia airport. The first third of the film takes us back to his youth as he graduates from senior school, falls in love with his childhood best friend, and reluctantly leaves to do his military service. After unsuccessfully applying to the Academy of Medicine, he learns that he was denied entrance because of his problematic family history (both his grandfather and father tried to escape from Bulgaria). By the time he finally makes it back to Sofia, his love, Neli, is dating another man. Slavi takes up drinking, gets into trouble with the militia and eventually decides to defect to the West, significantly, to mend his broken heart rather than for political reasons. After staying at a refugee camp in Austria, where he has a short-term affair with a Serbian woman, he travels to the United States. An American friend helps him to buy a truck and Slavi hits the road. Eventually he settles in Chicago. A few years after the fall of the Berlin Wall he returns to Bulgaria where he is reunited with Neli. The film depicts Slavi as a man without roots, desperately searching for a home, rather than as a political dissident. Indeed, as he prepares for his interview at the Austrian refugee camp, Slavi is coached in how to act like a political dissident by an old Bulgarian friend he encounters in the camp. His friend advises him to say that he left Bulgaria because he was 'repressed by the Bulgarian authorities' and to lie that he has never travelled outside Bulgaria before because, as his friend puts it, 'what kind of repressive regime would rob its citizens of their freedom and then let them travel abroad freely!'

The film paints a realistic picture of the emigration experience, emphasising the loneliness and alienation Slavi feels even though most of the people he meets are well meaning: the American Jim, who wins a large insurance case, gives Slavi thousands of dollars to buy a truck and the Native American owner of a souvenir store in Utah advises him to buy an arrow, an amulet that is supposed to bring Slavi's lost love, Neli, back to him. Slavi manages to support himself financially but he never becomes integrated either in Austrian or in American society. In Austria he communicates only with other refugees, developing a close relationship only with another emigrant (a Serbian woman). In New York he spends his time with the African American Jim and an Arab co-worker. In both countries we see him only at his place of work, never at home, because 'home', the film implies, cannot be recreated anywhere else: the only 'true home' is the one circumscribed by Bulgaria's cultural, geographical and historical borders.

In addition to depicting Slavi's growing sense of homelessness, the film paints a stark picture of post-communist Bulgaria. Bulgarians' initial intoxication with their newly found freedom eventually gives way to disillusionment and resignation: Neli's husband, a promising theatre actor, roams the bars, drunkenly performing the trick with which he used to impress his school chums, and Neli's best friend sells newspapers at a little kiosk in Slavi's home town. Neli is the only one who has been moderately successful, working as a doctor in the local hospital. In short, while Slavi's initial decision to emigrate might have appeared rushed, the immature act of a young, romantic man with a broken heart, in retrospect it turns out to have been a wise choice given how all those who stayed behind have fared after the long-awaited changes in the political system. The happy ending to the romantic story, however, prevents us from dwelling on the depressing post-communist reality.[6]

Kamen Kalev's second film, *The Island*, a radical departure from the gritty realism of *Eastern Plays*, follows a Parisian couple, Sophie and Daneel, as they travel on holiday to a Black Sea island. When they arrive in Bulgaria, Sophie learns, to her surprise, that her boyfriend of four years, whom she thought was German, was actually born in Bulgaria, where he lived in an orphanage until he was ten when a German priest took him to Germany.

Figure 8.1 *The Island*: Sophie learns that Daneel is from Bulgaria after they arrive there for a beach holiday.

After the lovers miss the boat back to the shore, the vaguely ominous atmosphere hanging over the island steers their already rocky relationship out of control. When Daneel runs into a woman he is convinced is his biological mother and starts having weird dreams, or delusional fantasies, Sophie returns to Paris, leaving him alone on the island to experience a quasi-spiritual transformation triggered by an intimate communion with nature, a transformation in the course of which he sheds his Western European/corporate persona and reconnects with his Bulgarian/wild/authentic self.

Like its own pseudo-spiritual premise – the idea that each one of us harbours multiple personalities – *The Island* suffers from multiple personalities/generic identities: it starts out as a drama exploring a couple's deteriorating relationship, then switches to a psychological thriller as the couple arrive on a mysterious island populated by weird people (that is, Bulgarians) before transforming again into an odd reality show (or a critique thereof) in the third act. Putting aside the absurd premise (the two lovers have been together for four years yet somehow Sophie never suspected the real nationality of her boyfriend), it appears that, by focusing the story on Daneel, a Bulgarian man who returns to Bulgaria after more than twenty years abroad, Kalev presumably wanted to explore the issue of borders or limits: both the limits of personal identity and, on a larger scale, the limits of national identity. Though the film appears to trace Daneel's personal journey – from a corporate slave to a New Age prophet, a Bulgarian Jesus who lectures *Big Brother* audiences about their spiritual enslavement by the media and by big-money business – it also provides a commentary on what being Bulgarian means twenty years after the fall of communism. Despite its New Age rhetoric, however, which might make it seem more 'modern' than other films exploring the loss of Bulgarian identity, *The Island* rehearses the familiar health/illness metaphor that renders emigration as a sort of illness, the only cure for which is a return to the homeland. Daneel's Western European identity is summarily dismissed as a facade disguising his 'true Bulgarian identity', which the film constructs in quasi-religious terms. Soon after Sophie returns to Bulgaria and rejoins Daneel on the set of *Big Brother*, Daneel disappears from the *Big Brother* house. Sophie, pregnant with their child, responds to his sudden disappearance by directly addressing the show's audience and asking them to call her 'Mary'.

The film presents us with two extreme and mutually opposed views of Bulgaria: the island and the *Big Brother* show. The choice of the island as the site where Daneel supposedly reconnects with his roots is significant as it locates the film within an established, conservative tradition of

Bulgarian films that continue to construct national identity in terms of elsewhere and elsewhen, relegating Bulgarian identity to a supposedly simpler past (Daneel's nostalgic childhood memories of holidaying on the island) and to a specific geographical area, the countryside or, in some films, the wild Black Sea Coast[7] not yet ruined by foreign developers, both 'uncorrupted' by post-communist developments. The third act of the film presents us with the exact opposite of this 'authentic' Bulgarian identity, neatly mirroring the corporate facade of the allegedly inauthentic, corporatised Western European identity glimpsed in the first act which condemns as inauthentic both Daneel's job and his girlfriend's parents' marriage for no reason other than that they are both Western: the new, Westernised facade of post-communist Bulgaria symbolised by *Big Brother*. Referencing Lars von Trier's *The Idiots*, in which a group of friends pretend to be 'retarded' as a way of getting in touch with their inner selves ('the idiots' within them) and criticising the pretensions of bourgeois morality, Kalev has Daneel volunteer to be a contestant in *Big Brother*, where he plays the role of a retarded man and 'freaks out' in front of the entire country before inexplicably dropping the mask one day and assuming another role, that of a prophet who takes it upon himself to lecture Bulgarians, on national television, about the inauthentic lives they live. There is no middle ground between these two extreme, caricatured images of present-day Bulgaria: the old Bulgaria as a wild, Black Sea island, a sort of eco-preserve untouched by the grabbing hands of Bulgarian and foreign capitalists; and the new Bulgaria, a despicable reality show that recreates, in the form of an entertainment, the spiritual and intellectual enslavement by the communist regime of surveillance (the original Big Brother). Though the film portrays the immigrant (Daneel) as suffering from an illness – the 'illness' of emigration – it also positions him, in the third act of the film, as a sort of spiritual leader for the whole country, a Jesus-like figure who lectures the Bulgarian people to break free from the capitalist matrix. Ironically, the only way he can reach his audience with this 'message of liberation' is from within the confines of the very reality he condemns (the 'fake reality' of the reality show). At the end of the film, in true Jesus fashion, having waxed philosophic for several months, Daneel questions Bulgarians' search for spiritual enlightenment, including their blind willingness to accept him as their spiritual leader. One day he vanishes from their television screens, leaving everyone as baffled by his mysterious disappearance as they were by his original appearance.

Most of the action in *Mission London* takes place at the Bulgarian Embassy in London. Through the character of the Bulgarian president's wife, a socialite of the first order who seems to be running the country by spending taxpayers' money on extravagant public relations events and dinners at Bulgarian embassies abroad, the film explores Bulgaria's inferiority complex manifesting as a maniacal desire to prove its European origins. The president's wife sends Varadin Dimitrov to London as the new Bulgarian ambassador to Britain. His first mission – to organise a charity dinner at the embassy and invite Her Majesty the Queen – turns into a nightmare as he is forced to work with the embassy's corrupt staff, all of whom are involved in bootlegging and other clandestine business deals with Bulgarian, Russian, Serbian, Macedonian and Jewish mobsters. Varadin contacts the 'Famous Connections' agency, which promises to secure the Queen's presence, together with other VIPs, at the charity dinner. As he learns too late, the agency, which specialises in celebrity lookalikes, intends to provide him with the Queen's double. While the film openly mocks Bulgarian politicians' desperate need to be accepted by Europe's cultural elite, it is equally scathing in its critique of the British, including Sibling, the director of the agency, and Lord Dean Carver, a drunken British parliamentary wheeler-dealer, who waxes poetic about the good old communist times when he visited Bulgaria and was invited on hunting trips by Bulgarian politicians, 'who may have lacked style but certainly had scale'.

The film draws a distinction between two generations of emigrants: the older generation which is the embassy staff that has been working there since before 1989; and the new generation, represented by Katia, who emigrated after 1989 and now works as a stripper and a cleaning lady at the embassy in return for free accommodation. Though the embassy staff must have been living in London for decades, their way of thinking is still painfully provincial. They live in one of the most multicultural cities in the world yet maintain close connections – that is, carry out their shady business deals – only with other Balkan and Russian expats. The term 'Bulgarian' is here used as shorthand for 'uneducated, uncivilized, barbaric, primitive, provincial, and gullible', in short, 'non-European'. By mocking Bulgarians' inferiority complex, however – the need to prove that we, too, are European – the film ends up sabotaging Bulgaria's real claim to a shared European identity. This is especially obvious in the experimental fire dance performance the Bulgarian president's wife organises as part of the charity dinner. The performance, whose scale and nationalist rhetoric recall the old communist grand parades and celebrations, traces the history of the Bulgarian nation, starting with the proto-Bulgarians – fearful barbarians – and ending with the rape of innocent Bulgarian virgins by the Turks. This familiar historical narrative remains inexplicable to the Brits, including the fake Queen, who, struggling to understand the meaning of all these semi-naked men dancing with spears among the flames, wonders if this represents 'the call of the wild'. The dance show dramatises Bulgarians' complex relationship with their own history: mocking it and revalidating it at the same time. Key moments in Bulgarian history and essential aspects of the national psyche are openly presented, and mocked, as barbaric, primitive, un-European, precisely as a way of demonstrating Bulgarians' claim to European identity. The implication is that the power to distance oneself from one's primitive, barbaric past, by objectifying it (presenting it through the eyes of another, here the Brits), demonstrates one's rationality and enlightenment, or Europeanness.

The film's tendency to self-exoticisation – portraying Bulgarians as exotic, wild, the Other of European – is complemented by an equally unsurprising turn to self-victimisation or, alternatively, blaming the 'bad Other', in this case the exclusive 'European club' that refuses to recognise Bulgaria's claim to membership of it. That membership which was temporarily suspended during the communist regime and which, in post-1989 accounts of Bulgarian history, is usually dismissed as an aberration in Bulgarian national history, a detour from Bulgaria's true, European destiny. Accordingly, the British in the film are portrayed as taking advantage of Bulgarians' gullibility and of their inferiority complex. Though, at first, 'Famous Connections' is wary of extending its services from private clients (rich Londoners who hire the Bulgarian stripper to act in various perverse scenarios) to political entities, they soon come around as they realise the huge profit that can be made from such a deal.

The character of Katia, who represents the new generation of emigrants, offers an insight into Bulgarian identity through the notion of 'passing', which has been central to postcolonial discourses of American identity (African American characters 'passing' for white; for example, in Douglas Sirk's 1959 film *Imitation of Life*). For a good part of the film, Katia appears in complete makeover, working as a call girl and dressed as none other than the epitome of 'Britishness', Princess Diana (tiara and all). The 'Famous Connections' subplot suggests that national identity might be just a mask or a role one plays for money: in fact, the film goes as far as to suggest that, not only can a Bulgarian girl 'pass for' a British princess but that British royalty itself is a well-crafted illusion. Thus, through what seemed to be a simple plot device – the 'practical joke' the agency plays on the gullible Varadin – the film drives home the idea of a multiple, fluid identity and of national identity as a construct.

Conclusion

Over the last several decades the scholarship on 'national cinema' has been informed by a persistent scepticism towards the idea of national identity, with Stuart Hall challenging the supposed unity of the nation by asserting difference in the specific context of black culture in Britain, Homi Bhabha defining postcolonial cultures and identities as 'hybrid', Andrew Higson advocating the study of a national film culture over that of a national cinema, and Stephen Crofts emphasising the importance of analysing the popular and generic aspects of national cinema while taking into account the cultural specificity of genres and nation state cinema movements.[8] The increased mobility of people within Europe has drawn into question the usefulness of the concepts of 'national identity' and 'national cinema' and introduced instead the notion of 'migrant', 'nomadic' or 'exilic' identity which, though they refer to a generalised discourse of displacement often described in liberating terms, cannot be separated from modernity's dominant orientalist tropes.[9] If there is one narrative trajectory or one deep structure of feeling that contemporary European films share, it is the narrative of migration and the feeling of homelessness experienced by an increasing number of Europeans, including Bulgarians. If we think of migration in terms of 'homelessness', and expand the notion of 'homelessness' beyond its narrow association with 'emigration' to include spiritual, rather than just geographical, homelessness and multiple or hybrid identity (if 'the self' is aligned with 'home', a multiple or hybrid identity is aligned with 'homelessness'), we can say that Bulgarian cinema is beginning to outgrow its long-standing investment in the idea of a pure *Heimat*. Nevertheless, it is still unclear to what extent we can see contemporary Bulgarian cinema – most of which still tries to 'resurrect' an 'authentic' Bulgarian identity – as a 'declined cinema'.

CHAPTER 9

The Point of No Return: From Great Expectations to Great Desperation in New Romanian Cinema

Lucian Georgescu (Romanian Theatre and Film University)

Preamble

April 2011: a Romanian in his twenties, a poor worker residing in the small Spanish town of Torrejón de Ardez, kills his pregnant, nineteen-year-old Romanian fiancée. The last minutes of the ordeal and the corpse are filmed with a webcam and shown 'live' via the Internet to the family of the girl in their country of origin. The criminal is arrested within minutes as the parents reel from the traumatic shock.[1]

This is neither a snuff movie nor the latest minimalist production of the New Romanian Wave which rose to worldwide fame in the first decade of the twenty-first century for its dark, sombre and depressive hyper-realist dramas. It is the depiction of only one of the many stories revealing some of the sombre results of the exodus of a population coming from a 'marginal space' of Europe, a nation that woke up from the communist nightmare confused about its identity, living a permanent 'frontier situation' and 'still in the search of the way ahead' (Boia 2001: 12–13, 27).

Twenty-five years after the fall of the communism, Romanian villages are depopulated. The locals, once not even allowed to hold a passport, are now leaving the country at an alarming and increasing rate. The often tragic results of this exodus are nevertheless profound, with dramatic long-term consequences. Thousands of children are left without proper supervision or education. The family, once at the centre of patriarchal society, has been destroyed in the desperate rush of parents towards the West. A good number of their children will later become criminals, closing a vicious circle. This is the dramatic resort of *Eu când vreau să fluier, fluier/ When I want to whistle, I whistle* (Florin Șerban, 2010, Romania/Sweden/Germany) and the philosophy behind *Periferic/Outbound* (Bogdan George Apetri, 2011, Romania), the film that closes stylistically the first decade of New Romanian Cinema. The young criminal from Torrejón de Ardez, Spain might easily have been

Paul, the protagonist from *Outbound*. The mirage of the West and escapist dreams are common themes for the majority of films of this new generation, starting in the 1990s with *E pericoloso sporgersi/Sundays on Leave* (Nae Caranfil, 1992, Romania/France) or *Asphalt Tango* (Nae Caranfil, 1996, France/Romania), *Telefon în străinătate/Long-distance Call* (Hanno Höfer, 1997), and continuing into the twenty-first century with *Occident* (Cristian Mungiu, 2002), *Italiencele/The Italian Girls* (Napoleon Toader, 2004), *Cum mi-am petrecut sfârșitul lumii/The Way I Spent the End of the World* (Cătălin Mitulescu, 2006, Romania/France), *Nesfârșit/California Dreamin'* (Cătălin Nemescu, 2007), *Fața galbenă care râde/The Yellow Smiling Face* (Constantin Popescu, 2008), *Boogie/Summer Holiday* (Radu Muntean, 2008), *Felicia înainte de toate/First of All, Felicia* (Răzvan Rădulescu and Melissa de Raaf, 2009, Romania/France/Croatia/Belgium), *Nunta lui Oli/Oli's Wedding* (Tudor Jurgiu, 2009), *Francesca* (Bobby Păunescu, 2009), *Dacă bobul nu moare/If the Seed Doesn't Die* (Siniṣa Dragin, 2010, Serbia/Austria/Romania), *Stopover* (Ioana Uricaru, 20120 Romania/Italy), *Oxigen/Oxygen* (Adina Pintilie, 2011), *Morgen* (Marian Crișan, 2011, Romania/France/Hungary), *Apele tac/Silent River* (Anca Miruna Lăzărescu, 2011, Germany/Romania).[2] It can be argued that the vast majority of the films included in the corpus of New Romanian Cinema have as a unifying theme, escape – personal, of a group, or of an entire nation – and as a common conclusion, its failure. This essay attempts to analyse the end of Romania's post-communist period of 'Great Expectations' and the failure of the Western myth, both of which have led to a nationwide sense of desperation that is palpable in all New Romanian Cinema productions. While the focus of many sociological studies 'is on the challenge for receiving societies' (Castles and Miller 2009: 16), I am less concerned by the shock to societies receiving immigrants than by the impact on the country of emigration and by the changes witnessed by that sending society to those left behind the border. While, from certain European vantage points, it may be possible that 'hard borders [have lost] some degree of their significance in post-1989 Europe' (Gott 2013a: 51), nevertheless the border remains etched in the collective imaginary of Romania. I also believe in the power of the imaginary, of films being 'representations of national identity' that 'textually reproduce many of the cultural, economic and psychological limitations facing the nation' (Gott 2012: 8) better than any official statistics could. The cinematic output of young Romanian film-makers is realistically portraying the current social status of a desperate nation, at the point of no return, with no open road in front. The essay is founded on the belief that the Romanian society faces an identity crisis profoundly affecting its genes and future, and that New Romanian Cinema offers a valid representation of this nation's altered state of mind.

Making the Invisible Visible: Film as a Reasearch Tool

In *Making Trafficking Visible, Adjusting the Narrative* (2010), Dina Iordanova raises a rhetorical question: 'Why would one avoid referring to films, however?' (113). Iordanova describes the moment when, after one of her talks, someone in the audience questioned the idea of using films as references in sociological research as 'an eye-opening experience, [which] alerted me to the striking absence of cinematic references from the work of social sciences scholars', given that many studies, 'although on contemporary social issues widely represented in cinema, persistently abstained from making any references to films or other texts of popular culture related to these same social issues' (110). Building on this highly pertinent question, I favour the idea that contemporary cinema is more than just a source of information for one interested in understanding social changes; beyond bringing 'to light what is invisible and [making] it visible' (Iordanova 2010: 84), the art of film is, in some cases, far ahead of sciences and research, an invaluable barometer of the climate of a nation, of a region or the entire world that is capable of revealing signs of sociological diseases that sciences have not yet noticed. Moreover this applies most greatly to 'marginal' nations or topics, and Romania is a perfect example in this respect: 'Romanians have always been on the margins and now they stand on the margin of the European Union, as candidates whose chances of being integrated into the European construct remain uncertain' (Boia 2013: 13). In spite of a decade of international success, the themes of the New Romanian Cinema are themselves marginal and have received much less worldwide attention than do war in the Middle East, African immigration, the Arab feminist movements or human trafficking to the West. When the world is preparing for the social shock of absorbing the Syrian war human flooding, would somebody consider the 'borderland of Europe' (Boia, 2013) and its emigration as interesting? Taking to the extreme the insight of Dina Iordanova and using the reading lens suggested by Mazierska and Rascaroli, for whom cinema mirrors 'the ever-increasing mobility of the population and have served as a reflection on the many and elusive shifts of borders, identities and cultures that we have been experiencing' (2006: 9), we would argue that films are not simply an excellent reference for scholars but could, in some cases – such as the very special one of a borderland nation – be worthy of research itself, as rigid figures are limited in comparison with the power of creative understanding. If Mazierska and Rascaroli are interested in how 'travel films have engaged with the notion of a changing European sociogeographical space, which has in turn produced new forms of national and transnational identity' (2006: 1), I am interested here in discovering through cinema the truth about the collapse of a nation undergoing twenty years of an unofficial New Europe social experiment.

The Genealogy of New Romanian Cinema

On 25 December 1989 Nicolae Ceaușescu, the last communist dictator, and his wife, Elena, are shot by a firing squad following an improvised court martial. The platoon soldiers are in their mid twenties, all of them born immediately after (or as a consequence of?) the Decree 770 which, in 1966, banned abortion. The tragic consequences can be spotted in the realistic fiction of *4 luni, 3 săptămâni și 2 zile/4 Months, 3 Weeks and 2 Days/4,3,2* (Cristian Mungiu, 2007, Romania/Belgium; henceforth *4,3,2*), the story of a teenager having an illegitimate abortion in the mid 1980s, while the social consequences are analysed by the documentary *Decrețeii/Children of the Decree* (Florin Iepan, 2005), describing a generation born at order which later kills its infamous parents. 'I was a mother for you' the new Medea, Elena Ceausescu, tells the young soldiers when her hands are tied before the execution. 'He was my father, he gave me the chance to live, to be myself', declares to the camera Laurentiu Ștefănescu, a member of the firing squad, speaking as a contemporary Cronus who had cut the testicles of his father Uranus. The godfathers of New Romanian Cinema, Cristi Puiu (born 1967) and Cristian Mungiu (1968) are 'children of the decree' themselves. The most awarded Romanian film of all time, Mungiu's *4,3,2*, in a way owes its existence to the experiment 770 of 1966, making Nicolae Ceaușescu himself the spiritual father of the most important Romanian cultural achievement of the last half of the twentieth century. Many of his children will see the first lights of freedom from behind the iron bars of the bedrooms where they are chained, rocking in their metal orphanage beds. When the red communist velvet unfolds, the Western world discovers the realities of a dysfunctional society pretending to care about its future generations. Thousands of children have been abandoned or have lost their mothers at birth and are kept behind the walls of institutions similar to concentration camps, such as the infamous Siret orphanage, still active more than twenty years after the revolution. Some of those who will manage to escape will be heading for the only salvation: the West. Nevertheless this national trauma cannot disappear without leaving some traces. Romania is still haunted by the ghosts of *omul nou* (the new man), a Frankenstein that Ceaușescu created and that director Lucian Pintilie imagined while in exile in France in his first post-revolution film, *Prea târziu/ Trop tard/ Too Late*(1996, Romania/France), as a Balkan yeti hiding in the caves of closed mines representing the former glory of industrial communism. It is obviously too late for a nation to escape its destiny, too late indeed, *trop tard*.

Crossing the Border: A National Obsession

After the 'obsessive decade' (as the period of Stalinist terror camps of the 1950s is generally referred to) and a period of thaw in the 1960s and 1970s in Ceaușescu-ruled Romania, escape to the West became a national obsession in the 1980s and continues to this day now that the western border has been opened. Any means of escape was used in the past: any possible type of transportation, including sailing on oxygen tubes on the Danube (*Oxygen*), or using other inflatable objects ranging from car tyre inner tubes (*Silent River*) to submarines (*The Way I Spent the End of the World*) and, in the post-communist migration period, modes of conveyance including buses (*Asphalt Tango*, *Francesca*), cars (*Dacia, dragostea mea/ My Beautiful Dacia*, Julio Soto and Ștefan Constantinescu, 2009, Spain/Romania), motorbikes (*Morgen*) or extreme post-modern fictional inventions, such as inflatable sex dolls (*Occident*). Last but not least as a means of escape is marrying a foreigner. The last method is almost omnipresent in the films we are considering and, in some cases, constitutes the key dramatic point of post-1989 films such as *Asphalt Tango, Occident, California Dreamin'*, *Oli's wedding* and *First of All, Felicia*. Missing love or confused feelings are fundamental issues for Romanians who are part of the generation facing the question of whether or not they were wanted by parents left without choice by the 1966 Decree. Indeed, given their generational issues, pretending to be in love to get out of a hurting country is not necessarily a bad strategy for a young person who might have a confused definition of affection.

Released in 1992, *Sundays on Leave* was the first feature to revisit the nation's communist-era border obsession. The action takes place in a small town where Cristina, the teenage girlfriend of a young soldier, falls in love with Dino, an actor planning his escape over the Danube. At the end of the 1980s, the river remained the only chance to get out of a country that had been transformed into an immense gulag. This theme is reprised in the 2011 film *Silent River,* based on the true story of Gregor, a Romanian-German who, together with a friend, Vali and his pregnant wife Ana, tries to escape only to end up on the Serbian shore having to take care of the woman whose husband is arrested. Once on the other shore of the river, the fugitives had few options, the best of which was to be sent by the Yugoslavian army into a refugee camp – the ultimate desire of Gregor. The communist regime had at the time a special deal with Belgrade: for each Romanian fugitive turned back by the Serbians, the Bucharest officials would pay an entire wagon of salt. The Yugoslavian government issued a law exempting from taxes any Serbian peasants that denounced fleeing Romanians to the authorities. The manhunt on the banks of the Danube reached its peak in 1989 when the action of *Sundays on Leave* takes place.

Oxygen, released in 2012, is symbolically set in 1984, the Orwellian resonance of the title being highlighted by the stylish photography of the deserted factories on the Danube and the neighbouring ghostly cities where the working class hides in grey buildings suggestive of a degraded socialist version of Fritz Lang's *Metropolis*. The plot is simple, based on a method that had on occasion been successful but, more commonly, resulted in the fugitives being shot or arrested: a man prepares his escape across the Danube using an industrial oxygen tube as a propeller. The characters are unnamed, rendering them as anonymous as the thousands of others who failed to escape. The film lacks dialogue, with the exception of inserts of communist propaganda television programmes, interrupted by the regular power cuts of the 1980s that threw the entire nation into the dark. Two symbolic characters complete this cinematic poem: an alcoholic musician, an Eastern European breed of a Jarmusch-Fellinian sad clown, and a Hemingway-type fisherman who kills his catch by hitting its head repeatedly shown in a slow-motion camera movement combined with the desperate struggles of the fish to breathe. The deeply symbolic scene is similar in its significations to the fish-out-of-water scene that opens the film *Morgen*: no oxygen, no escape.

The End of Illusions

In 1989 the communist regime collapsed.

> Already from the first moments of the revolution, the Romanians gained a number of freedoms whose taste they had forgotten. Among these were the right to travel abroad without restriction and the liberalization of abortion – the two great obsessions of the Ceaușescu period. (Boia 2013: 156)

The first decade of freedom was sunny and naive; anything was possible and few doubted that good things were to come. Romania was full of hope and the road to the West was wide open. An entire nation was striving to advance with the maximum speed possible on what is believed to be a road to prosperity and, of course, happiness. As a logical result, the first notable films of the young generation in the mid/late 1990s to early 2000s are – even though bitter – comedies, a rarity in New Romanian Cinema: *Sundays on Leave*, *Asphalt Tango*, *Long-distance Call* and *Occident*. Unlike other film-makers from the former Eastern Bloc, such as the Czechs,[3] Romanians and Romanian directors, are eager to travel in their movies or, more precisely, to run, and this is one of the reasons for which a significant number of film productions are road movies.[4] In *Asphalt Tango* the story follows the desperate attempt of Andrei to stop his wife Dora, a ballerina, from emigrating to France to become a dancer at a nightclub. Both Sorina and Mihaela, the heroes of two of the three stories forming *Occident*, are dreaming of marrying a foreigner and escaping from a present without a future.

Romanians waited half a century for the American army to come to liberate the country, and the national dream finally comes true in *California Dreamin'* (2007). Yet it is *trop tard* as Pintilie would say, the communist experiment has succeeded in transforming the nation into a population of *om nou*, on behalf of which the neo-capitalist society is operating another test, the transition from the *kolkhoz* (the Soviet collective farms) culture to the supermarket one, the result being hybrids of non-citizens, programmed with a singular focus: to escape the laboratory they don't recognise anymore as a country. The arrival of an American military train convoy on its way to the Serbian front brings immense hope to the inhabitants of the small town of Căpîlnița, to the musical theme of The Mamas and the Papas hit 'California Dreamin''. This is a comprehensive metaphor for the Western dream of a nation relying exclusively on exterior forces, with no trust anymore in its own capabilities. The only way out for Monica (Căpîlnița's young version of Emma Bovary) is having an affair with Captain Jones, commander of the military convoy and the ultimate American cliché. 'There is a dramatic reason for this escapism; the inhabitants of Căpîlnița are living into an existential provisional captivity, this interim status being characteristic of the country itself, blocked in a sombre temporal bubble' (Mitchevici, 193, my translation). The Iron Curtain melts away and is replaced by plastic supermarket bags covering both the dusty landscape and their dreams, easily blown by the wind over the now deserted barracks of the Western frontier. The border has been lifted. Or not?

No Border, No Hope, No Dreams

In August 1968, two years after Decree 770, Nicolae Ceaușescu celebrated the results of the most important achievement of the communist industry, receiving as a gift the first ever Dacia car, which would become a symbol of industrial national pride and the most important communist brand to survive to the present day. Two decades later, in December 1989 he will be hijacking one (an upgraded version, though, the 1300) in an attempt to escape an angry populace.

The name of the car comes from the Roman province of Dacia (which included a part of modern Romania), an 'outpost' in the 'barbarian world'; it was the only Roman province situated north of the Danube and was surrounded by territories not controlled by the Romans. Dacia was also a place worshipped in communist propaganda, which created 'the myth of pure Dacianism, a sort of nationalist religion for which Dacia represented the centre of the world' (Boia 2013: 43). The name was therefore sacrosanct; the national(ist) Dacia brand would, however, later be sold to the French Renault car maker in the mid 1990s, becoming a symbol of neo-capitalism. *My Beautiful Dacia*, by Soto and Constantinescu, is a 2009 documentary staged on the road, using the Dacia car as a metaphor for fifty years of history, a long travelling shot describing moments, places and parts of the nation which the urban-oriented New Romanian Cinema (with the exception of Marian Crișan's *Morgen*) has neglected. The film is a puzzle of situations and characters, all having in common love for the old car; the central story is the attempt of the Bujor brothers, Mircea and Marian, to travel with a Dacia to Spain where members of their family and village neighbours are agricultural workers. The goal of the trip is finding a temporary job in order to save money to return back home and build a new house in the village, the ultimate dream of most of seasonal agricultural workers. Mircea and Marian are now driving their old Dacia 1300 heading for Spain, the birthplace of the first non-Roman-born emperor, Trajan, conqueror of Dacia, where his descendants are today called *căpșunari* (strawberry pickers, a primary source of seasonal employment). It is an appellation the protagonists of *Italian Girls* are trying to hide from, pretending that, instead of strawberries in Spain, they had picked grapes in Italy, presumably a more glamorous undertaking. Jeni and Lenuța (*The Italian Girls*), Marian and Mircea (*My Beautiful Dacia*) and the mother of Silviu from *When I Want to Whistle, I Whistle* each documents examples of the current transnational migration that is transforming a quarter of the Romanian workforce into a permanently shifting population in constant motion between East and West. Their endless movement has a purely economic justification and represents their only compass on the road, giving them a financial 'home orientation, a key component of transnationalism' (Sandu 2013: 32). Romania has always been a site of emigration located 'at the crossroad of civilizations, an open space *par excellence*, characterized by a permanent instability and a ceaseless movement of people and values' (Boia 2013: 14). The regional situation has changed and 'since the 1980's [sic] Southern European states like Greece, Italy and Spain, which for a long time were zones of emigration, have become immigration areas' (Castles and Miller 2009: 8), with the Romanians now heading en masse to Italy and Spain.[5] Their native language is derived from Latin so, within a very short time, the eponymous protagonist of *Francesca*, the cousins of Paul from *Outbound* and Silviu from *When I Want to Whistle* are all able to attain fluency in the language of their adopted countries which are no longer cold, rigid Saxon countries (such as West Germany, the preferred immigration destination of the 1980s) but a place where they can feel more easily at home. In the 2011 national census, over 700,000 Romanians were declared to be living temporarily (more than a year) abroad but the results were considered incomplete as there are only a few members of each family left at home to respond the questionnaires.[6] Unofficially, the number of Romanians living in Spain and Italy alone is close to two million, meaning that 10 per cent of Romania's population and almost a quarter of its workforce have left the country, living more or less continuously abroad, as 'migration has become a life strategy' (Sandu 2000).

Those, such as the Bujor brothers in *My Beautiful Dacia*, are suspended between two countries, though in a fashion that has nothing to do with what Baudrillard would call a 'sidereal journey' (2008). The Bujors are not travellers but neither do they consider themselves immigrants. Their dialogue in the car heading for the West is centred on Romania, the country left behind, which mentally they never left. Distinctions between 'travellers' and 'tourists', categories too sophisticated for a poor country, are not present in the cinematic journeys of New Romanian Cinema. Instead, Romanian films are populated with pseudo-travellers scouting abroad for a better future, demonstrating the observation that 'the barrier between migration and tourism is becoming blurred ... [and] many migrants become settlers' (Castles and Miller 2009: 4).

The Bujors are non-citizens (suspended between spaces that lost their national identities in favour of an abstract Brussels-ruled entity) and non-tourists, as their primary goal for travelling is solely economic. They do not fit any of the four models of voyagers proposed by Zygmunt Bauman: pilgrims, strollers, vagabonds or tourists. Their closest prototype might be the vagabond, as they are out of the centre of the social world, 'the advanced troops of guerrilla units of the post-traditional chaos' (Bauman 1996: 28). They are humble citizens of an ever-changing continent, far away from their base camp-nation, while travel itself is a way of life, rather than a journey, for the Bujors and other tens of thousands of *căpșunari* or *stranieri,*[7] permanently on a road leading to nowhere. The dialogues on the road show a different perception of the West, as 'allowed to a direct contact Romanians have a different perception on foreignness than before 1989' (Boia 2013: 192–3) but this contact reveals a deep frustration of a nation that was cut from the West and now finds it impossible to get over the clichés of education received for half a century. As Boia puts it, 'the West continues both to attract and to repel. There is still a long way to go before the Romanians will be able to regard Westerners with the same detachment (or indifference) with which the Westerners regard them' (2013: 193). Leaving the country, even for a short time, 'has as a consequence the dismantling of the couples and the dissolution of the family, being a perpetual source of distress for the ones left home' (Corciovescu 2011: 51). Paradoxically, the dissolution of the border and the mobility to the promising West have led to a national desperation; no more chains, yet no more hope.

Morgen: There's no Tomorrow

As Romania is no longer an Eastern communist country, it has become a land of promise for others from even further East, using it as a passage in

Figure 9.1 Nelu crosses the border in *Morgen*.

their search for a better life. 'The experience of working abroad became a modernizing factor for Romanian society' (Sandu 2010: 272) and the West gave this Eastern, emerging capitalist country the gift of one of its most important inventions: the supermarket. This is the place where Nelu of *Morgen* works as a guardian of a consumerist society symbol built up in the middle of the former 'no-man's land' of the border that once seemed to be the last frontier.

Nelu is a silent hero who fights daily with the sadness of a life without horizons. From the supermarket where he spends most of his time as a security guard, he travels back to his isolated house in the middle of nowhere and sometimes goes fishing on the Hungarian border. *Morgen* is a perfect depiction of the atomic bomb kind of social effect of the transition from an absurd politically imposed society to another that is totally alien, hardly understood by a historically traumatised local population. Nelu did not make a decision to stay, he hasn't even thought about leaving, being suspended in a time bubble broken only by third-degree encounters, such as the one with Behran, the Turkish alien heading unrealistically for a dream-like Germany. *Morgen*'s Romania is almost deserted, a marginal place of Europe, a transitional zone used as an antechamber of the West, an extreme version of a 'non-place' (Augé 2009) on the verge of becoming a non-nation, as the members of its scarce populace look like guinea pigs used as subjects for testing the artificial foods of the fourth worlds of tomorrow. The brain drain is complete: since 2007 (the year when *Mr Lăzărescu* dies on the way to an illusory hospital) more than eight thousand doctors have left the country in just four years (Roman 2011) and the nation has lost not only its health but is still constantly losing its children who hate being deprived of love as in the case of the teenage criminal from *When I Want to Whistle I Whistle*. Silviu, a Romanian version of Rocco Parondi from Luchino Visconti's 1960 film, is desperately trying to compensate for the lack of maternal love and to protect his brother from suffering the same deception as himself when abandoned by a mother emigrating to work in Italy. For Silviu and his many brothers, '*morgen*' no longer means tomorrow. Twenty years after the revolution, Romanian society shows itself to be incapable of building a future for its next generations.

Conclusion

Romania is a frontier nation at the crossroads of East and West, a European outpost at the gates of the orient with a unique, contradictory mixture of two cultures within the same body and spirit. For centuries the Romanians have looked towards the West with the hope of a better future while struggling with the local, Eastern-dominated realities. The two powerful neighbours, the Ottoman and Russian empires, have always closely watched and brutally censored the local random heretical tendencies for freedom, because the West always meant freedom for Romanians, as it was once for the heroes of westerns, even though in a different way.

Years after World War II, in spite of the Stalinist-imposed regime which put one of Europe's most flourishing young nations in house arrest, the Romanians still hoped for the Western liberation. 'When are the Americans coming?' was a frequent question in the 1950s and even the 1960s asked by the peasants from remote villages, awaiting a never-coming miracle. Some of them even continued an absurd fight, as the heroes from *Portretul luptătorului la tinerețe/The Portrait of the Fighter as a Young Man* (Constantin Popescu, 2010), the tragic story of an improvised group of partisans who hold out, in the mountains, against the pro-Russian communists in the aftermath of World War II.

The 1989 revolution was an explosion of liberating young energy, a moment of national epiphany when everything seemed possible. The fall of the Wall, the disappearance of frontiers, the absence of any limit, in both physical and spiritual ways, were challenges for these people, desperate to win freedom but not necessarily prepared to deal with that freedom. A long period of social, political and, last but not least, axiological confusion followed: the new capitalist way of life; the stampede for acquiring social and material status; the lust for possessions of an emerging new society; a nation of eternal commuters willing to gain the material values that their Western cousins have long enjoyed – the Romanians wanted it all and they wanted it now, no matter what the cost.

The productions of New Romanian Cinema reflect in their neo-realist style the social and moral changes of the post-communist era to a greater extent than scientific research could. Contemporary Romanian cinema is nurtured by a major disillusion in the wake of the collapse of the dreams of the generation of the 1989 revolution: the films of these young auteurs portray the drama of a nation that lost its compass on the way towards the West.

CHAPTER 10

'Weirdness', Modernity and the Other Europe in *Attenberg* (2010, Athina Rachel Tsangari)

Jun Okada (SUNY Geneseo)

As part of a distinctly 'other' Europe, but not particularly falling under classic postcolonial categories, Greece and Greek cinema offer interesting insights into the state of contemporary European cinemas and global art cinema. Besides the illustrious career of Greek auteur, Theo Angelopoulus, Greek cinema has stayed largely on the periphery of more globally known European cinemas. In fact, the work of Angelopoulos has been deeply invested in Greece's transnational identity within Europe, particularly in the travel between East and West in *Topio stin omichli / Landscape in the Mist* (1988) and in *To vlemma tou Odyssea / Ulysses' Gaze* (1995),[1] which meditates on the notion of the 'first gaze' of Greek cinema being dispersed across multiple borders among the Balkans. The sudden popularity of Greek cinema in the late 2000s is surprising given that 'it emerged in the context of an almost total alienation of audiences from Greek cinema throughout the 1970s, 1980s and for a large part of the 1990s' (Papadimitriou, 497). During this period, Greek audiences preferred popular genre cinema and abandoned the largely state-funded art cinema which was stymied by an inability to find distribution, leaving the only exhibition venue for 'quality' Greek cinema to the Thessaloniki Film Festival, founded in 1960. (Papadimitriou, 498) More recently, starting in 2009, a spate of independent films from Greece, notably *Attenberg* (Athina Rachel Tsangari, 2010, Greece), *Kynodontas/Dogtooth* (Yorgos Lanthimos, 2009, Greece) and *Alpeis/Alps* (Lanthimos, 2011, Greece/France), have garnered some attention, not only because of the uniqueness of the films' sense of absurdity but by the very fact that this new wave of films has made the nation of Greece more known to the world. What is, indeed, unique about the new Greek cinema is how the press has labelled it as not simply a new wave but a 'weird' Greek new wave. *The Guardian* has described it thus:

> The growing number of independent, and inexplicably strange, new Greek films being made has led trend-spotters to herald the arrival of a new Greek wave, or as

some have called it, the 'Greek Weird Wave'. Whether or not the catchy label fits, if there is a wave, weird or otherwise, Lanthimos and Tsangari are undoubtedly at its crest. *Dogtooth* won a prize at Cannes and earned an Oscar nomination; *Attenberg's* Ariane Labed won best actress at the Venice Film Festival last year.

So far, what we know of the new Greek cinema is that it is lauded and that it is 'weird'. The purpose of this essay, therefore, is to unpack this label of 'weirdness' with which the press has conveyed the mystery of the New Greek cinema. Though the Guardian article quoted above indicates Greece's economic meltdown as a reference point for these films' weirdness, I want to connect this concept to Greek cinema's historical marginalisation within Europe. In my view, 'weirdness' is the strangeness of being European and not European, both culturally and geographically. According to the European Union, Greece is 'located near the crossroads of Europe and Asia', at various points belonging to Asia Minor, the Balkans and, at the same time, being the classical origin of Western European thought and culture. In addition, this marginalisation stems from the instability of Greek cinema's past, particularly in its reliance on imports from Western Europe over many decades. What is more, the dominance of Western European and American popular culture in Greece over the twentieth century has amounted to a palpable cultural imperialism that has shaped how contemporary Greek film-makers have thought about its place within the cultural and economic margins of Europe. Though neither France nor Britain colonised Greece, the legacy of this cultural imperialism connected to a sense of loss becomes a key subject in the films of the Weird Greek Wave. It is, in fact, because of Greece's ambiguous historical position as both a part of and apart from Europe in the twentieth and twenty-first centuries that has informed the Greek New Wave cinema's specific aesthetic of mimicry that is unique among cinematic expressions of postcoloniality. Specifically, I focus on *Attenberg*'s employment of the spectacle in which characters wordlessly pantomime a range of actions in scenes that, together, suggest that Greece's cinematic identity has relied on a cultural masquerade.

Part of this predicament has to do with expectations of what a Greek national cinema should be in 2012 which, in reality, exceeds outdated notions of nation and belonging. In other words, the unpacking of 'weirdness' requires a search through layers of possible theoretical paradigms – national cinema, postcolonial studies, affect theory – in order to reveal not only the complexities of a new Greek independent cinema but also what it means for global art cinema and European cinema. I read *Attenberg* through a meditation on two kinds of mimicry – both postcolonial and affective – as ways of understanding the 'in-betweeness' of Greek cinema whose very marginality implies new ways of reading contemporary independent films. I argue that the critical reception of *Attenberg*'s 'weirdness' stems from the film's interrogation of language's inadequacy to reveal experience, specifically that which relates to belonging, to both family and nation, sources that articulate identity from a limited and predictable, structural, semiotic, Freudian perspective. As *Attenberg*'s main character is released from conventional expressions of desire, the film suggests a new kind of belonging beyond the biological family and the political nation state. Interactions and revelations of affect, therefore, allow for belonging to both the larger family of living organisms: other mammals, other humans beyond the biological family, and also, to things which move and which move us that have inevitably arrived through the processes of globalisation.

Unpacking the weirdness of *Attenberg* is complicated by the fact that Greek cinematic production has been historically erratic and has frequently relied on imports from Western Europe and the United States to make up its box office receipts. Independent film has made up the bulk of so-called Greek national cinema. Perhaps *Attenberg* would fall under the category of what Rosalind Galt and Karl Schoonover call the 'impure' global art cinema. In *Global Art Cinema: New Theories and Histories*, they argue that the critical value of contemporary global art cinema reveals itself through its imprecise relationship to national cinemas and international cinema (7). Most certainly, the new Greek wave would be a solid candidate for impurity as a low-budget, independent art film emerging from a very peripheral 'other' European nation. And yet, impurity does not begin to describe the uniqueness of *Attenberg*'s narrative and style.

Superficially, *Attenberg*'s narrative is a conventional and seemingly universal coming-of-age story about a twenty-three-year-old virgin, Marina, who is dealing with the imminent death of her father, Spyros, while figuring out her sexuality which exists in tension not necessarily with homosexuality or heterosexuality, but with asexuality. The possibility of an asexual subject is one element of many that suggest a way of thinking beyond assumptions about identity formation. This superficially straightforward Electra narrative is set against a backdrop of a post-industrial Greece which resembles the austere landscapes of Michelangelo Antonioni's *Il Deserto Rosso/Red Desert* (1964, Italy/France), a reference that links the film to the tradition of modernist, European art cinema. In tension with the romantic, grey deadness of contemporary Greece, the characters come alive to cultures that emerge solely from outside the nation's borders: 1960s French pop songs, British television, American punk rock. Aesthetically, *Attenberg* takes its cues from both Godard's irreverent self-reflexivity and Antonioni's postmodern alienation. Therefore, while it appears as yet another exemplar of so-called European art cinema, Tsangari's film challenges the primacy of this tradition by meditating on the ambiguity of Greece's place within this art cinema continuum. In other words, *Attenberg*, specifically, and the new Greek cinema in more general terms, offers an opportunity to challenge the meaning of Europeanness by analysing the historical divisions that exist between Greek cinema and European cinema.

National Cinema, Mimicry and the 'Other' Europe

In thinking about the ways that film studies categorises cinema, theories of national cinema and postcoloniality seem at first to be most apt in contextualising Greek cinematic output. For instance, we must consider *Attenberg* to be identified first as a product of the nation. As Andrew Higson has argued, national cinema as a theoretical concept rests on 'the tension between "home" and "away", between the identification of the homely and the assumption that it is quite distinct from what happens elsewhere' (Higson 2000: 60). And yet, the text itself reveals itself not to be literally or figuratively about these tensions but rather fits into a post-national sense of belonging that includes discourses of the transnational and globalisation as part and parcel of its universe.

Greek cinema established itself by copying other cinemas from Hollywood and France and, in so doing, began a pattern of 'coloniality' that bears traces in the way that contemporary Greek cinema thinks about its own identity:

> The ways in which early Greek film culture linked the Greek narrative of national destiny to the cinematic geoculture are fairly consistent with what the Peruvian sociologist Anibal Quijano has called coloniality ... Coloniality produces colonial subjects, subalterns, without the raw exercise of imperial/colonial power. It is internalized and works at the level of cognitive processes and psychic dispositions. (Tsisiopoulou, 75)

Therefore, on one level, the tensions in *Attenberg* revolve around the pleasures and problems of globalised culture. Greek national cinema is ideal for thinking about the in-between state: those states and cultures that have been excluded from the grand narratives of postcoloniality yet still exemplify tension within its power dynamic. Moreover, Greek cinema's unusual lack of a history of co-productions makes it a uniquely isolated one within the European context, a sense of which is intimated in *Attenberg*.

It is this contextual lens through which contemporary Greek cinema uses postcolonial textual strategies as a way in which to articulate itself and imagine itself in the global cinema market as well as in film history. New Greek cinema's successful reception as 'weird', therefore, has come out of a concerted effort to differentiate itself from other European cinemas in the absence of other clear markers of difference. In his book, *History of Greek Cinema*, Vrasidas Karalis says:

> As a small market with limited investment capital, Greece could neither sustain a developed and organized system of film production with international distribution and appeal nor, even more importantly, attract international funding through co-productions, something that would give wider scope to co-productions. Greek cinema could not even attract foreign actors (as could, for example, Italian, and more recently, Spanish cinema) who would have given international appeal to local films. Almost all Greek movies were made for domestic consumption, addressing local problems within the parameters of specific historical circumstances. This contextual specificity of these movies is both what redeems them and what marginalizes them. (xi)

Given Greek national cinema's infrastructural marginalisation, and its identity as an 'other' Europe, it is clear that these issues, of marginalisation and overshadowing by other, more established and globally relevant and fiscally supported European cinemas, would be an important part of its discourse. The very fact that resources had to be borrowed from the more economically viable national cinemas suggests a relationship of servitude and of feudalism, in addition to cultural imperialism. Also, the enclosed, almost incestuous nature of the idea that 'almost all Greek films were made for domestic consumption' suggests an insularity that has been allegorised most famously in Yorgos Lanthimos's *Dogtooth*.

One strategy that *Attenberg* uses to address the material austerity and cultural isolation of Greek cinema is a very self-conscious form of mimicry, specifically, of imported cultural forms from Britain, France and the United States. These instances of mimicry find their analogue in Homi Bhabha's classic concept of postcolonial mimicry in which characters in postcolonial texts imitate the behaviour of the colonisers as a way in which to gain cultural capital. Since the state of Greek cinema falls under coloniality, if not full colonisation, the role of cultural imperialism in *Attenberg* is an important aspect of its discourse. The film's overriding narrative concern is the main character Marina's inability to feel desire or a want a sexual relationship which predictably coincides with the impending death by cancer of her father, Spyros, who is also her only living parent. This plot is overridden by scenes that take us out of the narrative in which the three main characters (the heroine, her father, and her best friend) act out scenes inspired by other cultures, namely British television and the hit French pop tune 'Tous les garçons et les filles', a 1962 hit song by French pop chanteuse Françoise Hardy about youthful, amorous, female longing. That the entire film takes its title from the close-but-not-quite Greek translation of television naturalist Sir Richard Attenborough's name, 'Attenberg', suggests that mimicry is not merely that of animal nature but of a very self-conscious, post-cultural imperialist one that allegorises how the world has learned about being human from institutions such as the BBC. And also how that intercultural mimicry and hence translation, is by its very nature imperfect. Marina's affect and emotion, which are muted and blank in most other interactions with humans, are aroused only by imitating Sir Richard Attenborough's wild animals. Not to be outdone by Europe, American alternative culture gets a shout when Marina, who adores the music of American punk band Suicide, finds a fellow fan in the Engineer and proceeds to dance ecstatically and spectacularly in a poignant musical interlude to their 1977 song 'Ghost Rider'. The scenes of spectacle, in which Marina acts out varying levels of intensity, seem to be the only arena in which passion is allowed.

These references to Attenborough, French pop music and American punk rock are perhaps not an overt critique of so-called cultural imperialism. In fact, they are most certainly love letters to these cultural icons. Yet, in the light of the historical marginalisation of Greek national cinema and the function of the new Greek wave as recuperating this absence, they suggest that Greece's relationship to the rest of Europe and the West has been one largely of estrangement. Greek cinema is the cinema that Europe and Hollywood, and even independent cinema, have forgotten. That the characters take tutorials on behaviour from the likes of Sir Richard Attenborough and Françoise Hardy reveals its very lack of identity in the absence of pre-existent roles to fulfil in the cinematic global economy. By suggesting that desire and longing are supplied via cultural import from Britain and France, *Attenberg* infers that Greek cinema has not really lived and that, by default, its operational mode is in the mimicry of others.

A crucial element in *Attenberg's* coloniality is the incorporation of Frenchness. Among the film's various mysteries lies the central fact that a French actress, Ariane Labed, portrays the heroine of a film exploring Greek national identity. What is more, Marina shifts diegetically between Greek and French identity positions. While cross-cultural casting has always been a fact of cinema, given French cinema's historical dominance in Europe and the film's consistent ambivalence about various forms of identity – gendered, sexual, national – *Attenberg*'s textured use of Labed traverses diegetic and discursive lines to the point where it becomes a necessary part of the film's expression of an unstable Greek identity. Ariane Labed is a French national who was born in Greece and spent the first six years of her life there. As a young adult, Labed lived in Greece as a working actress with a theatre troupe and stayed on to make films after having met Tsangari and Lanthimos (Asseraf 2012). When she filmed *Attenberg*, Labed did not speak Greek fluently and had to learn and speak her lines phonetically (Clarke 2011).

Though the use of Labed's masquerade as a Greek national could have stopped here, what is interesting is how Labed's Frenchness is allowed to seep through the film in both direct and indirect ways. For example, the intrusion of Frenchness appears most pointedly in a scene in which Labed's character, Marina, teaches her friend Bella how to sing the famous Françoise Hardy pop song 'Tous les garçons et les filles'. Marina plays the guitar and sings each line of the lyric in a monotone, yet perfectly unaccented French, which is followed by a much more imperfect parroting of them by Bella. The song bridges over a transition from Bella and Marina inside a bedroom to a laconic dolly shot of people playing night tennis as Marina's and Bella's rendition shifts to the Hardy recording from 1962 which, in turn, ends up on a two shot of the women walking arm in arm, at night, down a lane lined by droves of young men hanging out. Aptly, the song is about a girl who cannot find love despite being surrounded by all the boys and girls who seem immersed in love. Topically, the song helps to narrate Marina's predicament of a lack of desire for romance. Marina's superior French proficiency is never explained narratively, so one must either take a stab in the dark at a backstory or perhaps, more to the point, read it through the mechanism of colonial and affective mimicry as a leitmotif in the film. In the same way that Sir Richard Attenborough teaches Marina how to act, and hence, how to feel, through mimicking gorillas, she, in turn, teaches Bella, perhaps, how to embody a particular kind of romantic, nostalgic position of youthful yearning through the filter of Frenchness. What better way to transmit this than through an iconic French pop song of the 1960s about being alone among a sea of lovers. Though Bella at first doesn't seem to need instructions on feeling or affect as she is the sexual opposite of Marina, it is clear, through the plaintive tones of this simple song, that what Bella lacks is the feeling of love if not lust. Where Marina is unable to enact animal, sexual affect, Bella is only able to have sex with various men because she lacks the ability to form emotional intimacy. And it is appropriate in the context of postcoloniality that the young, quite literally disaffected Greek characters of *Attenberg* require an outside influence to animate them back into some semblance of feeling.

Though the use of 'Tous les garçons et les filles' is a gentle suggestion of the French colonial imprimatur into Greek national identity, it is later a more forced and mysterious postcolonial intrusion of Frenchness that is ultimately inassimilable. At one point later on in the film Labed's character suddenly starts to speak French in a conversation with Spyros. In this scene, Marina's father tells her how it will be after he has died and she responds. Spyros wants to be cremated abroad where he can have an atheist burial, something that cannot apparently be done in his homeland. Marina suddenly says, in French, 'what shocks me is you plan things without me and then announce them in the end'. This is the only perfectly spoken French in the film, yet, again, nowhere in the plot is it ever suggested that Marina is French or has spent time in France. This verbal exchange abruptly throws us out of the narrative in the precisely Brechtian manner practised by Godard while also telegraphing the looming presence of the French cultural dominance over assumed Greekness. As remarked on earlier, one of the signs of success in the European film economy has been a pattern of having foreign stars in your films, a marker of success that Greek cinema had never reached. Therefore, that Labed's Frenchness bleeds through the narrative in a number of ways – dialogue, singing French pop songs – reveals a self-awareness about the importance of the markers of Frenchness to the contemporary cinema of the 'other' Europe. Rather than straight homage or straight critique, Tsangari suggests the necessity of Greek cinema to engage in a sort of ventriloquism in the vacuum of a strong cinematic tradition that has as much to do with its own economic history as it does to its ambivalent relationship to European superpowers. That *Attenberg* decides to point attention to this fact is yet another way in which an emergent Greek national cinema makes itself distinct as both European and other.

It is well established that France, and particularly the French New Wave, remain the matrix from which the contemporary art cinema evolved. Therefore, as an exemplar, both stylistically and industrially, of art cinema, *Attenberg* refers to French culture and the signatures of art cinema to identify with belonging to this tradition. The film's narrative is a fairly conventional one but its style, particularly its enactment of Marina's lack of desire and alienation, is what identifies it as such. Specifically, *Attenberg* follows in the 'parametric' tradition as outlined by David Bordwell in which a film's style dominates plot in its overall formal organisation. Bordwell's parametric prototype is French New Wave cinema – specifically *Pickpocket* (1959) by Robert Bresson and any given film by Godard. Bordwell points to Godard's 1960s films as the *sine qua non* of the art cinema, and which is redolent with self-reflexivity and deconstruction of both Hollywood conventions and European cinema (275). Like Godard's heroines, the characters of *Attenberg* take part in their own self-conscious mimicry of representations but, in the context of Greek cinema and its economic struggle, this self-reflexivity has decidedly different connotations.

While *Attenberg*'s intertextual devotion to French cinema could be read as a capitulation to the dominance of the West, upon closer examination, I think the film opens toward a new cinematic tradition that confronts the incorporability and untranslatability of Western European culture within Greek culture. The idea that European art cinemas are completely heterogeneous and beholden to economic, aesthetic and even psychic dominance by France is a fact that is confronted and transformed in the new Greek cinema. Though resting comfortably within some of the stylistic signatures of European art cinema, it is through the trope of self-conscious mimicry that *Attenberg* allows for both an homage to, and critical analysis of, Greek cinema's reliance on cultural exports and its history of being in the shadow of Western European film traditions.

Affect and Mimicry

On the one hand, *Attenberg* is a film that ponders Greek national identity in a quickly shifting, ethnically and geographically ambiguous new Europe. Yet its inner mechanisms reveal a resistance to expected ways of speaking about nation. Affect, as defined by theorist Brian Massumi, is a method of textual inquiry that transcends the so-called primacy of language and structure as ways of understanding. Specifically, *Attenberg* is a case study for illustrating the 'two orders of reality' that Brian Massumi describes in his book *Parables for the Virtual* (2002). In other words, *Attenberg* can be read on the conventional semiotic, symbolic, ideological track as a classical narrative film, and all of its national/postcolonial implications, on the one hand, but, on the other, it offers several examples of cinematic affect as an active resistance against such traditional 'reading'.

Mimicry as a motif in *Attenberg* can arguably be seen as a function of coloniality and postcoloniality but, because of the film's equally meaningful interrogation of the disconnect between feeling and action, the possibility of affect enters the film's universe. In *Attenberg*, the typical ways of conveying narrative meaning – through the psychological cues of facial expressions, dialogue and soundtrack music – are replaced by what Massumi calls 'prepersonal intensities'. Prepersonal intensities refer to affective states that precede subjectivity and, therefore, language: in other words, the way in which infants and animals react to phenomena by levels of intensity, and not by specific emotions, which are necessarily linked to semiotic values. By conveying events through instances of prepersonal intensity, rather than through the signification of emotions, *Attenberg* simultaneously expresses the inadequacy of language to convey the meaning of sexuality, of love, of death and, importantly, of being human in a postnational environment. Precisely because Marina is a character who can only feel and express things through comparative intensities of affect gained through the enactment of a song or the mimicry of an animal, affect becomes a significantly viable generator of meaning within *Attenberg*'s diegesis, as well as a possible pathway for the viewer beyond conventional modes of spectatorship.

Though national and postcolonial contexts are keys to understanding *Attenberg*, given Greece's specific cinematic history, mimicry also operates as something that is not merely motivated by these issues. Clearly, in the postcolonial context, the desire by the marginalised to belong to the centre lies at the heart of mimicry. And yet, at its base, mimicry functions as a way, simply, to feel the feelings one ought to feel even to be a desiring subject. In other words, 'going through the motions' or mirroring is a pathway to genuine feelings and desires. Therefore, the mimicking behaviour in *Attenberg* operates not merely as a way in which to reveal the coloniality under which Greek cinema has existed. Because one of the motivating narrative strands in *Attenberg* involves a young woman who cannot feel desire, mimicry for her is a means to desire. Therefore, mimicry operates at a prepersonal, pre-identificatory process. And thus, only when Marina watches animals on Sir Richard Attenborough's television programme does she show any change in physical comportment and facial expressions. Marina doesn't react to kissing her friend Bella. She gamely goes through the motions of sexual intercourse with her new lover, the Engineer. Yet, she shows no passion in the way that people in films show passion. Marina comes alive only when she imitates the gorillas and birds from television. In some ways, we could compare the two Marinas and label the difference as intensity.

On the one hand, the fact that the film takes its very title from the garbled Greek translation of the name of British broadcaster and naturalist, Sir David Attenborough, points to the historical relationship between Western Europe and Greece and reflects on the failure of translation, of unincorporability of certain kinds of 'Westernness', and by extension, cultural imperialism, into contemporary Greek identity. All of these explanations are based on the structural understanding of language. Upon closer examination, however, the mechanism that reflects this mistranslation is that of the affect that Attenborough's television programme has on the main characters in the film. Attenborough's 1979 television series for the BBC, *Life on Earth*, and its most famous moments, those of his contact with a family of gorillas, are featured prominently in *Attenberg* and, in fact, provide the hinge on which the film demonstrates main character Marina's otherwise emotional and affective detachment. The famous clip shows Attenborough's contact with the gorillas as he exclaims

> There is more meaning and mutual understanding in exchanging a glance with a gorilla than any other animal I know . . . they live in the same sort of social groups, largely permanent family relationships. So if there were a possibility of escaping the human condition and living imaginatively in another creature's world, it must be with a gorilla.

Following this proclamation, Attenborough plays with the gorillas. This clip is one of the most famous from *Life on Earth* precisely because it illustrates something beyond linguistic explanation: affect.

Marina watches this clip with her father, and her reaction is to mimic a gorilla. Marina's 'aping' of Attenborough and his gorilla friends reflects 'meaning and mutual understanding', something that is not accessible through verbal communication. The mimicry of gorillas continues on to the mimicry of other animals in long scenes of Marina and her father acting out on his deathbed a sizeable swath of the animal kingdom. These long takes, in which Marina screeches and opens her arms in imitation of a bird's wingspan or grunts and sniffs like a primate, demonstrate how one might express various emotional states: sadness at the impending death of one's only living parent, deep parental love, fierce filial love and despair at being left alone in the world. In some ways, the animal mimicry that is acted out between Marina and her father, and also between Marina and her best friend Bella, indicates an alternative to a sexual liaison. The 'incest taboo', which extends to the incest taboo among friends and the taboo of lesbian sexuality, perhaps, reveals a true alternative to sex as the only act in which to express a certain kind of pre-verbal intensity, a 'realness' according to a Lacanian/Freudian reading. By enacting the behaviour of wild animals, which are themselves non-verbal, *Attenberg* allows for another avenue of expression of taboo love.

In *Attenberg*, characters have difficulty in doing the things 'normal' humans do, specifically in the realm of sex and love. Marina, the main character, for example, is constantly analysing the mechanism of sensation, giving a play-by-play account of how something feels, not emotionally, but physically, to her body. For example, a tongue feels 'like a slug' in her mouth. By contrast, sex scenes in most films operate as a common and necessary spectacle, a vehicle of visual pleasure. The notion that scenes of sex play out a kind of Freudian primal scene has also been taken for granted in the annals of film theory. But in the scenarios laid out in the Greek Weird Wave cinema, instead of 'natural' scenes of physical intimacy, we are given various situations which the participants analyse with detachment and precision. The film also frequently uses dancing, singing and the motif of non-human animal behaviour to express the otherwise ineffable.

Attenberg is very attentive to a resistance against traditional semiotic reading. The film opens on what has been described as 'the worst kiss in screen history'. The scene begins on a long take in close-up against a blank, white, stucco wall before two young women walk into a medium close-up, moving towards each other from the opposite sides of the frame. Now, the temptation to call the action that follows as 'kissing' would be to miss the nuances and awkwardness of what actually transpires on screen. The two young women, Marina and Bella, awkwardly and mechanically stick their tongues in each other's mouths to demonstrate what might physically be described as the motions one goes through in the act of French kissing. The event as it is filmed has a number of possible meanings: a scene of romantic passion, adolescent same-sex experimentation or, perhaps, a rudimentary attempt to elicit a pornographic look. Yet the dialogue that accompanies the image is interestingly at odds with it:

Bella: Did you like it?
Marina: I've never had something wriggling in my mouth before.
Bella: How does my tongue feel?
Marina: Like a slug. It's disgusting.
Bella: You have to breathe, or you'll choke.
Marina: Should I open again?
Bella: Half open . . . That's it.
Marina: Okay, get in there . . . You're all slobbery. I'm going to throw up.
Bella: If it's not wet in there, it won't work.

Ostensibly and visibly, this is a lesbian kiss but, narratively, it is one friend teaching another how to kiss. Often, illicit or experimental lesbian relationships in coming-of-age dramas appear with their own set of predictable cinematic codes. This is particularly true of films with female main characters. On the one hand, this opening scene, which became something of a minor cause célèbre in distinguishing this film above so many other coming-of-age indie films in recent years, could be seen as erotic, giving the film a garden variety element of titillation that has been the reliable staple of European art cinema for generations. Labelled in this way, the film is forced into a given set of expectations that is severely limited by the accepted rules of spectatorship. When viewed through the lens of scopophilia, the shared genetic trait of all narrative films, the existence of such scenes seems not as unusual or 'weird' at all. But, when looked at more closely, the effect, or affect as it were, of this scene is one of awkwardness and mystery, particularly in the light of the film's context of animals and the relationship between human and animal behaviour that envelops the film. For example, what follows the awkward kissing scene between Marina and Bella is a catfight, and not in the typical, metaphorical, linguistic sense of an argument between two women. The camera placement shifts from medium close-up to medium long shot and the two women suddenly emerge from their slug-like tonguing to become crouching, hissing cats. In other words, the scene ends with Marina and Bella play-fighting like alley cats or wild cats or even, perhaps, mountain lions skirmishing over territory. Most of the characters in *Attenberg*, in fact, turn into animals at the drop of a scene change, as if they are working a method-acting seminar. The lack of a narrative explanation forces us to contend with how affect works as a solution to narrative, cinematic problems.

What prevents the film's animal antics from being merely pretentious is the role that affect plays in its motifs of animals and animal behaviour as a textured, palpable means of indicating intensity. According to Brian Massumi, 'affect always precedes will and consciousness' (29). Indeed, he writes,

> at any moment hundreds, perhaps thousands of stimuli impinge upon the human body and the body responds by infolding them all at once and registering them as an intensity. Affect is this intensity. In the infant it is pure expression; in the adult it is pure potential (a measure of the body's readiness to act in a given circumstance). (29)

What Marina is trying to get at in the opening kissing scene is not the answer to a predetermined set of questions such as, 'Am I a lesbian?'. For example, when Marina is being French kissed by Bella, she describes it as slug-like: neither good nor bad, straight nor lesbian, but through an animal metaphor. This is a 'weird' moment because it goes against expected interpretations of physical contact and experience. Therefore, an interpretation of Marina's action and reaction in this scene as affect unmoors the film from predictable gendered, sexual identity positions by considering the pre-linguistic, animal nature of humanity.

What is more, affective mimicry provides a solution to the overdetermination of the structured Electra narrative. According to Massumi, 'structure is the place where nothing ever happens, that explanatory heaven in which all eventual permutations are prefigured in a self-consistent set of invariant generative rules' (27). On one level, *Attenberg* provides precisely the kind of stale structure that Massumi critiques. It demonstrates a classic Electra narrative through the construct of a father and daughter coming to terms with their relationship in the absence of a mother. Marina's mother and Spyros's wife died when Marina was a child, hence, father and daughter are the only ones who remain in the family, with Marina's hypersexual friend Bella filling in as potential love object for both Marina and her father. In the hospital where we first learn that Spyros is ill, Marina confesses that she has imagined him naked and that it bothers her as an image though she does not reject it. Marina asks him if he ever imagines her naked. He responds by saying no, never, that a father's mind represses such thoughts about his own daughter. Marina asks if it is taboo. Spyros responds that there is a reason why mammals have taboos. It assures the propagation of our species without defects. This scene clearly allegorises Freud's *Totem and Taboo*, a highly criticised work that laid out how primitive cultures create myths to prevent incest. Freud's book became the urtext for the ideas that underpin Claude Lévi-Strauss's study of myths which, of course, lead to structuralism and post-structuralism themselves. Therefore, one could very easily read these scenes, which spell out the issue of incest taboos, as obstacles to the heroine's maturation. This would be a predictable path.

Though it is tempting simply to read this structural surface, we discover that intimations of incest on the part of Marina comprise only one possible solution that Marina attempts in her journey towards feeling and desire, and thus, maturation. Marina 'tries out' sexual contact with Bella, her best friend, an incestuous relationship with her father, and even compulsory heterosexuality, but they are all left wanting. One of the first conversations which occurs in the film is one in which Marina's best friend talks about a dream she has about a tree that grows penises like fruit. Bella is Marina's foil and is as promiscuous and hypersexual as Marina is questioning and asexual. Bella's dream of the penis tree illustrates a striking contrast to Marina's predicament of feeling alien to sexuality as it is conventionally portrayed and enacted. On the other hand, Marina, in her fear of suspected asexuality, dreams of breast trees instead of penis trees. And yet, she says that she is not aroused by women's breasts but that she admires them. The only solution to her predicament in trying to feel human and alive appears in her private enactments of animal behaviour from Sir David Attenborough's television series.

Therefore, in every instance in which Marina is given a way out of her lack of desire and her asexuality, she rejects it and, what she takes up in lieu of the banality of sex is the intensity with which she is able to mimic a gorilla or a gull or any number of animals in the spectacular menagerie that

Tsangari offers as a solution. Thus, in a reaction to the structural determinants of the Electra narrative (and other classical structures), allowing for affect and, in this case, a character who finds solace not in narrative conclusions to narrative problems but in the spectacle of affective mimicry, is the solution out of the problematic structure of narrative and of language. Unlike structured narrative interpretations, Massumi informs us that:

> Nothing is prefigured in the event. It is the collapse of structured distinction into intensity, of rules into paradox. It is the suspension of the invariance that makes happy happy, sad sad, function function, and meaning mean. Could it be that it is through the expectant suspension of that suspense that the new emerges? As if an echo of irreducible excess, of gratuitous amplification, piggy-backed on the reconnection to progression, bringing a tinge of the unexpected, the lateral, the unmotivated, to lines of action and reaction. A change in the rules. (27)

Conclusion

Mimicry – both postcolonial and affective – are responses to the very specific estrangement of Greece from the rest of Europe. Key to this estrangement comes in the discourse of Spyros, a socialist who calls himself a 'toxic remnant of modernism' and bemoans the loss of Greece's physical beauty to failed industrialism, both of which are evident in the film's stark cinematography. Spyros's death indicates even more the neither-here-nor-thereness of Greece as his dying wish is for an atheist burial which is not available in his homeland and, therefore, must be done outside its borders. When Marina goes to a funeral director, she inquires about the countries he might be sent to. The coffin salesman replies, 'well, we work with Bulgaria, Monaco, and Germany. Hamburg to be exact. I wouldn't recommend Bulgaria as your first choice. It's the cheapest option, if you don't mind me saying. They mainly serve people from the Balkans.' Marina responds, 'We're Balkan, too.' He says, 'I mean the former Eastern Bloc. You know, atheists. I propose sending him to Hamburg where services are more advanced.' This exchange, about the impossibility of a Greek national to be buried in his own country because of his personal beliefs, drives home the theme of estrangement-from-self that undergirds the film's fascination with the process of mimicry. Ultimately, Greece is a postcolonial no-man's-land, caught between the rest of Europe and what lies beyond, between the past and the future, and unsure of its position in space and time.

In the same way, Marina seeks a way out, not literally out of Greece, but outside predictable responses to life, sex and death. The 'weirdness', therefore, ascribed to this film is one that reflects the film's suggestion of affective mimicry as a reasonable way to get out of the dead structure of semiosis. In the end, affective mimicry and the audience's ability to interpret it, whether as 'weirdness' or something else, suggest a new frontier for global art cinema. *Attenberg* strikes the balance by being familiar enough as a work of art cinema, with its self-reflexivity and musings on post-nationality and postcoloniality, as well as expanding the possibilities that exist beyond predictable narrative and genre structures. By offering affective states as solutions to structure, *Attenberg* and its ilk present possibilities for a cinematic resurgence whose epicentre may well proliferate in the 'other' Europe.

CHAPTER 11

Lithuania Redirected: New Connections, Businesses and Lifestyles in Cinema since 2000

Renata Šukaitytė (Vilnius University)

Since the 1990s Lithuania, like other countries of the former Soviet bloc, have gone through rapid political, economic and social reforms and gradual geopolitical 'redirections' from the East, especially Russia, towards the West, particularly the European Union. These processes were mirrored in the national and regional cultural artefacts which were frequently promoted under umbrella terms 'Central', 'East Central', 'New Europe' and alike. These terms, however, as Ewa Mazierska and Paul Coates incisively note, 'did not enter cultural discourse after the fall of communism' but had existed long before this event (Mazierska 2010: 6) because 'East Central' and 'Central' have different connotations than 'East' for many nations that joined the EU in 2004. It should be noted that the umbrella term 'Baltic Countries', which served for indicating the cultural otherness of Lithuania, Latvia and Estonia within the Soviet Union, also had been circulating in the public discourse much before the 1990s, and can be seen as a certain tactic for situating these three republics within the cultural tradition of the Central-Northern Europe, especially countries located around the Baltic Sea. National cinemas, including Lithuanian, have been contributing significantly to the reflection of these new 'redirections' and existing binarisms within the European Union, dividing it into old (Western) and new (Eastern) Europes.

In her essay 'Reliving the Past in Recent East European Cinemas' Roumiana Deltcheva discusses the ongoing processes of cultural and geopolitical redirection and repositioning of Eastern European cinemas and the crystallisation of new cultural and political identities after the relocation of former centres and peripheries of power (Deltcheva, 197). She notes that different countries from the former Eastern bloc 'have undergone a differentiated economic and political development' which led to the integration of the Baltic States, the Czech Republic, Hungary, Poland, Slovakia and Slovenia into the European Union on 1 May 2004, and to the emergence of a new cultural, political and economic 'binarism along the Central-versus-Eastern axis' (198). It is worth noting that the 'new binarism' and attempt to distance the nation from the Soviet past and identity are quite noticeable in the majority of Lithuanian cinematic productions of the 2000s, where a new national identity is developed between two poles: from the similarity to 'old Europeans' to the difference from them and from former Soviet 'brothers'. This also relates to the efforts of Lithuanian politicians and intellectuals to reposition Lithuania from Eastern Europe to the Centre (by measuring and marking a geographical centre of Europe in Lithuania in 1989) and even to the North. After ongoing political and economic tensions with Slavic neighbours, especially Russia and Poland, Lithuania very visibly redirected co-operation towards the North. This course towards new cultural and economic alliances is well represented by recent film productions, which have been made in co-operation with new partner countries: *Lošėjas/The Gambler* (Ignas Jonynas, 2013, Lithuania/Latvia), *Santa* (Marius Ivaškevičius, 2014, Lithuania/Finland) and *Redirected/Už Lietuvą!/Redirected* (Emilis Vėlyvis, 2014, Lithuania/UK) and ongoing projects, the main co-production partners of which are from Latvia, Estonia and Finland.

The slow and problematic transition from 'Eastern' towards 'Western' society and the uneasy crystallisation of new cultural and political identities for Lithuania have been the target of several recent Lithuanian films, most notably by the nation's most internationally acclaimed auteur, Šarūnas Bartas, and most commercially successful director, Emilis Vėlyvis. Both use different stylistic and genre approaches to deal with essentially the same issues. The aforementioned geopolitical and geocultural changes have been accompanied by the emergence of new phenomena, such as migration and transnational networking and intercultural work experiences. These developments have also resulted in types of characters moulded as a consequence of the emergent lifestyles of capitalist Lithuania. Lacking fundamental values, such as diligence, dedication and honesty, these new characters possess many features of the postmodern figures defined by Zygmunt Bauman as the 'vagabond' and the 'player' (Bauman 1996: 28–32). Selfish, aimless and lacking goals or structure, these characters tend to approach life as if it were a game. The characters of Lithuanian films could be called adventurists, possessing multiple identities, playing games and making risky businesses deals simply to bring some change and energy into their boring lives. This chapter will examine the historical, cultural and economic contexts framing the relationships of these adventurists from various generations to contemporary Lithuanian identity and cinema before proceeding to an analysis of contemporary films that are reflective of these new realities. A picture emerges in post-Soviet Lithuanian cinema of an uneasy period of transition between East and West, with transnational exchanges becoming commonplace but often involving the black market or otherwise 'mysterious' transnational networks.

The Space of Disappearance and New Repositioning

As it did in the other Baltic States, Lithuanian national cinema existed before 1991 when the world *de jure* recognised the restoration of an independent state, and before the withdrawal of the Soviet army from the state's territory in 1993 rendered that independence official. The world discovered the phenomenon of Lithuanian cinema, however, only at the beginning of the 1990s, particularly after young Lithuanian film-makers received recognition at a number of international film events. Most notably, Audrius Stonys's documentary *Neregių žemė/ Earth of the Blind* (1992)[1] won the European Felix (now called a European Film Award) for the 'Best European Documentary', and Šarūnas Bartas's feature fiction *Trys dienos/Three Days* (1991) premiered at the Berlinale and was nominated for a European Felix in 1992 under the category of 'Young European Film'. Bartas and Stonys were part of a new generation of national film-makers (a list that includes Arūnas Matelis, Valdas Navasaitis, and others) that emerged when Soviet Lithuania was transforming into a cultural and political space of 'disappearance'. After the 11 March 1990 declaration of independence, it took more than a decade to restore the status of Lithuania as a 'European' state. Acbar Abbas's term 'disappearance', used to describe Hong Kong's status as a state and its cinema in the 1990s (2006: 72–99), aptly illustrates the situation of Lithuania and Lithuanians who suddenly discovered themselves faced with the evaporation of the previous state and their cultural identity. According to Abbas, 'disappearance connotes not simply a vanishing without a trace, an absence, but an elusive and problematic presence . . .' (2007:114) which, for most of Lithuanians, meant living in spatial and temporal heterotopias – an independent capitalist state with the domestic and mental relics of communism. In other words, Lithuanians experienced a kind of diffraction of previously existing time zones and the splitting of previously existing unbroken spaces, and the constitution of new spatio-temporal constructs. To paraphrase the insights of Michel Foucault, they emerged in the epoch of simultaneity: in the epoch of juxtaposition, of the near and far, of the side by side and of the dispersed (1986: 229).

Lithuanian cinema has responded and adapted to this specific historic situation by rejecting traditional realism and its representational schemes because the transformations of social and political life had become too difficult to represent. This is especially noticeable in Lithuanian films of the early 1990s, namely *Praėjusios dienos atminimui/In the Memory of a Day Gone By* (Šarūnas Bartas, 1990), *Dešimt minučių prieš Ikaro skrydį/Ten Minutes Before the Flight of Icarus* (Arūnas Matelis, 1991), *Rudens sniegas/ The Autumn Snow* (Valdas Navasaitis, 1992) and *Earth of the Blind*, all of which represent the memory of days gone by and a *déjà disparu* cultural space.

It should be noted that, during the Soviet period, Lithuanian national cinema (especially films produced in the 1960s and 1970s by auteurs Vytautas Žalakevičius, Marijonas Giedrys, Almantas Grikevičius and Raimondas Vabalas) was regarded as a form of cultural maintenance, a means of sustaining national identity and countervailing the cultural dominance of mainstream Soviet cinema which originated from an environment that was stronger in industrial and ideological terms. Therefore, film-making could be considered as a certain tactical response to the condition of 'statelessness'. From the point of view of national identity, it is significant that the Lithuanian language was used in these films and that they contained political and cultural subtexts (expressed via songs, references to art works or historical/cultural figures) that appealed exclusively to, and were comprehensible only to, Lithuanian audiences. Moreover, these films were mainly produced in the Lithuanian Film Studio by Lithuanian cineastes and contained local stories aimed at local audiences. The distinctiveness of the national auteur cinema in the Soviet context has been accurately defined by the State Institute of Cinematography- (VGIK) trained Lithuanian film critic Saulius Macaitis:

> First of all, this kind of filmmaking cannot be called Soviet. Talented Russian filmmakers of the time, sensing the 'thaw' attempted to rethink their own revolutionary history without forgetting to praise their idols. Lithuania has never been the country of revolutions. Thus, young filmmakers chose a different path for their work than Russian directors.
>
> [...] In the best films of the time, the issues of tragic divisions in post-war Lithuania when brothers killed each other transcended a concrete geopolitical level and reached a universal dimension. Another issue, namely that of survival without losing conscience and basic human values, was raised in films associated with the so-called poetic Lithuanian filmmaking. (8)

These films were usually placed into a category known as 'black Lithuanian film' by censors from the State Committee for Cinematography, *Goskino*, because they did not demonstrate a positive attitude towards Soviet life and Soviet people. As such, they often risked being 'shelved' or being allowed only for internal distribution (that is, only in the cinemas of the Soviet Republic of Lithuania) and, thus, to stand against, to use Hamid Dabashi's words, 'the over-riding presence of an absence' (cited in Abbas 2007: 114).

Even after independence, however, the challenges of 'marginalisation' and 'invisibility' remained crucial for Lithuanian film even when Lithuania joined the World Trade Organization in 2001 and following integration into the European cultural, political and economic space after European Union membership in 2004. Lithuanian film-industry players, especially the ones representing older generation, found it difficult to adapt to global markets and successfully function within them, and, as Mazierska puts it, to 'close various gaps between the old socialist East and capitalist West [. . .]' (2011:74).

Liquid Identity and a New Man in Perpetual Motion

Stuart Hall suggests that cultural identity is 'a matter of "becoming" as well as of "being"'. He argues that '[cultural identity] belongs to the future as much as to the past. It is not something that already exists, transcending place, time, history and culture,' it undergoes constant transformation (706). In this section I shall analyse Lithuanian film-makers' attempts to reflect the crystallisation of a new Lithuanian identity and the emergence of new subjectivities which are signifiers of new types of work, family and urban forms, and other conditions in the post-industrial and neo-liberal society. I shall also examine cinematic representations of transnational economic, political and sociocultural proximities and interconnections that produced, on the one hand, new and controversial lifestyles and, on the other, harmonious and smooth societal developments. As is the case in Eastern European cinema in general, contemporary Lithuanian cinema focuses on 'a new array of characters' that include 'morally ambiguous protagonists' as Dina Iordanova names them (2012: xvi). These are typically smugglers or nomads of the urban variety [unlike the primordial provincials seen in a range of Polish or Hungarian films, such as Wojciech Smarzowski's *Dom zły / The Dark House* (2009, Poland), Xawery Żulawski, *Wojna polsko-ruska / Snow White and Russian Red* (2009, Poland) or Kornél Mundruczó's *Delta* (2008, Hungary/Germany)], operating outside the Foucauldian 'disciplinary society'. Such protagonists are quite typical in films produced in the 2000s by different generations of Lithuanian film-makers, namely Bartas, Kristina Buožytė, Ignas Miškinis, Valdas Navasaitis, Algimantas Puipa, Emilis Vėlyvis and Kristijonas Vildžiūnas. Therefore, these protagonists could be scrutinised from the point of view of new societal and economical phenomena which developed in the post-Soviet and transnational labour and migration environment, after Lithuania had joined the European Union, the Schengen Area zone and the World Trade Organization, which brought opportunities for mobility and to do business and make deals transnationally. Moreover, good knowledge of Eastern and Western business 'cultures' and the relatively large community of Lithuanian emigrants in the Western countries made Lithuania an attractive 'point of contact' and 'transit country' for all kinds of deals characteristic of transnational markets, including the 'black' market. The effects of the aforementioned geopolitical and economic transformations have been most dramatic in the local labour milieu, in lifestyles and in societal norms. In the remainder of this section I shall look into the ways in which these issues are represented and reflected on in a selection of films that notably includes Navasaitis's *Perpetuum Mobile* (2008, Lithuania), Vildžiūnas's *Nuomos sutartis/The Lease* (2002), Buožytė's *Kolekcionierė/Collectress* (2008) and Miškinis's *Artimos šviesos/Low Lights* (2009, Lithuania/Germany).

In his essay *From Pilgrim to Tourist – or a Short History of Identity*, Bauman describes the contemporary postmodern world which 'is retailoring itself to the measure of the vagabond' (1996: 28–9), as a 'life-game' in which its players – all types of consumers – keep changing in the course of playing, and look ceaselessly for 'open options'. He argues that this figure of contemporary man – 'a gamer' – rapidly changes identities and adopts new ones like someone might change costumes. He/she avoids long-term commitments and attachments to one place or community, vocation, 'loyalty to anything and anybody', and lives in a kind of 'continuous present' (1996: 23–4). For Bauman the contemporary 'vagabond' is the result of 'the scarcity of settled places' (1996: 28–9). This description of a 'postmodern gamer' and 'vagabond' perfectly corresponds to the protagonists of *Perpetuum Mobile*, *The Lease* and *Aš esi tu/You am I* (2006, Lithuania/Germany), *Collectress* and *Low Lights*. For instance, the characters in *Perpetuum Mobile* – Ronas, Adi and Dina – assemble in a bar, co-owned by Adi and a mysterious elderly barman, spending their days drinking, gambling, chatting with bar visitors and local prostitutes, making dirty deals with strange businessmen, strolling along the streets of Vilnius and doing various other trivial, pleasant and adventurous things. They enjoy each moment of life, have no long-term commitments or attachments to anybody, are open to any new opportunities 'destiny' offers and do not worry about anything; even a television report on the forthcoming global financial crisis makes no impression on them. Ronas is a divorced and unemployed biologist whose current

Figure 11.1 Gamers taking risks in *Perpetuum Mobile*.

interests are mainly limited to alcohol, women and gambling. He rarely sees his parents, ex-wife or his son. Even important family events fail to entice him to spend some time with the family and fulfil his paternal duty. Precarious social and financial conditions do not weigh on him at all, as his wealthy female friend (an architect) offers him a comfortable shelter, allowing him enjoy his freedom with friends and the adventurist Dina. It seems that none of Ronas's male friends are in close relations with women, nor do they have stable careers; they could be perceived as typical males in midlife crises. As for Dina (who works sporadically as a model), she is best described as an archetypal contemporary 'femme fatale'. She makes fools of Ronas and Adi and absconds to the United States after stealing a considerable sum from the bar, causing significant problems for Adi.

The characters of *Perpetuum Mobile* fancy the contemporary urban nomadic lifestyles of Bauman's 'vagabond' and 'player', practising these life strategies in order to avoid 'being bound and fixed' (Bauman 1995: 91). They lack a definite, fixed identity, partner or place of residence, and work as if their life model was based on the cycles of nature – 'defoliation, vegetation and migration' – as Adi and Ronas put it in the final sequence of the film. The two friends end up penniless, abandoned by the woman, and kicked out of the bar, yet still looking forward to new 'games to play' and new identities to nurture. This stance is perfectly compatible with

Bauman's theorisation of the vagabond whose movements are 'unpredictable' and who 'has no set destination', for nobody knows 'where he will move next, because he himself does not know nor care much' (1996: 28).

Similar to the protagonists in Navasaitis's film, the characters of films, such as *Low Lights* (Linas, Tadas and Tadas's wife), the *Collectress* (Gailė and the video editor) and *The Lease* (two middle-aged business ladies and a flat lessor), try to prevent their everyday life and professional identity from conforming to 'societal norms' and everyday boredom by taking part in bizarre and hazardous adventures. In these films well-paid and reputable professionals (a speech therapist, businesswomen, insurance agents) suddenly, after experiencing personal crisis, decide to change their societal roles and free themselves from everyday monotony and responsibilities. They temporarily inhabit what Bauman describes as the 'the world-as-player', a 'world of risks, of intuition, of precaution-taking' where 'there are neither laws nor lawlessness, neither order nor chaos. There are just the moves – more or less clever, shrewd or tricky, insightful or misguided' (1996: 31). These players follow certain laws but they are very nearly out of control and beyond being governed, and thus unpredictable. They can be perceived as certain transformers of the Foucauldian 'arts of governing' and constitutors of a new 'kind of cultural form, both political and moral attitude, a way of thinking', which Michel Foucault called 'the art of not being governed quite so much' (Foucault 2007: 45). For instance, Gailė, the protagonist of the *Collectress*, works in a modern clinic specialising in speech therapy. She spends most of her time in the clinic training her patients and participating in professional conferences. After the death of her father, she suddenly finds herself incapable of feeling and expressing emotions and, therefore, decides to restore her numbed sensations with the help of video therapy. To implement her experimental 'treatment' she hires a very skilful freelance video editor. The man is well paid for shooting and editing various provocative situations: deliberately slamming the door on a puppy in her clinic; recklessly driving her boss's car; making love with her sister's fiancé; even endangering her own and the video editor's life while provoking a gang of youths. These activities are staged and partly performed by Gailė. The woman is so involved in this new experimental game therapy that she is ready to sacrifice her job and relationship with her only sister. Meanwhile, the 'editor' wants to give up this bizarre and stressful job, especially when he begins to fall in love with Gailė. Unfortunately he cannot afford to stop working for her because of the debts he has accumulated through his addiction to gambling and drinking. Gailė exploits his misfortune, becoming a kind of 'governor' of the man. She pays back his gambling debts (while revealing herself as a highly qualified gambler) and thus makes a long-term deal with him. Notably in *Collectress*, similarly to *Perpetuum Mobile*, we encounter a type of 'creative worker' operating outside the standard labour relations, laws and order. They live and work primarily in accordance with their own regulations and timetables. For example, the video editor edits film shots in the way he prefers, disregarding his clients' requests, and scrupulously 'plans' drinking and gambling hours in his agenda while sometimes forgetting about 'business' meetings. Both characters of the *Collectress* are sporadically 'governed' by others, or by each other, in order to sustain the very process of the activity. Decidedly, Gailė and 'the editor' are more engaged in the processes of gambling and collecting new emotions than in achieving any tangible results.

Despite the quite rapid 'Westernization' of Lithuanian life and the relatively smooth integration into European, as well as global, economic and political milieus, insecurity and uncertainty remain attendant features of the Lithuanian society. This is related to unstable social relations (especially within the family), decreased reliance on family support, and a precarious economic situation – manifested by financial instability, high unemployment rates and the vulnerability of small businesses – that has generated instability in the labour market. And this 'culture of uncertainty', as Andrew Beck indicates in his writings about cultural workers, does not 'just affect cultural workers in the workplace; it also produces a state of mind and being where security is sought after, worried about, lost and mourned' (6). This lack of security and satisfaction clearly manifests itself in the living and working situations of post-Soviet Lithuanians represented on cinema screens, notably in Vildžiūnas's films *The Lease* and *You am I*. For instance, in *The Lease* we observe the inner drama of the heroine, a middle-aged businesswoman who, having just experienced the collapse of her second marriage, must deal with her estrangement from her sister and daughter. Moreover, she has no proper working and living space: she lives in a temporary flat and desperately moves her office from one location to another as if trying to escape from something or somebody. Her life changes with the intervention in her claustrophobic realm of a young adventurist–entrepreneur involved in a very unethical and non-transparent business: he lets his flat to single, pretty, middle-aged women and dates them for as long as the lease is valid. In both instances, this transience symbolises the inability to find one's own place in the new, post-Soviet world.

In *You am I* we witness the mental and physical escape from the everyday routine and stressful life of a middle-aged architect, also divorced, who leaves the city for the countryside where he constructs a tiny tree house above the river and, in this way, enjoys his quiet existence. These traumatic images of a 'transition generation' reveal their inner imprisonment (or inner exile), their unreadiness to live in a constantly changing world and their inability to cope with new challenges resulting from increasing consumerism and human alienation and decreasing social solidarity and equality. Ultimately, they are not ready and able to handle the steadily growing responsibility of an individual (especially an intellectual) having to cope with his/her own fears and uncertainties. This situation echoes the description offered by Bauman in *Liquid Times: Living in an Age of Uncertainty* where he claims that 'although the risks and contradictions of life go on being as socially produced as ever, the duty and necessity of coping with them has [sic] been delegated to our individual selves' (Bauman 2007: 14).

Linas, Tadas and his wife, the protagonists of *Low Lights*, are in their thirties and – unlike the characters in *The Lease* and *You am I* – live a life practically free from fear and uncertainty. They feel the need to challenge the boredom of everyday life, however, and the certain commodification, even standardisation, of interpersonal relationships in work and family life. Linas, a freelance interior designer and restorer, finds his own way of dealing with the aforementioned contemporary urbanised man's 'obstructions' while engaging himself in odd 'travel games' played on micro (within a city) and macro scales (beyond the city). Tadas and his wife live a 'normal' life, have decent and stable jobs in an insurance company, and, as they are regarded as reliable consumers by the banking sector, are granted credit to buy a new car and a fancy apartment in a new district of Vilnius. But is this all they require to be a happy couple? Every day they dress in grey 'bureau' clothes, leave their home at the same time, travel the same itinerary to the office and back home, and each day repetitively exchange the same phrases with each other and with their clients. When the couples meets in the morning or late evening, neither speaks to the other, even on the subject of their work which they do not really enjoy. Average, boring people, whose everyday life is 'colonized by the commodity', they need 'liberation', 'entertainment' and 'distraction' in order to change this situation, or, as Henri Lefebvre, puts it to 'break with the everyday (. . .) and not only as far as work is concerned, but also for day-to-day family life' as leisure 'tends to come into being entirely outside of the everyday realm' (2003: 229). An adventurist, Linas realises the 'problem' facing his friend, and proposes to Tadas a kind of 'distraction', and a way for 'liberation', in the form of an unusual aimless drive inside the city, having no definite destination or clear point. Tadas's wife also engages in this night-time travel game; she follows the two men, interacts with stylish youngsters, temporarily 'borrows' a fancy car and finally enjoys a drive and a smoke with the two men.

Low Lights is structured as a road film, and contains elements of 'the urban road movie'. The term was employed by David Laderman to describe films in which urban mobility visibly dominates the plot (Laderman, 175). This cinematic form is well suited to examine the identity crisis experienced by young Lithuanians who lead their monotonous family lives and boring careers aimed at domestic comfort, financial and social security, and, in this way, find themselves trapped in a contemporary commoditised world. The cinematic form of a road movie, as Mazierska and Rascaroli claim, 'has the ability to mirror and interpret phenomena such as shifting European borders; the formation of new personal, national, regional and international identities; the transformation of communities; and, more generally, the character of movement in postmodernity' (2). Thus, the night journeys of the three protagonists could be viewed as a metaphor for the lack of adventurism, openness and happiness in a Lithuanian society desperately attempting to adjust to, and adopt, Western lifestyles.

Migration and Transnationalisation

Migration, both to and from Lithuania, has been poorly reflected in Lithuanian cinema despite the fact that, since the 1990s, more than 600,000, of a population of 3.5 million, have left the country. This trend continues; according to the data of the International Organization for Migration Vilnius Office, each year more than thirty thousand people migrate to other countries, mainly within the European Union, while the number of temporary residing and working foreigners (from the European Union and elsewhere) is one of the lowest in the European Community (International Organization for Migration, 5–8).

The reasons behind the high level of emigration and low immigration are purely economic and relate to the nation's relatively high unemployment rate and lower than the EU average minimum wage. Another important factor is the formation of so-called 'emigration networks' (especially in the United Kingdom, Ireland, Norway and Spain) in which family members and friends function as networkers and encourage further emigration. This has a strong effect on the social and economic life of Lithuania, as almost every family has members or friends temporarily working, or already settled, in foreign countries. The migrants' contribution to the Lithuanian social and economic life is enormous, with remittances accounting for more money than the nation receives from European

Structural Funds. Moreover, emigrants influence the emergence of new business models and new lifestyles in the society as the greatest number of immigrants entering the country are Lithuanians who come back after temporary residence and work abroad (mainly from the European Union and Russia). In society a negative opinion of migration prevails, however, because, in public discourse, the downsides of emigration (demographic decline, population aging, negative consequence to families, etc.) are emphasised. The aforementioned phenomenon is quite rarely reflected on the Lithuanian screen and is limited to a handful of feature films, such as, *Nereikalingi žmonės/ The Loss* (Maris Martinsons, 2008), *Emigrantai/ Emigrants* (Justinas Krisiūnas, 2013) and the short fiction *Laikinai/ Temporarily* (Jūratė Samulionytė, 2011). In these films the image of migrants is quite stereotypical and does not differ much from the ones depicted in foreign movies.

It should be noted that, since the Soviet occupation in the 1940s, the population of Lithuania has been in gradual decline. From the 1940s to the 1990s, the nation lost one-third of its inhabitants as a result of war, expatriation, Stalinist-era killings and the drastic deterritorialisation and reterritorialisation policies of the Soviet Union. Here I would like to invoke Deleuze's and Guattari's theories of deterritorialisation and reterritorialisation. The first is highlighted as a movement by which something escapes or departs from established relations and exposes new organisations. It is always bound by correlative developments to reterritorialisation which does not literally mean returning to the original territory but, rather, the ways in which deterritorialised elements recombine and enter new formations. According to philosophers, these processes have destructive consequences because deterritorialisation and reterritorialisation shatter the subject (1987: 421). Actually, for Soviet nations, this forced internationalisation had mainly negative consequences and caused both spiritual and cultural degradation (especially in Siberia and Middle Asia). This theme emerged on Lithuanian screens only after the 1990s, mainly in works of Bartas (for example, *Three Days*), *Mūsų nedaug/ Few of Us* (1996, Lithuania/France/Portugal/Germany), *Septyni nematomi žmonės/ Seven Invisible Men* (2005, Lithuania/France/Portugal/Holland) and in Puipa's *Žaibo nušviesti/ Hit by Lightning* (1995) and Gytis Lukšas's *Duburys/ Vortex* (2009). Interestingly, Lithuanian films of the Soviet period focused mainly on inner migration processes – such as the relocation of people from villages to cities – which were related to the industrialisation and modernisation of the country and were perceived by Soviet authorities as a positive societal shift as it served to create modern Soviet person. Other types of internal and external migrations were viewed disapprovingly and were considered to have negative consequences for such a small nation. Those who left the country and moved to the West were primarily depicted as selfish traitors and pre-Soviet Lithuania bourgeois (a former army officer in Raimondas Vabalas's 1966 *Laiptai į dangų/The Stairs to Heaven*). Cinema depicted the representatives of new (Soviet) Lithuanian intelligentsia choosing to stay in the country and work with their comrades despite being offered promising careers elsewhere in the Soviet Union (a young scholar in Vabalas's 1980 *Rungtynės nuo 9 iki 9/The Contest from 9 to 9*). Generally, migration from other Soviet Republics to Lithuania was also not widely represented even though Soviet policies strongly encouraged such deterritorialisation. For example, in the case of mixed marriage, a young couple might be awarded an apartment while young professionals could get better-paid jobs outside their native Soviet republic. Mixed couples were quite rare in Lithuanian cinema and depicted only when they faced a crisis which could be solved solely by a foreign partner's complete cultural integration into the Lithuanian nation, as was the case in *Perskeltas dangus/The Split Sky*, (Marijonas Giedrys, 1974).

As I have already mentioned, in the 2000s Lithuanians' ability to travel internationally and to do business and make deals transnationally were greatly enhanced by Lithuania's integration into the European community in 2004 and entry into the Schengen Zone a few years later. Moreover, Lithuanians' knowledge of both 'Eastern' and 'Western' business 'cultures' and the relatively large network of émigrés in Western countries made Lithuania an attractive transit site and point of contact for dealing on the transnational market. This includes the black market, particularly the fields of human trafficking and the smuggling of drugs, cigarettes and alcohol. These geopolitical and economic factors have had a dramatic effect on the Lithuanian economy and – unlike migration – have been quite widely reflected in contemporary Lithuanian cinema. For instance, in Puipa's film *Miegančių drugelių tvirtovė/The Fortress of Sleeping Butterflies* (2012) the main character, Monika, a wealthy middle-aged genealogist, temporarily accommodates in her old villa three young girls deported from Germany – former forced prostitutes – and takes great care of them. The trope of 'mysterious' transnational work is also prominent in the previously discussed films, *Perpetuum Mobile* and *Low Lights*, in which the protagonists escape to the United States after stealing friends' money (in the case of Dina) or return from the United States after being kicked out of the country because of involvement with illegal activities (in the case of Linas). In certain films, however, such as the comedies *5 dienų avantiūra/5 Day Scam* (Žeraldas Povilaitis, 2008) and Emilis Vėlyvis's *Zero II* (2010) and *Redirected*, or the mixed-genre film *Indigène d'Eurasie/Eastern Drift,* 2010, Lithuania/France/Russia) by Bartas, we encounter representations of foreign 'wheeler-dealers' coming to Vilnius for some non-transparent business while French and Russian 'mafia' types (mainly drug dealers) roughly handle their partners/competitors in Vilnius. In the case of *5 Day Scam,* it is the Greek, Eros Giannakakis, a pop music 'expert', who comes to Vilnius to look for new pop music talents (especially young females) for a European television show. In *Zero II,* a mysterious Asian, the so-called 'Jackie Chan', is caught with a large amount of 'goods' and is kept imprisoned by local mafiosi. In *Redirected* a bunch of British gangsters is tracked by a bigger British gang from whom they stole a significant sum of money.

In the aforementioned films, especially *Zero II* and *Eastern Drift,* Lithuania is represented as a dynamic, transcultural transit country, slightly 'wild' but also quite 'civilised', where even certain criminals have manners and principles, namely Genia in *Eastern Drift* and Sylvester in *Zero II.* For example, *Zero II* starts with a shot of a huge poster of 'Vilnius – European Capital of Culture 2009' fixed on the city limit to welcome arriving city guests. In the next shot we get a slightly controversial picture of this 'city of culture'; a police officer uses sexual services and sells Lithuanian policemen's uniforms to criminals, all right next to the poster. Thus, the two sides of this post-Soviet country (official and unofficial) are marked and reveal that inter-European and transnational economic, political and sociocultural proximities and interconnections can bring chaos and mess as well as seemingly harmonious and smooth developments. As Steven Vertovec argues, 'globalization itself has not produced a smooth, borderless, integrated global order, transnationalism has not entailed consistent kinds of social formations or practices' and as 'transnationalism is manifestation of globalization, its constituent processes and outcomes are multiple and messy too' (Vertovec, 2).

The similarly controversial situation of Lithuania's transnationalisation is addressed in *Eastern Drift* in which, during the opening sequence, an image of an unnamed harbour in France is seen to a background of pleasant ambient music. The idyll is suddenly distorted by the emergence of Genia, the protagonist played by Bartas himself, and his 'confession' in accented French:

> The time went by and the Soviet Union collapsed. It was total chaos, so it was easy to take an advantage [. . .] I've been traveling a lot, and spent much time in France. I don't really have any home. Paris, Moscow, Vilnius, Minsk, Warsaw. I have plenty of enemies [. . .] Life is short. The major part of it is over. I didn't even notice. I would like to live a normal life. Wherever you are you're just a guy with no roots other than a criminal past. A Eurasian native.

For those who know Bartas's films, this monologue is unexpected and surprising, especially when Genia speaks for himself in the first person and doing so as if it gives a voice to the post-Soviet 'subaltern' who, for quite a long time, had been represented and whose voice had been subsumed by the 'bigger brother' Russia. Genia is an educated dealer and smuggler from 'New Europe', mimicking the typical image of an Eastern European male seen in Western media and film. In contrast to the protagonists of Bartas's earlier films (with the exception of *Freedom* and *Seven Invisible Men*), Genia undertakes his journeys and implements his illegal deals intentionally and meaningfully, and without any possibility of escaping the business. Thus, the newly (re)constituted transnational character (bridging West and East) can be perfectly depicted in Deleuze's concept of 'a new race of characters' who are a 'kind of mutants: they saw rather than acted, they were seers'. These are the inhabitants of newly emerged specific constructs: 'any spaces whatever', deserted, but inhabited, abandoned warehouses, waste sites and cities under demolition or reconstruction process' (Deleuze, xi). This depiction of post-war Europeans represented in a neorealist cinema is quite close to Bartas's description of Eastern Europeans after post-1989 political and economic shifts. His films can be perceived as furnishing a bridge that links post-communist Eurasia to Western Europe. These works, however, do not really belong to post-1989 European cinema that manifests a new Europe and explicitly articulates, in words of Luisa Rivi, a 'post-1989 European cinema and European identity firmly grounded in the specific post-Cold War historical juncture and sensibility' (Rivi, 64). Instead, Bartas depicts different post-communist nations healing historical traumas, grappling with the issue of the post-1989 identity and the damage of an artificially created and imposed (Soviet) multicultural and multinational belonging. Bartas's films implicitly indicate the increasing threats of moral and mental deprivation in dystopian societies.

Conclusion

In this chapter I have attempted to reveal how the process of a slow and challenging economic, cultural and political transformation of post-Soviet Lithuania is represented in the number of films produced during the first decades of independence. These films chart Lithuanian society's unsteady transition from a certain space of 'disappearance', which characterised the aftermath of independence from the Soviet Union, towards an independent state that is an integral part of the European Community, as well as the desire to construct a new regional identity within 'Northern' Europe.

These films comment and reflect upon the existence of individuals in the constantly shifting and globalising world that promises a seemingly stable and secure life. The films under discussion reveal a condition of people who have suffered in the recent past from dramatic and drastic deterritorialisations and reterritorialisations, and who, therefore, had to develop tactics – of a 'player' and a 'dealer' – in order to survive and function in a new and foreign sociocultural and economic order and to manoeuvre between the political and economic agendas of the Eastern and the Western worlds. The transitional status of the Lithuanian people and state is explicitly signified by the titles of the films discussed above: *Zero II*, *Redirected*, *Eastern Drift* (released under the title *Indigène d'Eurasie*) and *Perpetuum Mobile*.[2]

CHAPTER 12

Lessons of Neo-liberalism: Co-productions and the Changing Image of Estonian Cinema

Eva Näripea (The National Archives of Estonia and the Estonian Academy of Arts)

The primary purpose of this chapter is to chart the terrain of post-Soviet Estonian cinema from the perspective of international co-operation and financing. The main issue concerns the impact of transition to the neo-liberal variety of capitalism on both the production processes and filmic text in terms of the dynamics of 'national' and 'transnational' currents on the cinematic field. To contextualise the changes that have occurred over recent decades, parts of the chapter will provide 'flashbacks' to the questions of trans/nationalism and co-production practices during the Soviet period. These historical shifts and (metaphorical) 'journeys' reflect the geopolitical position of Estonia in the border zone between 'East' and 'West'. Both co-productions analysed in the final section of this chapter – Peeter Simm's *Kõrini/Fed Up!* (2006, Estonia/Germany) and Marko Raat's *Lumekuninganna/The Snow Queen* (2010 Norway/Estonia) – address a deep-seated sense of 'liminality' in the collective Estonian psyche which is torn between a desire to belong to the 'advanced North' (in global as well as regional terms) and a persistent spectre of historical 'Eastern' subjugation. The two case studies, introducing examples of popular and auteurial modes of expression, offer insights into screen manifestations of the human condition in the neo-liberal age, flows of finances and talent, distribution patterns and audience reactions. The investigation of production processes of these films accentuates a number of risks involved in the co-productive mode, especially in relation to small cinema cultures in search of their identity.

Cinema and Nation: Struggles with the 'Other'

Estonian cinema has rarely fit neatly within the notion of 'national cinema'. During Soviet times, ideological instructions, aesthetic norms and technical know-how were largely determined centrally in Moscow and transferred to the republican studios as non-negotiable directives. Overall, the Soviet cinema industry functioned as a transnational enterprise: multinational talent from the various Soviet republics was trained exclusively in Moscow; the work of republican studios was centrally co-ordinated in terms of ideological tenets and control, as well as allocation of finances; the configuration of crews and cast was regularly international; and the resulting films were distributed on the Union-wide cinema and television network. As the scarcity of state support and the extremely small size of the local market had prevented the Estonian film industry from establishing a viable national tradition during the interwar period, post-war audiences regarded the Soviet cinematic invasion as a by-product of Russo-Soviet imperialism and, hence, approached it with a fair amount of suspicion, if not outright contempt. Moreover, though the initial wave of 'cinematic troops', loyal to the Soviet cause and perceived as ignorant, even incompetent intruders of foreign descent, were soon replaced by image-makers of local background and screen projections of decisively local, sometimes even subversive nature, the Estonian audiences never quite embraced the output of Tallinnfilm, the 'subsidiary' of *Goskino* (USSR State Committee for Cinematography), as an undisputed part of national, that is, contra-Soviet culture (Näripea 2012).

Interestingly, the collapse of the Soviet Union in 1991, preceded by the abolishment of film censorship in 1988, was not immediately accompanied with a change in the public image of Estonian screen culture as a 'national' phenomenon. Rather, the untrammelled influx of spectacular and uplifting Hollywood blockbusters threw into sharp relief the bleak social realism preferred by local film-makers finally liberated of the obligation to provide airbrushed images of Soviet past and present. The high production values, too, stood in stark contrast with the more than modest resources at the disposal of the newly established local small production companies. Such contrasts with dominant Western output contributed to the sense of alienation that continues to haunt Estonian spectatorship to this date. In part, this is also due to the fact that many local film-makers gravitate towards the auteurist mode of cinematic expression. Those who do choose to appeal to entertainment rarely succeed in earning the affection of audiences precisely because of unequal competition with the hegemonic Hollywood product.

Cinema and Neo-liberalism: New Directions

The collapse of the Soviet Union led to the abolishment of the vertically integrated film industry. Though the Estonian state continued to fund

Tallinnfilm until 1993, film production was soon completely separated from the state on the institutional level (unlike theatres which continued to be owned by the state). Once all (single- or double-screen) cinemas were privatised they went out of business one after the other and were, in due course, replaced by multiplex cinemas and a few art house establishments that were typically situated in the major urban centres of Tallinn and Tartu. In 1993, the institution-based system of financing was replaced by a project-based system. Initially, the minister of culture and education formed a council of film-makers whose task was to consider and evaluate grant applications. Thus, funding of films was put in the hands of film-makers themselves and was based on a model in operation in Scandinavia that started in the 1960s. In 1994 the Cultural Endowment that had operated in interwar Estonia was restored, with the funds to be distributed not only to film-making but also to other fields of professional and amateur art coming from alcohol and tobacco sales taxes, a percentage of which (about 3 to 3.5 per cent) was allocated for the endowment.

In 1997 the Estonian Film Foundation (since 2013 the Estonian Film Institute) was established to support, with tax-payers' money, film production as well as distribution. The budget of the foundation has grown annually, as have production numbers (ranging from one feature film in 1997 to ten in 2012), although film-makers continue to complain about insufficient funding. In 2012, the budget of the Estonian Film Foundation for funding development, production and distribution of local films (including feature-length and short films, documentaries and animation) was €3.8 million (Baltic Films, 5).[1] The Cultural Endowment contributed an additional €1.7 million which included support to film culture in general (publishing, research grants, film events and so on), and the Estonian Ministry of Culture €571,000. The pan-European MEDIA programme has supported the development and distribution of Estonian films since 2002 with a total of €1.8 million. Eurimages, set up in 1989 to fund European co-productions, funded between 2002 and 2012 nine projects with Estonian involvement to the sum of €3.3 million.

To a significant extent, the dynamics of Estonian cinematic ecology, as well as those of culture in general, have been determined by the fact that, after the dissolution of the Soviet Union, the Estonian political establishment, alongside other Baltic states and Russia, opted for a path of radical and uncompromised neo-liberal capitalism. This was characterised by a gradual dismantling of the social welfare system, in contrast to Visegrád countries, which opted for an embedded type of capitalism (see Bohle and Greskovits) that balanced marketisation with social protection and services. In Estonia, neo-liberalisation has had the effect of commodification of culture and glorification of 'creative industries' which, according to the dominant political position, should, in principle, be self-sufficient and independent of any state subsidy, either surviving on the 'free market' or perishing if there is no demand. Thus, from the governmental point of view, which echoes prevailing public perception, the local film industry appears to be already too dependent on tax-payers' resources while, from the film-making community's vantage point, the scarcity of public funding has thrown it into a more or less vegetative state of existence, or at least keeps it from realising its full potential. The project-based funding model, very much a symptom of neo-liberal economy, has turned creative talent, as well as technical crew, into a modern-day precariat, without a stable income, basic social guarantees and overall sense of security; in short, a perfect example of neo-liberal labour 'flexibility' (cf. Jäckel 2003b, 19). According to David Harvey, this commodification of cultural forms is an expression of 'accumulation by dispossession', the key feature of neo-liberal order (Harvey 2005b, 148), which testifies to 'a radicalized return to nineteenth-century principles of the free market' (Kapur and Wagner, 2) and which affects most severely the weakest cohorts of society. Even if the public funding of film culture has grown from next to nothing to slightly over €6 million[2] in 2012 (equal to the average budget of 1.2 European films, see Kissa; or 2.4 Danish films, see Direitinho), the overall (political) attitude considers cinema to be a business that should not rely on public subsidies which serve to distort the free market.

The neo-liberal frame of mind reveals itself also in a special emphasis on entrepreneurship as the preferred and publicly promoted mode of image-making practice. While, traditionally, cinema has been regarded in Europe (including the former Eastern bloc) first and foremost as an art form – admittedly one that perhaps requires a more intensive management of resources, creative processes and outcomes than older media – and an effective tool for shaping dominant values and perceptions, or, to put it bluntly, an instrument of propaganda, the global spread of neo-liberalism has coincided with the rise of business-like attitudes towards the 'cinematic merchandise'. Two recent documents offer useful insights into prevailing (political) perspectives on the Estonian film industry and their fundamental conflict with those of film-makers. On the one hand, the language used in the Ministry of Culture's report 'Directions of Cultural Development 2020', clearly presents a vision of local cinematic ecology in 2020 as primarily a commercially geared endeavour, stressing the internationalisation of the Estonian film industry by means of co-productions and export of both technological skill and geographical potential. Perhaps especially revealing is the statement that '[t]he state supports film production to the extent that creates preconditions for the continuity of professional filmmaking in Estonia', suggesting that any (artistic) development beyond that depends solely on the film-making community's ability to find and/ or earn additional resources (Estonian Ministry of Culture). On the other hand, 'Directions of Estonian Film 2012–2020' (Estonian Film Institute), the result of discussions among the film-making community itself, initiated by the Estonian Film Foundation in 2011, underscores that, while film is a branch of economy, it is also an art form, a vehicle for (national) identity and, importantly, a form of cultural diplomacy which, as such, serves a wider public interest and deserves larger public investments (cf., for example, Jäckel 2000b: 131). Still, the official policy of the newly reorganised foundation, now the Estonian Film Institute, highlights the need to decrease the dependence of local film-making on state subsidy, as its new head Edith Sepp explains:

> previously we have produced [films] only based on cultural incentives, but the state cannot support this on its own, since this requires constant investments. We must increase production volumes, and this can only be done by way of outsourcing, coproducing, minority coproducing. (Taruste)

In short, for policymakers, the lifeline of Estonian cinema appears to be its integration with global circuits of media production which are, alas, dominated by 'profit-driven and power-thirsty media entrepreneurs' (Jäckel 2000b: 146) whose interests obviously contradict those of a minuscule national cinema. At the same time, my interviews with producers and directors indicated that, in their opinion, this point of view is merely an excuse for the reluctance of the neo-liberally minded political establishment to provide sufficient support for economically 'unviable' culture.

Cinema and the Geography of International Co-operation: From Socialism to Capitalism

To facilitate or, rather, enforce the 'friendship of nations', the architects of Soviet-colonial ideology supplemented the oppressive measures of the 'military-industrial complex' with various instruments of cultural assimilation. In cinema, declared early on the most effective medium of mass communication and propaganda, this included setting up, or reorganising, centrally controlled film studios in newly conquered territories, such as those established and/or revamped after World War II in Estonia, Latvia and Lithuania; sending Soviet (Russian) film-makers as 'ideological watchdogs' to those and more distant countries of the Soviet bloc;[3] and promoting co-production practices across and, even beyond, its sphere of influence in an effort of cultural diplomacy.[4] In Soviet Estonia, co-operation with 'sister republics' was quite common, mostly in terms of supplementing local talent with film-makers from other parts of the Soviet Union. Notably, these visiting (and, importantly, invited) artists – most often actors, cinematographers and occasionally scriptwriters – came predominantly from the republics situated in the western part of the USSR, that is, Latvia, Lithuania, the Ukraine and Belarus, while the script consultants were, as a rule, appointed by the central authorities in Moscow. The latter practice can doubtless be considered another exercise in censorship and control. Collaboration with communist countries beyond the USSR was much less common in Estonia. Perhaps the most remarkable exception is the case of Polish director, Marek Piestrak, whose science fiction film *Test pilota Pirxa/The Test of Pilot Pirx* (*Navigaator Pirx* in Estonian, 1978) and fantasy adventure *Klątwa Doliny Węży/ Curse of Snakes Valley* (*Madude oru needus*, 1988) were co-productions between Tallinnfilm and PRF Zespoły Filmowe and Zespół Filmowy Oko, respectively (see Näripea 2010b). Some collaboration was also done with Finland: for instance, on Lennart Meri's documentary *Linnutee tuuled / Winds of Milky Way* (1978) which was made in co-operation with Tallinnfilm, Finnish OY Mainos-TV-Reklam Ab and Hungarian state radio and television. Finally, Estonia, and, in particular, its capital city Tallinn, which features a unique medieval Old Town, provided ready-made 'Western' locations for countless Soviet productions (see Näripea 2004).

Film-makers in post-Soviet Estonia were quickly forced to learn to swim in new capitalist waters if they wished to avoid a rapid demise. As early as 1992, Peeter Urbla directed *Balti armastuslood/Baltic Love Stories* in co-operation with his own production company Exitfilm and Finnish Filminor OY, and *Daam autos/Lady in the Car*, produced by Russian Novoye Vremya, Estonian Freya Film and Finnish Filminor OY. For obvious reasons – cultural as well as geographical vicinity – Finland has remained one of the major co-producing partners for Estonian studios, together with Latvia and Russia. Yet Denmark also established its collaborative presence fairly early into the post-socialist era. Most importantly, after providing rather substantial assistance on shooting *Den sidste viking/ The Last Viking* (1997), directed by Jesper W. Nielsen (and produced by Danmarks Radio, Trust Film Svenska and Zentropa Entertainments) in Estonia, in 1997 Exitfilm was invited by Peter Aalbaek to join the Danish Zentropa network, and is now co-owned by Peeter Urbla (51 per cent) and Zentropa ApS-Denmark (Exitfilm). Between 1993 and 2004 Exitfilm provided production services to eleven feature films from Nordic countries,

Britain, Germany and France, including, perhaps most famously, Lukas Moodysson's *Lilya 4-Ever* (2002, primarily produced by Swedish Memfis Film), partly shot on location in Tallinn and Paldiski, Estonia. In the early to mid 1990s, when almost complete lack of state support to the local film industry threatened to wipe it out altogether,[5] film-makers found some relief by offering their services to foreign productions that attempted to capitalise on post-Soviet exotica, such as the Finnish thriller *City Unplugged* aka *Darkness in Tallinn* (*Tallinn pimeduses*, 1993, directed by Ilkka Järvilaturi, produced by Finnish FilmZolfo and New York-based Upstream Pictures; see Näripea 2010a), the American made-for-television 'Christmas film' (Laaniste) *Candles in the Dark* (1993, directed by Maximilian Schell, produced by Family Productions), and *Letters from the East* (1996, directed by Andrew Grieve, produced by British Lantern East, German Lichtblick and Exitfilm as a minority partner). These undertakings were perhaps especially instructive in terms of acquainting the ex-Soviet talent and crew with capitalist industry practices and production culture. Overall, in the 1990s, animation film, the flagship of Estonian cinema, fared somewhat better than live-action film-making, whether narrative or documentary, because the internationally acclaimed anima-auteurs, such as Priit Pärn, were able to attract funding and find employment in the Nordic countries, securing a smoother transition from one production environment to another (see Robinson). They were also relatively more successful in terms of international recognition and critical praise, even if within the limits of their own niche market. For example, a hand-drawn animation *1985* (1995, directed by Priit Pärn, co-produced by Estonian Eesti Joonisfilm, Finnish Yleisradio OY and British Cine Electra Ltd), dedicated to the centennial of cinema, received awards at several distinguished festivals, such as those in Zagreb (1996, Grand Prix) and Ottawa (1996, Best Design Award). Since 2000, out of sixty-two feature films made in Estonia or with involvement of Estonian studios or funding, thirty are co-productions or co-financed projects.

Negotiations of the 'Old' and the 'New' Europe: *Fed Up!*

Peeter Simm, who made his directorial debut in 1977, has perhaps been the most prolific and consistent co-producing film director in post-Soviet Estonia. All five feature films he has directed since 1994 are co-productions: *Ameerika mäed / American Mountains* (1994) was produced by French 47ème Parallèle, Hungarian Budapest Filmstúdió and Estonian Lege Artis Film, the latter owned and run by Simm himself;[6] *Head käed / Good Hands* (2001) was made in co-operation between Estonian Allfilm and

Latvian Studija F.O.R.M.A.; *Fed Up!* (2006) was a collaboration between Estonian Ruut Film and German Saxonia Media Filmproduktion; *Georg* (2007) was produced by Estonian Allfilm and Lege Artis Film, Russian Tsentr Natsionalnogo Filma and Finnish Matila Röhr Productions; and Lege Artis Film's latest collaboration with Latvian Studija F.O.R.M.A. and Byelorussian Belarusfilm resulted in *Üksik saar/Lonely Island* (2012). Despite (or perhaps because of) all this experience, the film-maker has repeatedly spoken out about the inherent difficulties of co-production practices.

Conceived as the story of relationships between a couple of German crooks and two Estonian prostitutes (Aarma 18),[7] *Fed Up!* finally[8] appeared on screen as a 'tragicomic road-movie' (Feldmanis) with four main characters, travelling from Leipzig, Germany to Estonia. Kaminsky, a dispirited and nearly suicidal former tap dancer, jilted by his wife for a wealthier suitor, decides to take one last trip to Estonia to deliver a jukebox to his friend as a present. To make the journey, he agrees to drive a truck carrying a load of theatrical supplies. Soon his path crosses with Stella, a talented Estonian cellist who moved to Germany soon after the collapse of the Soviet Union to launch a musical career before ending up playing in a third-rate commercial string quartet. Tired of being exploited by her German impresario, including sexually as it seems, she opts for a return to her homeland. By coincidence, a young Estonian man, Hunt, hides some money he has robbed from a bank in Leipzig in Kaminsky's truck. Hunt is picked up by Manfred, a crook turned undertaker and man of God who was hired as a getaway driver by Hunt's boss, and the two chase Kaminsky's truck in Manfred's hearse. This gallery of characters seems to suggest a dynamic of work relations typical of the situation in post-socialist Europe, where the 'Old' continent initially appears as a promised land of new opportunities. Both Stella and Hunt, a swimmer who worked as a lifeguard in Germany before being forced to take up a criminal career, had relocated to the West in the hope of fulfilling the potential of their respective talents, only to see their dreams falling apart in the face of the harsh neo-liberal reality. The exploiters and antagonists of this story are German: Radtke, a shady businessman arranging bank robberies and other questionable dealings; and Stella's impresario Robert whose intentions towards her are less than honourable, both in professional and personal terms. Yet these national oppositions are contested by the fact that Kaminsky and Manfred, identified as German even if the name of the former sounds Slavic, are also taken advantage of by their countrymen. Furthermore, Leipzig as a city in the former German Democratic Republic, itself forms a part of the 'New Europe', thus undermining the binary East–West opposition. This impression is also confirmed spatially, as the film avoids showing either Germany or Estonia as a place more significantly 'developed' or 'underdeveloped' in comparison with the other, thus abstaining from Eastern and/ or Western 'exoticism' and stereotyping. Finally, Stella (or rather Maarja Jakobson, the actress playing Stella) states in the beginning of the film that 'There are three things that everyone should know about the Estonians. First, Estonians are not Russians. Second, Estonians are not Germans. Third . . . There is no difference . . . Yes, there is no difference.' This self-reflexive non-diegetic insert highlights once more the transnational ethos of the film which also finds expression in its happy ending, a perfect, if somewhat sentimental, image of the new 'unification of European nations'; Stella and Kaminsky fall in love and Manfred and Hunt decide to donate the retrieved money to an Estonian village church and also collaborate on the construction of its new roof.

At the time of its making, the film's budget of €1,188,757, which took about two years to raise and represented a modest sum in a German or wider European context, was the largest ever in post-Soviet Estonia. Sixty per cent of the funding came from Estonia, from public funds and private sponsors, granting Ruut Film the title and (veto) rights of the main producer. On the German side, the largest supporters were Filmförderungsanstalt (German Federal Film Board)[9] and Mitteldeutscher Rundfunk (Central German Broadcasting, the public broadcaster for federal states of Thuringia, Saxony and Saxony–Anhalt), with Telepool, München handling the distribution. In securing the German part of the budget, the producers experienced difficulties owing to the small size of the Estonian market (Aarma) and the high proportion of Estonian talent. In addition to director Peeter Simm, two of the four scriptwriters (Simm, Valentin Kuik, Honert and Thomas Steinke), the cinematographer (Rein Kotov) and the composer (Sven Grünberg) were Estonian. Two leading roles were cast with German actors, however, Heio von Stetten (Kaminsky) and Thomas Schmauser (Manfred), mainly to appeal to the tastes of the German audiences, thus guaranteeing the funding from the German television station and the distributor (Ilisson). In retrospect, Artur Talvik, the film's Estonian producer, considers the choice of von Stetten as a mismatch in a feature made for theatrical release, as in Germany he is mainly famous for appearances in television films. The backing from the German Federal Film Board came with a requirement to spend 150 per cent of their contribution in Germany which translated into four shooting days in Leipzig and Rostock, even though, according to Talvik, it would have been at least four times cheaper to shoot in Estonia (Ilisson).

The co-production mode presented some specific restrictions and (mainly) cultural negotiations which perhaps most clearly manifested themselves in the aforementioned numerous rewrites of the script, as the sense of humour of the co-producing partners varied to a considerable extent, with Germans gravitating towards 'safer' solutions (Ilisson); a vivid example of economic (self-)censorship. Simm also reports difficulties in the working process, partly because of the language (the film was shot in German) but especially because of the German actors whose working methods differed remarkably from those to which Simm was accustomed. Talvik has aptly summarised the disparity of the two film-making cultures by saying that the production of *Fed Up!* felt as if 'a group of [Estonian] guerrilla soldiers faced a well-trained [German] army' (Koppel, 102).

Most Estonian critics denounced the film as shallow and bland entertainment (for example, Jõerand 89–91), devoid of local character and the sharpness of Simm's familiar style (for example, Tomberg 2006), or critiqued it for being too 'German' (Leppik). Others saw its light playfulness and universality as positive traits (Feldmanis; Mirme). *Fed Up!* also failed to win popular acclaim; during the opening weekend, it received 547 admissions in Estonia, reaching a domestic spectatorship of about three thousand over the first year (Tõnson 2006). While the German television viewers received it somewhat more favourably, and the film also travelled to other German-speaking countries, its overall lack of international success was an unexpected disappointment to the producers.

A Nordic Fairy Tale? *The Snow Queen*

Marko Raat, one of the first graduates of the local film school set up in 1992, caused a small sensation with his debut, a documentary, *Esteetilistel põhjustel/For Aesthetic Reasons* (1999, produced by Det Danske Filminstitut/ Workshop Haderslev and Nordic Baltic Media Network, producer Karl Jensen). The film features Andres Kurg, an Estonian critic and historian of architecture who travels to Denmark and asks various institutions for permission to relocate to Denmark for aesthetic reasons because he admires the Danish modernist architecture of the 1950s and 1960s. The provocative film, made on a shoestring budget, was funded entirely with Danish resources, made with assistance by Danish cinematographer and editor, and was declared the film of the year by Estonian film critics. In addition to documentaries that provide intriguing insights into the Estonian art world and neo-liberal urbanism, Raat has made three feature-length films and one short narrative film, all relatively low budget. Two of the features are co-productions: *Agent Sinikael/Agent Wild Duck* (2002, produced by Estonian Suhkur Film and Estonian–Danish Exitfilm, in collaboration with Peter Aalbæk Jensen and Zentropa) and *The Snow Queen* (2010, produced by Estonian F-Seitse and Norwegian Pomor Film).

The Snow Queen is loosely based on Hans Christian Andersen's acclaimed fairy tale from 1845. Raat concentrates on a narrative ellipse in Andersen's tale: what happened to Kai after the Snow Queen bewitched him and took the boy to her icy domain. Advertised as a 'fairy tale for adults', the film transfers the story to a contemporary, yet no less fantastic setting, visualised in hauntingly beautiful imagery. In Raat's rendition, the Snow Queen (or simply 'Woman', as indicated in the credits) is a successful businesswoman in her late thirties/early forties whose name is never revealed. Meanwhile the boy, now called Jesper, seems to be in his mid teens, slightly older than in Anderson's version, and Gerda's role as his girlfriend is played down. The Woman suffers from terminal cancer and seeks desperate help from a witch who prescribes a cold environment and the 'blood of a virgin boy' as a potential cure, though in vain, as the story's fatal ending demonstrates. Following his advice, the Woman moves to a modest cottage on a frozen, supposedly magical, lake in a valley surrounded by snowy mountains and hires a contractor to enclose it in a wall of ice blocks. She floods the entire house with water and turns off the heating, transforming the house into a surreal, glacial realm.

The stunning images of this phantasmal frozen terrain, where boundaries between interior and exterior, both human and environmental,

Figure 12.1 *The Snow Queen*. Courtesy of Kaie-Ene Rääk.

get decidedly blurred, seem to evoke the idea of a world pervaded by a distressing sense of coldness, metaphorically speaking, devoid of emotional warmth, meaningful connections and intimacy. What I read as a perceptive critique by Raat of universal shallowness is reinforced by the short-message-service-like dialogues which were dismissed by local critics as simply banal (Ruus 2010; Tõnson 2010).[10] Furthermore, the fact that the Woman is wealthy, yet childless and unmarried, suggests that, in neo-liberalism, 'prosperity' is achieved at a price, especially for women, and that this notion is inevitably linked with profound individualism. In turn, the role of community is diminished, including on the national level. As both *Fed Up!* and *The Snow Queen* demonstrate, loneliness and social atomisation are recurring themes in recent Estonian films. Examples of this include *Sügisball/Autumn Ball* (2007, Estonia) and *Püha Tõnu kiusamine/Temptations of St Tony* (2009, Estonia/Finland/Sweden), both by Veiko Õunpuu, and *Kirjad Inglile/Letters to Angel* (2011, Estonia/Finland/Lithuania/Mauritania) by Sulev Keedus. This thematic tendency coincides with certain broader, global currents as, according to Elizabeth Ezra and Terry Rowden, 'transnational cinema's narrative dynamic is generated by a sense of loss' (Ezra and Rowden, 7). Raat's film, indeed, attests to a move away from local and explicitly national concerns towards a transnational mode of expression. Among other things, this is evident in the somewhat 'neutered', abstracted spaces of *The Snow Queen*, similarly to many other post-Soviet Estonian productions, including *Fed Up!*, where the characteristics of geographical locations are obscured (Mazierska 2010) in one way or another. Moreover, its visceral, bodily effect is comparable to recent films by Lars von Trier and Alejandro González Iñárritu. Still, the film's Nordic sources, names and wintry environs dovetail with a long-standing drive in Estonian society to identify itself as a part of a Nordic, rather than Eastern (European), sphere of culture. Moreover, by choosing to use Estonian actors and to present the story in the Estonian language, to avoid the 'Europudding' effect, a decision which certainly limited the film's chances of wide international exposure, *The Snow Queen* retains a clear sense of its 'nationality', testifying to the fact that '[t]ransnational cinema arises in the interstices between the local and the global' (Ezra and Rowden, 4).

The budget of *The Snow Queen* was €861,529, with €576,483 coming from the Estonian Film Foundation, Estonian Cultural Endowment and Estonian Ministry of Culture. The Norwegian partners invested €210,954 (including €90,857 from the Norwegian Film Institute, €85,178 from FilmCamp, a Norwegian regional resource and infrastructure company, and €34,919 from Pomor Film). An additional €39,998 was contributed by the

MEDIA programme which specifically focuses on promotion of European films outside their country of origin. While the production of *Fed Up!* was initiated on the basis of a long-standing friendship between Simm and Honert, *The Snow Queen*'s search for partners began in the pan-European framework of cinematic co-operation; Raat participated in the Sources 2 training scheme set up by a Dutch foundation with the support of the MEDIA programme for European film professionals working in the field of script and story development. The workshop took place in FilmCamp, situated in a northern Norwegian municipality of Målselv, where Raat was advised to team up with Pomor Film as a Norwegian co-producing partner. FilmCamp, funded by private investors, finances productions shot in the region, which determined in part the location of shooting the exterior scenes of *The Snow Queen* but also matched the diegetic need for a snowy environment, especially because Estonian winters are unpredictable in terms of wintry weather. The Norwegian Film Institute insisted on the involvement of local talent, hence the choice of Norwegian cinematographer and production designer (Marius Matzow Gulbrandsen and Jack van Domburg, respectively). While Raat recalls no restrictive demands made on the content or aesthetics of the film, and the collaboration between the creative talent was generally productive and pleasant, the management of the production process was described as rather stressful, and both Raat and the film's Estonian producer, Kaie-Ene Rääk, admit to clashes in working cultures and have expressed their preference to avoid the co-production mode in the future. As an auteur film, *The Snow Queen* was targeted at a niche market anyway, yet the low domestic admission numbers (1,317 spectators over the first year in Estonian cinemas) testify that it failed to reach its potential audiences. It opened theatrically in neighbouring Latvia, being screened for two weeks in an art house cinema, but never in Norway or any other Nordic countries, perhaps because the Norwegian producers, who hold the rights to the Norwegian market, did not regard the comparatively small Norwegian investments worth the effort of recouping. In addition to television rights sold to stations in Estonia and Switzerland, the film was distributed through the festival circuit (including in Montreal, Helsinki, Mumbai, Lübeck, Cairo, Aubagne, Brussels and Cork), receiving some acclaim, most notably the best director award at the Cape Winelands Film Festival (South African Republic, 2011).

Conclusion

These two examples demonstrate in relief the inherent risks of the co-production mode. Even if policymakers foster the illusion of a shared

European identity, complications in the production process indicate significant cultural differences among the various film-making (and financing) communities. Such differences necessitate negotiation which, in turn, has an impact on the final product. Further dangers, especially with low-budget productions, are presented by the choices of casting and language. Actresses and actors of smaller cultures and languages, even if they present their roles in more widely spoken languages, as was the case with *Fed Up!*, are clearly at a disadvantage when it comes to cross-national audience appeal. *Fed Up!*, featuring a German-speaking cast with two leading roles by Estonian actors, remained alien to both German and Estonian spectators. Furthermore, as a film targeted at a mainstream audience, its production values fell short of the Hollywoodesque glamour expected by such spectators. The distribution reach of *The Snow Queen* was undoubtedly affected by the choice of local cast and language, in addition to the idiosyncratic auteurial narrative mode and visual expression, which also proved discouraging for the film's domestic audience who failed to embrace its transnational qualities. All in all, neither film managed, for different reasons, to enter the field of 'national cinema' proper on the home turf even though, for the attentive viewer, both of them provide revealing insights into, and metaphors of, the human condition in the neo-liberal world order that continues to shape the realities in Estonia and beyond.

In sum, the terrain of co-production is a contested one, both in Estonia and in Europe. On the one hand, it does result in larger budgets and presumably wider possibilities, both in terms of production values and (potential) audience reach, yet, on the other hand, the local producers and directors find it cumbersome to navigate, and audiences are not always willing to embrace its 'transnational' outcomes as equal to works of 'national' cinema. Hence the extra resources found beyond state borders may not necessarily facilitate the production of works that meet the expectations of national (or international) spectatorship, and may also fall short of functioning as profitable commodities and/or cultural ambassadors. Moreover, Anne Jäckel has correctly observed that the preference of large-scale commercial productions on both national and European levels might jeopardise the cultural diversity based on cinematic experimentation and innovation (Jäckel 1997: 119). As in Europe, however, cross-border collaboration remains a necessity in the foreseeable future, both in terms of financial support and cultural negotiation, the film-makers will probably adapt and learn to make the most of the situation.

CHAPTER 13

Decentring Europe from the Fringe: Reimagining Balkan Identities in the Films of the 1990s

Danica Jenkins and Kati Tonkin (University of Western Australia)

During the Cold War the Iron Curtain marked a clear-cut division between 'us' and 'them'. From the point of view of Western Europe, the continent was inhabited by two distinct 'tribes': the civilised 'West' and the exotic, often uncivilised 'others' (Buchowski 2006: 465). The fall of the Berlin Wall in 1989 disrupted these boundaries and brought an uneasy shift in collective identities, provoking, as Michał Buchowski summarises, 'confusion, uncertainty, cognitive dissonance, symbolic disorder, a liminal stage in the rite of passage ... that needed to be worked out' (2006: 465). The incertitude over remapping Europe triggered a revival of orientalism towards the East; as the East Central European states[1] sought to reassert a 'Western' or 'European' identity after decades of cultural and political subjugation, the most eastern of the formerly communist countries were relegated to an 'orientalist fringe' of the new Europe (Iordanova 2008: 72). In the case of the Balkans,[2] echoes of the nineteenth- and early twentieth-century labelling of the region as 'violent' (Bakić-Hayden 917–19) and 'oriental' (Livanios, 300) were frequently heard in Western media and political discourse after 1989, specifically in the context of the Yugoslav Wars of Secession in the 1990s and the ongoing project of European unification. Emphasising the importance of narrative in providing meaning to the way individuals and collectives identify themselves, their histories and their social realities – and, importantly, those of others – Igor Krstic maintains that cultural texts such as films play a vital role in constructing, reflecting and subverting narratives of identification (Krstic). Through a comparative analysis of two transnational projects by Balkan-born directors, *Pred doždot/Before the Rain* (Milcho Manchevski, 1994, Macedonia/France/UK) and *Podzemlje/Underground* (Emir Kusturica, 1995, France/Germany/Hungary/FR Yugoslavia/Bulgaria), the Balkan-produced film *Lepa sela, lepo gore/Pretty Village, Pretty Flame* (Srđan Dragojević, 1996, FR Yugoslavia) and the British production *Welcome to Sarajevo* (Michael Winterbottom, 1997, UK), we explore how the Western gaze viewed late twentieth-century Balkan conflict through the prism of orientalism and, by so doing, narrated a causal trajectory of historical Balkan violence against which Western progress and civilisation could be affirmed. By replicating and subverting aspects of these narratives, the films at once foreground them as ideological constructions and actively participate in their reimagining. At the same time, this cinematic reconception of the Balkan 'other' decentres the West, thus contributing to broader 'metadialogues' of European identity, including those of Western Europe, in the post-Cold War environment.

Savage Europe: Narratives of Balkan Violence

From the perspective of the West, the Balkans have long occupied a peripheral position in Europe. The habitual labelling of the region as 'savage Europe' and 'oriental Europe' during the nineteenth and early twentieth centuries 'did not imply any recognition that the peninsula was an integral part of Europe' (Livanios, 300); instead, it signified that, while in a geographical sense the region was part of the European continent, in a cultural sense it was not.[3] As Dmitris Livanios has remarked, 'the Balkanites were located in Europe's geographical backyard, but they were rarely, if at all, invited to join the family's dinner table' (300). In 1876, during the Great Eastern Crisis, German Chancellor Bismarck declared that the Balkans were 'not worth the healthy bones of a single Pomeranian Grenadier'.[4] When European Commissioner for External Relations, Chris Patten, quoted these words in a speech to the German Bundestag in 2004, however, it was in order to reject this view of the Balkans and declare that '[t]he people of the Western Balkans[5] are our fellow Europeans' (2004). Yet Patten's inclusive attitude contrasted sharply with the more ambivalent, if not rejecting, views expressed during the Yugoslav Wars of Secession in the 1990s. In a strong echo of the orientalising rhetoric of the turn of the century, Western media coverage of the wars frequently contrasted the '"ancient hatreds" of the south Slavic peoples' with the 'civility' of the West (Bakić-Hayden, 929).

The interplay between the perception of the Balkans as mired in recurrent ethnic conflict and the process through which the East Central European states sought integration into the European Community/European Union during the same period cemented the peripheralisation of the region. Almost immediately after the revolutions of 1989 and the collapse of Communism across Central and Eastern Europe, the European Union, then still a predominantly Western European organisation, began signalling it was open to Central European[6] desires to join 'the

European club'. The central pillar of the East Central European states' bid for European Union membership between 1989 and 2004 was that the Iron Curtain had created an artificial division between countries that had been politically and culturally close (O'Brennan 2006: 14): countries that have shared the norms and values of a collective European civilisation (Schimmelfennig 2001: 71). This argument appeared to be largely accepted by the European Union,[7] at least after the Copenhagen Summit of 1993 (O'Brennan 2006: 22), which took place against the backdrop of wars raging in Europe's south-eastern periphery. But analysts have suggested that, while the catchphrases 'return to Europe' and 'unification of Europe' implied acceptance of Central Europeans as 'European', the enlargement process was, in fact, predicated not on an assumption of shared identity but on Western European presumptions of political and cultural difference between EU15[8] and countries east of the former Iron Curtain, including the East Central European applicant states. Merje Kuus has argued that the discourse which underpinned the eastern enlargement was 'broadly orientalist' since it assumed 'essential difference between Europe and Eastern Europe' and framed 'difference from Western Europe as distance from and a lack of Europeanness' (2004: 473), this implying a synonymy between Western Europe and 'Europe'. Rather than rejecting such assumptions, Kuus contends, the East Central European states contributed to the persistence of stereotypes of 'Western superiority and Eastern inferiority' by adopting them in their own rhetoric (2008: 181). By identifying a civilisational border between 'Central' and 'Eastern' Europe – including the Balkan region – the accession states sought to 'shift the discursive border between Europe and Eastern Europe further east and to thereby move themselves into Europe' (Kuus, 2004: 479). Their success cemented the perception in the West of the Balkan states as unambiguously 'eastern'.[9] The wars breaking out on what was frequently referred to as 'Europe's doorstep'[10] were cited as evidence of Balkan 'otherness', signifying the distance and difference of the Balkans from the Western European 'centre' at the same time as the East Central European states were demonstrating their compatibility with this centre (Bakić-Hayden, 923–4).

This perception was supported by what Dina Iordanova describes as a 'putative' narrative of Balkan violence that was used by the West to establish a 'direct causal link between the present-day state of affairs and concrete past events' in Balkan history (2008: 74). Drawing on Maria Todorova's discursive concept of 'Balkanism', which refers to way the Balkans have been othered as 'a repository of negative characteristics against which a positive and self-congratulatory image of the "European" and "the West" has been constructed' (1994: 453), Iordanova argues that many cinematic representations of the Balkan conflicts perpetuate Balkanised narratives of cyclical and irresolvable violence (2008: 72). These narratives evince the continuing orientalist construction of the Balkans in the present day (56). Using the term 'teleology of conflict'[11] (73) to describe how the 'causes' of Yugoslavia's demise are often arbitrarily sought in Balkan history, Iordanova states that a 'journalistic dominance' over discourse on the wars favoured the use of culturist tropes over contemporary economic and political factors to delineate the roots of 1990s ethnic violence (72). As a result, sensationalist descriptions of the wars, which draw on the trope of a 'clash of civilisations' between 'ancient enemies', correspond to orientalist dialogues that portray the Balkans as a 'dark and primitive periphery doomed to trouble' (72–3). The films under study challenge persistent assumptions of Balkan remoteness from Western Europe by decentring these narratives and the Western gaze that upholds them.

Iordanova claims, however, that the orientalist framing of the Balkans as a site of recurrent violence is not simply a 'Western project' but has also been 'embraced, internalised and partially carried out by many consenting Balkan intellectuals' (2008: 56) in a process which parallels the East Central European states' adoption of Western European stereotypes. She contends that the deployment of Western narrative devices by Balkan directors reflects a broader Balkan effort to 're-enter Europe' whereby, feeling 'obliged to be apologetic' for not being a desirable partner within the European realm, intellectuals are prepared to mirror stereotypical representations of themselves as part of an 'admission bargain' (67). Maintaining that cinematic auto-orientalism is simply a further manifestation of this wider practice (67–8), Iordanova argues that it is seemingly 'more convenient' to perpetuate self-exoticism than it is to counter the dominant Western narrative model (68–9). As such, she contends, most Balkan film-makers remain uncritical of the Western gaze on the Balkans and fail to question the Eurocentric construct at its heart (1998: 263–4). Yet a deeper interrogation of the registers of cinematic representation and signification reveals that, what Iordanova describes as 'voluntary self-exoticism' (2008: 56), can, in fact, challenge, rather than support, Western orientalism by encouraging viewers to contemplate the very politics of Balkan representation.

The Circle is not Round: Reconfiguring Narratives of Balkan Violence in *Before the Rain*

Before the Rain is one film that Iordanova proposes does 'little more than perpetuate and facilitate the Eurocentric gaze' (2008: 64). Set in Macedonia and London during the Bosnian War, the tripartite circular narrative follows the interconnected stories of: Zamira, an Albanian Muslim girl accused of murdering a Macedonian man from her village; Kiril, a young Orthodox monk who has taken a vow of silence and hides Zamira from her Macedonian pursuers; Aleks, a disillusioned expatriate war photographer who returns to his Macedonian homeland after a sixteen-year absence; and Aleks's lover, Anne, a London photographic editor. The film has attracted criticism from other Balkan scholars who assert that it reinforces traditional stereotypes of the region and gives credence to teleological speculations of violence in the context of the Yugoslav Wars of Secession. Slavoj Žižek, for example, denounces the film as an ideological product of the Western gaze that portrays the Balkans as 'a spectacle of a timeless, incomprehensible, mythical cycle of passions, in contrast to decadent and anaemic Western life' (1995: 38). Iordanova similarly contends that the film depicts contemporary Macedonia 'as a land of tribal culture and medieval ethos' (1998: 269) where 'nothing can be done to change the cycle of Balkan self-destruction' (2000: 153). Vojislava Filipčević agrees, stating that the film's emphasis on historical narrative prevents it from transcending its Balkanised context (12), despite the director's insistence that, while the film 'was inspired by the events unfolding in Yugoslavia, . . . it was *not about* them' (Manchevski, 130; emphasis in original).

A cursory viewing of the film supports these opinions to some extent. When the paramilitaries searching for Zamira reach the monastery, for example, they remind the priests that their Orthodox ancestors endured 'five centuries of Turkish [slavery]'. The invocation of a bygone era as a means to persuade the priests to surrender the young Albanian Muslim can be read as supporting Western assumptions that the 'wheels of Balkan history are turned by the persistent rhetoric of the past' (Filipčević, 17). We concur with Victor Friedman, however, who argues that *Before the Rain's* tendency to be interpreted through the prism of journalistic fatalism is 'not a failure of the film but of the gaze' (2000: 143). While Iordanova explicitly accepts this assessment (2008: 84), she fails to grasp Friedman's more salient point which he makes by quoting Keith Brown's reading of the film as not corresponding to a single reality but aiming rather to 'illuminate the existence of different modes of imagining by which realisms are constituted' (2000: 143; Brown 1998: 173). Iordanova implies that using the same narrative devices as Western films about the Balkans precludes any subversion of Western orientalism and that Western othering of the region can be countered only by employing an entirely different discursive framework (2008: 68). Yet, despite its narrative circularity, *Before the Rain* encourages viewers to contemplate the Western ideological construction of Balkanised narratives. The narrative's dischronology becomes a means of 'performatively critiquing the stereotypical portrayal of violence in the Balkans as a permanent historical construct' (Marciniak, 67), and the film's circular structure, though imperfect, appears to draw on Balkan experiences of conflict in a manner that is mindful of stereotypical Western representations of violence in the region. By reperforming the Western gaze with an inherent 'carefully designed quirk' (Manchevski, 129) – a temporal narrative flaw which prevents the three parts from linking together in a full circle – Manchevski simultaneously subverts the orientalist rendering of the Balkans as a timeless space outside of 'progressive' Western European history and foregrounds the very notion of 'narrative' as a contrived historical construct. The 'quirk' results in both Alexander's and Zamira's deaths being anticipated before they occur and in Anne responding to Kiril's phone call to Aleks in London before it could have been placed. The final alteration of the film's leitmotif from 'time never dies; the circle is not round' to 'time does not wait; the circle is not round' can therefore be read as a call to action against determinism: for Balkan peoples to challenge vestigial Cold War European binaries by self-consciously forging their own, new narratives in the post-1989 political-cultural climate. In this sense *Before the Rain* decentres the Western gaze by reconfiguring, rather than reiterating, normative narratives of Balkan violence.

Awakening the Ogre: Spectres of the Past in *Underground* and *Pretty Village, Pretty Flame*

Like *Before the Rain*, Kusturica's *Underground* and Dragojević's *Pretty Village, Pretty Flame* use the backdrop of the Yugoslav Wars of Secession to explore Balkan identities and history. *Underground* narrates a satirical history of Yugoslavia from 1941 to 1992 in three parts: War, Cold War and War. After tricking his partisan comrade, Blacky, into hiding in a cellar and stealing Blacky's girlfriend, Natalija, Marko quickly becomes one of Tito's closest associates and a powerful illegal arms dealer. Under the pretence of ongoing war against the Nazis, Marko suppresses Blacky and the partisans underground for several decades and oversees their illicit production of weapons – a deception that eventually causes the ruination of their friendship, their lives, and Yugoslavia itself. *Pretty Village, Pretty Flame* flashed backwards and forwards between Tito's Yugoslavia and the Bosnian War in order to tell the story of boyhood friends Halil, a Muslim, and Milan, a Serb, who find themselves on opposing sides when war breaks out. Through flashbacks to their pre-war lives, the film attempts to shed light on why hostilities between former friends and neighbours erupted so suddenly and vehemently. Delving deeper into the Balkan psyche than Manchevski in *Before the Rain*, Kusturica and Dragojević both provide Balkan narratives with a psychological dimension. Jerzy Jedlicki observes the crucial role that historical remembrance plays in ethnic warfare, discerning not only how genuine or apparent memories of the past aggravate current conflicts but also how these memories are modified in the process (226). Defining 'collective memory' as a complex of beliefs 'shared by at least a part of the national community, and relating to a given segment of the national history', Jedlicki explores how motives and arguments drawn from history 'fan the flames' of current animosities and make them seem irresolvable (226). Anthony Oberschall contends that Balkan peoples nurture two distinct mind-frames: an 'ethnic cooperation and peace frame' which operates most effectively when there is a strong central power in place, and a 'crisis frame' which manifests itself when the unifying power weakens or dissipates (983). As nationalist narratives rapidly filled the political and ideological void created by Tito's death, mass media propaganda distorted collective memory and awakened the 'crisis frame' after decades of dormancy (990).[12] Triggered by fierce competition for political power and uncertainties over state boundaries and minority status, the worst recollections of old enmities and hatreds turned neighbour against neighbour in an expanding spiral of aggression and reprisals (982). The provocation of contemporary warfare among those in the Balkans as a 'response to a former insult'[13] thus projected an image to the rest of the world of a conflict predicated on the past which, in turn, appeared to confirm Western narratives of historically determined Balkan barbarism. By confronting the Balkan past through the concept of 'historical memory', Dragojević and Kusturica cinematically disinter that which has been suppressed in Balkan history and illustrate how such suppression has engendered the cyclical patterns of Balkan violence that have been stereotyped and othered by the West. Both films therefore deconstruct the narratives of Balkan identity upon which Western orientalism depends.

The fragile moral order which was established in Tito's Yugoslavia necessitated the disavowal of historical facts that conflicted with the new multi-ethnic nation's unified image. Official state rhetoric under the 'Brotherhood and Unity' slogan served to conceal World War II experiences of fascist collaboration and inter-ethnic hostility by implanting 'new' memories of the war built upon the myth of brave Yugoslav Communist partisans (cf. Krstic; Coulson 94–5; Gow and Carmichael 45–7). Drawing on Lacanian psychoanalysis to explain how the awakening of latent war memories contributed to the resurgence of violence in the post-Yugoslav era, Žižek likens the reconstruction of memory to a 'return of the dead':

> Why do the dead recur? ... [B]ecause they were not buried correctly ... because something was missing at their funeral. The recurrence of the dead is a sign of a trouble in the symbolic rite, in the process of symbolisation; the dead recur as collectors of a not settled symbolic debt.[14]

The scale of devastation inflicted by the historical 'ghosts' of tabooed World War II memories must be understood as the result of their 'incorrect burial': the failure to confront and reconcile experiences of wartime trauma owing to the widespread psychological whitewashing under Yugoslav ideology. Kusturica and Dragojević cinematically perform this 'return of the dead' by narrating that which has been silenced, yet not truly forgotten, in the course of Balkan history. In so doing, they not only deconstruct the internal Balkan ideologies which have reinforced the region's peripheral positioning through their precipitation of ethnic conflict but also actively participate in the reimagining and rewriting of these narratives that have historically supported Western stereotypes.

Krstic suggests that Kusturica's underground cellar and Dragojević's 'Brotherhood and Unity' tunnel are metaphors for the Balkan subconscious and that what resides within them represents all that the official Yugoslav public sphere suppressed (2002). *Underground*, in particular, deals largely with the reconstruction of history that was required to uphold the Brotherhood and Unity myth. Žižek asserts that every ideological system has an obscene 'hidden reverse' which, built upon a series of 'inherent transgressions', contradicts the system's public face yet functions as a condition of its stability.[15] These transgressions must, for that reason, 'remain under the cover of night, unacknowledged, unutterable'.[16] In Kusturica's film, Marko and Natalija's rapid consolidation of power after World War II is depicted in contradistinction to – and also as a result of – their oppression of Blacky and the other workers within the underground tunnel. Marko's maintenance of authority is underpinned by his dealing in illegal arms; the munitions from which he profits financially and politically are built by those he keeps trapped in the cellar through the fiction of an ongoing war. The underground workshop thus serves as a metaphor for the 'hidden reverse' of Yugoslav Communism, allegorising all that was silenced in order for Tito's Brotherhood and Unity ideology to reproduce itself. By rendering visible the 'inherent transgressions' of Marko's power and the manner in which these are concealed behind his public face, Kusturica reveals that the construction and perpetuation of Yugoslav social reality were predicated on suppressing aspects of Balkan history which conflicted with the state-enforced fabula of unity.

Just as Marko's carefully constructed world crumbles and violence erupts when his underground prisoners resurface, in *Pretty Village, Pretty Flame*, the carnage of war is portrayed as the consequence of awakening a monstrous ogre from its slumber in the Brotherhood and Unity tunnel. In the film's opening sequence, the young Milan and Halil avoid the tunnel for fear that the ogre within will, if disturbed, 'burn all the villages'. If the ogre is interpreted as a metaphor for 'the fear of difference',[17] the monster incarnates the psychological repression of memories of inter-ethnic conflict necessitated by their contradiction of Yugoslavia's official doctrine of unity. The burning villages therefore represent the violence that ensued from the rousing of latent memories during the Yugoslav state's disintegration, and the ruination of Milan and Halil's friendship symbolises the destruction of coexistence between Yugoslav 'brothers' of different ethnicities that once prevailed. Thus, while a superficial viewing of these films appears to reveal a repetition of Western stereotypes through the apparent portrayal of Balkan warfare as a psychological predisposition, deeper analysis demonstrates that each director has attempted to exhume the 'inherent transgressions' of the past through narrative. Through this process, the ghosts of Balkan history are symbolically granted the 'burial' that is required to transcend them.

Maintaining that one cannot 'forget' what was once a massive trauma, Jedlicki declares that there remains a choice between the 'deliberate stirring of memory so as to feed the dreams of retribution' and 'letting the ever-recurring nightmare become finally a historical recollection' (231). This choice is crucial to the forging of new Balkan narratives in the wake of the Cold War. *Underground* and *Pretty Village, Pretty Flame* enact several tropes that urge reflection on, rather than revenge for, the past. Though these tropes self-exoticise, they are not, as Iordanova contends, a means for the directors to self-denigrate their way into European status; instead, they act as a vehicle through which Balkan peoples can apologise for themselves, *to* themselves. Stefan Jonsson asserts that 'figures of monstrosity are conjured up by an imagination afflicted by historical trauma' in order to make sense of the injuries of war (11). Keeping this idea in mind, a closer examination of the films reveals that their recurring motifs of drunkenness, madness and monstrosity – despite reproducing Western stereotypes of Balkan barbarism – are mirrors with which to reflect on the past in a manner that does not call for vengeance. *Pretty Village, Pretty Flame*, for example, represents the Yugoslav Wars of Secession

Figure 13.1 *Underground*: 'drunkenness, madness and monstrosity' at the wedding of Blacky's son Jovan.

retrospectively as a kind of debauched, drunken affair. Halil's closing reminiscence to Milan about being 'nice and drunk' frames the film's explicit violence as the result of inebriation – in other words, a psychological lapse in control. The perpetual bacchanalia of *Underground's* protagonists likewise projects this perspective, particularly when the drunkenness climaxes at the wedding of Blacky's son Jovan, as heavily intoxicated guests squabble over unsettled affairs (cf. Iordanova 2008: 113).

The sense of deranged lunacy communicated through these scenes is underscored by the intermittent screen presence of Natalija's mentally handicapped, wheelchair-bound brother. Yet, while Dragojević and Kusturica here seem voluntarily to replicate the orientalist vision of the 'irrational, chaotic and primitive Balkan "Other"' (Rivi, 92), this does not imply their assent to Western relegation of the Balkans to a European fringe. Rather, through deliberate self-exoticism, the directors expose the monstrosity of the Balkan past and suggest that a confrontation with suppressed, traumatic memories will bring about the self-forgiveness required to transform the 'ever-recurring nightmare' into a foregone recollection. Ironically, it is by consciously performing the impaired moral standards frequently attributed to them by the Western gaze that these 'new' narratives begin to eclipse the orientalist stereotypes and peripheral positioning upon which this gaze depends.

Beyond the East–West Dichotomy: Films from the Balkans and *Welcome to Sarajevo*

The desire to transcend the Balkanised past through new, multifaceted narratives of identity is compelling in an age when the broader concept of 'Europe' is evolving beyond the Cold War dichotomy of East versus West. Some Balkan directors participate in this shift by decentring the West from its ideological positioning as 'Europe'. Dragojević, for example, wryly engages with the debate surrounding Balkan admissibility to Europe by mocking the West's long-term identification of itself with civility and the Balkans with violence. In *Pretty Village, Pretty Flame*, the Serb soldier nicknamed Viljuška ('Fork') wears a fork around his neck to symbolise the sophistication of fourteenth-century Serbian kings compared with their English and German counterparts who, he proclaims, still 'ate using their hands'. This declaration reflects discussions about Balkan belonging in Europe and corresponds to arguments that the Balkans were not only a 'cradle of European culture' but, in some respects, civilisationally more developed than Western Europe (Iordanova 2008: 37). Similarly, in *Before the Rain* Manchevski challenges assumptions of Western supremacy by denying the West a position outside Balkan history. Western culture projects its superiority through the credo that 'barbarism resides elsewhere ... in that other world ... steeped in medievalism and bloody cruelty' (Marciniak 79).[18] Manchevski rejects this notion by placing the nightmares of Balkan history in Western as well as in Balkan contexts (Filipčević, 20). When a shootout between men of Balkan ethnicity occurs in the sophisticated London restaurant where Anne and her estranged husband Nick dine, Nick's ironic declaration of relief that the men are 'not from Ulster' undercuts the rendering of their enmity as 'an inexplicable Balkan affair'.[19] Manchevski thus disallows the representation of Western Europe as a superior civilised space that has overcome ethnic conflict (cf. Marciniak, 69), as Nick's unwitting reference to the recurring sectarian violence in Northern Ireland exposes the non-exceptionalism of inter-ethnic Balkan hostilities. By debunking Western conceptions that ethnic violence occurs 'elsewhere',[20] Manchevski creates a narrative of cultural interconnectedness which discredits the Eurocentric binarism of perceived distance between the 'civilised' West and the 'barbaric' Balkans. Furthermore, if this assumed remoteness has long provided a comfort to Western Europe, a reminder not only of Western commitment to humanitarian values but also the persisting barbarism of the 'other world' that requires Western guidance (Marciniak, 2003: 79),[21] Manchevski's drawing of connections between London and Macedonia in *Before the Rain* undermines the West's belief in its superior role as 'rescuers and leaders in maintaining the world's "order"' (Marciniak, 79). Such subversion questions the basis of Eurocentrism and calls on the West to recognise the spuriousness of Balkan orientalism. Filipčević contends that this interconnectedness is underpinned by the casting of both Balkan and international actors as 'displaced or rootless characters who traverse continents' (8). Iordanova likewise argues that the casting in Balkan films of actors familiar to a Western European audience is intended to forge an emotional connection to the Balkans (2008: 62). Manchevski's casting of well-known French actor Gregoire Colin as the Macedonian monk, Kiril, however, can be read as an example of his emphasis on East–West interconnection.

The cinematic interrogation of Balkan identity and history by Manchevski, Kusturica and Dragojević challenges the notion of the West 'as' Europe by destabilising Western stereotypes that serve to other the Balkans and dismantling those which exalt the West. By provoking a disjunctive shift in Western narratives that are predicated on Cold War divisions, these directors thus implicitly call for a reimagination of the Western self. Winterbottom appears to have recognised the need for self-examination as he explores a Western 'crisis of self' in *Welcome to Sarajevo*. The film depicts a group of British and American journalists, stationed in the besieged city of Sarajevo, who are outraged at both the lack of coverage their frontline reports receive back home and the inadequate humanitarian support given to Bosnia during the war. After first staging the orientalist dichotomy of the 'civilised' West's confrontation with the tribal warring of the Balkan other, Winterbottom poses an ethical dilemma that questions Western cultural superiority. Henderson's 'humanity' is measured and tested against the 'inhumanity' of Sarajevo (Molloy, 82) as he crusades to help local children escape Bosnia and decides to adopt the orphaned Emira. It is here that his moral compass is thrown into doubt when the girl's biological mother pleas for her return to war-torn Bosnia from the safety of England.

From the outset, and in contrast with the other films examined, Winterbottom frames the film's narrative from the perspective of the West by constructing the prologue as a news report given by Henderson, who is pictured against grim footage of refugees escaping a Serbian mortar attack in Vukovar. This strategy encourages viewers to recognise the film as a construction and raises questions of framing. Winterbottom establishes Western negligence and culpability as key themes through the transition of Van Morrison's 'The Way Young Lovers Do', released on the album *Astral Weeks* in 1968, from non-diegetic to diegetic usage during the opening credits, which encourages viewers to attribute its late 1960s politico-cultural milieu to the film's narrative setting. The allusion to the failures of the West during the Vietnam War encourages viewers to approach the depiction of the West's involvement in Bosnia critically. The idea of Western European self-reproach for having allegedly failed to 'maintain' its 'neglected backyard' (Iordanova 2008: 67, 69–70)[22] is likewise examined: Winterbottom satirises the failure of the West to conciliate in Balkan conflict by portraying a European United Nations convoy official as justifying the lack of intervention with the statement that besieged Sarajevo is 'still only the fourteenth most dangerous place on Earth' – a sentiment that is underscored by real footage of a European Union Peace Negotiator advising those in Bosnia against 'living under the dream' of Western arbitration and salvation.[23] Winterbottom's engagement with the West's retrospective guilt over its failure to help Sarajevo's besieged inhabitants[24] indicts the West for effectively sustaining the Balkan violence it depended upon for its own civilised distinction.

By highlighting these 'sins of the West' (Molloy, 81) through the prism of Western journalism, Winterbottom participates in the debate over Western culpability raised by both Manchevski – who implicates the West directly in perpetuating Balkanised narratives through Aleks's realisation that an innocent man was murdered for his camera[25] – and Dragojević – who characterises the American journalist, Lisa, as an exponent of the Western gaze when she is accused by the Serb soldiers of exacerbating Balkan violence through gross misrepresentation in the Western media. On this level, Henderson's decision to cease being a neutral observer and participate in the rescue of the orphans can be read as a celluloid attempt to atone for the West's inflammation of Balkan conflict as much as its failure to conciliate or provide adequate aid. On a deeper level, however, Henderson's moral dilemma over adopting Emira, which ensues when his assumption of the girl's future well-being in England is disrupted by her Bosnian mother's plea for her return, challenges the West's entitlement to view itself as the Balkans' 'civilised superior'. Henderson's personal interrogation thus poses questions of the wider Western conscience and, through this enquiry, commands a reimagining of the Western self and its responsibilities. Thus, although *Welcome to Sarajevo* has been criticised for simplifying and stereotyping the Balkan conflict along orientalist lines,[26] Winterbottom's invocation of Western culpability through music, cinematic irony and a narrative of ethical responsibility indicates an attempt to exhume cinematically spectres of the past in order to confront them directly and cease their repetitive perversion of present and future identities. This exploration of Western responsibility responds – albeit indirectly – to the decentring of Cold War European identities. While Winterbottom stops short of directly implicating the West in the perpetuation of Balkan history – in contrast to the Balkan directors Dragojević and Kusturica – his firm denial of Western absolution over the Bosnian crisis points to a need for Western Europe also to engage in a renegotiation of identities in the age of the new Europe.

Conclusion: Decentring Cold War European Identities

While some critics contend that the films examined in this chapter confirm Western presumptions of timeless Balkan barbarism and European progress, each of them challenges aspects of the dominant Western narrative of Balkan remoteness from European norms of civility. By foregrounding Balkanised narratives as Western ideological constructions, the directors not only draw attention to the need for their rewriting but also engage directly in this process through film-making. Manchevski's appeal to break the cycle of violence is addressed not only to Balkan peoples but also to complacent Western Europeans who, in condemning recurrent ethnic conflict on Europe's south-eastern fringe, conveniently forget or discount Western Europe's own history of perennial internecine warfare. Cinematically exhuming the ghosts of the past, Kusturica and Dragojević urge reflection on, rather than revenge for, past wrongs because it is only through reflection that self-perpetuating narratives of violence may be rewritten. As a Western European director, Winterbottom responds to the call to rewrite these narratives by challenging the West to re-examine its role in their perpetuation. All four films must therefore be understood as cultural texts which contribute to the hermeneutic understanding of contemporary Balkan identities in the post-Cold War context, as they actively engage with new, meaningful dialogues on Balkan identity and contribute to broader 'metadialogues' of European identity in the post-1989 decentring and reimagining of Europe

Part III

Spectres of the East

CHAPTER 14

Through the Lens of Black Humour: A Polish Adam in the Post-Wall World

Rimma Garn (University of Utah)

Marek Koterski is a Polish film director virtually unknown to American audiences. He has recently come to the attention of critics and viewers alike and is gradually gaining recognition as a prominent auteur. Ewa Mazierska considers him the greatest Polish director since Andrzej Wajda (Mazierska 2013: 159). Koterski's *oeuvre* should be examined in its entirety as it represents an unusual phenomenon: a coherent narrative spanning an octology of eight tightly connected feature films.[1] All eight films revolve around the same protagonist, a Polish intellectual named Adam (the director's alter ego), as well as his everyday life and family.[2] Adam Miauczyński is an everyman living in the rapidly changing world of Eastern Europe, a world by which he is somewhat baffled. Koterski's octology – and, most pointedly, the two films in it that this chapter focuses on, *Dzień świra / The Day of the Wacko* (2002, henceforth referred to as *Wacko*)[3] and *Wszyscy jesteśmy Chrystusami / We're All Christs* (2006, henceforth *Christs*) – takes a sceptical look at both the Polish communist past and post-Wall present, yet also suggests a path towards salvation that the director sees not in political changes but in spirituality and humanity. Within Polish cinema and culture, Koterski is hardly alone in his assessment of recent Polish history and the fraught progression from communist past to post-communist present, seeing political and economical changes as going from bad to worse and bemoaning – together with his protagonist – the artist's precipitous fall from the status of national prophet (Mazierska 2013: 145–59). What does make him unique is his original cinematic style, the poignant psychological assessment of self and others, and his black humour.

The choice of the protagonist's first name appears quite straightforward: Adam was the first man, and Koterski's protagonist is the 'everyman'. The often used diminutive form of this name, Adaś, suggests his infantile connection to his mother and turns the adult man into a child, the role he seems to play even as an adult. The last name, Miauczyński, hints at the miaowing of a cat and evokes the director's name, Koterski (*kot* is Polish for 'cat'). Oppositions between dogs and cats, as well as between men and women, pervade the octology, and this last name suggests that Adam does not belong to the stronger or more aggressive camp.

Spanning more than a quarter of a century, from 1985 to 2011, Koterski's octology covers a time of dramatic transformation in Poland and the whole of Eastern Europe as totalitarianism was replaced by various shades of democracy, anarchy and capitalism, often leaving chaos, social breakdown and even war in its immediate aftermath. Koterski's octology provides us with a unique look from the perspective of an artist and an ordinary 'little Pole' at the impact of these transformations on private life. The two films which are the focus of this chapter offer an unexpected point of view that reframes the notion of contemporary Europe. Adam sees no difference between communist and post-communist Poland in the way the authorities treat intellectuals, with a disregard that exacerbates his private psychosis and depression (as *Wacko* suggests); only love, faith, and the next generation – not political change – offer an escape from personal frailties and the stifling experience of the past (as *Christs* intimates).

The search for national identity is a pressing issue for each and every country of the former Eastern bloc in the post-Wall world. For Poland, this search is a particularly complex project for a number of historical and cultural reasons. As Tamara Trojanowska insightfully explains:

> Robbed by the eighteenth-century partitions of the typical nineteenth-century European modernity, and ruined by its twentieth-century totalitarian experiments – Nazism and Communism – Poland emerged twenty years ago free, but deeply scarred. Marred by the discontinuities of its social, political, cultural, and economic structures and networks, and struggling with the neglected, contentious and deeply divisive narratives of its immediate past, the country remains unsure of its role in the current phase of the European identity-building project and ambivalent in attitudes to its own conflicting traditions. (Trojanowska, 2)

The search for identity in this emerging world is at the heart of Koterski's octology. His protagonist, Adam Miauczyński, a frustrated Polish intellectual, rejects the reality he finds around him. Not only is Adam lost in his own era, he is deeply disturbed by the changing role of the intelligentsia in Polish society:

> The romantic Miauczyński's defeat is the defeat of the Polish intelligentsia. From the time of the partitions to the fall of communism, they ruled the people . . . They used to be intellectual and moral leaders, but this is no longer true. At least that would seem to be Koterski's conclusion as . . . he exposes the complexes, inhibitions and incurable pessimism of a Polish intellectual despairing over his general impotence, low wages and lack of prospects. (Wróblewski, 182)

A large portion of Koterski's octology, six out of eight films, was produced after the cataclysmic changes Eastern Europe faced in 1989. The two films this chapter focuses on, *Wacko* and *Christs*, examine and re-examine the political, social and spiritual issues facing the new Poland with particular poignancy. *Wacko* shows a middle-aged Adam (49) in post-communist Poland, yet his whole personality, from his quirks to his worldview, is the product of a communist past. We see one day in his life, from morning until night, as he performs rituals that help him survive his mundane existence, lashes out on his loud neighbours, teaches poetry to indifferent students, visits a teenage son from his failed marriage, drops in on his mother who never hears him, goes to numerous doctors who cannot help him, escapes to the beach seeking (but failing to find) relaxation, and finally goes to sleep hating his life and certain of the impossibility of changing anything.[4] The plot is unified by the single subjective perspective of the protagonist, supported by his darkly ironic background narration.

In *Christs* an older Adam (55) looks back on his life and compares his memories to those of his son, Sylvester. The differences are both comic and tragic. Adam tries to make sense of a failed life filled with alcoholism, loneliness and fear, a life that unravels in front of us against the background of Christ's passion. The plot of this film, full of temporal leaps and loops and overlapping subjective perspectives on the same events, cannot be easily linearised, and that was exactly the intention of the director. The whole film constitutes, in a sense, a difficult conversation between Adam and Sylvester which takes place in Adam's apartment in contemporary Poland at the beginning of the twenty-first century. Their memories and flashbacks take us not only to Sylvester's painful experiences of childhood and youth in the grip of drug addiction, and further back to Adam's marriage and the alcoholism he battled in the 1970s and 1980s, but also to another generation, to the life of Adam's parents and to the alcoholic father who introduced his child to alcohol. Moreover, both Adam and Sylvester, while struggling with their respective addictions, turn out to be warriors in a cosmic battle between Good and Evil, supported by Adam's guardian angel and tempted by the Devil in angelic disguise. These three generations, in communist and post-communist Poland, could either repeat the patterns of their fathers or break them, both in private and public life, and the director suggests that political changes alone do not bring the solution a 'small man' seeks.

Depictions of the West, often alluded to by foreign languages, do not play a prominent role in the octology. Whenever the West is evoked, it is presented comically or as a source of foreign, unusual and prestigious goods, such as a child's bicycle, Levi jacket or a fancy dress. Koterski's characters either learn a foreign language – usually unsuccessfully, be it English, German, Russian or Hungarian – or throw in a phrase in a foreign language without much thought or even without understanding it. In *Ajlawju* (1999), the film that precedes *Wacko* and whose title playfully transcribes the English 'I love you', Adam goes to America, yet the trip proves a cruel irony of fate: the internship that Adam was so eager to get earlier in his life comes at a moment when he is in love and reluctant to leave his girlfriend. As a result he sees nothing around him while in Chicago and longs to return. He brings a gift for her, a fancy dress that she refuses to wear, leading to a row.

In the two films under discussion a similar pattern is maintained: the English language is presented in comical situations and consumer goods from America turn out to be useless or even dangerous. In *Wacko* Adam tries to learn English (even while on the toilet) without hoping ever to be successful with it. He tries to help his son with English grammar but ends up exploding in frustration upon learning that his son apparently has never heard of Shakespeare. Like Kieślowski, Koterski incorporates foreign phrases that suggest an authorial commentary on the protagonist and his problems.[5] The three memorable English phrases in *Wacko* – 'to go to pieces', 'to be or not to be', 'who would you like to be?' – seem to comment on Adam's life and predicament. A bright Levi jacket, which Adam brought his son from America also incites concern, with Adam worrying that people are ready to kill to acquire it. Meanwhile in *Christs* Adam brings his son a bicycle from America but falls on it when drunk and breaks it; in another scene, drunken Adam uses English when talking to a street vendor who misunderstands him and Adam winds up buying faux fox fur that his wife rejects. Both foreign languages and foreign consumer goods thus appear distant, irrelevant and useless, suggesting that the new Poland is a world in and of itself and one has to learn to live in it without relying on the West.

Black humour, startling naturalism, tragic overtones and angst over personal and universal questions permeate all Koterski's films. Moreover, his post-1989 films also address political and social issues. They occasionally comment on the distant West but mostly on the bleak world of communist Poland and on its 'product', Adam, trying to understand and to fit into the new world around him. A number of scholars relate this black humour to cultural roots and periods of historical cataclysm. Olga Reizen summarises this phenomenon:

> It is quite well known that the more rotten something is in any nation, the blacker is its humour. Thus, black humour appears during the crucial moments of the 'rotten

> nation' of history, either during wars, stagnation periods, or revolutions ... Our [Soviet] socialism has created a real superman – Homo sapiens who can consider as quite normal libraries that are closed or ruined, churches used as stores, and personal dignity looked on as some irrelevant factor at all levels ... The ability to laugh at oneself is either a sign of high culture or of great despair, or both. In any case the colour of such laughter is black. (Reizen, 94–5)

Moreover, Reizen suggests that, while the culture of any given nation may offer more or less fertile ground for black humour, it tends to gain currency in totalitarian regimes where the public has been trained by censors to appreciate and decode metaphorical thinking. Black humour in Polish, Czech, Georgian, Russian, Yugoslavian and other Central or Eastern European arts supports this proposition.

Black humour runs on both comedy and horror and strives to entertain as it horrifies: most often it depicts such topics as disease and death, war and crime, addiction and taboos. Koterski's black humour focuses in particular on disease and death. His octology uses humour to denigrate life and love, reducing the former to eating, drinking and the scatological, and the latter to mechanical sex (with the notable exception of *Christs*). When a totalitarian system takes away one's privacy, dignity and hope, when a system that replaces it appears to do the same, when the cornered little man is further ruined by his own addictions, what is left for him but laughter? Koterski's black humour is the weapon he uses to fight the empty rhetoric of politicians and unmask these public and private enemies of the little man.

East and West, communist and post-communist Poland, the public and the private, the role of the individual in a society undergoing a rapid makeover; Koterski's films address all these issues, yet the director suggests that it is not politics and societal transformation that matter. In *Wacko*, black humour, at times, leaves the audience squirming uncomfortably as it colours Adam's dealings with public and private life. In *Christs* Koterski goes even further in his re-examination of the communist past and ridicules attempts by people to blame history for their own shortcomings. His peculiar brand of black comedy still helps to balance incongruous elements, horror and humour, yet more and more the focus of investigation shifts from the contemporary and political to the universal and eternal – to the inner world and basic humanity.

The Day of the Wacko: A 'Groundhog Day' in the New Europe

If 'humour is just another defence against the universe', as Mel Brooks claims, then black humour is, perhaps, a bitter attempt to deal with an absurd, horrifying, disintegrating universe, the universe that Adam sees around him. The term 'black humour' has been subject to a variety of interpretations, and Reizen's explanation of its roots and symptoms appears to be most convincing. Some critics might prefer the term 'tragicomedy' in describing Koterski's octology, a concept suggestive of something less grotesque and less horrifying than black comedy. Mazierska chooses to discuss Koterski's *oeuvre* in this way, focusing on more light-hearted and comic features of his first six films. She makes a convincing case for this choice of terminology by arguing that, while Koterski's films are always imbued with an aura of tragedy, they overflow with irony and comedy: from his films' titles to the praise of 'Schadenfreude' in *Wacko* and the 'gap between the human ideal and reality' to the 'different types of irony', including Koterski's self-irony and the irony of fate, the range of his comic devices is quite impressive (Mazierska 2007: 217–21). This chapter, however, will focus on the motifs specific to black humour that make the spectator uneasy and thus more susceptible to Koterski's images and messages.

Black humour can be imagined as two intersecting continuums: those of humour and horror. Terry Heller suggests that 'humour and horror appear to be mutually exclusive effects in the sense that when they are juxtaposed, three general possibilities emerge: horror subsumes humour; humour subsumes horror; or they tug equally at the reader, suspending him between them' (Heller 205). While in *Wacko* humour prevails over horror, in *Christs* this relationship is reversed, and both films contain a number of scenes where humour and horror pull equally at the viewer. The scatological is an important element in Koterski's black humour as it allows him to juxtapose the lofty with the basest in a most striking contrast, making the viewer uncomfortable and thus most susceptible to the director's message.

> What is satirically grotesque about such a subject [the scatological] is obvious: proud, self-delusional man ever aspires to elevate himself and his dignity, whereas the satirist destroys such upward mobility by reducing man to defecating animal before our eyes. (Clark, 116)

Koterski realises this metaphor quite literally in *Wacko* when Adam, enraged by the piles of dog excrement all around his apartment block and seeing a dog under his balcony as the final offence, runs to a place under his offender's balcony to 'return the favour'. Koterski forces us to consider the possible reasons for, and meaning of, his protagonist's strange behaviour: that of a cornered animal responding to the pressures of a hostile society. As Clark explains:

> [T]he satirist utilizes bathhouse and scatological humour to serve purposes that go beyond chamberpottery, beyond the merely comic, debunking, and anticlimactic . . . An element of the grotesque is added, and the bathroom parodies and exposes many facets of human folly and vice . . . Here bodily function, the daily necessities of nature, and the toilet itself become symbols and analogs . . . for the broader concerns and larger failings of men. (124)

Koterski uses scatological motifs and the lavatory as a setting for some of Adam's most poignant monologues, often regarding his country and its politics, contemporary life and his non-existent role in it.

In *Wacko*, Koterski comments on both communist and post-communist Poland along with its burning political and social issues through his alter ego, Adam, all in a fashion at times subtle and at times grotesque. Critics argue that Eastern European artists have taken on greater responsibility for conveying the meaning of historical and cultural changes than artists elsewhere in the world. The origin of this special role comes from centuries of repressive state rule. Only bards and writers had the courage to speak truth to power, the traditional role of the 'holy fool'. As David Paul puts it:

> Long before the invention of the motion picture, art and literature played a political role in the region [Eastern Europe], as writers, poets and even musicians considered themselves called to articulate the destiny of the nation. Latter-day filmmakers, then, are part of a long tradition that defines the role of the cultural intellectual, in part, as a spokesman for a societal cause . . . These roles have woven themselves permanently into the complex mosaic of art, literature, drama and film in Eastern Europe. (Paul, 7)

Adam, as a poet and an educator, bemoans the loss of the traditional role of the intellectual who used to address crowds and move them to start revolutions. He thinks back and comes up with a poignant, if surprising, conclusion: for centuries Polish intellectuals were spiritual leaders of the nation, yet teachers in communist Poland were not granted this status. In post-communist Poland his frustration is doubled: he is still ignored as a teacher and now, additionally, as an intellectual. In a memorable scene on payday, getting his salary, Adam reflects on his studies in philology and his present job. As he leaves the cashier's window, the bitterest of his monologues is delivered in a school bathroom as he is relieving himself:

> . . . And then [after his student days] poverty and disappointment. Then, despair and silent aging . . . And paralyzing disregard by the government. From tyranny through democracy, everyone has treated teachers like shit. Why does every authority treat me like nothing? Democrats or communists, they all treat me like shit. Damn! They make me feel like a stray dog.[6]

This scene combines a number of elements of black humour in order to keep the viewer suspended between humour and horror, while also alluding to earlier scenes in the same film as well as foretelling episodes from the next one, *Christs*. As Adam walks from the cashier's window to the lavatory and mulls over his disappointments, his thoughts are accompanied by the same Chopin funeral march that he spitefully left for his neighbour to listen to earlier. The famous music, in an unduly familiar arrangement, keeps reiterating the march's tragic section, over and over, never getting to the melodious middle section with some notes of hope. Adam throws burning matches at the ceiling, and they end up forming a grotesque face that smirks down at him like some malevolent 'Big Brother'. He thinks bitterly of the traditional role of the intelligentsia: 'And we are supposed to be the heart of the land. This land.' The very same concern for 'this land' comes back in Koterski's next film, *Christs*, when the Polish pope talks of Poland's fate and faith.

Adam is embittered by the general decline of the intelligentsia's authority but he is also subject to the same collective trauma that left its mark on generations of ordinary Poles who lived under totalitarianism in communist Poland (the PRL or Polish People's Republic):

> People born in Poland before, say, 1975 and who remained in the country, have been subjected to the trauma of dealing with an absurd, if not disturbing, reality, as well as to the trauma of having gone through the systemic quake that put an end to the PRL ... The most significant outcomes of such prolonged traumatic experiences are helplessness, a general sense of fear and lack of faith in the good will and good sense of those in charge. (Murawska, 2)

Exactly these feelings – helplessness, fear and distrust towards authority – underlie Adam's attitude towards the contemporary world. When Adam watches political debates on television, he is overcome by frustration. After listening to a number of politicians, Adam comes to the podium and confesses the bitter truth: 'I do not believe in anything. How can I believe when you don't give a damn even about my greatest effort? You can promise me anything you want ...' His confession is met by general laughter and followed by the memorable image of a Polish flag being torn in different directions by politicians and bleeding as if it were living flesh.

One more passionate and bitter monologue regarding the nature and fate of his country runs through Adam's head as he relieves himself (or tries to) in a train lavatory, a moment of slapstick imbued with black humour:

> Since I can remember these seats always fall down by themselves. Why? Through the decades, imbeciles supervised by imbeciles put a toilet so close to the wall that its

seat must fall down. Decades, Jesus Christ . . . is this a bad metaphor for the Polish fate?

By juxtaposing the lofty and profane, by comparing the country itself to a lavatory with a seat that cannot stay up, the director bemoans, through Adam, the demise of the intelligentsia, a general failure to hold anything sacred and the lack of hope for improvement even in a new Poland.

The film depicts the political and social phenomena that trap Adam in a sort of existential cage of subjective horror. One such phenomenon is the erosion of what it means to be masculine. Adam struggles to find himself somewhere between the two polar extremes that predominate the idea of masculinity in post-Wall Poland. Mazierska describes this duality:

> These shifts [in the way men and women perceive their roles in society] are conceptualized by two apparently contrasting paradigms: the rise of masculinism . . . and the less widespread idea that Polish men are in a state of crisis . . . The second paradigm is rooted in the idea that the end of communism . . . brought men some drawbacks. They include the loss of status resulting from shrinking opportunities to be heroic, which for Polish males was regarded as the most noble destiny, promoted in Polish literature, art and mythology, especially of Romantic origin. (Mazierska 2006: 114)

Adam is nourished by the Romantic tradition. He discusses the greatest Polish Romantic poet, Adam Mickiewicz, with his pupils and repeatedly attempts to write a poem of his own in the same vein. The gulf between the Romantic world of his imagination and reality, his inability and

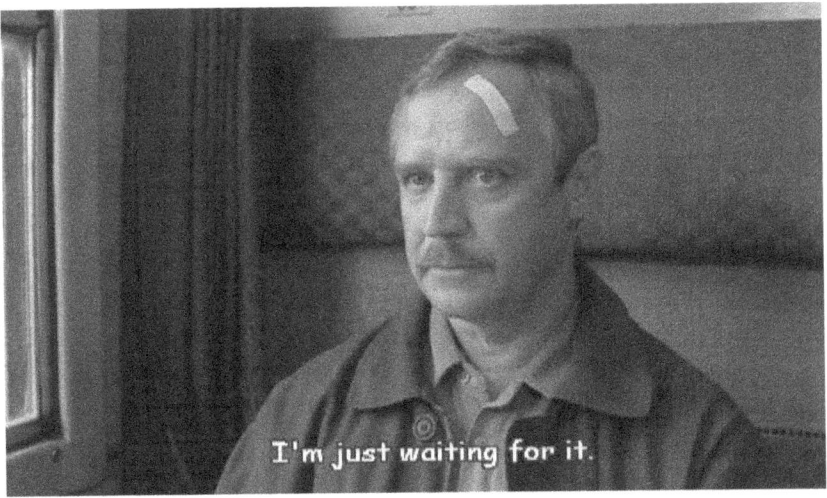

Figure 14.1 Adam on the train.

unpreparedness to confront his lack of masculinity – all these elements contribute to the black humour of the film.

While shaving in front of a mirror, Adam thinks of the macho men in films and suddenly turns into one. This transformation of a neurotic Adam into a pistol-packing cinematic 'tough guy' – complete with slick hair and 'wife-beater' vest, who quickly wipes the shaving cream off his face, grabs a shot of whisky and lights up a smoke – is grotesquely funny yet also quite telling. Emasculated by politics and society, Adam retaliates with an exaggeratedly masculine pose and a 'macho' demeanour borrowed, ironically, from the kinds of films that intellectual Adam must despise.[7]

In another example, Adam is sitting on a train trying to get away from the city and his life when a female passenger asks for help with her luggage.

> She: Could you take my luggage down, please?
> He: No.
> She: What? Excuse me?
> He: No. Nobody helps me.
> She: You're a man! . . .
> He: A man is a 'Man' if he takes out the garbage, fixes the outlet, or gives up a seat on a bus or a tram. I feel no need to be a real man. But you are a real man.

This seemingly shocking gender reversal should come as no surprise. Adam sees women as having taken over men's traditional power and roles. What is he left with, when stuck between the cult of masculinity and its crisis? Crushed by debilitating contempt of both society and politicians towards the intelligentsia and by his own inability to cut the umbilical cord from his mother, Adam becomes an infantile Adaś.[8]

Wacko takes the political and social issues facing contemporary Poland and refracts them through the lens of a 'loser', a frustrated intellectual. This process highlights the lack of difference between 'then' and 'now', forcing the viewer to contemplate the striking similarities between the past and the present. Even though society has changed, and post-Wall Poland is supposedly progressing, things remain fundamentally the same.

Black humour in *Wacko* is a well-chosen vehicle for conveying Adam's attempts to deal with the political and social, the public and private aspects of his life. The octology may be viewed as a form of directorial self-therapy; in order to heal himself, Koterski has to bring Adam's deepest inner essence to the fore and expose it. It is for us, the viewers, to decide who will dare 'cast the first stone' at Adam's weaknesses and shortcomings laid bare. Using Adam as his Everyman, Koterski seems to suggest that black humour of the darkest shade is a more appropriate approach to post-Wall Polish society than rose-tinted spectacles.

We're all Christs: Towards the Light at the End of the Tunnel

Christs, made four years after *Wacko*, tackles political issues as well but in a completely different vein. It also casts them in a more sombre light: the director seems to view the situation in post-communist Poland as getting progressively worse. This film has a much more complicated structure than *Wacko*. Instead of focusing on one main character and showing just one typical day in his life through the prism of his own perception, *Christs*, which deals with questions of faith and the fate of Poland, is complex, both on the levels of form and message. Two main characters, father and son, talk about their lives and compare memories, which differ drastically, about lives disfigured by addiction, depression, despair and the desire to commit murder and die. The son's recollections trigger Adam's memories as well, and the vicious circle of addiction and abuse comes to the fore in his thoughts as he looks back on his own childhood. The narration is anything but linear: in addition to all these intersecting and overlapping layers of memories, the lives of Adam and those closest to him are juxtaposed with Christ's passion and the crucifixion.[9]

On the one hand, we are shown an ordinary life in communist Poland, as Adam's memories take us back, in a series of flashbacks, to the 1970s and 1980s, when people eagerly complained about the system but did nothing to change it. On the other hand, in a key scene at Adam's favourite bar, a crucial moment in Polish and world history is shown. Four drinking pals watch and comment on televised coverage of Pope John Paul II's visit to his Polish homeland and his address to the crowd in Warsaw's Victory Square. He is commonly credited with starting the process that led to the fall of communism in Poland. Following the Pope's visit, Solidarity gained strength and momentum.

Koterski uses this episode to ridicule those who blamed the political system for problems that actually stemmed from their own weakness and apathy. Adam's voice is echoed and surrounded by his own 'Greek chorus', his three drinking pals who share his thoughts and dissatisfaction with themselves and the country:

Adam:	So many years taken away from me! Those damned Soviets!
Friend one:	So many years . . .
Adam:	My life was supposed to be completely different!
Friend two:	Why am I wasting my time here?
Adam:	I'm an expert on culture but they all take me for a sucker!
Friend two:	Why is it my lot to live in such a country?
Adam:	. . . In a constant hopelessness. . .

Friend one: To be ruled by some morons and butt-heads!
Friend three: A band of thieves! Brawlers!
Friend two: And clowns!

While Adam's companions lament that they drink because of Poland, their own life or to kill the pain of existence, he responds, 'And I drink in general'. Adam's refusal to find a specific reason or a scapegoat for his drinking is comical. Yet, at the same time, it is disturbing: an everyman drinking 'in general' stands as a universal representative of an all too common societal curse. As Adam and his mates watch the Pope on television, they are in awe of this remarkable man. In a fit of drunken exuberance Adam tries to reproduce one of his famous gestures: the imaginary binoculars the Pope pretends to use to represent communists watching the rest of the world from behind the Berlin Wall.

The actual final section of the Mass celebrated by Pope John Paul II in Warsaw in June 1979 addressed both faith and the fate of Poland. Without being overtly political or direct, the Pope's words suggested that Poles who love their country should contribute to changing its fate:

And I cry – I who am a Son of the land of Poland and who am also Pope John Paul II – I cry from all the depths of this Millennium, I cry on the vigil of Pentecost:

Let your Spirit descend.
Let your Spirit descend.
and renew the face of the earth,
the face of this land.
Amen.[10]

Adam and his drinking companions keep reiterating the final words of the speech, which Adam garbles, 'Send the Holy Ghost... whatever... land, this land!' The jarring juxtaposition of the Pope's words with Adam's drunken rant and his companions' empty complaints about the system is not meant to denigrate religion. Rather, it exposes the apathy of ordinary people stuck in their ways and comfortable with their customary complaints. At the same time, it bares the craving of adrift post-Wall souls for a meaningful existence, for spiritual connection, for a glimpse of hope. The black humour of this scene is perhaps more dark than funny but it resonates nonetheless.

Gradually, as a result of his alcoholism, Adam plummets from the social ladder, transformed from a respected professor of cultural history[11] into a nobody, 'processed' and humiliated at the police sobering-up station before being repeatedly beaten and robbed at a landfill. The landfill suggests associations with two prominent Polish films that feature the same setting: Kieślowski's *Trois couleurs: Blanc / Three Colours: White* (1994, France/Poland/Switzerland) and Andrzej Wajda's *Popiół i diament / Ashes and Diamonds* (1958). Yet, in each of them, the symbolism of the landfill is different. In Wajda it may be viewed as standing for the death of Christ and of Poland, as well as for the misguided life and senseless death of the protagonist; in Kieślowski it is a parodic nod to Wajda and an ironic encapsulation of the reality facing a post-communist Poland; in Koterski it is a symbol of the ultimate fall of humankind from which spiritual rebirth is possible (Falkowska, 150; Garn, 501–2). A new, fantastic social order replaces the ordinary one in this film: Adam is now suspended between good and evil, between a guardian angel and the devil. Another dichotomy stressed in the film – men and women – is gradually replaced by a dichotomy of victims and victimisers. Anybody – man, woman or child – can end up in either role. Victimisers become akin to the Roman soldier thrusting his spear into the side of the crucified Christ that suddenly appears on the screen amid twenty-first-century housing complexes.

When Koterski deals with Adam's private life in this film, the familiar black humour, evident in *Wacko* returns, but with a tenor that is more sombre and less comical: grotesque scatological motifs take the form of drunken urination; the farcical catalogue of diseases, doctors and pills is replaced by a deadly addiction to drugs and alcohol; thoughts of death and imaginary dying turn into real attempts at suicide and murder. Yet, at the same time, this film features comical incongruity in the form of discrepancies between two planes: between Adam's memories and those of his son; between Adam's recollections and the actual past. They are comical in their familiarity: Adam is not lying, because he believes his version of the past, and that makes him all the more pathetic and human.

When the four alcoholics drink, eat and urinate simultaneously, this visual device emphasises their loss of individuality. When drunk, Adam wets his bed, his son changes his trousers but can do nothing about his soaked mattress; the next morning Adam, unaware of what has happened, comes to his son to complain about the wet clothes in a comical tone of childish reproach and confusion. When Adam ends up repeatedly confined at a sobering-up station, a deeply unsettling scene takes place. Tied to his bed and unable to move even his head, Adam keeps crying out to his son. His drunken neighbour, unable to make him stop, comes up to him and urinates in his face. It is difficult to erase this scene from one's memory or to imagine a more degrading fall. Such episodes stretch the boundaries of black humour: they stray so far in the direction of horror that they are no longer laughable. Having reached this new low, and finding himself in a landfill, Adam compares himself to a urinating dog and decides to start a new life: 'Enough of seeing the world from the bottom, like a dog beaten for peeing in the living room'.[12]

Both murder and suicide are often referred to in this film. The film begins with the son's confession that he wanted his father to die. Numerous instances of violence, suicide and murderous thoughts occur throughout the film, and none is surprising: thrown into the depths of despair, addiction and abuse, the helpless characters lash out – at themselves and those around them. And yet there is hope. When Adam, lying on a pile of rubbish in the landfill, imagines his son talking to his companions about his dead father – 'He drank, went mad, and died' – this is a crucial moment that drives him towards change. He gets up and walks away from another circle of drunkards. Adam thinks of his son in a way that Poland should be thinking of its next generation, of its future: 'I don't want him to have to talk like that. I can't do this to him! He can't live happily with that stain. He won't have faith that he can succeed.'

When all else fails, when no hope seems to be left on this earth, a modern-day guardian angel, swearing with frustration, comes to their rescue: he saves Adam from an attempted suicide, from recurring instances of accidental near death and, most importantly, from drinking. With this image of a down-to-earth guardian angel that curses and wears some kind of a construction worker orange uniform with ridiculous, precariously attached cardboard wings, Koterski reminds us how misleading appearances are. The guardian angel observing his charge from a lifeguard's tower through binoculars, as father and son slowly walk on the beach, supporting each other, suggests that hope is out there and that the next generation has a chance to create a new and better Poland. While the situation in post-communist Poland appears to be grimmer for ordinary people than depicted in *Wacko*, this film ends on a more positive note.

Koterski skilfully balances the dark with the comic, and the nature of human perception and memory provides rich material for the latter. The mismatch between Adam's imagination and reality is at once funny and sad. Adam claims to have loved his son and never to have hit him. Yet, when his wife was pregnant with him, he violently opposed her desire to keep her pregnancy and kicked her belly to force a miscarriage. He brags to his mates that he is able to separate his public and private lives: 'My drinking never affects my job. I either drink or work.' We, however, witness him drinking with students, throwing up on his supervisor and losing his job. Yet Adam is being sincere, for he seems truly to believe what he says. Another frailty of the human mind the film explores is the selectivity of memory.[13] Adam becomes aware of this while comparing his recollections with those of his son. Adam remembers taking his son to a number of doctors; his son remembers just one time at the dentist, when his father abandoned him and returned drunk. Similarly, Adam remembers something to be proud of: seven years of holidaying with his son in the mountains, without drinking. His son, however, remembers only one holiday out of all these years, one that involved his father drinking and womanising.

The sordid side of life as shown in this film – its tragic moments of cruelty, abuse, addiction, suicide and murder – come close to overpowering its humour, yet the comical incongruities of self-perception versus the perception of others, and self-perception from various points in time that are interwoven with them, are just palliative enough to allow the viewer to appreciate the complexities Koterski places before them. Through these incongruities of perception and memory he focuses on the private, on universal and eternal human frailties, rather than on the public and modern. Koterski reframes the debate over the new Europe and casts it in different colours. Adam is Polish, yet he is also a citizen of the former Eastern Europe and of the new Europe. He combines uniquely Polish features with those that resonate with European and international audiences. Adam is not alone. Generations of citizens of the Eastern European countries face the same predicament as he does: finding their new identities in the new Europe, reversing the collective trauma of life in the totalitarian system that shaped them.[14] Time and again Koterski reminds us to look first in the mirror, and that it is better to look in the mirror through the lens of dark humour than rose-tinted spectacles. Black comedy can make the sight of truth palatable, allow people to find their true strength and offer a helping hand to the next generation.

Conclusion

These two films by Marek Koterski deal with Poland's fate and the attempts of its 'Adams', that is, of typical Polish intellectuals of his generation, to fit in. In them Koterski appears to have re-evaluated his view of the earthly and the heavenly. Political changes, even those as dramatic as the fall of the Berlin Wall and the collapse of communist Eastern Europe, do not alter much in the lives of ordinary people. Only in faith and love, Koterski suggests, can salvation and hope be found. Black humour is Koterski's satirical weapon aimed at both East and West, at past and at present, a weapon that blasts away at the deceptive surfaces and reveals what truly matters. When Adam, in the depths of degradation in *Christs*, makes his landfill confession, he finds a piece of paper with the Apostle Paul's words on love: 'If I had all the knowledge and had not love – I'd be nothing. Love forgets all evil. Love can bear anything, endure everything.' This miraculous coincidence, this sudden reminder of Adam's only source of hope, is one of the film's major ideas.

The ending of *Christs* brings us back to the very first scene, father and son sitting at a table having a difficult conversation. But the last exchange is quite different from the first one. It is a confession of love:

Father: I want you to know one thing, son.
Son: Yeah?
Father: You had every right to wish I was dead.
Son: Just like that? It's not a bad thing?
Father: You had . . . you have every right to hate me.
Son: What a relief. But can I love you?
Father: You can. And can I love you?
Son: Sure! But you already love me.
Father: That I do.

Koterski's message seems to be quite straightforward: love is the key. Love has a profound significance in Roman Catholicism: it is the essence of God, it is one of the three divine virtues enumerated by the Apostle Paul in the very text that Adam finds in the landfill (love or charity, faith and hope), and the most important of them. Koterski suggests that only love offers hope as well as the solution that no political transformation can ever provide, both for individuals and for society.

Made in 2002 and 2006, *Wacko* and *Christs* give us a unique opportunity to trace the artist's development and his shifting perception of political events, the new Poland and new Europe. *Wacko* is a more comical film, yet it has a tragic conclusion: 'nothing changes, and life is not worth living'. The latter film, *Christs*, is harder to watch and more earnest, yet it offers its reward, a 'light at the end of the tunnel'. Even if, in a certain sense, Koterski might be succeeding Andrzej Wajda as the new, quintessentially Polish director, in another crucial sense he is following in the footsteps of Krzysztof Kieślowski in that he transfers his attention from the political and social to the spiritual, universal and eternal. And, fortunately for his audience, he above all manages to remain an original and unique auteur, a skilled practitioner of the powerful art of black humour.

CHAPTER 15

East Germany Revisited, Reimagined, Repositioned: Representing the GDR in Dominik Graf's *Der rote Kakadu* (2005) and Christian Petzold's *Barbara* (2012)

Nick Hodgin (University of Lancaster)

Book and box-office sales vary but publishers, broadcasters and producers recognise that, more than twenty years after the collapse of the East German state, the interest in the German Democratic Republic, from the thanatouristic curiosity in the GDR's dark sites and misdeeds to the desire to know more about the everyday life histories, is sufficient to warrant continued investment. Conflicted memories, new revelations and diverging opinions have been a mainstay of post-GDR discourse, in some cases almost eclipsing the texts themselves, as was evident in the reception to *Das Leben der Anderen/ The Lives of Others* (Florian Henckel von Donnersmarck, 2007, Germany) and the reporting of Angela Merkel's selection of *Die Legende von Paul und Paula/ The Legend of Paul and Paula* (Heiner Carow, 1973, GDR) as her favourite film (doubtless with an eye on the East German constituency and the 2013 election).

East German autobiographies, memoirs, and documentary series arguably enjoy good ratings because these programmes, featuring ordinary East Germans talking about their lives in the GDR, offer more nuanced accounts than had previously been the case and, in so doing, shift post-GDR discourse from the victims and villains narrative to one that privileges private experience over broad historical surveys, an emphasis, then, on personal, rather than professional, accounts which broadly corresponds with what Maier (5) terms the 'dialectic of Herrschaft [domination] and Gesellschaft [society]'. Surveys and questionnaires bear out the East Germans' somewhat proprietorial approach to accounts of lives lived, a suspicion that is well founded given that West Germans have tended to mediate East German history (Ahbe 2011). But, while many people rationalise this approach, arguing that it goes some way to providing a normalised portrait of the GDR, critics (including numerous politicians) have attributed the inaccurate history and conspicuous errors that characterise many young people's knowledge of the GDR to the increased focus on the politics of the everyday, arguing that this is what happens when ostensibly objective historical accounts are eclipsed by a range of subjective histories narrated according to limited personal experience and selective or inaccurate memory. The Sabrow Commission, established in 2005 to assess the different modes of remembering the GDR and to make recommendations regarding memorialisation proposals, observed the disjuncture between Eastern and Western accounts of the GDR and noted, too, problems in the secondary education treatment of the GDR as well as a general trivialisation of the state. Their report, which also underlined the need for a differentiated interpretation was not welcomed by all, with critics arguing that an increased focus on everyday life in the GDR would 'relativize the extent of repression under the regime' (de Simine, 96). Luthar and Pušnik stress the importance of recognising the banality of everyday life under socialism and the need to rescue the microhistory of domestic space which has been obfuscated by the focus on male-oriented activities, and of avoiding the 'articulation of cold war values' on which the totalitarian paradigm has continued to rely (4).

The purpose of this chapter is to consider the ways in which two post-millennial portrayals of the GDR, Dominik Graf's *Der rote Kakadu/The Red Cockatoo* (2005, Germany) and Christian Petzold's *Barbara* (2012, Germany), each attempts to reimagine the East German past: the early 1960s in Graf's film, the early 1980s in Petzold's. The East German state was terra incognita for many in the West and intranational movement continues to be largely occidental in orientation; thus, the media's provision of images has been crucial in defining the ways in which we see the East, both past and present. Though there have been so many films made about the GDR that it is impossible to establish clear taxonomies, one can point to certain tendencies, thematic preoccupations and formal similarities. Few films offer new interpretations of the GDR but settle instead for homogeneous and reductive accounts which reinforce the limited (and, one might argue, deliberately limiting) master narratives.

What is interesting about the films under review is that both offer a means of re-evaluating our ideas about the GDR (and its representation) but without departing from conventional representation. Indeed, their box-office success is probably more attributable to their conventionality than to their iconoclasm. Both films demonstrate a clear engagement with genre cinema, specifically melodrama, albeit in ways very different from one another. 'Recourse to drama', as Nietzsche maintained, 'betrays that an artist is more a master of false means than of genuine means' (440) and this, arguably, holds true for many of the portrayals of the GDR. Hake has spoken of the 'gradual disappearance of history into media simulations and filmic spectacles' (212) and noted how conventional film-makers are in 'their reliance on visual pleasure and their validation of the personal in position to the political'. Graf and Petzold, however, each uses melodrama to problematise prevailing ideas about the GDR and its representation. If, as Rancière suggests, 'politics comes about solely through interruption' (13), the films under discussion constitute a political cinema through various moments of (formal and discursive) rupture.

Hope, Remembered: Dominik Graf's GDR

In popular culture, the best-known memory narratives by the so-called Trabant Generation, focus on life in the 1970s and 1980s in books and films whose recollections are, in many cases, a mixture of self-awareness, irony and melancholia. The autobiographies and life stories of older generations, those born in and before the GDR, are, by contrast, often more serious, reflective accounts. These provide a range of experiences and interpretations, from those who were in power and find that that the GDR was essentially sound in theory if not in practice, to those whose recollections offer a more complex, self-analytical approach to their past, exploring, as Bathrick puts it, 'the inchoate subliminal region of social life, where an individual self and the power of the state become proximate' (230). Film portrayals of the GDR have seldom reached back further than the 1970s; the more commercial aspects of the *Ostalgie* trend, whose films became the 'dominant cinematic mode of remembrance' (Fisher, 195), focus principally on the Honecker era of real, existing socialism and not the erratic and fluctuating hard-line Stalinism that characterised the Ulbricht era. Until recently, there has been no equivalent fascination for earlier decades, though that has begun to change with dramatisations of hinge events, such as the Berlin blockade and the Berlin Wall, and the republication of texts that chronicle the first decades of the GDR, notably Brigitte Reimann's *Ankunft im Alltag*, one of the GDR's key socialist realist novels.

Given the interest in the GDR *Alltag*, the Berlin-based production company, X Filme, producers of some of the most critically and commercially successful recent films in Germany, must have been confident that *The Red Cockatoo*, a melodrama focusing on a group of young people growing up in Dresden in the months before the building of the Berlin Wall, would perform well at the box office. Not only was the topic on trend, its script was co-written by Michael Klier, who was held in high regard by critics, while Dominik Graf, one of the most respected film-makers in Germany, had signed up as the director.[1] Both the film poster of the three young protagonists in hip period outfits sitting on an iconic Schwalbe scooter against a multicoloured backdrop and the stylish website, featuring a rock 'n' roll soundtrack and numerous stills of the young, attractive actors, must have led some people to think they were going to see a colourful celebration of the GDR. But anyone expecting an *Ostalgie* film will have been disappointed. Though the film begins with archival footage that situates the film historically (namely scenes of Gagarin's space flight in April 1961), which is reminiscent of both the optimistic tone and visual arrangement of the opening sequences in films, such as *Helden wie Wir/Heroes Like Us* (Sebastian Peterson, 1999, Germany) and *Good Bye, Lenin!* (Wolfgang Becker, 1999, Germany), Graf's GDR is one in which state oppression is immediately brought into play. This is not the whimsical, vaguely inept Stasi state glimpsed in *Sonnenalle/Sun Alley* (Leander Haussmann, 1999, Germany) and other films, but a state whose representatives are ruthless and brutal in their treatment of its citizens. Despite Graf's focus on the Stasi and their tactics, which range from subtle manipulation of those seeking to infiltrate the Red Cockatoo music club, to physical abuse, his film does not dwell solely on the GDR as a totalitarian state. Klier's script drew on his own adolescence in Dresden (shortly before emigrating to the west) and was for Graf an opportunity to present a story of everyday life during a period when, according to the director, many young East Germans were still optimistic about their state (Suchsland 2006).[2]

Graf has also insisted that his film is not a historical drama but, rather, a love story which brings in the wider political and historical context only in the final stages of the narrative. His resistance to the label may in part be explained by the director's aversion to the earlier post-unification GDR narratives. Yet Graf also suggested in one interview that his film challenged the top–down narratives of what he provocatively terms 'imperialist history' and that, for him, the conflicting cinematic portrayals of the GDR are reminiscent of the 1980s 'Historians' Debate' which had revolved around opposing historiographical approaches, approaches that were shaped by, and fed into, political discourses. Where some historians sought to free German history of its National Socialist focus and thus facilitate a restored national pride, others argued that German history was uniquely problematic. German unification further exacerbated the debate with historians on the right, their confidence boosted by political triumphalism, regarding this caesura as a return to a national history; this triumphalism would seek to delegitimise the GDR, its historiography, politics and, as a consequence, its population's life stories.

Graf argues that his film offers a version of the GDR that would connect with the experiences of ordinary East Germans, privileging the social memory of the GDR over what Pierre Nora terms 'the terrorism of historicized memory'(1989: 14). Graf rejects both the historical narratives provided in contemporary history culture and, by implication, 'histotainment', and cautions against documentary films' provision of historical facts and the authority attributed to witness testimonies, arguing instead for a more dialectical approach, the mediation of history through the politics of memory which, borrowing from Assmann, we might term 'mnemohistorical' (1997: 9–10). His determination to bring some balance to those historical accounts that simply contribute to the narrative of the GDR as the Stasi state does not, however, mean indulging the fondly remembered GDR adolescence in the way that other films do – or, at least, were seen to do. The director's attitude towards the GDR and towards its subsequent representation is less a question of rescuing social memory from the totalising narratives of history than it is representative of the left's mourning for the GDR's unrealised potential.

The historical framing of the film (signalled by the intertitles' regular countdown towards the date of the Berlin Wall's construction) is significant. The film opens with a reference to one of socialism's greatest achievements, the first manned space mission, and ends with perhaps its most infamous gesture, the construction of the Berlin Wall. These two events are, of course, intended to symbolise both the high hopes of socialism and its corruption. *The Red Cockatoo* initially outlines the conflict between state and citizens as a clash between generations before sketching out the broader ideological contexts and underpinning the hopes and aspirations of the so-called 'fatherless generation'. According to Mary Fulbrook, this generation was, despite the real opportunities available to them in the form of education and upward mobility through the GDR's functionary system, not just 'unwilling to commit themselves to the new cause' in the way the previous generation had, but was 'widely opposed to any political ideology, including communism' (345). But for Luise (Jessica Schwarz), the GDR remains a project to be worked on, and, though victimised by representatives of the state, she apparently remains committed to socialism's guiding principles. This is evident in the exchanges with Siggi (Max Riemelt), her admirer, who is considering leaving the GDR. At times, her attachment to the GDR is voiced indirectly through criticisms of the West. She notes, for example, that 'executioners still run the economy' in the Federal Republic of Germany, which echoes the GDR's historical accusations and prefigures the charges made by the 68ers (the 1968 generation) in the west that many National Socialists had gone on to enjoy successful post-war careers.[3] Other comments transcend the historical context and will resonate with some contemporary sentiments, notably that the West is less meritocratic than it purports to be; that the West is a superficial society (a sentiment, in fact, more typical of her parent's generation if we are to follow Fulbrook's analysis (2011: 349), and somewhat contradictory given her interest in Western pop culture and the status accorded fashion in the Kakadu). There are also clear, unambiguous endorsements which, likewise, echo contemporary attitudes towards the GDR. 'I am sure we have the right conditions to become the better state' she comments at one point; later she argues that 'the right people need to steer the state and not the old guard'. Despite these utterances, Luise's commitment to the GDR is evidently more a matter of private belief in the GDR's utopian vision, a confidence in the state's potential, than it is of being politically active.

Such utopianism is a significant development in films about the GDR. While other post-unification films have focused on state corruption, or on the conflict between individuals and the regime, or broadened the view of the GDR by considering everyday lives, very few films have acknowledged the sincerity of feeling or the high hopes that many East Germans held for their state. Such focus would have been inconceivable in the immediate post-GDR period when the East Germans had overwhelmingly voted for unification; and any consideration of the GDR's ideological aspirations was politically questionable thereafter – certainly in terms of popular culture. Positive memories of lives lived in the GDR rather than of the GDR were more frequently articulated but these were seldom ideologically inflected. These statements, then, are instances, or interruptions, in which Graf creates some space to reflect on socialism's potential. Graf's film establishes the historical context for the GDR's aspirations evident in the rebuilding of Dresden and references to the *Aufbau* of the East German state. The film also references several times the destruction of Dresden – the ruins are to be seen in the background still; Siggi is suddenly distracted during an intimate moment with one girl when he sees her scars sustained in the firebombing; Luise and Wolle's relationship has its origins in the same Allied attacks. The *Aufbau* motif is thus as much an issue of physical restoration as it is of ideological renewal, a symbolic acknowledgment of the GDR's attempt to construct a new and better society. Referencing what came before the GDR lengthens East German history and thus lends the narrative a seldom-acknowledged contextual depth and chronological meaning; according to this account, the state arose, first and foremost, not in opposition to the West but out of the ashes of the NS past.

A poet, whose work is condemned by the authorities and whose unofficial publication (privately arranged by Siggi) threatens eventual prosecution, the sexually and intellectually confident Luise is coded as both feminist and dissident. Luise's attempt to make sense of the GDR, her hopes for the state together with her youthful exuberance and irreverence, cause friction not just between her and the system but also between her and the two men in her life, the Apollonian Siggi, a sensitive artist who is torn between her free spirit and the freedom of the West, and the Dionysian figure of Wolle, her husband, an irreverent rebel with little concern for his actions. Dilemmas of this kind were a stock theme in early East German film and literature. Making the right choice meant choosing the side of socialism, if not for what it already offered then for what it might yet offer. Graf bemoaned the lack of characters such as Maria Morzeck (from Kurt Maetzig's celebrated DEFA classic *Das Kaninchen bin ich/I am the Rabbit* (1961, GDR), which went unseen until after the GDR's collapse) in contemporary German film, and Luise, the independent, intelligent, creative, politically progressive socialist, can be seen as an attempt to address this absence.

A parallel may also be drawn with films such as *Berlin Ecke Schönhauser/Berlin Schönhauser Corner* (Gerhard Klein, 1957, GDR), particularly given the films' chosen milieus and their focus on East German youth culture at a time when the state was looking East while many young East Germans were looking West. But, though connections can be made with some East German productions (notably, those films that were removed by the state but which have since, rather problematically, become part of the DEFA canon), there are some clear divergences. The two DEFA films referred to might have suffered at the hands of the East German authorities, who pronounced them provocative and 'unsocialist', but they did clearly side with the GDR project, if not with its managers. The young Berliner played by Ekkehard Schall in Klein's film, whose rebellious nature but thoroughness at the workplace made him too ambiguous a hero for SED (Socialist Unity Party of Germany) ideologues abandons his refuge in West Berlin and returns home. Maria Morzeck, meanwhile, (constructively) criticises inconsistencies in the East German legal system but, finally surmounting various difficulties, is able to look forward to a bright future in the young state (a reformist's happy ending that was denied the director). While Graf cannot conclude his film with didactic codas of this kind, *The Red Cockatoo* does clearly acknowledge the optimism, however vain this might have been, that the GDR could have become the better Germany, something Graf acknowledges when he says that the GDR he presents 'belongs to my desired image of Germany had it had had the opportunity to become a different country' (Sterneborg).

His film does not therefore fit with Robert Rosenstone's assertion in his essay on the historical film that 'the message delivered on the screen is almost always that things are getting better or have gotten better or both' (56). Instead, *The Red Cockatoo* attempts to reposition East German history, to arrange it according to coordinates seldom acknowledged in post-unification discourse, by which I mean the GDR's successes and its idealism, as compromised as these were. Graf's film never actually waves the flag for communism but it does indicate why others might have chosen to – the GDR's prehistory (the Nazis' war, the Allied bombing) offers us pause for thought; criticism of the FRG's post-war order provides further context (and here Graf is umbilically tied to Western 68er rather than the SED even if the rhetoric is not dissimilar). Ostensibly, the film is a generic composite, a rites of passage–thriller–melodrama. But for all the generic conventions and topoi, the film also upsets typological expectations: the marketing for the film gestures towards *Ostalgie* but the film is not nostalgic for the past per se but for its past potential; it celebrates not youth but the possibilities of youth and inscribes what superficially is a mainstream drama with the ideological sensibilities that characterised those films withdrawn by the East German authorities.

The film ends with a retrospective voiceover in which Siggi, who fled to the West only days before the construction of the Wall and whose relationship with Luise was thus permanently severed, reflects on his life in the GDR, commenting that 'time has preserved both Luise's beauty and her ideals' and that she remains 'the epitome of those ideals'. The final line is a eulogy for, and not a defence of, a lost cause. Graf, then, stands in line with other left-wing intellectuals clinging still to an idealised socialism, and to the hope for a future Utopia that is retreating ever further into the past.

The GDR as Generic Collage: Petzold's *Barbara*

On its release, Petzold's film was frequently compared with *The Lives of Others*, an evaluation prompted more by their topical similarities and their apparent commitment to authenticity, a preoccupation with a faithful representation of history that in Germany especially has become an increasingly limiting consideration in the critical reception of historical dramas, than any true overlap. Despite some correspondence in cinematography (defined more by absence, there is none of the retro-fitted glamour and ironic kitsch associated with *Ostalgie*) and the fact that these are imagined East German lives whose temporal coordinates roughly coincide, the resulting depictions diverge in important ways.

While both focus on the nexus between state and individual, Petzold's film is far more concerned with providing a version of the GDR that eschews the binarism of *The Lives of Others*. Though also quite different from Graf's film, formally especially, there is at least an isomorphic

Figure 15.1 Barbara (Nina Hoss) moving forward but often looking backwards in *Barbara*.

connection with *The Red Cockatoo*. The two films are connected chronologically (Barbara is roughly the age that Graf's Luise would be in 1980) and thus offer audiences access to two points of this generation's imagined continuum. If Graf's film depicts the dreams and hopes of the fatherless generation at a time where such aspirations, whether private or collective, still exist but are increasingly compromised, Petzold's film initially reveals a GDR in which such private hope has all but faded. The differences between the films are especially interesting given that Petzold, like von Donnersmarck and Graf, turns to melodrama. The female protagonist, caught between life-changing decisions, between two different men, a victim of sinister forces (elements at play in both *The Lives of Others* and *The Red Cockatoo*) are all common to melodrama. But, in contrast to Graf's redeployment of genre in an effort to challenge master narratives and to revisit leftist utopianism, Petzold seeks in his film to re-present the GDR by reconceptualising genre, simultaneously observing, manipulating, and subverting its conventions. Saying of his own efforts that he feels as though he works 'in the cemetery of genre cinema, from the remainders that are still there for the taking' (Abel 2008) suggests a Frankensteinian labour, the end product of which bears some resemblance to, but is significantly different from, the model from which it draws inspiration.

In *Barbara*, Petzold follows the eponymous protagonist, a talented medical doctor whose exit application has resulted, as punishment, in her exile to a provincial hospital from the Charité in Berlin. Barbara (played by Petzold's long-time associate, Nina Hoss) does not seek to establish a new life in the province but to survive her relocation, opting for an ostensible, near-mute, passivity which she maintains despite the physical and psychological intrusions of the Stasi as well as the attentions of a colleague, André (Ronald Zehrfeld). Her intention to flee the GDR with her Western lover, a visiting businessman, enables her to endure the manipulations and advances of the state's security agents and fellow worker, while her professional duties, to which she is committed above all else, provide the only other area on which she focuses her energies.

Barbara offers the educated and cine-literate viewers an abundance of references to scholarship, literature, art and film history. An assured and erudite interviewee, Petzold has been instrumental in shaping the discussion of his own work and, in the case of this particular production, has made reference to several films whose influence, whether stylistically or in terms of moral or ethical deliberations, might not otherwise have been discerned: from William Friedkin's *French Connection* (1971, United States) to some of Rock Hudson's medical dramas. He has acknowledged, too, artists, writers, film theories and theorists, among them Walter Benjamin, Gilles Deleuze, Hermann Broch and Gerhard Richter. Abel (2013: 96) has commented on the relation of the latter's images to some of those in Petzold's films, and the artist's compositional techniques are sporadically referenced in *Barbara*, as in the penultimate scene in which Barbara and Stella, a former patient and escapee from a youth penal centre, move across the beach to their rendezvous with the scuba-diver who will deliver them from the GDR. Hans Fromm's camera work employs a completely different colour scheme from previous night scenes. Richter's influence is discernible in the scene's tonal composition, the blues and greys of the coastal landscape against which Barbara's pallid face appears both overexposed and almost superimposed, recalling the imprecision and opacity of Richter's work. Caspar David Friedrich, too, is briefly and multiply referenced in the seascape and through the *Rückenfigur* image of Barbara, a visual citation made even more recognisable in the marketing posters. These references are by no means the only examples of Petzold's inventive collaging of disparate influences. The fairy-tale tradition is invoked when Barbara enters a dark wood (complete with empty wicker basket) to meet her lover, a lupine businessman from the West, a relationship that may anticipate the later perception of the West's subsequent devouring of the innocent East. Elsewhere, the film's use of landscape plays an important role. Nature does not signal a means of escape but is a site of oppression and danger; the film thus subverts *Heimat* topoi, re-presenting the subject's experience of the rural not as an opportunity to commune with nature or become part of a community but as one defined by isolation and risk. The route along which Barbara cycles cuts between a bank of trees and flat fields; our identification with her paranoia (gesturally communicated by her furtive glances and anxious expression) is augmented by the sound of the trees, their aural presence an unusually loud recording. Indeed, the film's sound design is carefully arranged with everyday noises used to increase tension, whether the wind, the jarring buzz of a doorbell, or the snap of surgical gloves being pulled on shortly before a strip-search.

Though, initially, it looks to offer audiences the reassurance of recognition, by gesturing towards melodrama, *Barbara* disrupts generic expectation by consciously undermining the very genre it invokes. Passion is largely absent; at best it is underplayed, interrupted. Barbara's encounter with her lover is more furtive and desperate than it is passionate, a rendezvous that is made less romantic still by his post-coital gift/payment of Western cigarettes and, afterwards, his colleague's lewd interest in the encounter ('was it at least worth it?'). Music, too, is notable by its absence. While music in meldodrama 'often replaces words [. . .] to underscore the emotional subtext' as Fisher (202) argues it does in *The Lives of Others*, its absence in *Barbara* increases the tension. Paradoxically, Petzold's exclusion of music to accompany scenes where one might expect a soundtrack to heighten urgency, to emphasise emotion, whether terror, longing or dread, does not mean the exclusion of affect, for silence, too, becomes oppressive.

It would be wrong to suggest that Petzold redefines the portrayal of the GDR, for the film does not so detach itself from conventional representations as to render the familiar wholly unfamiliar. Indeed, one might note that *Barbara* features images and themes whose routine appearance in post-unification discourse have become a cliché. The encounter between a Trabant driver and the Western businessman in his glistening Mercedes is the most obvious of these. Yet, its inclusion is not incidental nor, I would suggest, a question of relying unthinkingly on stock signifiers. The director dwells on this chance meeting and even returns to it when the Mercedes driver tells his colleague about the encounter. Why, more than twenty years after unification, does Petzold use such hackneyed signifiers, ones whose shelf life seemed finally to have come to an end in post-millennial depictions of the GDR? While some directors (such as Andreas Dresen) avoid the contrived markers of East Germanness, Petzold not only engages with them, he foregrounds them, highlighting how limited post-unification discourse has been in order, arguably, finally to break out of it. That discourse has, of course, evolved over a quarter of a century (more than half as long as the GDR existed) but the recourse to clichés and stereotypes continues; my suggestion, then, is that Petzold is, in a sense, parodying conventional representations. If the metaphorical dualism of Trabant/Mercedes is part of the visual grammar of post-unification discourse, then its use here is to undermine it, not by avoiding it but by dramatising it, by drawing attention to such overworked juxtapositions. Ever alert to the meaning and power of signs, Petzold makes deliberate use of the cars to remind us of the reductive either/or binarism that has long characterised post-unification accounts of the GDR, using cliché as parody, for parody as, William Brown notes in his discussion of Deleuze, 'defeats cliché' (2013: 125).

In contrast to the verbose protagonists of *The Red Cockatoo* seen discussing options, voicing opinions, sermonising, exclaiming, Petzold's characters are reticent, their conversations piecemeal, the dialogues often out of balance. André's attempts to foster discussion flounder because of Barbara's suspicion and careful restraint; only professional considerations give rise to any mutuality of exchange. Nevertheless, the dialogue in *Barbara*, as in *The Red Cockatoo*, includes a number of ideological statements that affirm the guiding principles of socialism and present a critique of the West, and which, in earlier depictions of the GDR, would have been imaginable only if voiced by the state's representatives and not those with whom viewers are expected to identify. André's reminder to Barbara that her education was due to the 'workers' and peasants' state' is not quite homologous to Luise's quasi slogans; belief in the GDR's potential had largely disappeared by 1980 and it was no longer possible to defend the GDR's moral high ground. It does, however, echo the sentiment that the GDR was a *welfare* dictatorship. Similarly, the unbidden assurance Barbara's lover makes that she will not need to work once in the West, a promise which goes uncommented, reminds us that, with regard to female emancipation, West German society was some way behind that of the GDR. The reasons for the significant number of women in the East German workforce was, of course, as much a question of labour shortages as it was a matter of genuine emancipation; nevertheless, the abiding memory is that, in terms of professional self-realisation, women could be better off in the GDR, and Barbara's decision, finally, to stay in the GDR is as much an acknowledgement of this as it is a recognition that André respects her professional role. The film is not an apology for the GDR, of course; plenty of instances testify to its repressive nature. But here, too, the film resists the one-dimensional portraits highlighted as problematic by Dresen in his criticism of *The Lives of Others*. The latter's argument, namely that Stasi officers would be better portrayed if they were shown to be ordinary family men at the weekend and ruthless civil servants during the week, is evident in Petzold's film in which the Stasi officer, who organises Barbara's intimidation with little regard for the trauma caused, is also seen to be bereft at his wife's terminal cancer (Hodgin 2011: 84). André, whose role as informer is outlined in the first scene and is soon obvious to Barbara, is presented as a victim of the system, with a backstory providing the contextual information for his Stasi association. His behaviour demonstrates that he serves the Hippocratic oath before any hospital or Stasi protocol, though Petzold ensures that the level of commitment to his role as informer is ambiguous. While the discovery of collaboration and its repercussions is (and continues to be) a tried-and-tested narrative concern in GDR period films, this is much less a consideration for Petzold who undermines the potential suspense and impact of such revelations by establishing André's connections from the start without fully relinquishing its invocation of the thriller genre. Just as the director routinely confounds certain generic expectations, so, too, does he challenge our perceptions of the East German past.

A clue to Petzold's approach to representing the GDR may be found in an earlier scene where André and Barbara discuss the print of Rembrandt's *The Anatomy Lesson of Dr Nicolaes Tulp* hanging in the small laboratory. André's thoughts about Rembrandt's famous perspectival inversion, namely the right-handed arm on the corpse's left side, the perspective offered in the medical atlas transposed to the cadaver, might serve as André's oblique caution to Barbara about the dangers of misperception. The director has indicated that the scene is intended as a commentary, via Sebald's discussion of the image, on the ruinous effect that the 'Objectification of the Enlightenment in the everyday politics' has, likening Rembrandt's scientists to communism's 'corrupt functionaries' [my translation] (Hinrichsen), from which we may infer that the prone figure of Aris Kindt to symbolise the East German people similarly overlooked. But one wonders whether Petzold's inclusion of this picture might not also serve as an acknowledgement of the problems of representing reality. Thus, Sebald's contention that 'the much admired verisimilitude [. . .] proves on closer examination to be more apparent than real' (16) holds true not just for our engagement with Rembrandt but for our engagement with the depictions of the GDR. The concern with modes of representation makes the references to Caspar David Friedrich and to Gerhard Richter more than visual allusions. Petzold may not be as 'preoccupied by the impossibility of representing historical fact' as Mary Jacobus (56) says of Richter but, in all its multilayered and intertextual references, its invocation and subversion of genre, *Barbara* may be reminding us of the constructedness and multiplicity of memory.

Conclusion

What does distinguish *Barbara* from many other films made about the GDR is the choice the protagonist finally makes. The state's power to intrude into its citizens' private lives makes clear the reasons for Barbara's desire to escape but, as with the protagonists of Petzold's other films, Barbara does not finally escape; she sends the young girl in her place and returns to the hospital. Protagonists in earlier post-unification depictions were seldom granted such agency. In films such as *Das Versprechen/The Promise* (Margarethe von Trotta, 1995, Germany), they are the victims of history, their fates decided by circumstances beyond their control. Petzold, like Graf, positions his protagonists at a point where they must choose whether to stay in the GDR or whether to leave. The dilemma of departure in fact reconnects Petzold's and Graf's films to pre-1989 narratives. Rita famously faces the predicament of whether to follow her love to the West in *Der Geteilte Himmel/Divided Sky* (Konrad Wolf, 1964, GDR), finally deciding to stay in East Germany. In Roland Gräf's film, *Die Flucht/The Escape* (1977, GDR), the protagonist, also a doctor, faces the dilemma of how to reverse the plans to escape when his situation unexpectedly improves. Choosing to abandon the GDR could never have been permitted in those DEFA films; one reaffirms the possibilities seemingly still available in the GDR, the other hints at opportunities for improvement (and underlines, as had Klein's film two decades earlier, that escape can be fatal – the doctor, who has found new professional and personal reasons to stay in the East, is killed by the men who would take him to the West). The reasons for Barbara's decision are deliberately ambiguous. Is it because she wishes to save another victim (Stella)? Is it because of her attraction to André? Is it the realisation that the freedoms of the West are not without compromise? In contrast to the explicit eulogy wistfully narrated at the end of Graf's film, Petzold provides a characteristically anticlimactic ending: Barbara simply returns to her station, sitting silently between her colleague (and Stasi informer) and a failed suicide. I am less inclined to view this teleologically as a decision that anticipates the end (of the GDR) that is yet to come but rather as Petzold's attempt to provoke interpretation, to require the viewer to ruminate on Barbara's decision. Where Graf ambitiously seeks to widen the purview of the East by exploring the utopianism that has largely been subsumed within totalitarian discourse and only rarely considered in film, Petzold avoids the grand narratives, opting for a formally diverse and complex narrative, an approach reminiscent of Lyotard's *petit récits* (Kearney, 208), to provide a polysemic portrait of the GDR, one requiring a greater degree of what Bordwell terms 'inferential elaboration' (2012: 50). The further the GDR recedes into the past, the more problematic may be the representations of that state, that time, as future generations will have recourse to ever fewer first-hand accounts, to those whose memories of the GDR have frequently challenged, endorsed, rejected the post mortem analysis. The subtle, self-reflexive approach favoured by Petzold may prove too elusive for those who lack closer knowledge or understanding of the East Germans' forty-year existence or the wider contexts of the Cold War and of its representation. Similarly, acknowledging the East Germans' optimism as Graf in particular does, seeing this not teleogically (frequently rendered as dream-become-nightmare) but chronologically, will probably feature in still fewer accounts than those we have already seen. It would be inaccurate to claim that either film constitutes a radical intervention in post-GDR discourse but they do mark important shifts in its representation. A quarter of a century after the state's collapse, the need for such differentiation is crucial.

CHAPTER 16

Barluschke: Towards an East–West Schizo-history

Kalani Michell (University of Minnesota)

In 1997, after a five-year respite from film-making at the Berliner Ensemble, Thomas Heise, an East German author and director for theatre and film, now self-employed in the West, makes a film about somebody who is professionally trained in the art of changing sides. Somebody who has learned how to migrate in between, and adapt to, the different geopolitical spaces of the East and the West, as well as how to apply these skills to other situations in life. This somebody, Berthold Barluschke, worked as a secret agent for the East German Ministry for State Security (MfS); lived in Sweden, Spain, Columbia and New York under a West German identity; married a German-Jewish-American physician in the United States; so fully assumed his alias that he listed this West German name, Knut Dammasch, on his daughter's birth announcement; had a romantic relationship with his party functionary; changed sides to work for the West German Federal Intelligence Service; was accused of selling off the assets of the East German National People's Army after reunification; and, in this film, still has difficulties keeping track of who he is and where he is.

Berthold Barluschke first appears in this film when he is leaving. The camera observes Bert and his other self, his reflection in the mirror, as he paces around the living room. He yells out: 'Danny, come on! Anna . . . Joanna! Hurry up!'[1] When Bert leaves the room, the camera doesn't follow him but stays behind to observe the space. With Bert out of the picture, a roll of bubble paper occupies the centre of the frame. There are boxes stuffed with plastic sheeting, artwork around the room that has yet to be packed and, in the reflection of the mirror, a table covered with bottles and glasses. The room is still in use. Bert returns and waits in front of the piano, fidgeting and scratching his beard. Then he finally gives in, striding across the room and out the door for a second time. The camera is left alone to look at the same not-so-empty frame once again. Viewers can hear him in the background: 'Danny, come on, it costs money when the film is running! And so on . . . and the time of these people . . . one should not needlessly waste it.' Bert is aware of the film crew, his presence on screen and the audience that he needs for his stories. In the next shot, he is standing in front of the piano with his family and an arrangement of pets, directly addressing the camera as he talks about a cartoon image he once saw in the *New Yorker*. As he tells his story, he leans back on the piano, strokes his chin, gesticulates now and then and smiles. But he is having trouble explaining this image while ignoring his wife and children who are laughing and trying to keep the pets from attacking one another. His wife, though she appeared to be completely preoccupied, then recalls and fills in the caption of the image for him: 'To you and yours'. As if it were meant for the caption contest in the *New Yorker*. Bert repeats it. The screen turns to black and the title sequences fades in: 'BARLUSCHKE/a film by Thomas Heise'. It seems that, as rehearsed in this scene, viewers will be tasked with managing the chaos and filling in the captions for the images they see from now on.

This first scene in *Barluschke* restages the family, but also its chaos and divisions, at the very moment in which it is breaking down. Berthold Barluschke, who was born in the East, and Joanna Haas, who was born in the West, are separating. During Bert's lengthy reflections on his time as a spy for both the East and the West in this film, he repeatedly describes his life in terms of a film itself: 'I often had this feeling [. . .] it is all just a film'. When he tells stories from his past about being a spy, a husband and a father, he is also, then, selecting and replaying for this film, *Barluschke*, the particular films that he knows all too well about his many previous lives. The characters' stories in this film are always already intertwined with the idea of filmic stories and, over time, they illustrate that the narratives of the East and the West are fragmented, often incoherent, but never completely separate. In German film scholarship, the relationship between German productions from the East (for example, those associated with the East German state-controlled film company, *Deutsche Film Aktiengesellschaft*, or DEFA films) and those from the West is customarily characterised by a non-relation. This film, however, forces one to consider their common tumultuous experiences. How is it possible to write what Thomas Heise has repeatedly demanded from film scholars and critics alike, namely the necessary 'schizo-history' of the East and the West together, side by side? (Heise 2012) The place of post-war German cinema cannot be articulated in all its complexity without such a schizo-history, which would first of all entail an alternative approach to the Cold War logic of isolating and/or fetishising productions from the West and the East. *Barluschke*, which could very well be seen as the first film openly to address the schizo production of the East–West image, is, after all, interested in how the joint family, the failed family of the East and the West, can be reconceptualised, with all its chaos and divisions, without being reduced to national terms. None of the family members shown in the theatrical display in this opening scene is able to be considered solely on the basis of their nationality. A more complex understanding of the Barluschke situation is required to fill in the appropriate captions for the remaining images to come.

Even the name 'Barluschke', the title of the film, cannot be read strictly along the lines of a biographical interpretation.[2] 'Barluschke' is only one of the names that belongs to the spy in this film, along with the names Bert, Knut and Dammasch. 'Barluschke' is also the surname that belongs to his children, Anna and Danny, to his sister who committed suicide in the German Democratic Republic (GDR) and to his father and his mother, of whom Bert often speaks. *Barluschke* is never just about Bert Barluschke, just as he is never only Bert from the small East German town of Mittenwalde. Bert is a spy by profession and '[u]nder the conditions of the politics of secrecy, the political (and aesthetic) subject is always already caught between truthfulness and play-acting' (Horn, 42). Thus, as Bert meticulously recollects and re-enacts his duties as a former spy in the film, his positions and his trustworthiness as a narrator are constantly called into question, even by Heise in their conversations. In one interview, Bert is describing how he was trained to respond to unexpected situations that could catch him off guard, again perceiving the characters he plays as specifically filmic characters: 'You have perhaps a certain repertoire [as a spy] . . . and then you just select the appropriate film and . . . let it run.' Heise responds: 'That's what I mean, Bert. Sometimes I have the feeling that I'm seeing the repertoire.' After Bert acknowledges this, almost too hastily, and the two sit in awkward silence sipping wine, it becomes clear that it is not the objective of this film to pin things down, to fix biographies, identities and histories, but to complicate the approach to the 'Barluschke' family portrait.

This uncertainty about the facts and the characters' motivations was a polarising factor in the initial reception of *Barluschke* which won the prestigious *Silver Dove* at the International Leipzig Festival for Documentary and Animated Film. Some critics praised the elusiveness of the characters: 'The "Barluschke case" [. . .] is immensely captivating because Heise doesn't entirely reveal his characters. It's even difficult to get the facts straight. "Barluschke" is like a knot you can try to untie, but which you can never fully unravel' (Hohenberger, 15).[3] Others found this same characteristic of the film to have the opposite effect: 'Heise's collage of sounds and images, due to what it leaves out, exudes an air of sympathy with Barluschke that appears strangely out of place' (Baer and Koepnick, 49). 'Place' is an interesting term to use, even if unwillingly, to describe a film that is about constantly being out of place and switching places. It begs the question: *which* place? Why is it that critics at this time would either like to see a denial of a sense of place for the 'facts' and the characters in *Barluschke* or a stable place for them?

The place of *Barluschke* in Heise's *oeuvre* is also not immediately self-evident. Contrary to the other productions which are represented on his website through summaries, reviews and stills, Heise provides hardly any context for this film.[4] His characterisation of it is surprisingly brief: '*Barluschke* tells the story of the agent Berthold Barluschke who, in the second half of the twentieth century, first becomes a Stasi henchman for the GDR and then for the West German Federal Intelligence Service in the Federal Republic of Germany' (Heise, 'Barluschke'). This is deliberately reductive for a film that thoroughly complicates the double-agent formula in the documentary form. As one critic wrote, '[i]f this story were the plot of a fiction film, nobody would believe it' (Reinecke, 15). Below Heise's stubbornly incomplete description of the film on his website, this failure of a summary, is what he has labelled the 'postcard' for the film: a set of four identical black-and-white photographs of a baby whose eyes have been covered with a black bar in all but one of the images. The word 'BARLUSCHKE' is stamped in red across all the photographs, as if they had been classified and settled. Beneath this series of images are four sentences:

'Identity is a myth.'
'The family is happy.'
'Nothing remains.'
'Work is work.'

In the film, these are, at best, incredible understatements, if they are not proven to be wrong altogether. Identity may be a myth, but the family is not happy, there is much that remains and there are not separate spheres for work and play, or *Dienst* and *Schnaps* in German. The production details of the film are listed below this image series, followed by a still of Bert in the living room looking into the camera with a framed painting next to him of a front door and windows. Beneath this still on the website there is only a long blank space – a void in the place where context is typically provided.

His website isn't the only place where Heise refuses to elaborate on *Barluschke*. In his nearly 500-page book, *Traces: An Archaeology of Real*

Existence (*Spuren. Eine Archäologie der realen Existenz*, 2010), Heise provides background information and production materials related to the films that have come before and after *Barluschke*, but there are barely any traces of *Barluschke* itself. Even though it is only referenced once, this film nevertheless occupies a meaningful position in his text. In the last of the three interviews about his film-making aesthetic, which frame and punctuate the materials he provides about his other films, a reference to *Barluschke* has the last word. This passage becomes the transitional point between the materials that relate to his individual works and it is followed by a section that Heise designates as 'Reste', 'The Rest' or 'The (Archival) Remains'. At the end of the final interview, Heise is asked about whether anything is missed 'through this improvisational, intuitive film-making approach', which is characteristic of his film-making style (Girke qtd in Heise 2010a: 424). Heise replies with an anecdote about the desire to find allegorical purposes in the image:

> When we were shooting *Barluschke* in Paris there was an image that I originally wanted to include: below, in the metro station 'Les Halles', the black inhabitants of the city were on their way home to the outlying areas of the city. In between there were anti-terror troops marching through the subway tunnels and sealing up the garbage cans. Up above, on the surface, everything was white. Pretty white girls, attractive looking, are drinking coffee and chatting away in the sun. Maybe we would have tried to capture a specific meaning in these shots and therefore we were better off leaving them be. I believe one doesn't miss anything. To miss something means to pursue certain things and events, to pursue luck. (Heise 2010a: 424)[5]

Below this, to conclude the chapter, is a photograph of a boy holding a black, red and gold flag. 'Child with flag, 1960, Photo: Private' (Heise 2010b: 492). At the beginning of 'The Remains' section of the book on the very next page, Heise writes that he was born in 1955. The child is of his generation. The photo was taken the year after the East German flag was augmented to include the hammer and ring of rye, and the year before the Berlin Wall was erected. Which flag is this child holding? One from the East or one from the West? And where is he? To whom does he belong? In German, '*Flagge zeigen*', to show the flag, means to take a certain position. The flag in this image makes such an attempt increasingly problematic.

Heise takes the ambiguity of place and identity in the Barluschke situation as a point of departure, not subsequently to differentiate between the stories that belong to 'the East' and those that belong to 'the West', not to force a demarcation between these two terms. Heise resists the temptation to force allegories upon images. Rather, he takes the Barluschke situation as a point of departure for exploring the joint schizo-history of the East–West family film culture. If, etymologically, 'schizo' recalls the notion of a 'split' mind that is characterised by 'a breakdown in relation between thoughts, feelings, and actions' and 'the occurrence of delusions and hallucinations',[6] then *Barluschke* would present many opportunities for exploring this schizo-history of the East and the West in which Heise is interested. As a family that has constantly been in the process of switching sides – from the father who is a spy for the East in the West, then in the East, then for the West, to the mother who is from the West, living under a different Western identity in the East and then fleeing back to the West – the Barluschke family encourages this kind of back-and-forth observation or, in its extreme form, this kind of paranoia. It is also a family for which 'film' is a constant reference point – from the father who regards his life as a series of films, to the filming conditions of the family frequently alluded to in *Barluschke*, to the family's home movies that, towards the end of the film, completely take over the frame. One of the complications in writing this East–West schizo family film history is precisely the uncertainty of the Barluschke situation: how to document statements that may or may not be real, characters that may or may not be criminals and places that may or may not have been relevant, for example.[7] Simply because Bert, Heise's informant, 'succeeded in saying practically nothing' throughout the interviews does not mean that the project comes to an end (Heise qtd in Reinecke 1998: 15). The film is presented with the challenge of visualising this 'nothing said' and this placelessness of the Barluschke situation, the challenge of turning it into something productive. In *Barluschke*, 'the East' and 'the West', terms that convey a particular topography, geopolitics and nationhood, enter into a relationship that makes one inseparable from the other, and yet they are never equivalent nor completely reconcilable. While the experiment of this impossible family is shown as being in a permanent state of disarray, it is still needed, complete with its entire series of beginnings and ends, in order to move the project forward and reconceptualise the relationship between 'the East' and 'the West'.

Barluschke doesn't begin with interviews, but by observing the characters' interactions with each other, noticing their changes in behaviour, if any, when the camera's presence is felt, and by documenting the spaces they inhabit. After the title sequence, the film moves through the apartment that is in a state of flux. It inspects the hallway full of boxes, the kitchen appliances that have been unplugged, ready to be packed, and the dust that has collected on the surfaces over the years that is now exposed. Heise's voice-over narrates these images:

In the end all stories have a beginning and they don't find a conclusion. Out of one beginning arises the next, even before the first has found its conclusion, and is soon forgotten. And it happens this way again and again, until the end of time.⁸

This description of how temporality functions becomes a helpful method for understanding the various beginnings that this family experiences over a fifty-year period. The first 'facts' about the family Barluschke come from Heise, not from the interviews. The camera is again in the living room but now the furniture is gone, all the hallway doors are open and the carpets have been neatly vacuumed. The room has been emptied of its traces of life. As the camera slowly pans the space from left to right, Heise creates a beginning for one of the versions of this schizo relationship between the East and the West. He tells viewers that Berthold Barluschke was born in the Soviet Occupation Zone in 1945. Joanna Haas was born two years later in the Bronx. 'That is over fifty years ago.' It is important to keep these timespans in mind. This is a story that begins with the *Kriegskinder*, the children of war, with the post-World War II moment. Bert and Joanna marry in 1975 in New York. Twenty-two years later they are living in Paris. Today they are moving into separate apartments. Heise presents these facts in his iconic monotone voice-over; they are concise and don't reveal anything about the characters' motivations or psychologies. As a spectator, one might, at this point in the film, be on the lookout for a guiding narrative for the previous collection of clips: the elusive figure of Bert, marked by his spectral appearances and disappearances as well as by his double, his reflection, who almost always accompanies him; a wife that can no longer manage a life together with her angry and bitter husband; and a family home that is being vacated. This information, though almost too expedient to contextualise the scenes that have been shown, could ask spectators, at least for the moment, to consider the family as one possible guiding narrative. Perhaps this film is not, as Heise's website suggests, about a spy who changes sides but about the construction and the collapse of a family.

In the next scene, after the piano has been moved into the new apartment, Bert asks his daughter, Anna, to play for him while he eats his lunch. She reluctantly sits down and begins to play. A French flag can be seen behind her, if only for a second, blowing in the wind. The camera cuts to a close-up of Bert's lunch, which is half eaten, and his hand, out of focus, which is resting in the background. Then a photograph appears in a cutaway shot with the steady sounds of the piano in the background. It is a black-and-white photo of a smiling young man wearing a striped T-shirt. The camera focuses on his face for several seconds before slowly zooming out, revealing another black-and-white photo to its right. It quickly becomes clear that these are two photos of the same man. In the photo on the right, he is wearing a suit and tie but everything else looks almost identical: the same pose, turned slightly to the side, the same eyes and the same half smile. This looks like a much younger version of Bert, or two versions of Bert, as always. In this scene, the double is organised according to the structure of the shot/reverse shot. First one sees the subject on the left in the striped shirt. Then the subject on the right appears, the one in the suit and tie. The spectator glances back at the first subject to confirm that it is, indeed, the same face, the same person, in both images. One subject is negotiated with the other. Especially in its application of the shot/reverse shot, the film system is a place that is naturally prone to harbouring paranoia:

> [P]aranoia could be said to be latent to the structure of cinematic spectacularity in itself, in that it represents the radical alterity of signification [. . .]. To suggest this is to challenge the idea of the spectator's subsumption into an imaginary totality and to point to the potential splitting of that totality within the moment of its constitution. (Rose 1988: 145)[9]

When the frame of vision shifts from the gaze of one subject to another, the constitution of the subject is called into question. It is always on the verge of becoming objectified and losing its special status as the place of spectatorial identification.

These photographs do not lead to a recollection scene but are, instead, left without any narrative explanation. They are never mentioned or shown again in the film. Though the images in and surrounding this film are not organised in a didactic way, they gradually enter into suggestive relationships: there is a French flag in the window behind the daughter contrasted with the East or West German flag the child is holding in Heise's photograph; there are the daughter's hands working the piano keys and the father's hands that suddenly lie still; then, in the next shot, there is the mother, explaining her initial interest in preventive medicine. While working at a hospital in New York, it didn't take her long to realise that the causes for most of the diseases she was treating were not to be found in the end stages but in the patient's earlier years and experiences. To understand these disorders, one needed to look at the more complex beginnings. How can one decipher and situate the photographs of the young man that appear in this scene? Where do these images of such a complex beginning belong?

In the many interviews with Bert that follow, there is not much context provided for his earlier years, at least not by Bert himself. Indeed, he was always interested in surveillance, in cameras, 'the combination of art and technology', but the pressing question that is probably on the spectator's mind about the impetus for his employment with the MfS goes unanswered. Before he describes the moment when he was approached and asked to work for the Main Reconnaissance Administration of the GDR, the film shows his former teacher and girlfriend in Rostock. Standing on the dock, she tells the camera that this is the city in which Bert took courses in Latin American studies and from which they would often depart for their camping trips. She pulls several photos out of her pocket and narrates them: Here is Bert pitching the tent, there he is lying on the beach, this is Bert on his birthday and here are both of us in front of the tent. In retrospect, the viewer might wonder if these photos document the last carefree times that Bert was able to enjoy before becoming a spy for the East, if they are representative of the last moments of his 'normal' life. In a jarring transition, the film then cuts to a longer sequence of two sets of swinging doors. None of the members of the Barluschke family is present, only people from the street coming in and people from the building coming out. The camera is fixed, just watching the doors and listening to their screeches which are almost constant. 'People go in and out of the squeaky doors, anonymously, remaining unidentifiable' (Schenk 1998: 23). A Western identity, Knut Dammasch, is reborn in the East on a dock in Rostock, narrated via a series of schizo speech acts filmed in France. The Barluschke situation at this point involved two identities, Bert and Knut, and the division of the two was crucial. As he explains, Bert never met Joanna in the United States, even though that is where they married and had their first child. He doesn't even think today, over twenty years after his training as a spy began, that Bert ever met her: '*Bert* was never in New York. *Knut* was in New York. [. . .] I could never afford to be Bert Barluschke in New York. When? Maybe on Christmas in a very weak moment? [. . .] But apart from that I never assumed the identity of Bert Barluschke.' 'Bert' was stashed away in a drawer, and Joanna first met him in 1980 when she followed him to the GDR and he was allowed to pull him out. 'Secret agents or agitators need a social and rhetorical suppleness, such as the ability to defend positions without believing in them, to camouflage their identities or to blend invisibly into a crowd' (Horn 2006: 42). Even to this day, Bert knows how to talk to the camera. He never seems to say anything without an awareness of his addressee nor without a momentary process of negotiation. Before he addresses his audience, he first has to decide which self he would like to assume, which film he would like to play.

Heise often helps him along with this. He will take a fragment of Bert's performance that is being documented, such as his fanatical enthusiasm for a recording of *Zorba the Greek* by Mikis Theodorakis, and juxtapose it with larger events, such as the MfS reports on Bert's work upon his return to the GDR that Heise reads in the voice-over. Appropriately, the song from the ballet is *The Return of Zorba*. In the 1964 film directed by Michael Cacoyannis, a version of this song is first heard when the two main characters, Zorba and Basil, triumphantly arrive in Crete by car and are greeted by a swarm of local children. As Bert listens to the recording in his living room, he imitates the hand movements of a conductor and sings along: 'Ba, ba ba ba, bam bam badda badda bam!' But Heise's voice-over, which reads out the accolades that Bert received for his work with the MfS, and the sound effects of a typewriter soon interrupt Bert's concert performance. When Bert nods his head and sings along with the music, the voice-over tells the audience that Bert 'fulfils his assignments with discipline and vigilance'. Bert begins to talk to the camera about how interesting Theodorakis is but then he gets too excited by the music and has to take a break to sing along again.[10] The voice-over continues: 'Barluschke is a comrade with a great degree of political consciousness and a clear ideological position.' He is triumphantly greeted upon his return to the GDR. The Theodorakis piece becomes the caesura for Bert's file. Though Bert has chosen to select the identity of the educated music enthusiast for this scene, Heise challenges and seems to ridicule it. 'This man is introduced as a connoisseur, drinking red wine and playing the piano, but he leaves the film as the exact opposite' (Schenk 1997: 9). In describing Heise's strategy of oscillating between the micro- and macro-historical perspectives in his film *Material* (2009), a three-hour-long compilation of various material that Heise shot over the previous twenty years, Simon Rothöhler argues that Heise is interested in the notion of the fragment, the marginal cases in this film that could be representative of larger societal realities.

> *Material* does not, on the other hand, only resort to telling the history of German reunification from peripheral perspectives, to macroscopically enlarging microcosms in order to allow interference with, traces and adaptations of the 'whole process' to become visible. Heise's montage always returns to the places of 'big history' [. . .] but shows them from deconstructed perspectives – when seen in comparison with the imagery and the visual grammar of cable news networks. (Rothöhler, 109–10)

Heise continuously comes back to the places of big history – here, Bert's employment with the MfS as documented in these records with their particular discursive strategies – while keeping the fragments of a micro-history in clear sight.

By the time the concert reaches its dramatic end, the conductor has calmed down, the voice-over has concluded and the faint sound of warning bells at a railway crossing can already be heard in the background. Once the setting visually changes, a Trabant, or Trabi, an iconic East German car, abruptly races through the frame over the railway tracks. The warning bells are still ringing as the camera turns, in an extremely slow pan, to the right to show the red-and-white barrier lowering itself down before the train comes rushing by. The film cuts to an old phone box and an open phone book at the station. The sound of the ringing phone carries over into the next shot, which documents the tunnel to the commuter train, and a sign labelled 'Eichwalde' on a deteriorating building in the distance. This is the town in the former GDR to which Bert brought his family, Joanna and the children, once his work in the United States was complete. Bert's voice can be heard over the images as he states that he was, with one exception, always completely honest with his case officer. Joanna appears in an interview, discussing Bert's unique situation when he was working in foreign trade with the 'Iberma' company in the GDR, which allowed him to travel outside the country. Then the camera is back at the station, scanning advertisements for Sparkasse, a savings bank, and Real, a grocery store, before returning to the tunnel leading down to the train platform.

The camera is back on the Sparkasse advertisement but this time films a close-up of the face of the man on the left. Bert is now speaking in a voice-over about a specific somebody. 'He was, I believe, maybe twenty-five or twenty-six years old when I first got to know him at the Iberma Company.' The camera slowly moves to the right, across the graffiti between the two faces. 'He was often in Mittenwalde. He was my party functionary.' The camera moves up to the face on the right which, like the other face, has a little heart drawn next to it. The double is back. *Herzlich willkommen*. Welcome.

Figure 16.1 *Barluschke*, directed by Thomas Heise

The voice-over and compilation of images in this scene – the Trabi travelling short distances, the train travelling long distances, the phone call that goes unanswered, the double, the dark stairway – set the tone for two subsequent scenes that mark a shift in the aesthetic register of the film. The first of these scenes displays rows of military vehicles in stunted slow motion. White text is typed out at the bottom of the screen and is accompanied by the sound effects of a typewriter. Theodorakis's music returns but this time it is *Zorbas*, or *Zorba's Dance*, the most well-known song from the soundtrack. In the 1964 film, Zorba acknowledges that he dances when overcome with extreme emotions, whether joyous or painful, and in the final scene in which Zorba shows his foreign friend how to do his dance, he experiences a bit of both. After the first few chords of this song in *Barluschke*, Bert chimes in: 'I have a rather selective memory'. The sound- and imagescapes are overwhelming: in addition to listening to the music, the sound effects of a typewriter and Bert's statements that appear out of context in voice-overs, viewers are looking at both the text at the bottom of the screen, which is extracted from reports about Bert's role in the illegal sale of GDR assets, and the jerky documentation of military vehicles which are implying these very assets.[11] Bert's statements about his dealings with the East and the West during the tumultuous reunification period are vague and jump from one subject to another – from his contact with the West German Federal Intelligence Service and the Defence Ministry, to his belief in the necessity of his 'work' and his longing for some kind of 'objective control' by capturing moments on camera. Bert's sound bites, as divergent as they are, allude to feelings of paranoia, of being seen without seeing. His devotion to the different roles he assumed as a double agent has only intensified during the reunification period. Instead of renouncing his commitment to any particular 'side', to 'East' or 'West', Bert continues to operate within 'the paranoid universe of stealth, where each side is trying to determine its strategies in terms of what it can see the other side seeing about itself' (Klein and Warner, 8). By decontextualising and then juxtaposing Bert's statements about a major historical event which, for many, is tied to a subsequent sense of confusion and uncertainty, his memories, even if they come across as unclear, contradictory and unbelievable, nevertheless communicate certain aspects of this historical reality. Though '[a] situation of reciprocal watching, of tacit assurance that the other is watching and knowing, would seem to insure against fundamental misapprehension', Bert's monologue foregrounds the difficulty of filtering meaning from noise when working under paranoid habits of surveillance (Klein and Warner, 19).

Then, in the next scene, more noise. The images of vehicles and the text at the bottom of the screen are abruptly interrupted with television snow. The film changes the channel. This is not Heise who is filming Bert on this new channel. The quality of the image is grainier and the framing conditions are not as static. Trained in the previous sequence to notice the periphery of the frame, viewers recognise that there is white text stamped in the lower right-hand corner of this image: 'Rhineland-Palatinate, Easter 1994'. It soon fades and is replaced by 'Home Video B. Barluschke'. In the first home movie clip, Bert is explaining that, owing to a lack of equipment, it is impossible to create the proper distance between the subject and the camera, which is a curiously telling comment given the collection of home movie snippets to come. Though home movies typically record private, everyday moments of the familial life, the Barluschke films turn these adjectives on their heads. The videos are no longer private, the family does not have everyday problems and arguments and it is barely a family. In one clip, Danny is being meticulously recorded while Bert scolds him: 'I was so looking forward to going on a trip with you and then you show up here looking like a *pig*.' In the next shot, Bert is speaking to someone outside the frame: 'I just want to get my life together under orderly circumstances!' He says this as he is holding a marijuana bong. Since he found out that he has HIV, Bert states that he knows what is important. The film cuts to him inspecting the tea towels that Danny folded. Danny scolds him back: 'Now you're just mad that you have nothing else to complain about, right?!' The juxtapositions would be comical if they weren't so painfully accurate. A family fight ensues. The television snow returns. Joanna is sitting at the table looking exhausted while Bert lectures her. She eventually stands up and sighs: 'Your mental status is so crazy.' Bert talks about his CIA codename, his flight from the East and Ingelheim, a city in Rhineland-Palatinate, in former West Germany. Sometimes he is speaking directly to the camera, such as when he describes how he survived the reunification period as a spy by simply being honest. Television snow returns. He had deposited things in Switzerland. Then another family shot in the kitchen. They avoid eye contact, staring down at the table. 'There is a man sitting [at] the table. Is that his boyfriend? We never get to know. It continues to be a secret' (Löcker, 32). 'Home movie images function less as representations than as *index* inviting the family to *return to a past already lived*' (Odin, 259). Except these movies are not watched by the family but by the viewers of *Barluschke*. Through them, viewers return to a past already lived, the previous seventy minutes of the film documenting the schizo-history of this family. Judgements made about characters based on their initial interviews are reassessed. The information they communicated about their family might have seemed true and meaningful before. Is it still meaningful now? Is it ever possible to separate information, a signal, from noise here? What happens when noise becomes more meaningful than the signals?

Conclusion

In *Barluschke*, the schizo-history of the East and the West cannot be told through a definitive filter for signal and noise. Neither can it be communicated through 'objective' documentary work capturing the subjective stories told by Bert, Joanna, Anna and Danny. This film might seem to be breaking the 'rules' of documentary film-making in these last few scenes which depart from the 'more impartial' interview format. According to such rules,

> [l]ip-synchronous sound is validated as the norm; it is a 'must'; not so much in replicating reality [. . .] as in 'showing real people in real locations at real tasks'. [. . .] Real time is thought to be more 'truthful' than filmic time; hence the long take [. . .] and minimal or no editing [. . .] are declared to be more appropriate if one is to avoid distortions in structuring the material. The camera is the switch onto life. Accordingly, the close-up is condemned for its partiality, whereas the wide angle is claimed to be more objective because it includes more in the frame, hence it can mirror more faithfully the event-in-context. (The more, the larger, the truer [. . .]). (Minh-ha, 94–5)

These scenes towards the end of *Barluschke* demand a more diverse and complex method for depicting a history and a reality which are equally perplexing. The close-ups of the double at the railway station narrated by Bert, the military vehicles moving to *Zorba's Dance*, the B. Barluschke home movies and a subsequent scene, which documents a trip to La Défense by car and a particular corner of Paris with the sounds of Bach's *Invention No. 2* in the background, are still part of this documentary production. *Barluschke* documents a reality that 'is more fabulous, more maddening, more strangely manipulative than fiction' (Minh-ha, 98). Rather than trying to simplify this reality, the film embraces it, positing the schizo family history as a schizo film history and therein opening up a space for, and drawing attention to, the fabulous, maddening and manipulative narrative structures that constitute this East–West schizo-history. Such a history has a variety of jumping-off points. There is a potential beginning in the early childhood films of Joanna, in the photographs of young Bert or in the home videos of Anna and Danny. As Heise says, 'out of one beginning arises the next, even before the first has found its conclusion'. The splitting up of the East–West family documented in this film isn't the conclusion to the story. It is, rather, another beginning.

CHAPTER 17

The Limits of Nostalgia and (Trans) National Cinema in *Cum mi-am petrecut sfârșitul lumii* (2006)

Mihaela Petrescu (University of Pittsburgh)

There are several historical and practical reasons in the light of which Romanian cinema could be characterised as marginal.[1] Unlike Poland, Czechoslovakia and Hungary, Romania did not develop a significant film school during the Cold War. During the 1990s only few and poor-quality films were produced and, today, there is no Romanian film industry in the sense of a commercially viable enterprise, and the country has only a few cinemas and small audiences. In this bleak landscape Cristi Puiu's film *Marfa și banii/ Stuff and Dough* (2001) constituted a turning point for Romanian cinema as it ushered in what critics have called Romanian minimalism. Characterised by raw realism, dark humour, attention to detail, hand-held camera, location shooting, low-key performances and low budgets, Romanian minimalism has propelled recent Romanian films into the international limelight.[2] Over the last decade and a half, Romanian films have received several prestigious prizes at reputable international film festivals, most prominently in Cannes and Berlin, and they have been celebrated as the breakout star of European cinema.[3] Cătălin Mitulescu's feature film debut *Cum mi-am petrecut sfârșitul lumii/ The Way I Spent the End of the World* (2006) does not display the celebrated Romanian minimalist style. In terms of its production, the film is also not striking as it illustrates a widely spread trend in recent Romanian cinema towards international, particularly French–Romanian, collaborations. Uricaru states that the majority of contemporary Romanian films rely on financial support from abroad: France's policy to help foreign cinema has been particularly propitious for Romanian–French collaborations, as have been funds received competitively through the MEDIA (Measures to Encourage the Development of Audio Visual Industries) and the Eurimages programmes (Uricaru, 441–2). In this sense, *The Way I Spent the End of the World* is a Romanian–French co-production between Strada Film, the director's own production company, the Centrul Național al Cinematografiei (Romania's Centre for National Cinematography) and

Les Films Pelléas (France), while the film also benefited from the support of the Sundance Institute (USA), from which Mitulescu received the award for best European script in 2005.[4]

Mitulescu's film does, however, stand out among contemporary Romanian films owing to its unique narrative strategies. Thus, it distinctively blends humorous and dramatic focuses on life in Cold War Romania and on the revolution that brought about the demise of the country's Communist regime with a portrayal of the relationship between Eastern and Western Europe before and after 1989.[5] The film's transnational, universal appeal, which emerges from the lyrical-ludic portrayal of childhood and a young woman's coming-of-age story dovetails with overtly Romanian narratives which are shaped by their setting in communist Romania during 1989, the last year of Nicolae Ceaușescu's dictatorship. While it is marked by nostalgia for childhood and adolescence, however, Mitulescu's work does not reveal the nostalgic gaze towards the past that infuses the opening scenes of Mungiu's *4 Months, 3 Weeks and 2 Days*, a gaze that is balanced out later in that film by critical views of communism.[6] Neither is *The Way I Spent the End of the World* an example of the popular *Ostalgie* trend that is present in German films such as *Sonnenallee/Sun Alley* (Leander Haußmann, 1999) and *Good bye, Lenin!* (Wolfgang Becker, 2003), and which Jennifer Kapczynski defines as a 'retro aesthetic' (Kapczynski 2007: 80) that functions through brand recognition of GDR products and as a form of 'oppositional memory for East Germans who feel that their personal history has been delegitimized in the course of reunification' (Kapczynski 2007: 83).[7] In contrast to Mungiu's introductory sequences and the *Ostalgie*-infused films, *The Way I Spent the End of the World* shows the limits of nostalgia for Cold War Romania by meticulously weaving together three narrative threads that highlight the country's uniquely grim experience of communism. These threads comprise episodes that: satirise Ceaușescu; attempts to leave the country illegally; and a humorous, imaginary twist on the events that ultimately brought about Ceaușescu's ousting. They conjure up Romania's economy of penury, its political persecution and pervasive censorship, and thus recall what historian Vladimir Tismăneanu has termed Romania's 'dynastic Communism' (Tismăneanu, 16, 187–232) and reveal the implausibility of a nostalgic cinematic portrayal of communist Romania's final years. By both using nostalgia and revealing its bounds, the film attempts to come to terms with the past without glossing over its atrocious strains or the harmonious human bonds.[8] Furthermore, the film's look to the future turns its clear-cut Cold War paradigm, in which only Eastern Europe stands in for negative values, into a more ambivalent understanding after

1989. Thus, as the concluding scene suggests, through her employment on an international cruise liner, Eva, the female lead, gains access to the West and claims her space – limited as that may be – in a globalised, transnational world. There is a sense, however, that Eva's place in this crosscultural Europe is marked by uncertainty and negativity from the Western side. This echoes the adverse Western reception Romanian migrants faced throughout the 1990s and prefigures its vitriolic development in 2007 (after Romania joined the European Union) and in 2014 (when Romanians were legally permitted to find employment anywhere in the EU).

The Universal Appeal of *The Way I Spent the End of the World*

Mitulescu's film portrays universal stories that intertwine humorous episodes from the life of seven-year-old Lalalilu (Timotei Duma), nicknamed Lali, with the coming-of-age story of his seventeen-year-old sister Eva (Dorotheea Petre).[9] Both plot lines are deeply nostalgic. For example, nostalgia for childhood marks the scenes that show the loving relationship between Lali, Eva and their parents, the pranks and games Lali plays with his two best friends, Tarzan (Marius Stan) and Silvică (Marian Stoica), as well as his joyful interactions with various neighbours. Lali embodies a prototypical boy whose curiosity, good cheer, and sense of adventure bring to mind the literary figures Tom Sawyer and Huckleberry Finn as well as Ionică, the famous child protagonist of Ion Creangă's book *Amintiri din copilărie*, a classic of Romanian literature. Lali is a jovial, energetic, though sickly, youngster whose trademark is an irreverent, almost subversive, humour of which he is, however, unaware. In one of the first scenes of the film, for instance, Lali asks his mother if Ceauşescu also had baby teeth, a remark whose innocently subversive humour mocks Ceauşescu's media image which revolved around his status as infallible political leader and did not allow for any mundane associations.[10] Lali's open-mindedness is emphasised through the fact that his friend Tarzan is of Roma descent, a detail through which Mitulescu's film points to an idealist atmosphere of ethnic conviviality.[11]

Concomitantly, through the figure of Eva, the film comprises nostalgic portrayals of first love and its complications, and of Eva's sexual awakening. Eva's budding love relationship with Alex (Ionuţ Becheru), the son of a *Securitate* (communist Romania's secret police) employee, is cut short when he betrays her trust: even though Alex himself had accidentally smashed Ceauşescu's bust, he votes for her exclusion from their senior school while he eludes reprimands at his father's intervention. At her new school, Eva meets Andrei (Cristian Văraru) whom the authorities had relocated to her neighbourhood after discovering his parents' dissident activities. Andrei is smitten with Eva but she does not reciprocate his feelings. Nevertheless, the two spend their summer vacation secretly training to swim across the Danube in an attempt to flee Romania illegally. After Eva changes her mind about the planned escape, she rekindles her relationship with Alex with whom she initiates her first sexual experience. As the film concludes, we find out that Alex died during the December 1989 revolution, and we witness Eva sailing away on board an international cruiser.

The two sets of nostalgic, universal plot-lines outlined above dovetail with the film's representation of Romania in 1989, a representation that feeds off nationally explicit elements. With his detailed attention to several of Romania's dire socio-economic and political aspects, which include austere food shortages, the rationing of electricity, gas, and television programmes, the state's forceful and mindless urban systematisation, as well as massive censorship, Mitulescu's film is imbued with critical references to his country's past. The film's national specificity emerges from three narrative threads that expose the limits of cinematic nostalgia for the cultural identity and the quotidian life of communist Romania. These threads include: firstly, humorous scenes that mock the regime; secondly, dramatic attempts to flee the country; and, thirdly, a fictional twist on the events that toppled Ceaușescu. In the following, I shall analyse these threads individually and point to the particular way in which each of them sheds light on the limits of nostalgia.

The Limits of Nostalgia for Cold War Romania

The first narrative thread consists of a poignant Ceaușescu masquerade performed by Lali and Eva's father, Grigore (Mircea Diaconu), and subversive acts of the figures Titi (Nicolae Praida) and Bulba (Corneliu Țigancu). The scene in which Grigore impersonates Ceaușescu to entertain his children is a telling example of the politically subversive humour that permeates the film. The masquerade satirises Ceaușescu's speech pattern and inability to pronounce certain words correctly alongside his facial expressions and his gestures. But, more importantly, it alludes to the country's severe food shortages and rationing of electricity and television programming, measures that Ceaușescu instituted in order to repay Romania's foreign debt.[12] In an ironic turn of events, Grigore's subversive performance of Ceaușescu begging for bread and promising to extend television programming is cut short by the interruption of electricity. For a viewer familiar with Romania's Cold War history, the act of asking for bread brings to mind the curtailment of basic food supplies that brought the country to the verge of famine towards the end of the 1980s when bread, oil, sugar and milk were rationed while meat, eggs, cheese and flour could be purchased only in small quantities after long hours of queuing.[13] Even if, historically, Bucharest was exempted from extreme rationing because of its prominence as the country's capital and the state's showpiece, the film suggests that its suburbs – the place where the narrative unfolds –were far from having sufficient food supplies.[14] In fact, this dearth of food is a recurrent motif throughout the film. It dominates the opening scene which portrays Lali's nightmare of having Ceauşescu take away from him a big wheel of cheese. It is also present in a sequence in which a slice of cheese is passed around from the mother, to Lali, to Eva, and back to Lali, who decides to split it three-ways. And it appears in episodes that depict Alex and his father, as well as Eva, Lali, and their parents, eating lettuce soup, a dish that had become a staple of the communist Romanian cuisine because of its easy-to-procure ingredients.[15] It is important to note that the severe scarcity of food that permeates Mitulescu's film stands in stark contrast to the nostalgia via brand recognition that Kapczynski considers defining for *Ostalgie* films (Kapczynski, 80). The abrupt interruption of Grigore's masquerade also evokes two other economic deficiencies that characterised Romania during the 1980s: the extreme brevity of television broadcasting and the mandatory daily suspension of electricity.[16] In rendering Grigore's humorous and politically subversive masquerade, the film briskly delineates itself from both Ceauşescu nostalgia and from nostalgia for the quotidian life during the communist past, a past which, in Mitulescu's vision, is inseparably linked to Romania's austere socio-economic realities.[17]

The regime is also mocked through the acts of the male side-figures, Titi and Bulba. Titi's actions are highly subversive both visually and aurally. Thus, he undresses to his underwear and starts to work demonstratively on his roof in order to show Vişan (Grigore Gonţa), Alex's *Securitate*-employed father, how little respect he has for him.[18] This humorous visual protest against the *Securitate* worker is also a protest against the state he represents, an aspect that becomes even more evident in the episode that depicts Titi mocking the policemen who come to take him in for questioning after his son Nucu (Cristian Nicolaie) is caught at the Danube trying to leave the country illegally.[19] By raising his hands in the air despite the officers' request not to do so, Titi performs yet another visually subversive act through which he seeks to reveal the oppressive methods of the Romanian state in dealing with its citizens.[20] In addition to these visually satirical actions, Titi also mocks the authorities verbally by loudly declaring that he respects the Romanian state, an assertion that strongly contrasts with the disrespect and invasive treatment he receives from the authorities. The regime is further ironised via a specific verbal act performed by Bulba, a slow-minded, grandfatherly figure. This act consists of Bulba's humorous promise to Lali to beat up Ceauşescu for upsetting the child. Interestingly, Bulba who, as the neighbourhood's fool, enjoys the freedom of a Shakespearean jester, employs phrases typically used in Romania by adults in order to pacify their scared children and assure them that they will punish the malevolent person who has upset the youngsters. While Bulba's assertion signals his powerlessness as he makes a promise he cannot keep, by using these particular expressions he also unknowingly ridicules Ceauşescu's self-aggrandising image as the caring father of all Romanian children and casts him as a source of evil and pain.

It is important to note that the subversive acts that mock Ceauşescu and his regime unfold in a specific space, namely at the outskirts of Bucharest in the north-eastern neighbourhood of Colentina, where Mitulescu grew up. In an interview, the director states that people there 'resisted [communism] differently, they were freer, had a purer soul, more untouched' (Stanciu). As the film suggests, Colentina is caught between a rural atmosphere, revealed by the prominence of dirt roads, stray dogs, and singing roosters, and the threat of impending demolitions as part of the regime's plans for urban systematisation.[21] The Colentina portrayed in the film is not an urban area but a so-called '*mahala*', one of the numerous rustic, often impoverished, sometimes charming neighbourhoods of which Bucharest had consisted since the eighteenth century, and which Ceauşescu wanted razed to the ground and replaced with blocks of flats. It is this space, with its gardens, its dusty roads, its greenery and close-knit group of neighbours, that functions both as Lali's bucolic playground and as a site of government mocking. This dual role of Colentina is also underlined visually through the use of colour. While overall the film is dominated by tones of grey and dark blue, Colentina – which is depicted with sombre colours for most of the film – also offers an important counterpoint palette. When it is a setting for Lali's childhood games, Colentina is shown in vivid, warm colours such as vibrant green, yellow and specks of red.

A second narrative thread that reveals the film's limits of nostalgia emerges from its engagement with attempts to flee the country by swimming across the Danube to reach former Yugoslavia.[22] While Nucu's failed attempt is mentioned only in passing when his father is detained as a possible co-conspirer, the plan, developed by Andrei and Eva, to flee via the Danube receives significant screen time. The film presents in detail their resistance training against hypothermia and their experiments to swim using a floating vest reinforced by small, self-propelling devices. While Eva and Andrei share some good laughs at their physical weakness, the pervading mood is one of gloom and dramatic suspense. The latter is increasing particularly during their quiet and stern train journey to the Danube, their pause on the riverbank, and the moment when, after she swims for a short distance, Eva ultimately decides to return home. We eventually find out that Andrei made it safely to the other shore and that he subsequently went to Italy from where he sends Eva and Lali postcards and gifts. Intriguingly, we are not told what happens to Nucu. To the careful viewer, his face is visible in one of the final scenes of the film which show Lali driving along the street while his friends and neighbours, among them Nucu, wave at him. Since the scene takes place after the Communist regime was toppled, one can speculate that Nucu, who was probably given a prison sentence, must have been set free. By portraying these attempts to flee, the film reflects critically on the lack of freedom to travel and to leave the country that governed Cold War Romania and thus, once more, points to the implausibility of cinematic nostalgia for said past.

Finally, the third thread presents a humorous and hyperbolic twist on the events that happened during the live broadcast of the mass meeting Ceauşescu ordered for 22 December 1989, a meeting that ended in chaos and led to his downfall and eventually to his and his wife's execution a few days later. At this meeting, Lali, who was supposed to recite a poem for Ceauşescu, uses his sling to fire a stone into the crowd, an act that causes a commotion which throws Ceauşescu off balance and which, in turn, sparks a mass protest. By cross-cutting between historic footage of Ceauşescu's speech, people fighting in the streets of Bucharest, and the fictional scene that depicts Lali on television raising his thumb to signal that everything is fine (Figure 17.1), Mitulescu highlights live television's ability to create history and points out the latter's constructed nature. Moreover, the film offers an ironic commentary on the double role television played vis-à-vis Ceauşescu: while it was instrumental in maintaining his self-aggrandising grip on the country, by broadcasting his moment of weakness, television also sparked his ousting and aided the revolution via long hours of live transmission, a unique feat in the world at the time. The portrayal of Lali's whimsical and fictional act furthermore points to a still extant gap in the research that scrutinises the Romanian revolution of 1989. Scholars have not yet clearly determined the source that caused the disturbance which famously interrupted Ceauşescu's speech and led

Figure 17.1 An unlikely hero, Lali, makes history, and underscores cinema's fictional nature.

to his startled facial expression caught live on camera, a reaction which, as historian Siani-Davies states, was 'the turning point in which they [the people] realized the frailty of Ceauşescu's grasp on power and the possibility that he could be overthrown' (2005: 84).

The sequence gives contour to an unlikely hero whose action bears the dramatic implication that people were so weary of Ceauşescu's tyranny that even children forged plans to get rid of him, as did Lali, Silvică and Tarzan.[23] Through Lali's act, the film problematises the negative view articulated in the phrase 'mămăliga nu explodează' ('polenta does not explode') which circulated in conjunction with Romania in 1989. The statement is contentious because by employing the noun 'mămăligă' as a metonym for Romanians – since historically 'mămăligă' has been the basic food of Romanian peasants and continued to be consumed during Communism due to the scarcity of food – it implies that they are too lethargic to change the Communist regime. On the one hand, Lali's endeavour hints at a lack of action of adult Romanians, a lack which is furthermore echoed in the stoic, barely audible statement of old Florică (Jean Constantin) who expresses his doubt that the people will ever get rid of Ceauşescu. The inaction of the adults also transpires from the father's Ceauşescu masquerade which features him as a subversive performer but not a man of action outside the limits of his home. On the other hand, Lali's hyperbolic and heroic deed makes Ceaușescu's fall possible. Moreover, it contributes to re-evaluating the negative cliché about the presumed apathy of Romanians, by indicating that members of the young generation, exemplified by Lali and his co-conspiring friends Tarzan and Silvică as well as by Alex who joins the revolution and dies, go beyond subversive masquerades and promises and literally act against the regime.

In blending these three narrative threads, the film reveals Romania's draconian censorship, which prohibited free speech and movement, as my analysis has shown. Additionally, Mitulescu also highlights the manner in which censorship infringed on two realms of art: film and music. The state's tight grip on film and cinema had Romanians resorting to organising videotheques, namely group viewings of VHS tapes with Western films. These film showings were held in student centres and workers' clubs and, after 1985, in people's homes.[24] We get a glimpse at this special status the VHS medium had in 1980s Romania, and implicitly also a critical nod against the state's acerbic censorship, in the scene in which Eva visits Alex who offers to show her a film on his family's VCR, an apparatus probably acquired because of his father's employment with the *Securitate*.

Censorship also heavily affected the sphere of music, and the film alludes to this encroachment through acoustic references to songs made popular by the 'Cenaclu Flacăra'. The latter – a prominent musical manifestation that unfolded between 1973 and 1985, which presented folk music, patriotic songs and poetry readings – makes its presence felt in the film through two melodies. One is the song 'Seara' ('The Evening'), which Eva is not allowed to perform during a school festivity, a detail that brings to mind the 1985 banning of the 'Cenaclu Flacăra', and the ensuing official negative reception that non-patriotic songs popularised through this venue received.[25] Through the second melody, 'Țara noastră-i țara noastră' ('Our Country is Our Country'), the film ironises Romania's exaggerated and hollow nationalism. The satirical undertone emerges from the listless manner in which the song is performed by senior school students in music class and during an official festivity, the melody's emphatic patriotism lost on the interpreters and the majority of their audience. A similar ironic view of the country's overinflated nationalism ensues from the dull way in which Eva and her peers sing the national anthem.

In addition to the narrative threads discussed above, the way in which the film depicts the West of the late 1980s also delimits nostalgia for Cold War Romania. Throughout the film there are several references to what the West stands for in contrast to communist Romania: it is defined by an unlimited availability of consumer goods and freedom of speech and travel. Against Romania's economic destitution, the West emerges as a cornucopia of consumer goods: the film shows that products deemed luxury items in Romania, such as denim jeans and sweets, are readily available in the West. This becomes evident in the scene in which Eva receives a package Andrei sent from Italy which contains chewing gum, chocolate and the prototypical Western fashion accessory, jeans.[26] The West's affiliation with freedom is illustrated in a lyrical scene that portrays an imaginary submarine ride to various Western cities organised for their families and friends by Lali, Tarzan and Silvică. Here, the West emerges as an object of people's longing for liberty and unrestricted travel as well as the actualisation of such longing.

The film's portrayal of East – in this case Romania – and West along straightforward, contrasting lines during the last years of the Cold War becomes rather blurred in the final scene which depicts Eva in a work uniform on the deck of an international cruise liner. The sequence is ambivalent, both narratively and visually, about Eva's future in the West. Narratively, the scene does not clarify what Eva's job is, whether it entails her living in Romania and travelling abroad periodically or possibly relocating to the West. Visually, the sense of apprehension and uncertainty is rendered by the fact that a disconsolate Eva, who smiles only vaguely at the news she receives from Lali's letter, has her eyes covered by a pair of dark, impenetrable sunglasses that increases the impression of sadness and denies further access to this figure. While Eva's pensive mood is caused by Alex's death during the revolution and to missing Lali and her parents, economic worries also weigh her down. In this context it is important to note that Eva sends part of her salary home. This detail implies that her parents' wages are no longer sufficient to cover their living expenses or that their employment status has changed, both possibilities alluding to post-communist Romania's socio-economic struggles with inflation and unemployment. Said detail, however, also positions Eva among Romania's post-1989 work migrants to the West, people who, historically, have consistently been viewed negatively by the West. Since the first stages of the Romanian work migration abroad in the early 1990s, and particularly after 1 January 2007, when Romania acceded to the European Union, and 1 January 2014, when Romanians in search of better employment received the right of free travel throughout the EU, the Western media have employed, and continue to use, discourses of threat, invasion and undesirability vis-à-vis Romanians.[27] Against this background, it becomes apparent that, though Mitulescu's film offers no direct information about the way the West perceives Eva, she will probably not encounter a positive reception.

Conclusion

By blending humour and dramatic elements, Mitulescu's film reveals a twofold understanding of nostalgia: while it is nostalgic about childhood and adolescence, it swiftly reveals the conceptual limits of nostalgia for Cold War Romania. This dual view of nostalgia allows the film to deal with the country's past in a reconciliatory manner without denying its abusiveness. Furthermore, the film's view of the future shapes its Cold War oppositional East–West model in which numerous negative values are graphed to the former into an ambivalent understanding post-1989 in which negativity and detrimental attitudes stem rather from the West. Moreover *The Way I Spent the End of the World* helps rethink the relationship between Eastern and Western cinema as it shakes up the paradigm of national versus transnational by presenting national stories with universal appeal. Ultimately, Mitulescu creates a cinematic fusion of disparate elements, a film that is concomitantly national and transnational both narratively and in terms of its production. This interlacing of national and universal features suggests that we should revise our understanding of the relationship between Eastern and Western cinema to a more permeable model.

CHAPTER 18

The Ideal of Ararat: Friendship, Politics and National Origins in Robert Guédiguian's *Le Voyage en Arménie*

Joseph Mai

How did the opening up of a binary Yalta Europe to a more diverse continent, with new possibilities of movement across borders, change the way French directors depicted national identity? Asking this question of Robert Guédiguian is revealing because it forces us to consider two distinct themes of personal identity in his work and a possible tension between them: class solidarity and national origins.

Guédiguian, who was raised in a working-class, communist family, has built a well-earned reputation for his hard-line, leftist political ideology, expressed, at times, through an acerbic but humanistic comedy, at other times through anger and tragedy. He is also known for having focused his camera on the history and socio-economic struggles of the inhabitants of Estaque, the working-class neighbourhood of Marseilles where he grew up. While Guédiguian remains close to the Communist Party today, he does not give the impression that the fall of the Berlin Wall was a tragedy. In fact, his dissatisfaction and dissociation from the party predates 1989 by a decade. As Martin O'Shaughnessy has written, Guédiguian 'chose deliberately to work in what [one] might call the ruins where the working class used to be, examining consequences of defeat, scouting around to see what, if anything, can be salvaged from the wreckage' (2007: 59). By moving from party politics to the cinema, Guédiguian sought to define his professional life through a communal practice that was not possible in an age of partisan grandstanding and failed collaboration between communists and socialists. Surprisingly often, Guédiguian names that activity *friendship*, and a friendship associated with resistance: the cinema was a 'communal practice allowing us to remain friends for a long time' (Guédiguian and Danel 2008: 47). Since 1980, Guédiguian has steered a straight course, self-producing his own films and working with a small group, including his spouse Ariane Ascaride, childhood friend Gérard Meylan, and Jean-Pierre Darroussin, all of whom are cast in Guédiguian's film of personal origins, *Le voyage en Arménie/Armenia* (2006, France).

Figure 18.1 Ararat: an ideal and spectral landscape.

With, and related to, ideology, identity for Guédiguian is wrapped up in the interactions of friends.

The question of national identity after the fall of the Wall resounds more closely with Guédiguian's immigrant roots. As his name indicates, Guédiguian is of Armenian descent (as well as German origins on his mother's side). A brief consideration of history helps explain the presence of many Armenians in Marseilles, and why the emotional pull of Armenian self-identification might be strong for someone like Guédiguian. This old nation has corresponded to an autonomous, independent state only briefly. Balloted among the Persian, the Ottoman, and the Soviet empires, Armenian culture had always been strongest in the provinces of today's eastern Turkey, near Mount Ararat.

Constant oppression culminated in the 1915–16 genocide at the hands of the Young Turks. Razmik Panossian has explained that, during the genocide, the 'central point (the provinces) of Armenian identity was eliminated', and that most of those who weren't killed were left to survive 'in the form of diasporacised refugees concentrated in the Middle East, with some in France, Greece and elsewhere' (2006: 232). In many ways, feelings of Armenian belonging are strongest in the post-genocide diaspora. Many survivors settled in Marseilles, where Guédiguian (whose grandfather came to Marseilles before the genocide to study theology but was actively involved in helping refugees) could be expected to feel this pull.

The independence of the former Soviet possessions in the early 1990s might have offered an ideal occasion for Guédiguian to reconnect with his origins. And yet Guédiguian is not especially known as a film-maker invested in personal origins or national identity. Though his films have always included characters of immigrant descent, their sense of belonging to origins of an ethnic or national variety is rarely emphasised. In fact, Guédiguian's attitude towards origins has always been rather indifferent, unlike his firm attachment to questions of economic class. Given his political commitment, this resistance is not so surprising. His characters have always self-identified in terms of their present and through their resistance to economic forces more than through national or ethnic origin in a way that corresponds more or less to the proletariat internationalism of slogans such as 'workers of the world, unite!' That this conviction has not really changed is substantiated in a revealing interview, conducted after the release of *Armenia*, in which he refers to himself as an 'old classic Marxist'.[1] Guédiguian's position on personal identity has thus never passed through an emphasis on nation, on being French, but through class.

Guédiguian finally did venture out of Marseilles and France to deal directly with his own origins in *Armenia*, released in 2006. Oddly enough, it is, once again, friendships (along with family and the cinema) that slowly brought Guédiguian to reconsider his ethnic origins. Being Armenian became a salient fact to Guédiguian when an uncle praised him for not changing his name when he became a film-maker. Gradually, Armenian groups began attending his screenings. Ascaride grew interested in Armenia through another project, and eventually both she and he would testify in the *Assemblée nationale* in support of recognising the genocide. Then a retrospective of his work brought him to Yerevan where he struck up a number of new friendships. Ascaride began to co-write a screenplay about Armenia, based vaguely on Guédiguian's personal story, and, finally, he took it up and then shot the film.[2] It is the self-identifications of important others and their concern for Guédiguian's self-identification as Armenian that put Armenia on his map. In this way the early fading of political rigidity gives way to friendships which, in turn, allow Guédiguian to return to his own national origins.

Friendship, Identity and the Communist Hypothesis

What is it about friendship that can reconcile Guédiguian's concern for class solidarity with an exploration of national identity? We can better understand this by looking at a like-minded linking of politics, national identity and friendship in the political writings of Alain Badiou over the same period. Like Guédiguian, Badiou writes in search of a productive reference point outside party politics, indeed, outside all electoral politics. He proposes, instead, a grand ideal, the 'communist hypothesis', which he hopes can orient political opposition against prevailing economic and cultural trends. He catches glimpses of the communist hypothesis in events such as May 1968 when intellectuals and workers formed 'a completely new alliance' and, more recently, in local and micro-movements in which unaffiliated political actors reject the figures of subjectivity, 'passive and stereotyped consuming individuals', imposed by neo-liberal globalisation (Badiou 2010: 39). This is another way of describing the communal activity that Guédiguian sought through his alternative production practices.[3]

These rallying points are located, Badiou argues in *The Meaning of Sarkozy*, 'outside of the police'. Where exactly, in any given situation, is not always clear but Badiou believes they can be found if the search is driven by what he calls an overarching 'performative' conviction – the single and unifying idea that 'there is only one world'. On a global level, the sentiment that there is only one world resonates nicely with the promise of the end of Yalta-Europe: the fall of the Wall in Berlin seemed to open up the global horizon of a new world. But, for Badiou, politics and the police have betrayed the promise and erected new walls. Globalisation has facilitated the dominance of neo-liberalism, engendered more inequality and exclusion, and deprived workers of 'the basic right to move around and settle where they wish' (55). The developing world is locked out of an economic progress that feeds the bloated bank accounts of the increasingly rich.

It is within this context that Badiou situates former French president Nicolas Sarkozy's position on national identity: to distract the 'consumer', politicians and complicit intellectuals exacerbate differences and 'national identity' through figures of division. Guédiguian's return to Armenia, for example, took place at a disquieting moment when France was experiencing civil unrest in the suburbs, when interior minister Sarkozy made his infamous '*racaille*' (scum) comment about the rioters, and not long before the so-called 'debate on national identity' was launched by then President Sarkozy. In 2010, President Sarkozy made his own voyage to Armenia (where he remains popular) and called for Turkey to recognise the genocide. The following year he lobbied the *Assemblée nationale* to adopt a later law making it illegal to deny genocide, including the Armenian genocide. Following Badiou, one might, however, contextualise Sarkozy's Armenian discourses with France's vehement opposition to Turkey's entry into the

European Union. Viewed through this edit, the celebration of Armenian culture might be seen as constructing a division between Armenia and Turkey (one that, in turn, serves divisions between France and Turkey and finally Europe and Turkey). Guédiguian's Armenian return will have to contend with this type of context.

Badiou's 'single world' contradicts precisely this type of barrier-building without denying the reality of self-identification with a national heritage (or any other rallying point of self-identification). He distinguishes, instead, between a world of sameness in which everyone is identical – a world 'closed in on itself' and 'different from another world' – and his ideal of a single world 'where an unlimited set of differences exists' (63). In a single world, 'the transcendental measure of identificatory intensities, and thus of differences, is accessible everywhere to all, inasmuch as it is always the same' (62). From this non-exclusive point of view, in a single world, everyone has a right to their intellectual and emotional investment in sources of identity. What is not allowed – and here is the important qualification – is for differences to be exploitable by a police state in order to drive wedges between groups in the name of protecting a few economic interests. This is a return of proletariat internationalism with an opening to origins.

We can now consider how friendship of a certain type might represent a kind of resistance against the neo-liberal figure of the consumer. The philosopher Todd May's work explores friendship as a figure among many other figures of human relations in the contemporary world. Borrowing, like most philosophical analyses of friendship, from Aristotle's influential terminology, we are not concerned with friendships of use (in which one person befriends another because they expect some precise benefit from the relationship) or friendships of pleasure (where we spend some superficial, good times together). In fact, May shows that human relationships of these types map quite neatly on to the figures of the consumer propagated in neo-liberal economics.[4] With Guédiguian (and Badiou) we are more concerned with what May (again following Aristotle) calls true friendships. These friendships actually teach us about ourselves and about the world, in part because they are friendships in which the flourishing of the other counts because the other is an end rather than a means for achieving something we stand to gain for ourselves.[5] The affection that binds friends together can only, it would seem, arise in a context of equality. Badiou also points to friendship as a model for the single world, with the caveat that friendship should not remain a 'weakened form of traditional humanism' but become political: 'a friend is someone who exists in equality with yourself, in the same world as you' (2010: 66). Equality is not a definition of friendship, and enmities are certainly possible, but it is a necessary condition.

This is the political face of Guédiguian's cinematic friendships. He and his troupe collaborate in ways that treat the other as an end. Together they create counter-figures of human relationships – friendships – that appeal to equality and resist performing a simple function in the machine of economic profit. His films are pedagogical in that they propose these more complex figures of friendship to viewers who, themselves, may exercise their freedom to identify them as relevant and defensible in their daily lives.

Indeed, this process and these figures are so important to Guédiguian's *oeuvre* that I cannot avoid some hierarchy here, and I hesitate to call *Armenia* a film primarily about national identity. Instead, it seems like an extension of this deeper project of friendship on to the terrain of national identity. This does not mean that the film is unrelated to the spirit of a number of films that deal with the return to national or original identification, often in 'return road movies', as Michael Gott has convincingly defined them (Gott 2013b). There is no reason for Guédiguian to ignore national identity: on the contrary, to do so would mean conceding to the police state one more tool for forging oppositions. I shall suggest, however, that Guédiguian's entry into the genre is less invested in a notion of self-understanding through origins than it is in proposing a more idealistic figure of identity, according to which, as he states in a speech inaugurating the 'year of Armenia' in 2007, every person carries within 'the village where he is born' and 'the entire world' (Guédiguian and Danel: 121). Guédiguian's figures of identity conform to the complexity and egalitarianism of his far-deeper friendships.

Armenian Friendships

Armenia begins in a cultural centre in Marseilles where Anna's daughter (played by Ascaride and Guédiguian's own daughter) performs a traditional dance in front of a painted backdrop of Mount Ararat. The film cuts to a dark medical room where Anna (Ascaride), a doctor, diagnoses an older man (her father, though in this professional context she uses his first name, Barsam) with a heart condition and orders an operation. He refuses and makes vague references to teaching her a lesson before he dies. Secretly, telling only his granddaughter (in a scene back at the cultural centre), he returns to Armenia. Anna is irritated to find her father's electricity shut off and, in his work shed [strewn with leather and cobbler's tools (cobbling is a common Armenian trade)], there is a travel guide to Armenia. Anna has no interest in her origins: she does not go to watch her daughter dance, and even the old men playing backgammon in the cultural centre – her father's friends – do not recognise her. But, to settle matters with her father, she leaves: a coerced road movie reflecting Guédiguian's own story of return.

Armenia is organised around a serious of encounters with people that Anna believes will help her in her quest to find her father in Yerevan. But, in accordance with the road-film genre, these fortuitous encounters and accidental departures take over from the overarching plot.[6] At first she is grateful when one of her father's friends puts her in touch with his nephew, Sarkis (Simon Abkarian), who travels to and from Armenia on business. But Sarkis is a slick-haired and ruthless, semi-legitimate businessman through whom Guédiguian introduces the viewer to an Armenia that has little to do with Noah's Ark or the genocide. En route from airport to hotel, from inside his luxury SUV (sports utility vehicle), and over the techno music blasted out by his driver, Sarkis explains his ferociously neo-liberal version of the new Armenia and offers his own figures of Armenians: communism has made Armenians lazy and envious but there are myriad new opportunities for doing 'business'; to be chauffeured in a car like his demands hard work that should be rewarded with respect; his family lives in France because it isn't 'too communist', though America would be a little better. His family safely stowed away in France, Sarkis represents the extreme opposite of a single world.[7]

Though unsympathetic, Sarkis forces Anna to confront some uncomfortable contradictions of her own. For, though she was a communist militant for twenty years and is still a leftist, she also drives a smart Mercedes. He jokes that he, too, would be a communist if he could afford it, and that it is much easier to be a communist in France, where 'actually existing socialism' (and its debilitating effects) never took hold, and where communism could be seen as a utopian dream. On-screen there are images of nondescript filling stations (and a few flower shops), hinting at a global conformism, in which Anna participates. Guédiguian himself has spoken of the 'Empire of consumption' that threatens Armenia just as the Ottomans and the Soviets had in the past. Anna's attitude shows irritation at Sarkis's neoliberalism but also at her own complicity and tepid convictions.

This friendship fizzles quickly and, unsurprisingly, Sarkis's chauffeur neglects to pick her up in her hotel the next day. The narrative shifts and, without the means to track her father, Anna's experience takes a different quality. Alexander Nehamas has argued that the cinema is an appropriate vehicle for exploring friendship because it often deals in inconsequential actions, unlike the novel or the epic (271). Here meet the apparent banality of friendship, below the surface of which Anna is able to borrow new perspectives and model ways of living, and the temporal drift (and the openness of self it implies) of the road movie (see Gott 2013b: 79).

Her next new encounter is with Schaké, a young apprentice she meets at a hairdressing salon while waiting for Sarkis. Anna is drawn to Schaké, even if at first she seems like a typical Easterner attempting to make her way to the West (she wears Western clothes and begs Anna to find her a job in France). She also resorts to topless dancing in a seedy nightclub and makes mysterious deliveries to Sarkis's chauffeur. But, in her, Anna also finds complexity, as well as the poverty and thwarted aspirations that affect the young working poor. Eventually Schaké shows Anna her home, a two-roomed shanty on the edge of town that she rents for her grandmother and her sister, and reveals that her parents have died in an earthquake. Her moral ambiguities turn out to be an effect of a world understood as divided: her poverty is a sign of her exclusion and her black marketeering a means of gathering the cash to cross into a better place. And yet, as Anna and others emphasise, the borders between Armenia and more affluent European nations remain less permeable for the poor like her than they do for Sarkis, and she will probably not succeed.[8]

Another new friend, Simon, is a French doctor who operates a free mobile clinic in Yerevan. Though a less central character, Simon represents an alternative attitude towards the medical calling: if Anna's professional life has produced social status, a professional disposition, and a nice car, Simon has dedicated himself to the poor who come to the clinic. Through Simon, Guédiguian also addresses the issue of healthcare in Armenia and other post-Soviet economies. Here the film echoes another serious point of Badiou's 'communist hypothesis', the conviction that every sick individual should have a right to 'the present conditions of medicine' (2010: 49). Armenia, the film suggests, is failing terribly in this regard, for there is no social security system, no state insurance, and little affordable medicine: this film about Armenian identity is highly critical of the status quo in Armenia itself.

Through Yervanth, the deepest of Anna's new friendships, she (and the viewer) learns a wealth of information about Armenia's meaningful sites of memory and its more recent historical context. Yervanth is a Marseillais ex-pat of Armenian origins who was a member of the ASALA (the Armenian Secret Army for the Liberation of Armenia) terrorist group in the late 1970s. He is in exile for his participation in an armed political bank robbery in France, arriving at the beginning of the territorial war over Karabagh (given to Azerbaijan by the Soviets) to become a founder of the Armenian army. He is still called the 'general' but he currently works in Yervanth as a kind of potentate in the same 'business' as Sarkis.

His approach, however, is the opposite of that of Sarkis; it is Yervanth, for example, who buys medicine and funds the dispensary operated by Simon. Yervanth and Anna, who share a connection with Marseilles and leftist politics, have deep conversations about politics, economics and national identities. It is essentially through conversation – central to all theories of friendship and to Guédiguian's cinema as a whole – that Anna comes to self-identify as Armenian herself.

Anna's friendships have strongly reinforced her convictions and have a positive impact on her actions, as can be seen in the violent narrative event that returns the film to action. All the narrative lines are connected: Sarkis's illegal medicine trade is threatened by his driver and Schaké who have been stealing it from the hospital and selling it on the side; Sarkis orders their murder; Anna saves the girl while shooting out the knees of Sarkis's henchmen; Yervanth (founder of the dispensary) helps them escape to the countryside and, finally, settles accounts with Sarkis while issuing a stern warning: medicine will be delivered as it has been, perhaps not in the most legitimate and official way, but to any and all and not according to profit. This is a micro-movement straight from the communist hypothesis: one world wins out, for now. If this action seems implausible (and it does), it is because of the overreliance on coincidence and on Anna's unexplained extreme marksmanship with a gun, not because her commitments are in doubt.

Anna has changed, and the film suggests that friendship makes identity more fluid in ways that may cause other frictions. For example, Anna, Schaké and Yervanth begin to resemble a family, even with the suggestion of a discrete erotic attraction between Anna and Yervanth.[9] She also grows angry with her husband on the telephone when he makes light of her sense of belonging in Armenia. One could pass a moral judgement on Anna for, in some sense, betraying her husband. But there are other possible outcomes: one might suggest a more fluid and utopian idea of human relationships in which her new commitments can be integrated into her previous ones. Or perhaps her relationship with her husband has run its course and a renewal of Anna's identity can come only from new friendships. We, of course, do not see her return to France, but Guédiguian has explored a similar narrative situation in tragic mode in the past.[10]

Without resolving the issue, Anna's realisation that personal identity is dynamic does help her resolve some of the conflict with her father when she finally locates him in a small village. Anna, in part, has always resented Barsam's maltreatment of her mother and now his return to another woman here in this village. But they are reconciled when Anna introduces Yervanth to him at a festive dinner. At first, Anna lacks the proper words to describe Yervanth but then settles on a firm 'mon ami d'Arménie' ('my Armenian friend'). Barsam draws attention to the resemblance between himself and Anna: 'One can have more than one country in life, more than one friend, more than one family. The misfortune is that they aren't opposed but live side by side. Who can stand that?' With her new perspective, it is precisely Anna who can now 'stand it', and she sees that it is restrictive to be proprietary towards her father. There is a utopian feel at this dinner in its bucolic setting: father and daughter share a symbolic peach; Anna meets the new spouse and her family; and Schaké finds love with an Armenian boy and will stay in Armenia. Everyone is allowed his or her emotional or identitarian investments which, in turn, do little harm to others.[11]

Landscapes of Identification

I have concentrated on friendships because they have determined much of the change in Anna's and the film's action. The friendships, however, develop over images of landscape in which one can detect a more direct commentary on national identity. Anna's growing Armenian identity, for example, can be measured through her increased attention to landscape. At the beginning of the film she takes no notice of the painted backdrop of Ararat before which her daughter dances. Even in Yerevan, the omnipresent images of Ararat – in her hotel room and on the street – seem like mere kitsch, while the mountain is barely visible at a great distance (and underemphasised by Guédiguian's camera) from her hotel window. But it is a sign of a vast progression in Armenian sentiment that later, outside the Hayravank Monastery, she is moved, even to tears, at the impression that she has of 'having lived here before in a distant past'.

Generally speaking, landscapes, and the legends and myths associated with them, are some of the most potent figures of national identification. For Armenians, the single most powerful natural emblem is Mount Ararat. Ararat is the mythical setting of Noah's landing and the Haik and Bel story which, according to Panossian, is 'taught to all primary students in Armenian schools around the world' (2006: 51). In the story, Noah's descendant Haik rebels against Bel's Babylon and returns to the mountain, making it a symbol of 'righteous rebellion' and 'justice', evoked by most nationalist movements. After the genocide, Armenian national identity was often articulated through anti-Turkish sentiment, claims put on lost territories, even armed reprisals in terrorist attacks (such as those of Yervanth's ASALA group). Because Ararat is still today located in Turkey, visible from Yerevan, the mountain continues, on a daily basis, to embody a painful loss. Some monumental art in Armenia has taken advantage of this odd situation in its spatial *mise en scène*: as, for example, in the Soviet-era Mother of Armenia statue in Victory Park, which stands massively brooding over Yerevan with her enormous sword in front of her, pointing toward Ararat.

Guédiguian, who has often emphasised the tensions between such official histories of landscapes and the way in which they are inhabited by his characters, avoids Ararat as a divisive national symbol. In fact, most images of the mountain in the earlier portions of the film are the tacky, touristic painting found in Anna's hotel. Instead, Guédiguian shoots a diverse range of landscapes and architectures: traditional monuments, such as churches, villages where women make bread in the old style, and flower shops. But there are also filling stations, building sites and a CNN building. Guédiguian also keeps to his practice of filming lower-class neighbourhoods (such as Schaké's), and the rubble on the outskirts of town.

The images of rubble actually grow into a founding counter-myth of Armenia told by Yervanth as he flies Anna in a military helicopter over the rock formations of the South Caucasus – not Ararat but smaller fragments of the same formations. He calls the rocks 'your country', and tells her a story of their creation that displaces the myths of Noah, Haik and Bel. On the second day, God, here called a 'worker', passes the Earth through a sieve to ensure that it is arable (this good earth is in part what the 'have' countries have inherited – 'like France', Yervanth insists). Like any good worker, God empties his sieve after his labours. He had forgotten, however, the barren rocks left inside, and which all fell to the ground in the same spot – Armenia. To belong to Armenia, the story suggests, and all the more so for a Frenchwoman, means to be connected to its dregs: to this barren land, to the earthquake-scarred hills that swallowed Schaké's parents (emphasised in another scene), and to Armenia's impoverished inhabitants and workers (like God himself).

If this vision of landscape includes all layers of Armenian society, it also has porous borders. From the helicopter, the camera sweeps across the barren rocks, the mountains bleeding out of the frame, with some craggy details in close-up, all accompanied by music that combines traditional-sounding melody with modern instrumentation. This open and overflowing frame corresponds to a lack, or perhaps a multiplicity, of ways of identifying with the land. Anna's daughter, the old men of the community centre, and all the other characters have their own, private attachments to Armenia. Anna's feeling of a distant incarnation as an Armenian at the Hayravank Monastery certainly contrasts with Yervanth's tempered nationalism, or the emotion that would be felt by an Armenian Christian believer. Guédiguian does not discount any of these points of access. In this way, the film reflects Panossian's conclusion on Armenian identity as a 'complex web of meanings and beliefs' characterised by 'fragmentation' (392).

Ararat lingers in the margins of the frame throughout the film until, in a sort of epilogue, Guédiguian chooses to foreground it and supply it with an alternative legend. Manuk, an aged chauffeur who has been showing Anna around Yerevan in Sarkis's absence, drives her to the airport to return to France. When he stops to retrieve a bumper that has fallen off his dilapidated car, he also asks Anna to step out and look at the mountain. In Armenian, he tells her that a human being needs a dream, and that his dream is Ararat. He brings up the Turks: 'one could imagine that the Turks are not like us, because of what they did'. But Manuk thinks that the Turks will return the mountain, not because of outside pressures or military force, but 'because they know it is our dream' and 'they will feel better after they do'. In this way, Manuk lifts the film's message of friendship – that, among equals, the pleasure of one gives pleasure to the other – to the level of nations that have clashed violently. If Anna and Barsam can have two families and two countries, then Armenia and Turkey can also coexist in peace. Self-identifying as Armenian can, even must, take place in a single world.

Manuk calls his vision a dream, and the final shots emphasise its blend of idealism and realism. Guédiguian places Ararat – the mountain itself rather than kitschy reproductions – squarely in the centre of the image, though it sits, of course, in the distance that history has produced. The mountain has a mirage-like thinness: its snow-covered summit stands out against the blue sky but its lighter base blends in with its background, making it seem to disappear. The real mountain appears to float like an unanchored abstraction, almost unreal, a spectre, much like Manuk's dream of fulfilment and international friendship. There is a small hope of attaining the friendship that moves Manuk, if we focus on what he remembers – that Ararat itself has nothing to generate profit: no natural resources, no gold, 'not even grass for goats'. But the cheap frames of the hotel paintings are replaced here, literally, with the real booms of building cranes and electric wires that frame the mountain. To see the ideal that Ararat represents, we have to perceive it beyond the new economic order that still stands to benefit from old divisions.

Guédiguian's trip to Armenia was followed by a similar revision of some myths of French identity. Not long after his return to France, in 2009 at the height of the 'débat sur l'identité nationale' (debate on national identity), Guédiguian released a film in which he revisits one of the most important legends of French identity, modern France's own Ararat: the resistance to the Nazi occupation (*l'Armée du crime/The Army of Crime*). In the film, Guédiguian again revises an image, this time a poster – *l'affiche rouge* – distributed by the Vichy authorities to advertise the arrest and execution of the Manouchian Group, the resistance cell whose story Guédiguian tells in the film. The poster highlights photographs of the cell members with their hair tussled and faces dirtied and a caption emphasising the foreignness of the Armenians, Poles, Spaniards, Jews, communists, and others in the group: 'Liberators? Liberation by the Army of Crime.'

Once again, Guédiguian celebrates the group's diverse origins but, even more, he celebrates the friendships that form the strength of their unity. The film also acknowledges a growing new friendship in Guédiguian's work, actor Simon Abkarian, Sarkis in *Armenia* and the cell's leader Manouchian here. By rehashing this little-remembered episode of the occupation, Guédiguian also reminds his viewers that this French myth is also foreign, Armenian (Polish, Jewish, communist, etc.), and French all at once.

Conclusion: Modest Film, Modest Identity

I began this chapter with Guédiguian's 'old Classic Marxist', conviction that questions of national identity were somewhat secondary, and I do not believe that this film reflects a change of mind. The epilogue of *Armenia*, shot in part in shot–countershot as Manuk describes to Anna his dream of Ararat, shows our heroine moved but mostly moved by the emotion of another person – just as Guédiguian seems more moved by the emotion of family and friends than by his own self-identification as Armenian. This seems fitting in a film that lacks some of the fire of Guédiguian's best work. Jean-Michel Frodon is harsh, but partly correct, in his reaction to the film which he calls 'an accumulation of Epinal images transplanted to Yerevan, mixing tourist videos and historical-political review as for a middle-school test' (2006: 40). I hope to have shown that Guédiguian wants to problematise such images, though his new friendships may, indeed, lead him to cram too much learning into too small a space. Frodon is right, too, in his diagnosis: 'What has been lost? Anger doubtlessly, and his usual form of naiveté which leaves space for humour.' Guédiguian seems unable to summon uninhibited pity and fear within the framework of national identity. Anna perceives herself primarily in friendships, and only secondarily as Armenian.

When we think of the transformations of Europe since 1989, we often think of how opened borders and the end of binary, Cold War international relations can lead to less rigidity in terms of national identity and reconnection to ties long lost. Guédiguian's work certainly bears this imprint. But it also reminds us that national identification is just one of many considerations that make up personal identity, along with class and friendship, and doubtlessly many more. For Guédiguian, the end of Yalta–Europe also promises potential points of resistance to the cultural figures of profit and enjoyment of the new, Sarkisesque global economic empire. In this film, he seems guardedly hopeful that voyages towards identity in the faraway margins of Europe can strengthen the figures of identity – friendships – that he has offered in the margins of Estaque for the past thirty years. His approach to the new Europe and its economic order is thus a decentring of polarities and a recentring of identity on friendship and equality.

Notes

Introduction

1. Walter Schwimmer's version/vision of Europe includes the Transcaucacus states of Armenia, Azerbaijan and Georgia (Grillo. 70).
2. Czech and Slovak cinemas stand out as potentially glaring omissions. This type of volume is to a considerable extent, however, a reflection of current scholarly trends and it is not at present fashionable to examine contemporary Czech cinema in an East/West context. As an example of this, we could point to the contribution by Czech scholar Petra Hanáková to a recent collection on a similar theme (Engelen and Van Heuckelom), entitled 'Staying Home and Safe: Czech Cinema and the Refusal to be Transnational'. In another recent work on Czech cinema, Jan Čulík makes a similar point, arguing that the home is the most typical space in post-1989 Czech cinema (2013). Indeed, there are exceptions to this, a couple of which were referenced in this introduction, and the desire to stay home in itself speaks to our topic; we ultimately did not find a contribution that would have offered something new on Czech cinema since 1989. For more on Czech cinema, we can suggest the aforementioned works by Hanáková and Čulík, along with *Czech and Slovak Cinema: Theme and Tradition* (2009) and 'The Czech and Slovak Republics: The Velvet Revolution and After' (2013), both by Peter Hames.

Chapter 1

1. Earlier in the film the cuckoo is associated with the notion of greed, thus indicating the means of capitalism's all-consuming emergence.
2. For example, Gerhard Klein's *Berlin um die Ecke*, Herman Zschoche's *Karla*, and Frank Vogel's *Denk bloss nicht ich heule*.

Chapter 2

1. For further bibliographical references and a selection of case studies devoted to the treatment of East/West mobility in post-1989 European cinema, see Engelen and Van Heuckelom (2013).

2. Over the past few years, the 1975-born Baier has been hailed as one of the most promising talents of francophone Swiss film, or – to quote Alain Boillat (2010: 211) – 'un des cinéastes romands les plus remarqués de la dernière décennie'. See also Mathilde Babel (2008) who has conducted sociological research in the domain of contemporary Swiss cinema. Taking into account the number of realised productions, Baier's collaboration with established directors and producers and the critical and public acclaim his films have gathered, Babel grants Baier the highest position in the ranking of young Swiss directors.

3. Film critics and scholars have drawn particular attention to Baier's undeniable 'narcissism' as a film-maker. On the one hand, Baier's tendency to invest his work with biographical elements can be closely linked to his professional background as a documentary film-maker (which, in turn, can be related to the traditionally strong position of documentaries in Swiss cinema). On the other hand, the prominent autobiographical streak which runs through his work seems to stem from a profound interest in the interface between fiction and reality (which also explains Baier's repeated use of reflexive tropes). See Boillat (2008).

4. The fragment goes as follows: 'Sutter died at 73. Congress did nothing. The affair was closed. The estate was not settled, but can still be claimed. Who wants gold? Who wants gold?' For the purpose of this article, the English quotes from *Stealth* have been taken – sometimes with minor modifications – from the English subtitles track available on the DVD edition of the film (Epicentre Films, 2007).

5. 'Sutter was a man of action. Indians told him of a land further to the West, beyond the Rockies, beyond the desert. Now he knew: California. It haunted him.'

6. The notion of 'soft masculinity' has been theorised in relation to various East Asian societies: for example, the concept of 'wen' masculinity in traditional Chinese culture. Wang (2005: 74) describes the typical characteristics of such effeminate male characters in the following way: 'Their masculinity seemed to lie in their intellectual ability or artistic creativity rather than in their physical strength, wealth, aristocratic background or other attributes that are more frequently associated with masculinity.'

7. Opposing the Austrian oppressors of his native Uri, Tell allegedly inspired delegations of the three Alpine cantons to set up a secret defence pact against the Habsburg enemy (an alliance which was concluded on a meadow close to Lake Uri).

8. Interestingly, Kudelski's Polish–Swiss background establishes a symbolic link between the two cities that take up a central role in *Stealth*. Born in Warsaw in the late 1920s, Kudelski left Poland during the Nazi and Soviet invasions and eventually settled in Lausanne where he studied at the Swiss Federal Institute of Technology and lay the foundations for his career

as a world-renowned inventor and audio engineer. See Graff (2008) on Kudelski's historical significance for Swiss cinema.
9. While it partly explains the title of the film, the 'theft' of the Swiss Radio vehicle should be seen as the narrative follow-up to a much earlier scene during which Lucie invites her brother to escape from the yearly Christmas dinner and 'run into the night like thieves' ('Seulement moi et toi en train de courrir comme des voleurs dans la nuit'). The phrase 'comme des voleurs dans la nuit' is a quote taken from the 1973 François Truffaut film *La nuit américaine/Day for Night* and points – along with other intertextual references – to *Stealth*'s profound entanglement with cinematic tradition.
10. Two architectural landmarks which appear in these 'urban' sequences are the famous Lausanne Palace and the Palace of Culture and Science in Warsaw. While the two buildings point to the different historical trajectories followed by the two cities and countries, the appearance of both palaces in a very similar visual configuration seems to be indicative of their equivalence.
11. After passing through Oświęcim/Auschwitz, the siblings' journey to Warsaw includes visits to historical landmarks such as the Monuments to the Heroes of the Warsaw Uprising and the Tomb of the Unknown Soldier. Interestingly, although there is no Germany-set scene in the final cut of the film, a self-drawn road map, which appears in close-up when Lucie is glancing through Lionel's Polish copy of *Sutter's Gold*, indicates that they also passed through the German city of Nuremberg. Worl War II also comes up in a conversation between Lionel and Henryk Baier's Jewish wife (who turns out to have lost all her relatives in the Holocaust).

Chapter 3

1. The recent awards attributed to Haneke's *Amour* (2012, France/Austria), ranging from the Palme d'Or at the Cannes Film Festival to the Academy Award for Best Foreign Language Film, bear witness to the critical importance of the work of this European film-maker as well.
2. On the 'Polish Plumber controversy' in France and the hotly contested issues of 'European integration' and 'clandestine passages between the West and the East', I recommend Aga Skrodzka-Bates's article in *Studies in Eastern European Cinema* (2011).
3. Laura Rascaroli's excellent study of three French-language road movies also identifies a 'redefinition of both immigrant and French identities, as well as of ideas of Eurocentrism' in cinematic creations characterised by 'transnationalism' (Rascaroli, 22). Rascaroli maintains that, of the three films under analysis, Julie Bertucelli's *Depuis qu'Otar est parti/Since Otar Left* (2003) is 'the only film in which France is still regarded a utopian destination by the characters; seen from beyond the post-Soviet eastern border, thus, France is still equivalent with old Europe. The film, however, shows how the repositioning of the West/East border after the dissolution of the Soviet Bloc is

challenging the idea of what being European means' (24). This reconsideration of what it means to be European and this repositioning of the border are important to Rascaroli's analysis of 'the centrality (or, indeed, marginality) of France to these films' (22).
4. Slavoj Žižek refers to 'movements backward and forward in time' in his analysis of Kieślowski's *The Double Life of Véronique* (Žižek, 2006: 20).

Chapter 4

1. Prominent examples of films set in Eastern Europe include Andrea Maria Dusl's *Blue Moon* (2002, Austria), the omnibus documentary *Über die Grenze / About the Border* (2005, Austria), and Paul Rosdy's documentary *Neue Welt* (2005, Austria). Examples of films focusing on Eastern Europeans in Austria include Barbara Albert's *Nordrand* (1999, Austria/Germany/Switzerland), Barbara Gräftner's *Mein Russland/My Russia* (2002, Austria), Jörg Kalt's *Crash Test Dummies* (2005, Austria), Götz Spielmann's *Revanche* (2008, Austria), and Anja Salmanowitz's *Spanien/Spain* (2012, Austria/Bulgaria).
2. See Mokre (2004) and Liebhart and Pribersky (2001) for detailed accounts of Austrian positions on Eastern Europe.
3. 'Der Osten hat mich immer interessiert. Ich finde dort viel Interessantes und Gutes und Tolles. Ich fühle mich dort wohl und kann in den Chor derer, die die "Rückständigkeit" des Ostens verteufeln, nicht einstimmen' (Grissemann 2007: 115). All translations are my own.
4. The tune is 'Serdtse' ('Heart') performed by Pyotr Leshschenko.
5. 'Die Gefahr für mich wäre viel größer, es nicht zu zeigen.'
6. 'Ich versuche mit meinen Filmen, einen ungeschönten Blick auf das Leben zu werfen, auf eine gesellschaftliche Realität zu schauen oder in private Bereiche vorzudringen, . . ., die wir aber gern verdrängen, weil es unangenehm ist hinzuschauen. Ich versuche die Zuschauer zu verführen, auf eine Wirklichkeit zu schauen und sich damit zu konfrontieren, weil ich glaube, daß das letztlich uns alle betrifft, . . .'
7. While the film itself intercuts between the two narratives, this chapter will treat each narrative separately.
8. 'Tschusch' is an Austrian pejorative, originally referring to foreigners from the former Yugoslavia but now denoting foreigners in general. Michael here intensifies the term by adding the prefix, 'Russian'.
9. Michael presents similarly condescending expressions when he and Pauli later check into a Ukrainian hotel and bemoan the non-Western amenities.
10. How the middle-class, minimally educated Pauli can speak Russian is never revealed. Presumably, he acquired this skill from his real father whose whereabouts are also unclear. At any rate, Pauli's proficiency further aligns him with the female, Eastern European figures who are in submissive positions to Western figures.
11. 'Schau mir zu'.

12. 'Perverse Spiele'.
13. 'Du hast doch gesagt, ich soll zuschauen.'
14. It is beyond the scope of this chapter to discuss this controversial setting in detail. The scenes here were shot on location and nearly all the people depicted are actual patients, many of whom suffer from dementia and Alzheimer's. Seidl has often assured that he obtained permission from the home and from its residents' families and that his actual cast members even had to work in the home to prepare for their roles. For many critics, though, the scenes in the home constitute exploitation and verge on a gratuitous exhibitionism that ridicules and exploits the patients.
15. Cf. Parvulescu 853–4 for an extensive discussion of these scenes.
16. 'Bei uns san'S Putzfrau.'
17. Olga's thoughts about this proposal remain unclear. She does spend a great deal of time with him and is moved when she later sees him in the morgue but gives no indication that she is seriously considering the offer. Erich's offer, indeed, seems motivated by her labour potential, not love or affection: he states that she could cook and take care of him. Seidl notes that a union between the two figures was planned in an early script (Grissemann, 231). With that outcome, however, the film would have affirmed Maria's predjudices.
18. Maria's make-up also establishes a link between the antagonists of the two narratives. The brown lipstick smeared around Maria's face gives the impression of a thin beard and moustache, structurally similar to Michael's facial hair. Olga's costume is equally significant in that it consists of white rabbit ears and fluffy tail, which recalls the iconography of the soft-porn Playboy magazine and highlights her position as the object of others' (voyeuristic) gazes.

Chapter 5

1. For discussions of Akın's polyphonic sound: (Göktürk; Kosta).
2. For discussions of multi-ethnicity and migrant populations of European 'global cities': (Meehan, 2007; Neill and Schwedler, 2007).
3. Spector et al. 2007; Poché 2007.
4. For the differences of cosmopolitanism between *In July* and *Head-On*: (Eren 2012).
5. Hamburg, as a sailors' city, has long been connoted with sexuality/prostitution but here it becomes a romanticised space for love.
6. Fran Tonkiss discusses the perception of immigrants as 'others' in cities.
7. *Head-On*, *The Edge of Heaven* and *Soul Kitchen* are especially polyphonic.
8. Discussing travellers in *Head-On*, Göktürk refers to multidirectionality of migration. (Göktürk, 155, 168)
9. These included Turkish newspapers (1960s) and music/video cassettes (1970s/1980s).

10. Yeşilçam is a commercially oriented popular cinema that emerged in the 1950s. It 'produced cheap, low-quality films with large profit margins and were solely aimed at the star system (. . .)' (Ellinger and Kayi, 580, 582)
11. For a discussion on European multi- and monolingualism: (Yıldız).

Chapter 7

1. The United States heavily invested in eugenics at the start of the twentieth century and was the first country in the world to implement eugenic policies in the early 1900s. See Stefan Kühl, *The Nazi Connection: Eugenics, American Racism, and German National Socialism*.
2. Wolf explains that her 'power feminism' stands in opposition to 'victim feminism', which she aligns with the 'old habits left over from the revolutionary left of the 1960s – such as reflexive anticapitalism, an insider–outsider mentality, and an aversion to "the system"' (Wolf 1993: xvi).
3. For an excellent analysis of the 'girl power' movement as a veiled expression of plain commercialism and commodity feminism, see Rebecca C. Hains, 'Power Feminism, Mediated: Girl Power and the Commercial Politics of Change'. Hains argues that 'By refusing to take a so-called "victim" perspective, by refusing to consider the validity of critiques of the capitalist system, power feminism and girl power neglect to develop tools to resist hegemony, putting too much faith in the marketplace's willingness to support change' (Hains 2009: 109).
4. See Natalya T. Riegg's essay on the post-communist challenges to the Western feminism's empowerment rhetoric in 'Revisions of the Visions: Feminism and Empowerment in Post-Transitional Societies' in *Feminist Conversations: Women, Trauma, and Empowerment in Post-Transitional Societies*.
5. In racial discourses, Eastern European whiteness functions as a flexible signifier which, depending on the ideological need, can stand for white or non-white. In the context of European migration, Anca Parvulescu discusses how the whiteness of the Eastern European migrant allows her to 'pass' as Western European. For an in-depth discussion of whiteness in the context of post-Wall Eastern Europe, see Anikó Imre, 'Whiteness in Post-Socialist Eastern Europe' in *Postcolonial Whiteness: Critical Reader on Race and Empire*.

Chapter 8

1. Todorov attributes the dichotomy between the ethnic/provincial and the universal/cosmopolitan to Bulgaria's unique geographical position, observing that 'as a country on the crossroads between Europe and Asia [Bulgaria] tends to *absorb and reflect* rather than promote or flaunt its own unique national character' (my emphasis).

NOTES   299

2. All films are Bulgarian productions unless noted.
3. In Krassimir Kroumov's *Pod edno nebe/Under the Same Sky* (2003) a teenage girl leaves her mountain village to look for her father in Turkey. Svetla Tsotsorkova's *Zhivot sas Sofia/Life with Sophia* (2004) traces the mental breakdown of a village woman as she awaits the return of her husband who has emigrated without her. Nadejda Koseva's *Ritualat/Ritual*, part of the omnibus European production *Lost and Found* (2005), focuses on a village wedding celebration which takes place in the absence of the bride and groom, who have emigrated to Canada, where they are shown getting married in a simultaneous private ceremony.
4. On the theme of migration in Balkan cinema see chapter 13 in Dina Iordanova, *Cinema of Flames: Balkan Film, Culture and the Media*. On the role of village–city migrations in the construction of Balkan national identity, see Mark Mazower, *The Balkans: A Short History*, pp. 24–36.
5. See Thomas Elsaesser (2008).
6. *Tilt* (Viktor Chouchkov, 2011), set during the late 1980s and early 1990s, addresses more critically the post-1989 aftermath although, like *Zad Kadur*, it rejects the possibility of recreating 'home' outside Bulgaria's literal borders.
7. *Ketsove/Sneakers* (Ivan Vladimirov, 2011) displaces the opposition city/village to city/beach, the Bulgarian Black Sea coast now serving as the new source of liberation, not from oppressive socialist ideology but from the equally oppressive capitalist ideology, of which the post-communist city is apparently the embodiment. *Krapetz/Three* (Kiril Stankov, 2013) performs the same kind of displacement.
8. See: Stuart Hall, 'Introduction: Who Needs Identity?'; Homi Bhabha, *The Location of Culture*; Andrew Higson (1989), 'The Concept of National Cinema'; Andrew Higson, 'The Limiting Imagination of National Cinema'; and Stephen Crofts, 'Reconceptualizing National Cinema/s'.
9. See Caren Kaplan, *Questions of Travel: Postmodern Discourses of Displacement*.

Chapter 9

1. 'Detenido por estrangular a su pareja embarazada y mostrar su cadáver por una webcam', *20 minutos*, <http://www.20minutos.es/noticia/1010731/0/mato/mujer/web/> (last accessed 29 September 2013).
2. This selection includes features and shorts. The representatives of the New Romanian Cinema – most of them graduates (notable exceptions being Cristi Puiu and Adrian Sitaru) of UNATC, the national film school, a short-film factory and one of the very few Romanian viable production platforms – have made their debut with short films while others have not had the chance to direct a feature so far.
3. 'Czech cinema, however, has been slow to embrace the open border as an avenue for and between conceptions of "East" and "West"' (Gott 2012: 8).

4. This is just one of the many reasons for the existence of productions from this genre but not necessarily the least. For more details on New Romanian Cinema road movies, see Georgescu 2012.
5. 'In 2004 (in Italy), 320,000 first-time residence permits were issued, with Romanians, Albanians and Moroccans comprising the principal beneficiaries. The total foreign population increased to 2.4 million, with the largest net growth among Romanians' (Castles and Miller 2009: 111). This is the production year of *The Italian Girls* where the two protagonists are returning from Spain but pretending to have been working in Italy, a perceived 'superior' immigration country.
6. INS (National Institute of Statistics) 2011, *The 2011 Population and Statistic Census*, available at <http://www.recensamantromania.ro> (last accessed 9 September 2013).
7. 'Although used with the journalistic purpose of drawing attention, appellations such as "strawberry-pickers" ("*căpșunari*"), "*stranieri*" or "Euro-commuters" ("*euronavetiști*"), which contribute to narrowing down the field of interest by emphasizing either a certain type of occupation, or the purpose and duration of experience, direct the approach towards a temporary phenomenon' (Matei, 2011: 97).

Chapter 10

1. *Ulysses' Gaze* was a coproduction involving Greece, France, Italy, Germany, Britain, the Federal Republic of Yugoslavia, Bosnia and Herzegovina, Albania and Romania. *Landscape in the Mist* was co-produced by Italy, Greece and France.

Chapter 11

1. All films in this chapter are Lithuanian productions unless otherwise noted.
2. I should like to express my sincere thanks to the editors of this book, especially Michael Gott for the thoughtful reading and valuable suggestions, and assistance in writing this text.

Chapter 12

1. The term 'local' is used here instead of 'national', which is problematic when discussing co-productions. The Estonian Film Foundation requires local involvement – the production company or one of the co-producers must be registered in Estonia – yet the talent (including the director) can be of other nationality. Additionally, 'national' in this context indicates the acceptance of a certain body of films by its domestic audiences, while 'local' also includes those that were deemed 'unsuccessful' (that is, not entering 'national culture' proper).

2. The economic crisis of 2007–08 and the subsequent austerity measures also influenced the state funding of the film sector, witnessed by a cut of approximately €1 million in 2009; currently, the state support of €6 million remains near the level of 2007.
3. For example, Vsevolod Pudovkin acted as the 'Soviet film "policeman"' (Cunningham 2004: 70–1) in Hungary, visiting the country twice in 1950–51; in 1947–48 Ilya Trauberg served on the board of directors of the East German film company DEFA (see Allan 1999: 4, 6), and the missions of film-makers, such as Abram Room and Sergei Yutkevitch to Albania and Yogoslavia, respectively, resulted in Soviet-Albaninan/Yugoslavian co-productions.
4. In 1956, the Soviet Union signed a co-production agreement with the left-leaning France (Jäckel 2003a, 238), and it has been estimated that, between 1953 and 1985, the number of extra-Soviet co-productions was more than a hundred, including with the United States, Norway, Japan and Finland (see Siefert 2012a; 2012b). In 1968, Sovinfilm, a special unit dedicated to cinematic collaboration with foreign countries, was set up, and Western film producers were encouraged to acquire services from the Soviet film industry in order to earn much-needed hard currency (Siefert 2012b: 36).
5. In 1994, the total annual state support for film production was €364,505, increasing gradually to €1,419,670 by 1999 (Ruus 2000: 15).
6. *American Mountains* is also the only film with Estonian involvement that received funding from the French ECO Fund, set up to propel film-making in the former Soviet bloc (see Jäckel 2000a: 235).
7. The concept came from Hans-Werner Honert, a German producer born in Leipzig and a classmate and room-mate of Simm in the State Institute of Cinematography in Moscow in the 1970s. Honert had worked as a director of television films in the East German Deutschen Fernsehfunk until 1990, and as a producer in Saxonia Media, the co-producing partner of *Fed Up!*, since 1995.
8. According to Artur Talvik, the Estonian producer of *Fed Up!* (see Ilisson 2005) the film's script underwent more than eleven rewrites.
9. As Paul Cooke (2007: 36–7) observes, the public funding system in Germany gravitates heavily towards subsidising projects with potentially high commercial appeal, which made *Fed Up!*, an upbeat comedy, a good candidate for support.
10. The critics also accused the film of ignoring the typical narrative conventions, making this enchantingly delicate film difficult to follow which, in my opinion, signals Raat's intentional avoidance of formulas characteristic of the nineteenth-century tradition of psychological realism that have been hijacked by the profit-seeking commercial cinema and that perpetuate the exploitative circuits of global capitalism.

Chapter 13

1. 'East Central Europe' is the term widely used in literature on the European Union to refer to the states which acceded to the EU in 2004.
2. The terms 'Balkans' and 'Balkan region' are used in this chapter to refer to the states which were part of the Yugoslav Federation and involved in the Yugoslav Wars of Secession during the 1990s.
3. Todorova writes that the Balkans have long been seen as 'geographically inextricable from Europe, yet culturally constructed as "the other"' (1994: 455).
4. Otto von Bismarck, speech to the Reichstag, 5 December 1876; quoted in Patten (2004).
5. The term 'Western Balkans' has been used by the European Union since 1998 to refer to those countries in south-eastern Europe which are not part of the European Union but aspire to EU membership: Serbia, Croatia, Bosnia and Herzegovina, Montenegro, Macedonia, Slovenia. Slovenia joined the EU in 2004 and tends to be considered part of East Central Europe. Croatia acceded in July 2013.
6. We use the term 'Central Europe' to refer to the regional identity of the Czech Republic, Slovakia, Hungary and Poland, and 'East Central Europe' to refer to the EU accession process. Intellectuals and political actors in these countries have for decades consistently referred to the region as 'Central Europe' and sought to distinguish it from both Eastern Europe and the Balkan region.
7. For instance, when the Accession Treaty was signed in Athens in 2003, German Chancellor Gerhard Schröder declared: 'With this step, the Union is finally overcoming the division of Europe into east and west': quoted in *The Guardian*, 18 April 2003.
8. 'EU15' refers to the member states of the European Union prior to the 2004 enlargement: Austria, Belgium, Denmark, Finland, France, Germany, Greece, Ireland, Italy, Luxembourg, the Netherlands, Portugal, Spain, Sweden, and the United Kingdom.
9. Having seceded relatively peacefully in 1991 and because of its long history of incorporation into the Habsburg Empire, Slovenia was in the unique position among the former Yugoslav republics of being an applicant for EU membership at this time. Along with Croatia, Slovenia was viewed as 'less eastern' than the southern and eastern Balkan states (Bakić-Hayden, 1995: 924).
10. Dusko Doder, for example, wrote in 1993 that 'the Europeans' had been 'unable to stop a civil war on their doorstep' (4).
11. Iordanova does not imply that the violence itself is 'teleological', but rather uses the term to explain how violence in the Balkans is *interpreted*: past conflicts are retrospectively construed as having laid the groundwork for current conflicts and current warfare projects future violence.
12. The manipulation of historical memory and its effect in activating and

strengthening Western stereotypes about Balkan conflict are satirised in *Pretty Village, Pretty Flame*. Laza, a simple-minded Serbian peasant, is so outraged by a television news report broadcasting atrocities perpetrated against Serbs by 'Ustasha criminals' and 'fanatics of Allah's Jihad', that he abruptly leaves a family gathering and marches to the nearest main road to hitchhike to Belgrade and volunteer for combat recruitment. When he expresses contempt for his newfound, yet lifelong, enemy to the truck driver who pulls over, declaring 'never again shall a German or Turk set foot here', the irony is that he does not realise – in spite of the vehicle's kitsch Turkish paraphernalia – that the driver is himself Turkish. Laza's inability to recognise his allegedly most loathed foe, despite his staunch reiterations of enmity, reveals both the irrationality and the power of memory reconstruction in the wake of Yugoslavia's demise.

13. D. Warszawski, *Obrona poczty sarajewakiej* [*The Defense of Sarajevo Post-Office*] (1995), cited in Jedlicki (1999: 229).
14. Žižek (1991), *Liebe Dein Symptom wie Dich Selbst: Jaccques Lacans Psychoanalyse und die Medien*, Berlin: Merve, 10; cited in and translated by Krstic (2002).
15. Slavoj Žižek, in Benson (1996); see also Slavoj Žižek (1993), 'Why are the NSK and Laibach Not Fascists?' *M'ARS*, 3/4: 4.
16. Žižek in Benson (1996); see also Žižek (2004: 54).
17. According to the film's producer, this was, indeed, the intended signification: Dragan Bjelogrlic, cited in Krstic (2002).
18. Marciniak cites Page DuBois (1991), *Torture and Truth*, New York: Routledge: 155.
19. Filipčević argues that the rendering of the dispute between the two Balkan men as an 'inexplicable Balkan affair' is achieved by leaving their argument untranslated for both the restaurant patrons in the film and the audience (2004–5: 20).
20. In particular, this scene rejects the West's detachment from Balkan violence set up by Manchevski earlier in the film, when Anne studies war photos in her London studio at a seemingly safe distance from the Macedonian conflict. See Marciniak (2003: 71) for further analysis.
21. Marciniak cites Page DuBois (1991: 155).
22. Iordanova asserts that the West frequently only includes the Balkans in the concept of 'Europe' as a 'neglected backyard' that required maintenance due to its geographical proximity to Europe proper.
23. The implication of negligence is likewise reinforced through the ironic use of Bobby McFerrin's song 'Don't Worry, Be Happy', which backdrops the juxtaposition of a UN plane landing in Sarajevo against a montage of bloody, real-life footage of the siege.
24. Winterbottom explains that he made the film to highlight the fact that no one in the West was taking any notice of the conflict: 'They were getting the pictures and stories out – which should have made the world realise what

was happening and get us to do something about it. But no one responded, not the politicians or the general public': Winterbottom, in an interview with Ingrid Randoja, quoted in Molloy, 81.

25. Aleks confesses to Anne in a letter that, while he was working as a photojournalist covering the Balkan conflict, he complained to a Serbian militiaman about the lack of 'action', and the militiaman responded by shooting a prisoner right in front of him. 'I took sides', Aleks writes, 'my camera killed a man'.

26. Patricia Molloy, for example, argues that, through Winterbottom's reduction of the Bosnian War to a series of 'ill-defined stereotypes', *Welcome to Sarajevo* merely explains the conflict as the 'inevitable outcome of a long history steeped in ancient ethnic hatreds' (79–85).

Chapter 14

1. Polish cinema offers a precedent for this sort of extended cinematic work: *Decalog* (Krzysztof Kieślowski, 1989, Poland/West Germany), consisting of ten parts corresponding to the Ten Commandments.
2. *Dom wariatów/The House of Fools* (1985); *Życie wewnętrzne/Inner Life* (1987); *Porno* (1990); *Nic śmiesznego/Nothing Funny* (1995); *Ajlawju/I Love You* (1999); *Dzień świra/Day of the Wacko* (2002, Poland); *Wszyscy jesteśmy Chrystusami/We're All Christs* (2006); *Baby są jakieś inne/Man, Chicks Are Just Different* (2011).
3. All films are Polish productions unless otherwise noted.
4. The plot of *Wacko* appears similar to an earlier American film, *Groundhog Day* (Harold Ramis, 1993, USA) yet this similarity allows the viewer to appreciate the profound differences between them all the more.
5. The protagonist of Kieślowski's *White* (*Trois couleurs: Blanc/Three Colors: White*, 1994, France/Poland/Switzerland), Karol, learns French and, at some point, the verbs on the language tape come closer to his experience and reveal his innermost dream: from 'eat' and 'sleep' to 'leave' and finally to 'please'. Pleasing his French ex-wife, who left him, and returning to her is the dream and the project of his whole life.
6. Here and throughout the chapter the quoted dialogue from both films comes from English subtitles by Marcin Leśniewski, with minor revisions.
7. Koterski may be referring here to the whole genre of action movies and/or a specific example of it, like Travis Bickle in *Taxi Driver* (Martin Scorsese, 1976, USA).
8. This diminutive form of Adam's name does not express affection, as such forms normally do, but rather reduces him to a child, emphasising his infantile indecisiveness and excessive dependence on his mother (Żurawiecki 125–30).
9. Audiences face the additional challenge of trying to identify the two or three

actors who play Adam, his son, ex-wife, and mother at various stages of their lives.
10. The text of Pope John II's Mass is on the Vatican's Web site: <http://www.vatican.va/holy_father/john_paul_ii/homilies/1979/documents/hf_jp-ii_hom_19790602_polonia-varsavia_en.html> (accessed 14 January 2014).
11. Throughout the octology Adam has various jobs yet he is always an intellectual with a creative vocation that fails to bring him satisfaction: a film director (in *Nothing Funny*), a writer (in *Ajlawju*), an underpaid and burnt-out school teacher of Polish (in *Wacko*), and an art history college professor (in *Christs*).
12. Koterski made a number of documentary films before working on feature films, and some of them dealt with addiction and ways to combat it. So his treatment of alcoholism and drug addiction in the octology is not that of an outsider but of a person with expertise and compassion.
13. Interrelationship between trauma and memory is an intriguing and productive topic explored by experts from a variety of angles: historical, cultural, psychological, medical, etc. While Koterski makes fun of Adam's selective personal memories he may be suggesting to the viewer a broader look at the memories of collective trauma survivors and of Poland's past.
14. Even though a recent Russian remake of *Wacko* (*День учителя / Day of the Teacher*, Sergei Mokritsky, Russia, 2012) is a weak imitation of the original, it may be seen as a proof that *Wacko*'s ideas and types are relevant not only in Poland but in other countries of the former Soviet bloc as well.

Chapter 15

1. In fact, it was somewhat surprising that this film should have been scripted by Klier (co-written with Karin Åström), a director whose own work is resolutely unsentimental and resistant to genre, as was evident in his bleak Berlin film *Ostkreuz* (1991 Germany).
2. All references to Graf are taken from this interview unless otherwise stated.
3. Translations of dialogue from Graf's film are mine.

Chapter 16

1. All translations are the author's except where otherwise noted.
2. Heise only later gave this film its subtitle: *Psychogram of a Spy* (*Psychogramm eines Spions*). Even in this context, however, it could be argued that there is not a clear equivalent in the film between 'Barluschke' (whomever or whatever that happens to be) and 'the psychogram', the process of mapping a person's behaviour and visually scoring his/her responses, which, for a spy, is almost an oxymoron.
3. In his review, Marcus Sailer also emphasises 'this man's [Bert's] lack of

transparency, who, according to his own statements, lived his life in films for thirty years' (Sailer, 12).
4. The inaccessibility of *Barluschke*, even at present as Ivette Löcker describes, is also worth noting: 'The film is not available [on] DVD, as are most of the other films by Thomas Heise. In the Municipal Library of Berlin the videotape is classified as "missing". Barluschke does not allow himself to be caught' (Löcker 22–3).
5. In the next sentence, Heise states that there is a song about this 'nonsense' in Bertolt Brecht's *The Threepenny Opera*: 'Go running after luck / But don't you run too fast: / We all are running after luck / And luck is running last.' (Brecht, 119).
6. As defined in the 2013 *Oxford English Dictionary*.
7. On the legal placelessness of the spy, see Abramov 2008: 'Indeed, in contemporary legal scholarship the difficult-to-capture crime of espionage is considered a "noncrime crime": the spy's actions are neither outlawed, nor permitted in international law. [. . .] Spies hold an excessive status with relation to the law up until the moment they are caught. Until then – that is, until legal mastery becomes possible – for all legal and political purposes the spy [. . .] inhabits legal placelessness' (Abramov, 10–11).
8. Before this part of the voice-over, Heise states that '[e]verything which sets men in motion must go through their minds, but how this happens depends very much on the circumstances'. Julia Zutavern has discussed the first part of this passage as a 'cryptic prologue' inspired by a quotation from Friedrich Engels (Zutavern 2009: 46; see also Engels [1886] 1996: 50).
9. 'When referring the concept of paranoia to a specific code of the filmic substance of expression, I am using it as a reference to the fundamental reversibility of the imaginary dyad' (Rose 1988: 155).
10. 'Barluschke compares his changing of sides in the film with Theodorakis' change of political allegiance' (Goldstein 2013: 100).
11. The text in this scene consists of excerpts from the 'Köppe-Bericht' (see Köppe). Many thanks to Thomas Heise for clarifying this.

Chapter 17

1. I am relying on Nasta's, Uricaru's, and Şerban's descriptions of the history of Romanian cinema.
2. For definitions of Romanian minimalism see Nasta, *Contemporary Romanian Cinema*, 155–200; Şerban, 'Romanian Cinema', 15; and Uricaru, 'Follow the Money', 429.
3. Cristi Puiu's *Moartea Domnului Lăzărescu/ The Death of Mr Lăzărescu* won the Un Certain Regard award at Cannes in 2005; Corneliu Porumboiu's *A fost sau n-a fost?/12:08 East of Bucharest* received the Caméra d'Or at Cannes in 2006; Cristian Nemescu's *California Dreamin'* got the Un Certain Regard award at Cannes in 2007; and Cristian Mungiu's *4 luni,*

NOTES 307

    3 săptămâni şi 2 zile/4 Months, 3 Weeks and 2 Days won the Palme d'Or at Cannes in 2007. Most recently, Călin Peter Netzer's *Poziţia Copilului/Child's Pose* received the Golden Bear at the Berlin film festival in 2013.
4. Mitulescu states that he renounced his initial plan to collaborate with Wim Wender's German production company because of bureaucratic issues and Germany's overall restrictive policies for international co-operations. He retained In-Ah Lee, Wender's producer, however, and Wender himself as executive producer. See Mitulescu's interview, 'Cătălin Mitulescu – Un debut aşteptat', 14–15.
5. There are several recent Romanian films that focus on the relationship between East and West during post-communism, such as *California Dreamin'*, *Occident* (Cristian Mungiu, 2002), *Felicia, înainte de toate/First of All, Felicia* (Răzvan Rădulescu and Melissa de Raaf, 2009), *Francesca* (Bobby Păunescu, 2009), and *Despre oameni şi melci/Of Snails and Men* (Tudor Giurgiu, 2012).
6. For an analysis of the nostalgic gaze at the beginning of Mungiu's film see Pârvulescu, 'The Cold War'.
7. For more on *Ostalgie* see also Paul Cooke.
8. This reconciliatory tone contrasts with that of *12:08 East of Bucharest* and *Hîrtia va fii albastră/The Paper Will Be Blue* (Radu Muntean, 2006).
9. For her role of Eva Dorotheea Petre received the Un Certain Regard award for best actress at the Cannes Film Festival in 2006.
10. A parody of the taboos that applied to Ceauşescu's visual representation is presented in the episode 'Legenda fotografului oficial'/'The Legend of the Party Photographer' in Mungiu's co-directed film *Amintiri din Epoca de Aur/Tales from the Golden Age* (2009).
11. As Bădeanu notes, the film's ethnic amicability between Romanians and the two Romani characters, Tarzan and Florică, is 'potentially historically inaccurate'. See Bădeanu, 'Life as a Hill', 421.
12. In 1981, when Ceauşescu decided to pay off Romania's foreign debt, the latter amounted to $10.2 billion. See Massino, 'From Black Caviar to Blackouts', 217.
13. On food shortages see Massino, 238–41, and Vinea, 100–9, 256, 272–4.
14. On Bucharest's special position with regard to food see footnote 48. in Massino, 248.
15. Food shortages are also depicted in the episodes 'Legenda miliţianului lacom'/'The Legend of the Greedy Policeman' and 'Legenda şoferului de găini'/'The Legend of the Chicken Truck Driver' in *Tales from the Golden Age*.
16. Mustaţă points out that 'by the mid-1980s, Romanian television broadcasting was reduced to two hours on weekdays and four to five hours on the weekends' (Mustaţă, 56)

17. For a critical analysis of Ceaușescu nostalgia see Georgescu, '"Ceaușescu Hasn't Died"' and Popescu-Sandu, 'Let's All Freeze Up'.
18. Vișan is often referred to as Ceaușică, a form derived from the name Ceaușescu, and meant to underscore Vișan's role as an extension of the system. While this appellation underlines the subversiveness of those figures who employ it, in reality defaming Ceaușescu's name posed great danger.
19. For more on cinematic representations of immigration, see Chapter 9 by Lucian Georgescu.
20. The officers do not want Titi to raise his hands because such a gesture would clearly indicate to onlookers that the authorities have detained somebody. Officials wanted to keep such interventions hidden from the population as much as possible.
21. One of the most infamous examples of this forcible systematisation in Bucharest is the Casa Poporului (People's House), a building for which, in 1985, Ceaușescu had one fifth of the city's historic centre destroyed and bulldozed 9,300 homes, a cathedral and more than a dozen churches. For more information see Vachon, 'Bucharest', 59.
22. Magheți and Steiner state that, between 1980 and 1989, more than 16,000 people attempted to cross Romania's borders with Hungary and Yugoslavia, including swimming across the Danube; of these, 12,000 were arrested. See Magheți and Steiner, *Mormintele tac*, 11, 21.
23. Another unlikely hero who causes the fall of a Communist regime, namely that of the GDR, is Klaus Uhltzscht, the protagonist of Thomas Brussig's novel *Helden wie wir*.
24. For more details on videotheques see Pârvulescu and Copilaș, 'Hollywood Peeks', 1, 6, 14. The practice of organising showings of VHS tapes in private homes is illustrated in the episode 'Legenda vânzătorilor de aer'/'The Legend of the Air Sellers' in *Tales from the Golden Age*.
25. The 'Cenaclu Flacăra' was suspended on 15 June 1985, after a concert held in the city of Ploiești led to five deaths and several hundred injured people.
26. For the status of jeans and the ways in which they could be procured from the black market in communist Romania see Bernic. Jeans were a desirable item in other East European countries as well. In the GDR, for instance, they were a treasured gift from relatives in the FRG while counterfeit jeans could be purchased from Vietnamese guest workers. For more on the status of jeans in the GDR see also Plenzdorf, *Die neuen Leiden*, 13–14 and 58–9.
27. For a critical summary of the vitriolic reception Romanian workers received in the British press in the light of their country's 2007 EU accession see Light and Young. For negative British perceptions of Romanians in 2014 see Dawar. For a critique of antagonistic German views about Romanian migrants in 2014 see Kuzmany and Verseck. According to Stan and Zaharia, polls conducted in 2008 indicate that only 35 per cent of the Spanish

Chapter 18

1. 'For a very long time I took very little interest in these questions of belonging. I was born in a neighborhood of Marseille that was very structured, and I've always divided the world between rich and poor, and not between German, Italian, Armenian, Arab, or Spanish. I continue to think, more or less, like an classic old Marxist, that this is the only conflict that really merits interest' (Goudet undated; all translations mine).
2. See Goudet for Guédiguian's detailed account which ends with an avowal: 'It is as if it were the Armenians who claimed that identity for me, as a somewhat noteworthy personality'.
3. O'Shaugnessy and others have demonstrated that Guédiguian contributed in the 1980s and 1990s to a reorientation of politics towards local militancy. Phil Powrie, for instance, points to a 1997 petition signed by Guédiguian in opposition to stricter immigration laws. In his discussion of this matter, Guédiguian used terms such as 'proximity' and 'community politics' in ways that fit well with friendship along the Badiouian lines sketched below (Powrie 2001: 137).
4. See May's thorough discussion of Foucauldian figures as 'moldings' of our lives and practices (May 2012: 20–35).
5. May: 'In particular, we want to retain the central idea that there are certain friendships that are concerned with the other for the sake of the other' (May 2012: 75).
6. In *A Cinema without Walls: Movies and Culture after Vietnam*, Timothy Corrigan suggests that such fortuitous encounters and accidents are among the distinctive marks of the road movie: 'unlike other genres, such as the detective film where characters initiate events, in the road movie events act upon the characters' (145).
7. I have no proof of a direct inspiration but the resemblance between 'Sarkis' and 'Sarkozy' (and its variations in 'Sarko') is suggestive.
8. I should mention that Guédiguian had, in fact, filmed a few scenes of *À la place du coeur /Where the Heart Is* (1998, France) away from Marseilles, in Sarajevo. This film does not explore the themes of personal identity as *Armenia* does (none of its characters has a direct connection to Sarajevo) but it shares some of its representation of the city and its people. For instance, it features a similar change in perspective in a character played by Ascaride, who travels to Sarajevo to find a woman who has mistakenly accused her son-in-law of rape. Again with the aid of a friendly chauffeur/interpreter, she travels through a battered landscape (this one the rubble of war-torn Sarajevo). There she gets a glimpse into the difficulties of people's daily lives, and quickly stops seeing them as a means to an end.

9. In one scene, for example, the three share a room and Guédiguian shoots a quiet conversation between Anna and Yervanth (naked from the waist up) while Schaké sleeps. Meylan and Ascaride's long experience of playing lovers and spouses certainly contributes to the erotic interest.
10. See *Marie-Jo et ses deux amours* (2002) where the narrative arrangement of Marie-Jo's two truly passionate loves wreaks havoc on all involved, leading to death.
11. This point about 'two countries' echoes Gott's use of Nira Yuval-Davis's notion of 'multilayered citizenship' and Patrick Weil's description of flexible and changing processes of self-identification to this film (Gott 2013a: 76). Why shouldn't Barsam be allowed to be both French and Armenian?

Bibliography

Aarma, J. (2006), 'Peeter Simm: Muud ma ei oska!', *Maaleht*, 2 February, 18–19.
Abbas, A. (2006), 'The New Hong Kong Cinema and the Déjà Disparu', in D. Eleftheriotis and G. Needham (eds), *Asian Cinemas. A Reader and Guide*, Edinburgh: Edinburgh University Press, pp. 72–99.
Abbas, A. (2007), 'Hong Kong', in M. Hjort and D. Petrie (eds), *The Cinema of Small Nations*, Edinburgh: Edinburgh University Press, pp. 113–26.
Abel, M. (2008), '"The Cinema of Identification Gets on my Nerves": An Interview with Christian Petzold', *Cineaste* 33.3 <http://www.cineaste.com/articles/an-interview-with-christian-petzold.htm> (last accessed 10 September 2013).
Abel, Marco (2013), *The Counter-Cinema of the Berlin School*, Rochester: Camden House.
Abramov, Tamar (2008), *To Catch a Spy: Explorations in Subjectivity*, doctoral dissertation, Harvard University.
Agustín, L. (2005), 'At Home in the Street: Questioning the Desire to Help and Save', in E. Bernstein and L. Schaffner (eds), *Regulating Sex: The Politics of Intimacy and Identity*, New York: Routledge, pp. 67–82.
Ahadi, Ali Samadi (2009), 'Director's Commentary', *Salami Aleikum* (DVD), Germany.
Ahadi, Ali Samadi (2013), 'Fakten und Hintergruende zum Film Salami-Aleikum', <http://www.cinefacts.de/News-Features/Features/Fakten-und-Hintergruende-zum-Film-Salami-Aleikum,1312364/6> (last accessed 10 June 2013).
Ahbe, T. (2011), 'Competing master narratives: *Geschichtspolitik* and identity discourse in three German societies', in N. Hodgin and C. Pearce (eds), *The GDR Remembered. Representations of the East German State since 1989*, Rochester: Camden House, pp. 221–50.
Ahmed, Sarah (2000), *Strange Encounters: Embodied Others in Post-Coloniality*, New York: Routledge.
Ahmed, S. (2007), 'A Phenomenology of Whiteness', *Feminist Theory*, 8: 2, 149–68.
Allan, S. (1999), 'DEFA: An historical overview', in S. Allan and J. Sandford (eds) *DEFA: East German Cinema, 1946–1992*, New York and Oxford: Berghahn Books, pp. 1–21.

Andreescu, Florentina (2013), *From Communism to Capitalism: Nation and State in Romanian Cultural Production*, New York: Palgrave Macmillan.
Anon. (no date), 'Brooklyn Funk Essentials', *Last. fm*, <http://www.last.fm/music/Brooklyn+Funk+Essentials> (last accessed 14 March 2014).
Anon. (2005) 'Cătălin Mitulescu – Un debut așteptat', *Filmul tău*, 14–15.
Anon. (2009), 'Offener Brief: Fatih Akin boykottiert Filmpremiere in der Schweiz', *MIGAZIN: Migration in Germany*, 4 December 2009, <http://www.migazin.de/2009/12/04/fatih-akin-boykottiert-filmpremiere-in-der-schweiz/> (last accessed 7 December 2009).
Arendt, Hannah (1958), *The Human Condition*, Chicago: University of Chicago Press.
Aristotle (1976), *The Ethics of Aristotle: The Nicomachean Ethics*, London: Penguin.
Asseraf, A. (2012), 'Interview: Ariane Labed talks to Antoine Asseraf', <http://www.filepmotwary.com/motwary/2012/02/interview-ariane-labed-talks-to-antoine-asseraf.html> (last accessed 15 March 2014).
Assmann, Jan (1997), *Moses the Egyptian. The Memory of Egypt in Western Monotheism*, Cambridge, MA and London: Harvard University Press.
Augé, Marc (2009), *Non-Places, Introduction to an Anthropology of Supermodernity*, London and New York: Verso.
Babel, M. (2008), 'Jeunes cinéastes romands. Se faire sa place dans le champ du cinéma suisse', in Alain Boillat, Philipp Brunner and Barbara Flückiger (eds), *KINO CH/CINÉMA CH. Rezeption, Ästhetik, Geschichte. Réception, esthétique, histoire*, Marburg: Schüren Verlag, pp. 85–97.
Bădeanu, A (2008), 'Life as a Hill. *The Curse of the Hedgehog* and *The Land is Waiting*', *Third Text*, 22: 3, 421–5.
Badiou, A. (2008), 'The Communist Hypotheses', *New Left Review*, 49, 29–42.
Badiou, Alain (2010), *The Meaning of Sarkozy*, London: Verso.
Baer, H. and L. Koepnick (1998), '"Raus aus der Haut": Division and Identity in Current German Cinema', *GDR Bulletin*, 45–51.
Bakić-Hayden, M. (1995), 'Nesting Orientalisms: The Case of Former Yugoslavia', *Slavic Review* 54: 4, 917–31.
Balibar, Étienne (2003), *We, the People of Europe? Reflections on Transnational Citizenship*, Princeton: Princeton University Press.
Balibar, É. (2009), 'Europe as borderland', *Society and Space*, 27, 190–215.
Baltic Films (2012), *Baltic Films: Facts & Figures*, <http://www.efsa.ee/public/files/Facts%26Figures%202012.pdf> (last accessed 18 March 2014).
Barluschke, film, directed by Thomas Heise. Germany: ö-Film, 1997.
Bathrick, David (1995), *The Powers of Speech: The Politics of Culture in the GDR*, Lincoln: University of Nebraska Press.
Baudrillard, Jean and Guillaume, Marc (2008), *Radical Alterity*, Los Angeles: Semiotext(e).
Bauman, Zygmunt (1995), *Life in Fragments: Essays in Postmodern Morality*, Oxford and Cambridge: Blackwell.

Bauman, Z. (1996), 'From Pilgrim to Tourist – or a Short History of Identity', in S. Hall and P. du Gay (eds), *Questions of Cultural Identity*, London: Sage, pp. 18–36.
Bauman, Zygmunt (1998), *Globalization: The Human Consequences*, New York: Columbia University Press.
Bauman, Zygmunt (2007), *Liquid Times: Living in an Age of Uncertainty*, Cambridge: Polity Press.
Bhabha, Homi K. (1994), *The Location of Culture*, London and New York: Routledge.
Beck, A. (2003), 'Introduction: Cultural Work, Cultural Workplace – looking at the Cultural Industries', in A. Beck (ed.), *Cultural Work: Understanding the Cultural Industries*, London: Routledge, pp. 1–11.
Benson, Michael (1996), *Predictions of Fire* (documentary), New York: The Cinema Guild.
Berdahl, D. (1999), '"(N)Ostalgie" for the present: Memory, Longing, and East German Things', *Ethnos* 64: 2, 192–211.
Bergfelder, T. (2005), 'National, transnational or supranational cinema: Rethinking European film studies', *Media, Culture & Society*, 27, 315–31.
Berghahn, D. (2009), 'From Turkish greengrocer to drag queen: reassessing patriarchy in recent Turkish-German coming-of-age films', *New Cinemas: Journal of Contemporary Film*, 7: 1, 55–69.
Berghahn, D. (2011), 'Queering the Family of Nation: Reassessing Fantasies of Purity, Celebrating Hybridity in Diasporic Cinema', *Transnational Cinemas*, 2.2, 129–46.
Bernic, Corina (2009), (ed.) *Primii mei blugi*, Bucharest: Editura ART.
Bernstein, E. and Schaffner, L. (eds), *Regulating Sex: The Politics of Intimacy and Identity*, New York: Routledge, pp. 67–82.
Betts, Paul (2010), *Within Walls: Private Life in the East German Democratic Republic*, Oxford: Oxford University Press.
Bewes, Diccon (2010), *Swiss Watching: Inside Europe's Landlocked Island*, London: Nicholas Brealey Publishing.
Blumenberg, Hans-Christoph (1979), *Arbeit am Mythos*, Frankfurt: Suhrkamp.
Bohle, D. and Greskovits, B. (2007), 'Neoliberalism, embedded neoliberalism and neocorporatism: Towards transnational capitalism in Central-Eastern Europe', *West European Politics*, 30: 3, 443–66.
Boia, Lucian (2001), *Romania: Borderland of Europe (Topographics)*, London: Reaktion Books.
Boillat, Alain (2008), 'Je(u) fictionnel. Les avatars de l'"auteur" Lionel Baier dans "Garçon stupide" et "Comme des voleurs"', in A. Boillat, P. Brunner and B. Flückiger (eds), *KINO CH/CINÉMA CH. Rezeption, Ästhetik, Geschichte. Réception, esthétique, histoire*, Marburg: Schüren Verlag, pp. 143–57.
Boillat, A. (2010), 'Le cinéma documentaire contemporain en Suisse romande: Jean-Stéphane Bron, figure de proue', *French Forum*, 35: 2–3, pp. 209–31.

Bordwell, David (1985), *Narration in the Fiction Film*. Madison, WI: University of Wisconsin Press.
Bordwell, David (2012), *Poetics of Cinema*, New York and Abingdon: Routledge.
Bori, E. (2010), 'Puppet Masters. Szabolcs Hajdu: Bibliothèque Pascal', The Hungarian Quarterly, 51: 198, 165–8.
Boyer, J. (1989), 'Some Reflections on the Problem of Austria, Germany, and Mitteleuropa', *Central European History*, 22: 3/4, 301–15.
Brady, M. and Helen H. (2011), 'Import and Export: Ulrich Seidl's Indiscreet Anthropology of Migration', in R. von Dassanowsky and O. Speck (eds), *New Austrian Film*, New York: Berghahn Books, pp. 207–24.
Brecht, Bertolt [1928] (1982), *The Threepenny Opera*, trans. Desmond Vesey and Eric Bentley, New York: The Limited Editions Club.
Brown, William (2013), *Supercinema: Film Philosophy for the Digital Age*, Oxford: Berghahn Books.
Brown, William, Iordanova, Dina, and Torchin, Leshu (2010), *Moving People, Moving Images: Cinema and Trafficking in the New Europe*, Glasgow: St Andrews Film Studies.
Brussig, Thomas (1998), *Helden wie wir*, Frankfurt am Main: Fischer Taschenbuch Verlag.
Buchowski, M. (2006), 'The Specter of Orientalism in Europe: From Exotic Other to Stigmatised Brother', *Anthropological Quarterly* 79: 3, 463–82.
Burns, R. (2007), 'Toward a Cinema of Cultural Hybridity: Turkish-German Filmmakers and the Representation of Alterity', *Debatte* 15: 1 (April), 3–24.
Burns, R. (2009), 'On the Streets and on the Road: Identity in Transit in Turkish-German Travelogues on Screen', *New Cinemas: Journal of Contemporary Film* 7: 1, 11–26.
Busek, Erhard (1997), *Mitteleuropa: Eine Spurensicherung*, Vienna: Kremayr and Scheriau.
Buß, Christian (2007), 'Parcours der Demütigungen', *Der Spiegel Online*, 18 October. <http://www.spiegel.de/kultur/kino/0,1518,512151,00.html> (last accessed 14 March 2014).
Byg, B. (2013) 'Is there still an East German Cinema', in C. Portuges and P. Hames (eds.) *Cinemas in Transition in Central Eastern Europe after 1989*, Philadelphia: Temple University Press, pp. 75–103.
Castles, Stephen and Miller, Mark J. (2009), *The Age of Migration: International Population Movements in the Modern World*, New York: Guilford Press.
Clark, J. R. (1991), 'Scatology', in J. R. Clark, *The Modern Satiric Grotesque and its Traditions*, Lexington, KY: University Press of Kentucky, 116–30.
Clay, Catrine and Leapman, Michael (1995), *Master Race: the Lebensborn Experiment in Nazi Germany*, London: Hodder & Stoughton Educational.
Clarke, C. (2011), 'First sight: Ariane Labed', *The Guardian*, 18 August, <http://www.theguardian.com/culture/2011/aug/18/first-sight-ariane-labed> (last accessed 15 March 2014).

Cooke, Paul (2005) *Representing East Germany since Unification: From Colonization to Nostalgia*, New York: Berg.
Cooke, P. (2007), 'Supporting contemporary German film: How triumphant is the free market?', *Journal of Contemporary European Studies*, 15: 1, 35–46.
Copilaș, E. and Pârvulescu, C. (2013), 'Hollywood Peeks: The Rise and Fall of Videotheques in 1980s Romania', *Eastern European Politics and Societies*, XX: X, 1–19.
Corciovescu, Cristina (2011), 'Chemarea Occidentului in Noul Cinema Românesc', in C. Corciovescu and M. Mihăilescu (eds), *NoulCinema Românesc – De la Tovarășul Ceaușescu la domnul Lăzărescu/The New Romanian Cinema – From Comrade Ceaușescu to Mr. Lăzărescu*, București: Polirom.
Corrigan, Timothy (1991), *A Cinema without Walls: Movies and Culture after Vietnam*, New Brunswick, NJ: Rutgers University Press.
Coulson, M. (1993), 'Looking Behind the Violent Break-up of Yugoslavia', *Feminist Review* 45, 86–101.
Creangă, I. (1983), 'Amintiri din copilărie', *Povești, Amintiri, Povestiri*, Bucharest: Minerva, pp. 155–225.
Crisan, Cezara (2012), 'Transnational Experiences of Eastern European Women and Feminist Practices after 1989', in Glenda Tibe Bonifacio (ed.), *Feminism and Migration: Cross-Cultural Engagements*, Dordrecht and New York: Springer, pp. 165–86.
Crofts, Stephen (2002), 'Reconceptualizing National Cinema/s', in Allan Williams (ed.), *Film and Nationalism*, New Brunswick, NJ: Rutgers University Press, pp. 25–51.
Čulík, Jan (2013), *A Society in Distress: The Image of the Czech Republic in Contemporary Czech Feature Film*, Brighton: Sussex Academic Press.
Cunningham, John (2004), *Hungarian Cinema from Coffee House to Multiplex*, London and New York: Wallflower Press.
Dassanowsky, R. von (2008), 'A Wave over Boundaries: New Austrian Film', *Film International*, 6, 31–44.
Dawar, A. 'How Romanian Criminals Terrorize our Streets', <http://www.express.co.uk/news/uk/380512/How-Romanian-criminals-terrorise-our-streets> (last accessed 14 February 2014).
Delanty, G. (2005), 'What does it mean to be a "European"?', *Innovation* 18: 1, 11–22.
Deltcheva, R. (2005), 'Reliving the Past in Recent East European Cinemas', in A. Imre (ed.), *East European Cinemas*, New York and London: Routledge, pp. 197–211.
Deleuze, Gilles (2009), *Cinema 1: The Movement-Image*, London: Continuum.
Deleuze, Gilles and Guattari, Félix (1987), *A Thousand Plateaus: Capitalism and Schizophrenia*, Minneapolis: University of Minnesota Press.
DeWitte, J. (2011), 'Bibliothèque Pascal (2010, Hungary)', *Examiner*, <http://www.examiner.com/article/bibliotheque-pascal-2010-hungary> (last accessed 18 March 2014).

D'haen, Theo (1995), 'Magical Realism and Postmodernism: Decentering Privileged Centers', in L. P. Zamora and W. Faris (eds), *Magical Realism: Theory, History Community*, Durham: Duke University Press, pp. 191–208.

Direitinho, José Riço (2012), 'The secret of Denmark's success', *presseurop*, 20 January, <http://www.presseurop.eu/en/content/article/1421171-secret-denmark-s-success> (last accessed 18 March 2014).

Doder, D. (1993), 'Yugoslavia: New Wars, Old Hatreds', *Foreign Policy* 91, 3–23.

Druxes, H. (2011), 'Female Body Traffic in Ulrich Seidl's *Import/Export* and Ursula Biemann's *Remote Sensing* and *Europlex*', *Seminar*, 47.4, 391–412.

DuBois, Page (1991), *Torture and Truth*, New York: Routledge.

Dyer, Richard (1988), 'White', *Screen*, 29: 4, 44–64.

Ebert, Roger (2011), 'Hanna', <http://www.rogerebert.com/reviews/hanna-2011> (last accessed 18 March 2014).

Eder, K. (2006), 'Europe's Borders: The Narrative Construction of the Boundaries of Europe', *European Journal of Social Theory*, 9: 2, 255–71.

Ellinger, Ekkehard and Kayi, Kerem (2008), *Turkish Cinema: 1970–2007*, Frankfurt am Main: Peter Lang.

Elsaesser, Thomas (2008), 'Real Location, Fantasy Space, Performative Place: Double Occupancy and Mutual Interference in European Cinema', in Temenuga Trifonova (ed.), New York: Routledge, pp. 47–63.

Engelen, Leen and Van Heuckelom, Kris (eds) (2013), *European Cinema after the Wall. Screening East–West Mobility*, Lanham, MD: Rowman & Littlefield.

Engels, Friedrich [1886] (1996), *Ludwig Feuerbach and the Outcome of Classical German Philosophy*, ed. C. P. Dutt, New York: International Publishers.

Eren, M. (2012), 'Cosmopolitan Filmmaking: Fatih Akın's *In July* and *Head-On*', in Sabine Hake and Barbara Mennel (eds), *Turkish German Cinema in the New Millennium: Sites, Sounds, and Screens*, London: Berghahn Books, pp.175–85.

Ericsson, Kjersti and Simonsen, Eva (2005), *Children of World War II: The Hidden Enemy Legacy*, New York: Berg Publishers.

Estonian Film Institute (2012), 'Directions of Estonian film 2012–2020', <http://www.efsa.ee/public/files/EF_arengusuunad_2012-2020.pdf> (last accessed 18 March 2014).

Estonian Ministry of Culture (2012), 'Directions of cultural development 2020', <http://www.kultuuripoliitika.ee/files/Riigikogu%20otsus.pdf> (last accessed 18 March 2014).

European Parliament (EP) (2007), 'And the LUX Prize for European cinema goes to ... "Auf der anderen Seite" ("On the Edge of Heaven")', Press Release, 24 October, <http://www.europarl.europa.eu/sides/getDoc.do?type=IM-PRESS&reference=20071023IPR12109&language=EN> (last accessed 14 March 2014).

Exitfilm (no date), 'Services, <www.exitfilm.ee/services> (last accessed 18 March 2014).

Ezra, E. and Rowden, T. (2006), 'General introduction: What is transnational cinema?', in E. Ezra and T. Rowden (eds), *Transnational Cinema: The Film Reader*, London and New York: Routledge, 2006, pp. 1–12.

Falkowska, Janina (1996), *The Political Films of Andrzej Wajda*, Oxford and Providence, RI: Berghahn Books, p. 150.

Feldmanis, A. (2005), 'Korralik ja normaalne eesti film', *Eesti Päevaleht*, 12 December, 13.

Fenske, Michaela (2006), *Marktkultur in der Frühen Neuzeit. Wirtschaft, Macht und Unterhaltung auf einem städtischen Jahr- und Viehmarkt*, Köln: Böhlau Verlag.

Fiddler, Allyson (2006), 'Shifting Boundaries: Responses to Multiculturalism at the Turn of the Twenty-First Century', in K. Kohl and R. Robertson (eds), *A History of Austrian Literature 1918–2000*, Rochester: Camden House, pp. 265–90.

Filipčević, V. (2004–05), 'Historical Narrative and the East–West Leitmotif in Milcho Mančevski's *Before the Rain* and *Dust*', *Film Criticism* 29: 2, 3–33.

Fisher, J. (2010), 'German Historical Film as Production Trend: European Heritage Cinema and Melodrama in The Lives of Others', in J. Fisher and B. Prager (eds), *The Collapse of the Conventional: German Film and its Politics at the Turn of the Twenty-First Century*, Detroit, MI: Wayne State University Press, pp. 186–216.

Fisher, Jaimey and Brad Prager (eds) (2010), *The Collapse of the Conventional: German Film and its Politics at the Turn of the Twenty-First Century*, Detroit, MI: Wayne State University Press.

Foucault, M. (1986), 'Of Other Spaces', in N. Mirzoeff (ed.), *The Visual Culture Reader*, London: Routledge, 1998, pp. 229–36.

Foucault, M. (2007), 'What is Critique?', in M. Foucault, *The Politics of Truth*, Los Angeles CA: Semiotext(e), pp. 41–82.

Fredric, Jameson (1992), *Postmodernism, or, the Cultural Logic of the Late Capitalism*, London and New York: Verso.

Frey, Matthias (2011), 'The Cinema of Ulrich Seidl', in R. von Dassanowsky and O. Speck (eds), *New Austrian Film*, New York: Berghahn Books, pp. 189–98.

Friedman, V. A. (2000), 'Fable as History: The Macedonian Context', *Rethinking History* 4: 2, 135–46.

Frodon, Jean-Michel (2006), 'Le voyage en Arménie', *Cahiers du Cinéma* 613 (June), 40–1.

Fulbrook, Mary (2011), *Dissonant Lives: Generations and Violence through the German Dictatorships*, Oxford: Oxford University Press.

Galt, Rosalind and Schoonover, Karl (2010), *Global Art Cinema: New Theories and Histories*, New York: Oxford University Press.

Ganeva, Mila (2004) 'No Histories just Stories: Revisiting Traditions in Berlin Films of the 1990s', in C. A. Costabile-Heming and R. J. Halverson (eds), *Berlin: The Symphony Continues: Orchestrating Architectural, Social and Artistic Change in Germany's New Capital*, New York: Walter de Gruyter, pp. 261–78.

Garn, R. (2007), 'The Implied Author in Kieślowski's *White*', *The Polish Review*, vol. LII, no. 4, 487–508.
Georgescu, D. (2012), '"Ceauşescu Hasn't Died" Irony as Countermemory in Post-Socialist Romania', in M. Todorova and Z. Gille (eds), *Post-Communist Nostalgia*, New York: Berghahn Books, pp. 155–76.
Georgescu, L. (2012), 'The Road movies of the New Romanian Cinema', *Studies in Eastern European Cinema*, 3: 1, 23–40.
Gerstenberger, Katharina (2008), *Writing the New Berlin: The German Capital in Post-Wall Literature*, Rochester, NY: Camden House.
Gibbs, John (2002), *Mise-en-Scène: Film Style and Interpretation*, London and New York: Wallflower.
Gocić, Goran (2001), *Notes from the Underground: The Cinema of Emir Kusturica*, London: Wallflower Press.
Goddard, M. (2011), 'Eastern Extreme: The Presentation of Eastern Europe as a Site of Monstrosity in *La Vie nouvelle* and *Import/Export*', in T. Horeck and T. Kendall (eds), *The New Extremism in Cinema: From France to Europe*, Edinburgh: Edinburgh University Press, pp. 82–92.
Göktürk, D. (2008), 'Sound Bridges: Transnational Mobility as Ironic Drama', in Miyase Christensen and Nezih Erdoğan (eds), *Shifting Landscapes: Film and Media in European Context*, Newcastle: Cambridge Scholars Publishing, pp. 53–171.
Goldberg, Andreas (2000), 'Medien der Migrant/Innen', in Carmine Chiellino (ed.), *Interkulturelle Literatur in Deutschland: Ein Handbuch*, Stuttgart and Weimar: Metzler, pp. 419–35.
Goldstein, A. (2013), 'Heise: Notes', in Olaf Müller (ed.), *Thomas Heise. Fragments of Seeking*, Pamplona: Gobierno De Navarra, pp. 92–105.
Golumbia, David (2009), *The Cultural Logic of Computation*, Cambridge, MA: Harvard University Press.
Gott, M. (2012), 'Borderless possibilities, hesitant voyagers: Mapping identity in three post-1989 Czech road movies', *Studies in Eastern European Cinema*, 3: 1, 7–22.
Gott, M. (2013a), 'Cowboys, Icebergs and "Outlaws": The Paradoxes and Possibilities of Crossing Borders in the Francophone Belgian Road Movie', in *Transfers: Interdisciplinary Journal of Mobility Studies*, 3: 2.
Gott, M. (2013b), 'Traveling beyond the national: mobile citizenship, flexible identities, and layered republicanism in the French return road movie', *Contemporary French Civilization* 38; 1, 73–95.
Gott, M. (2013c), 'West/East Crossings: Positive Travel in Post-1989 French-language Cinema', in L. Engelen and K. Van Heuckelom (eds), *European Cinema after the Wall. Screening East–West Mobility*, Lanham: Rowman & Littlefield, pp. 1–18.
Gott, Michael and Schilt, Thibaut (2013), 'Introduction', in Michael Gott and Thibaut Schilt (eds), *Open Roads, Closed Borders: The Contemporary French-language Road Movie*, London: Intellect, pp. 1–17.

Goudet, Stéphane (n.d.), 'Robert Guédiguian: "Par endroits, Erevan, c'est l'Estaque de mon adolescence ..."', *TV5monde*, <http://cinema.tv5monde.com/articles/robert-guediguian-par-endroits-erevan-c-est-l-estaque-de-mon-adolescence> (last accessed 16 June 2013).

Gow, James and Carmichael, Cathie (2000), *Slovenia and the Slovenes: A Small State and the New Europe*, Bloomington and Indianapolis: Indiana University Press.

Graff, S. (2008), 'L'influence des technologies dans l'émergence du cinéma-vérité: Stephan *Kudelski et l'invention* du magnétophone Nagra III', in Alain Boillat, Philipp Brunner and Barbara Flückiger (eds), *KINO CH/CINÉMA CH. Rezeption, Ästhetik, Geschichte. Réception, esthétique, histoire*, Marburg: Schüren Verlag, pp. 233–45.

Gramling, D. (2010), 'On the Other Side of Monolingualism: Fatih Akın's Linguistic Turn', *The German Quarterly* 83. 3, 353–72.

Grillo, R. (2007), '*European* Identity in a Transnational Era', in Marion Demossier (ed.), *The European Puzzle: The Political Structuring of Cultural Identities at a Time of Transition*, New York: Berghahn Books.

Grissemann, Stefan (2007), *Sündenfall: Die Grenzüberschreitungen des Filmemachers Ulrich Seidl*, Vienna: Sonderzahl.

Grønstad, Asbjørn (2012), *Screening the Unwatchable: Spaces of Negation in Post-Millennial Art Cinema*, New York: Palgrave Macmillan.

Guédiguian, Robert, and Danel, Isabelle (2008), *Conversations avec Robert Guédiguian*, Paris: Les carnets de l'info.

Gueneli, Berna (2011), *Challenging European Borders: Fatih Akın's Filmic Visions of Europe*, Doctoral Disseration, The University of Texas at Austin, <http://repositories.lib.utexas.edu/handle/2152/ETD-UT-2011-05-3035> (last accessed 18 March 2014).

Gueneli, B. (2014), 'The Sound of Fatih Akın's Cinema: Polyphony and the Aesthetics of Heterogeneity in *The Edge of Heaven*', *German Studies Review*, 37.2 [forthcoming].

Gupta, A. and Ferguson, J. (2008), 'Beyond "Culture": Space, Identity, and the Politics of Difference', in Timothy S. Oakes and Patricia L. Price (eds), *The Cultural Geography Reader*, Hoboken: Routledge, pp. 60–7.

Hains, R. (2009), 'Power Feminism, Mediated: Girl Power and the Commercial Politics of Change', *Women's Studies in Communication*, 32: 1, spring, 89–113.

Hake, Sabine (2008), *German National Cinema*, London and New York: Routledge.

Hall, J. (1995), 'Nationalisms, Classified and Explained', in Sukumar Periwal (ed.), *Notions of Nationalism*, Budapest: Central European University Press, pp. 8–33.

Hall, S. (2009), 'Cultural Identity and Cinematic Representation', in R. Stam and T. Miller (eds), *Film and Theory: An Anthology*, Oxford: Blackwell, pp. 704–14.

Hames, Peter (2009), *Czech and Slovak Cinema: Theme and Tradition*, Edinburgh: Edinburgh University Press.

Hames, P. (2013), 'The Czech and Slovak Republics: The Velvet Revolution and After', in P. Hames and C. Portuges (eds), *Cinemas in Transition in Central and Eastern Europe after 1989*, Philadelphia: Temple University Press.

Hames, P. and C. Portuges (2013), 'Introduction', in P. Hames and C. Portuges (eds), *Cinemas in Transition in Central and Eastern Europe after 1989*, Philadelphia: Temple University Press.

Harvey, David (2005a), *A Brief History of Neoliberalism*, Oxford: Oxford University Press.

Harvey, David (2005b), *The New Imperialism*, Oxford: Oxford University Press.

Heine, Matthias (2007a), 'Ulrich Seidl und die Pornographie des Elends', *Die Welt*, 19 October, <http://www.welt.de/kultur/article1279225/Ulrich_Seidl_und_die_Pornografie_des_Elends.html> (last accessed 14 March 2014).

Heine, Matthias (2007b), '"Wichtig ist, dass man auch lachen kann": Regisseur Ulrich Seidl über seinen Film *Import Export* und den bösen österreichischen Blick', *Die Welt*, 20 October 28.

Heise, Thomas, 'Barluschke' (1997), *heise-film.de*, <http://heise-film.de/?page_id=175> (last accessed 1 December 2012).

Heise, Thomas (2010a), '*Gespräch 3*', *Spuren. Eine Archäologie der realen Existenz*, interview by Michael Girke, Berlin: Vorwerk 8, 402–24.

Heise, Thomas (2010b), *Spuren. Eine Archäologie der realen Existenz*, Berlin: Vorwerk 8.

Heise, Thomas (2012), '*Material*: Post-Screening Discussion with Thomas Heise', interview by Rembert Hueser, Walker Art Center, Minneapolis, 19 October 2012.

Heller, T. (1993), 'Notes on Technique in Black Humor', in A. R. Pratt (ed.), *Black humor: critical essays*, New York: Garland Publishing, pp. 197–214.

Higson, A. (1989), 'The Concept of National Cinema', *Screen* 30: 4: 36–47.

Higson, A. (2000), 'The Limiting Imagination of National Cinema', in M. Hjort and S. Mackenzie (eds), *Cinema and Nation*, London: Routledge, pp. 57–68.

Hillman, R. and Silvey, V. (2012), 'Remixing Hamburg: Transnationalism in Fatih Akın's Soul Kitchen', in Sabine Hake and Barbara Mennel (eds), *Turkish German Cinema in the New Millennium: Sites, Sounds, and Screens*, London: Berghahn Books, pp. 186–97.

Hilper, S. (2012), 'Mutual Intrusions: Ulrich Seidl's *Import/Export* through Jean-Luc Nancy', *Studies in European Cinema*, 9: 1, 53–67.

Hinrichsen, J. (2012), 'Eingetrübte Romantik', *Monopol: Magazin für Kunst und Leben*, <http://www.monopol-magazin.de/artikel/20105165/Christian-Petzold-Barbara-Interview-Harun-Farocki.html> (last accessed 10 september 2013).

Hodgin, N. (2011), 'Screening the Stasi: The politics of Representation in Postunification Film', in N. Hodgin and C. Pearce (eds), *The GDR Remembered. Representations of the East German State since 1989*, Rochester: Camden House, pp. 69–92.

Hohenberger, E. (1997), 'Erscheinungsbilder. Die 21. Duisburger Filmwoche', *film-dienst* 50: 25, 14–16.
Horn, E. (2006), 'Actors/Agents: Bertolt Brecht and the Politics of Secrecy', *Grey Room* 24, 38–55.
Huber, C. (2008), 'Ulrich Seidl's Song for Europe', *Cinema Scope*, 33, 24–8.
Hudson, R. (2000), 'One Europe or Many? Reflections on Becoming European', *Transactions of the Institute of British Geographers*, 25: 4, New Series, 409–26.
Huyssen, A. (1997) 'The Voids of Berlin', *Critical Inquiry*, 24: 1, autumn 1997, 57–81.
Huyssen, A. (2003), 'Trauma and Memory: A New Imaginary of Temporality', in J. Bennett and R. Kennedy (eds) *World Memory: Personal Trajectories in Global Time*, New York: Palgrave Macmillan, pp. 16–29.
Ilisson, A. (2005). 'Produtsent : "Eestis saab korraga teha poolteist mängufilmi ja tegijad lahkuvad"', *Eesti Päevaleht: Ärileht*, 11 May, 6–7.
Imre, A. (2005), 'Whiteness in Post-Socialist Eastern Europe', in Alfred J. Lopez (ed.), *Postcolonial Whiteness: Critical Reader on Race and Empire*, New York: State University of New York Press.
Institutul National de Statistica (2011), 'The 2011 Population and Statistic Census', <http://www.recensamantromania.ro> (last accessed 9 September 2013).
International Organization for Migration (2011), *Migracija Lietuvoje: faktai ir skaičiai*, Vilnius: Tarptautinės migracijos organizacijos Vilniaus biuras.
Iordanova, D. (1998), 'Balkan Film Representations since 1989: The Quest for Admissibility (Ideology and Stereotypes, with Amended Filmography)', *Historical Journal of Film, Radio and Television* 18: 2, 263–80.
Iordanova, D. (2000), '*Before the Rain* in a Balkan Context', *Rethinking History* 4: 2, 147–56.
Iordanova, Dina (2008), *Cinema of Flames: Balkan Film, Culture and the Media*, London: British Film Institute.
Iordanova, D. (2010), 'Making Trafficking Visible, Adjusting the Narrative', in W. Brown, D. Iordanova, and L. Torchin (eds), *Moving People, Moving Images: Cinema and Trafficking in the New Europe*, St Andrews: St Andrews Film Studies, pp. 83–115.
Iordanova, D. (2012), 'Foreword', in A. Imre (ed.), *A Companion to Eastern European Cinemas*, Wiley-Blackwell Press, pp. xv–xvii.
Jäckel, A. (1997), 'Cultural cooperation in Europe: The case of British and French cinematographic co-productions with Central and Eastern Europe', *Media, Culture & Society*, 19: 1, 111–20.
Jäckel, A. (2000a), 'Diversity and pluralism in European cinema: The role of selective aids for cinematic co-productions in multicultural acceptance in Europe', in B. Axford et al. (eds), *Unity and Diversity in the New Europe*, Oxford: Peter Lang Publishing Group, pp. 229–47.
Jäckel, A. (2000b), 'Film policy and cooperation between East and West: The case of France and Romania in the nineties', *International Journal of Cultural Policy*, 7: 1, 130–50.

Jäckel, A. (2003a), 'Dual nationality film productions in Europe after 1945', *Historical Journal of Film, Radio and Television*, 23: 3, 231–43.
Jäckel, Anne (2003b), *European Film Industries*, London: BFI Publishing.
Jacobu, Mary (2012), *Romantic Things. A Tree, a Rock, a Cloud*, Chicago: University of Chicago Press.
James, C. (1994), 'Review/Film; "Blue" and "White" as Different as Night and Day', *New York Times*, 10 June, <http://movies.nytimes.com/movie/review?res=9 F07E1DA133AF933A25755C0A962958260> (last accessed 22 February 2014).
Jedlicki, J. (1999), 'Historical Memory as a Source of Conflicts in Eastern Europe', *Communist and Post-Communist Studies*, 32: 225–32.
Jonsson, Stefan (2000), *Subject without Nation: Robert Musil and the History of Modern Identity*, Durham: Duke University Press.
Jõerand, R. (2006), 'Eesti filmist 2005, möönduseta II', *Teater. Muusika. Kino*, 3, 88–94.
Judt, Tony (1990), 'The Rediscovery of Central Europe,' *Daedalus* 119: 1, 23–54.
Kaceanov, M. (2008), 'On the New Romanian Cinema', *P.O.V. Filmtidsskrift* 25, March, <http://pov.imv.au.dk/Issue_25/section_3/artc6A.html> (last accessed 14 February 2014).
Kamalzadeh, D. (2009), 'Lachattacke gegen die Angst vor dem Fremden', *Der Standard*, 29, <http://derstandard.at/1259282837975/Lachattacke-gegen-die-Angst-vor-dem-Fremden> (last accessed 20 May 2013).
Kapczynski, J. (2007), 'Negotiating Nostalgia: The GDR Past in *Berlin is in Germany* and *Goodbye, Lenin!*', *The Germanic Review* 82: 1, 78–100.
Kaplan, Anne and Ban Wang (eds) (2004), *Trauma and Cinema: Cross-Cultural Explorations*, Hong Kong: Hong Kong University Press.
Kaplan, Caren (1996), *Questions of Travel: Postmodern Discourses of Displacement*, Durham, NC: Duke University Press.
Kapur, J. and Wagner, K. B. (2011), 'Introduction. Neoliberalism and global cinema: Subjectivities, publics, and new forms of resistance', in J. Kapur and K. B. Wagner (eds), *Neoliberalism and Global Cinema: Capital, Culture, and Marxist Critique*, New York: Routledge, pp. 1–16.
Karalis, Vrasidas (2012), *A History of Greek Cinema*, New York: Continuum.
Kearney, Richard (1998), *Poetics of Imagining: Modern and Postmodern*, New York: Fordham University Press.
Kissa, L. (2013), 'Ciné Europe: Interview: Dennis Abbott & Aviva Silver, European Commission', *New Europe Online*, 3 May, <http://www.neurope.eu/article/cine-europe-interview-dennis-abbott-aviva-silver-european-commission> (last accessed 14 March 2014).
Klein, R. and Warner, W. B. (1986), 'Nuclear Coincidence and the Korean Airline Disaster', *Diacritics* 16.1, 2–21.
Konopka B. (2009), 'Interview with Bartek Konopka' *Visondureel*, <http://www.youtube.com/watch?v=lJA61bBRg1Q> (last accessed 30 March 2014).
Köppe, I. 'Köppe-Bericht: Abweichender Bericht der Berichterstatterin der Gruppe Bündnis 90/Die Grünen im 1. Untersuchungsausschuß,' *Der Westen*,

<http://stasi.derwesten.de/files/koeppe-bericht_ht.pdf> (last accessed 24 June 2013).

Kopp, K. (2010), 'Christoph Hochhäusler's *This Very Moment*: The Berlin School and the Politics of Spatial Aesthetics in the German–Polish Borderlands', in Brad Prager and Jaimey Fisher (eds), *The Collapse of the Conventional: The German Film and its Politics at the Turn of the New Century*, Detroit: Wayne State University Press, pp. 285–308.

Koppel, A. (2006), 'Maailm Berlinale filmipeeglis. Kus oleme meie?', *Teater. Muusika. Kino*, 6, 98–107.

Kosta, B. (2010), 'Transnational Space and Music: Fatih Akın's Crossing the Bridge: The Sound of Istanbul (2005)', in Jaimey Fisher and Barbara Mennel (eds), *Spatial Turns: Space, Place, and Mobility in German Literary and Visual Culture*, Amsterdam and New York: Rodopi, pp. 343–60.

Kristensen, Lars (2012), 'Introduction', in L. Kristensen (ed.) *Postcommunist Film – Russia, Eastern Europe and World Culture: Moving Images of Postcommunism*, New York: Routledge, pp. 1–11.

Krstic, I. (2002), 'Re-Thinking Serbia: A Psychoanalytic Reading of Modern Serbian History and Identity through Popular Culture', *Other Voices* 2: 2, <http://www.othervoices.org/2.2/krstic/> (last accessed 28 February 2014).

Kühl, Stefan (1994), *The Nazi Connection: Eugenics, American Racism, and German National Socialism*, New York: Oxford University Press.

Kumar, N. and Swiatek, L. (2012), 'Representations of New Terror: "Autoanomie" in the Films of Michael Haneke', *Journal of Postcolonial Writing*, 48: 3, 311–21.

Kuus, M. (2004), 'Europe's Eastern Expansion and the Reinscription of Otherness in East-Central Europe', *Progress in Human Geography* 28: 4, 472–89.

Kuus, M. (2007), 'Something Old, Something New: Eastness in European Union Enlargement', *Journal of International Relations and Development* 10: 2, 150–67.

Kuus, M. (2008), 'The Ritual of Listening to Foreigners: Appropriating Geopolitics in Central Europe', in N. Parker (ed.), *The Geopolitics of Europe's Identity: Centers, Boundaries and Margins*, Houndmills: Palgrave Macmillan, pp. 177–93.

Kuzmany, S. (2014), 'Stimmungsmache gegen Osteuropäer: Seehofers falsches Spiel', <http://www.spiegel.de/politik/deutschland/kommentar-zu-csu-forderungen-zur-freizuegigkeit-a-941517.html> (last accessed 5 February 2014).

Laaniste, M. (2010), 'Conflicting visions: Estonia and Estonians as presented in the cinema of 1990s and 2000s', *Kinokultura: New Russian Cinema, Special Issue 10: Estonian Cinema*, <http://www.kinokultura.com/specials/10/laaniste.shtml> (last accessed 14 March 2014).

Laderman, D. (2013), 'Traffic in Souls: The Perils and Promises of Mobility in La Promesse', in M. Gott and T. Schilt (eds), *Open Roads and Closed Borders: The Contemporary French-language Road Movie*, Bristol: Intellect, pp. 173–86.

Lefebvre, H. (1958), 'Work and Leisure in Everyday Life', in B. Highmore (ed.) *The Everyday Reader*, London and New York: Routledge, 2002, pp. 225–36.

Legast, L. (2007), 'Mon identité polonaise: *Comme des voleurs (à l'Est)* de Lionel Baier', *Décadrages*, 10, 110–14.

Leppik, J. J. (2006), 'Gut. Besser. Simmig?', *Sirp*, 10 March, 12.

Liebhart, K. and Pribersky, A. (2001), '"Wir sind Europa!" Österreich und seine Nachbarn am Goldenen Vorhang', in F. K. Hofer, J. Melchoir, and H. Sickinger (eds), *Anlassfall Österreich: Die Europäische Union auf dem Weg zu einer Weltgemeinschaft*, Baden Baden: Nomos, pp. 115–28.

Liehm, Mira and Liehm, Antonin J. (1981), *The Most Important Art: Soviet and Eastern European Film After 1945*, Berkeley, CA: University of California Press.

Light, D. and C. Young (2009), 'European Union Enlargement, post-Accession Migration and Imaginative Geographies of the "New Europe": Media Discourses in Romania and the United Kingdom', *Journal of Cultural Geography* 26: 3, 281–303.

Lim, Dennis (2006), 'Austrian filmmakers with a heart for darkness', *The New York Times*, 27 November, 14.

Livanios, D. (2006), 'The "Sick Man" Paradox: History, Rhetoric and the "European Character" of Turkey', *Journal of Southern Europe and the Balkans* 8: 3, 299–311.

Löcker, I. (2013), 'Comments on Barluschke', in Olaf Müller (ed.), *Thomas Heise. Fragments of Seeking*, Pamplona: Gobierno De Navarra, pp. 22–34.

Luthar, B. and Pušnik, M. (2010), 'Introduction. The Lure of Utopia. Socialist. Everyday Spaces' in B. Luthar and M. Pušnik (eds), *Remembering Utopia: The Culture of Everyday Life in Socialist Yugoslavia*,Washington, DC: New Academia Publishing, pp. 1–37.

Macaitis, S. (2002), 'The Sixties', in M. Beger, L. Jablonskienė, B. Pankūnaitė and R. Pileckaitė (eds), *The World of Lithuanian Images* (trans. A. Tereškinas), Vilnius: Contemporary Art Information Centre of Lithuanian Art Museum, pp. 8–9.

MacCabe, Colin (2011), 'Three Colors: A Hymn to European Cinema: *Blue White Red Three Colors by Krzysztof Kieslowski*', The Criterion Collection, 11–13.

MacEwan, R. (2010), 'Bibliotheque Pascal', *Australian Film Review*, <https://australianfilmreview.wordpress.com/tag/bibliotheque-pascal/> (last accessed 18 March 2014).

McLean, Adrienne (2004), *Being Rita Hayworth: Labor, Identity, and Hollywood Stardom*, New Brunswick, NJ: Rutgers University Press.

Magheți, D. and Steiner, J. (2009), *Mormintele tac. Relatări de la cea mai sângeroasă graniță a Europei*, Bucharest: Polirom.

Maier, C. (2009), 'What have we learned since 1989?', in 'Revisiting 1989: Causes, Course and Consequences', Special Issue, *Contemporary European History* 18 (3), 253–69.

Manchevski, M. (2000), 'Rainmaking and Personal Truth', *Rethinking History: The Journal of Theory and Practice* 4: 2, 129–34.

Marciniak, K. (2003), 'Transnational Anatomies of Exile and Abjection in Milcho Mancevski's *Before the Rain*', *Cinema Journal* 43: 1, 63–84.
Massey, Doreen (2005), *For Space*, London: Sage.
Massey, D. (2008), 'A Global Sense of Place', in Timothy S. Oakes and Patricia L. Price (eds), *The Cultural Geography Reader*, Hoboken: Routledge, pp. 257–63.
Massino, J. (2012), 'From Black Caviar to Blackouts. Gender, Consumption, and Lifestyle in Ceauşescu's Romania', in Paulina Bren and Mary Neuburger (eds), *Communism Unwrapped: Consumption in Cold War Eastern Europe*, Oxford: Oxford University Press, pp. 226–47.
Massumi, Brian (2002), *Parables for the Virtual: Movement, Affect, Sensation*, Durham, NC: Duke University Press.
Matei, Ştefania (2011), 'Media and migration. Layers of knowledge in Romanian written press', *Journal of Comparative Research in Anthropology and Sociology*, 2: 2, 85–102.
Material, film, directed by Thomas Heise. Germany: Ma.Ja.De. Filmproduktion, 2009
May, Todd (2012), *Friendship in an Age of Economics*, Lexington: Lexington Books.
Mazierska, E. (2006), 'Witches, Bitches and Other Victims of the Crisis of Masculinity: Women in Polish Postcommunist Cinema', in E. Mazierska and E. Ostrowska (eds), *Women in Polish Cinema*, New York: Berghahn Books, pp. 110–30.
Mazierska, E. (2007), 'Marek Koterski', in E. Mazierska, *Polish Postcommunist Cinema: from pavement level*, Oxford: P. Lang, pp. 201–22.
Mazierska, E. (2010) 'Eastern European Cinema: Old and New Approaches', *Studies in Eastern European Cinema*, 1: 1, 5–16.
Mazierska, E. (2010), 'Post-communist Estonian cinema as transnational cinema', *Kinokultura: New Russian Cinema*, Special Issue 10: *Estonian Cinema*, <http://www.kinokultura.com/specials/10/mazierska.shtml> (last accessed 18 March 2014).
Mazierska, E. (2011), 'Ucieczka od Polityki? Polskie kino po komunizmie', *Kino*, 6: 2011, 10–14.
Mazierska, E. (2013), 'Searching for Survival and Meaning: Polish Film after 1989', in C. Portuges and P. Hames (eds), *Cinemas in Transition in Central and Eastern Europe after 1989*, Philadelphia: Temple University Press, pp. 135–60.
Mazierska, E., Kristensen, L. and Näripea, E. (2014), 'Introduction: Postcolonial RTheory and the Postcommunist World', in E. Mazierska, L. Kristensen and E. Näripea (eds), *Postcolonial Approaches to Eastern European Cinema*, London and New York: I. B. Tauris.
Mazierska, Ewa and Rascaroli, Laura (2006), *Crossing New Europe: Postmodern Travel and the European Road Movie*, London: Wallflower Press.
Mazower, Mark (2000), *The Balkans: A Short History*, New York: The Modern Library.
Meehan, E. (2007), 'Rethinking the Path to European Citizenship', in W. J. V. Neill and H.-U. Schwedler (eds), *Migration and Cultural Inclusion in the European City*, New York: Palgrave Macmillan, pp. 17–32.

Minh-ha, T. T. (1993), 'The Totalizing Quest of Meaning', in Michael Renov (ed.), *Theorizing Documentary*, New York: Routledge, pp. 90–107.

Mirme, O. (2006), 'Enesetapja, röövel ja muusik – kõik teed viivad Eestisse', *Postimees*, 6 February, 16–17.

Mitchell, W. J. T. (2002), 'Imperial Landscape', in W. J. T. Mitchell (ed.), *Landscape and Power*, Chicago: University of Chicago Press, second edition, pp. 5–34.

Mitchievici, Angelo (2011), 'Nostalgia, marile speranțe și spectrul eșecului', in C. Corciovescu, and M. Mihăilescu (eds), *Noul Cinema Românesc – De la Tovarășul Ceaușescu la domnul Lăzărescu / The New Romanian Cinema – From Comrade Ceaușescu to Mr Lăzărescu*, Bucharest: Polirom.

Modrow, Hans, *Ich wollte ein neues Deutschland*, Berlin: Dietz Verlag, 1998.

Mokre, Monika (2004), 'Österreich und Europa: Ein schlampiges Verhältnis', in E. Brix et al. (eds), *Memoria Austriae I: Menschen, Mythen, Zeiten*, Vienna: Verlag für Geschichte und Politik, pp. 418–45.

Molloy, P. (2000), 'Theatrical Release: Catharsis and Spectacle in Welcome to Sarajevo', *Alternatives: Global, Local, Political* 25: 1, 75–90.

Morokvasic, M. (2003), 'Transnational Mobility and Gender: a View from Post-Wall Europe', in M. Morokvasic-Müller et al. (eds), *Crossing Borders and Shifting Boundaries. Volume I: Gender on the Move*, Opladen: Leske and Budrich, pp. 101–36.

Murawska, R. (2005), 'Of the Polish People's Republic and its Memory in Polish Film', *KinoKultura*, Special Issue #2, 2005: 1–19, <http://www.kinokultura.com/specials/2/murawska.pdf> (last accessed 14 March 2014).

Naficy, Hamid (2001), *An Accented Cinema: Exilic and Diasporic Filmmaking*, Princeton, N.J: Princeton University Press.

Näripea, E. (2004), 'Medieval socialist realism: Representations of Tallinn Old Town in Soivet Estonian Feature Films, 1969–1972', in V. Sarapik (ed.), *Place and Location: Studies in Environmental Aesthetics and Semiotics*, 4, Tartu: Estonian Literary Museum, pp. 121–43, <http://www.eki.ee/km/place/pdf/kp4_07_naripea.pdf> (last accessed 18 March 2014).

Näripea, E. (2010a), 'From nation-scape to nation-state: Reconfiguring filmic space in post-Soviet Estonian cinema', in R. Šukaitytė (ed.), *Baltic Cinemas after the 90s: Shifting (Hi)stories and (Id)entities*, Acta Academiae Artium Vilniusis, 56, Vilnius: Vilniaus dailės akademijos leidykla, pp. 65–75.

Näripea, E. (2010b), 'Transnational spaces of science fiction: An Estonian–Polish co-production *The Test of Pilot Pirx* (*Test pilota Pirxa / Navigaator Pirx*, 1978)', *Kinokultura: New Russian Cinema*, Special Issue 10: *Estonian Cinema*, <http://www.kinokultura.com/specials/10/pirx-naripea.shtml> (last accessed 18 March 2014).

Näripea, E. (2012), 'National space, (trans)national cinema: Estonian film in the 1960s', in A. Imre (ed.), *A Companion to Eastern European Cinemas*, Chichester: Wiley-Blackwell, pp. 244–64.

Nasta, Dominique (2013) *Contemporary Romanian Cinema, The History of an Unexpected Miracle*, London: Wallflower Press.
Nava, Mica (2007), *Visceral Cosmopolitanism: Gender, Culture and the Normalization of Difference*, Oxford and New York: Berg.
Nehamas, Alexander (2010), 'The Good of Friendship', *Proceedings of the Aristotelian Society* 110: 3, 267–94.
Neill, William J. V. and Schwedler, Hanns-Uve (eds), (2007), *Migration and Cultural Inclusion in the European City*, New York: Palgrave Macmillan.
Nietzsche, Friedrich (2011), *The Will to Power* (trans. W. Kaufmann and R. J. Hollingdale), London: Random House.
Nora, Pierre (1989), 'Between Memory and History: Les Lieux de Mémoire' *Representations* (26), 7–25.
Oberschall, A. (2000), 'The Manipulation of Ethnicity: From Ethnic Cooperation to Violence and War in Yugoslavia', *Ethnic and Racial Studies*, 23, 982–1001.
O'Brennan, John (2006), *The Eastern Enlargement of the European Union*, New York: Routledge.
O'Brien, Mary (2012), *Post-wall German Cinema and National History: Utopianism and Dissent*, Rochester NY: Camden House.
O'Connor, C. (2011), 'Bibliotheque Pascal: The Weird, the Dark, the Literary at the Cleveland International Film Festival', *The Plain Dealer*, <http://www.cleveland.com/moviebuff/index.ssf/2011/03/bibliotheque_pascal_the_weird.html> (last accessed 18 March 2014).
Odin, R. (2008), 'Reflections on the Family Home Movie as Document: A Semio-Pragmatic Approach', in K. L. Ishizuka and P. R. Zimmermann (eds), *Mining the Home Movie: Excavations in Histories and Memories*, Berkeley and Los Angeles: University of California Press, pp. 255–71.
OECD (2001), *Migration Policies and EU Enlargement: The Case of Central and Eastern Europe*, Paris: Organisation for Economic Co-Operation and Development Publications Service.
O'Shaughnessy, Martin (2007), *The New Face of Political Cinema*, London: Berghahn Books.
Panossian, Razmik (2006), *The Armenians: From Kings and Priests to Merchants and Commissars*, New York: Columbia University Press.
Papadimitriou, L. (2011), 'The National and the Transnational in Contemporary Greek Cinema', *New Review of Film and Television Studies*, 9: 4, 493–512
Papadimitriou, Lydia and Tzioumakis, Yannis (2012), *Greek Cinema: Texts, Histories, Identities*, Bristol: Intellect.
Parvulescu, A. (2011), 'European Kinship: Eastern European Women Go to Market', *Critical Inquiry*, 37: 2, 187–213.
Parvulescu, A. (2012), 'Import/Export: Housework in an International Frame', *PMLA*, 127: 4, 845–62.
Pârvulescu, C. (2009), 'The Cold War behind the Window: *4 Months, 3 Weeks and 2 Days* and Romanian Cinema's Return to Real-existing Communism', *Jump Cut* 51.

Patten, C. (2004), 'The Western Balkans: The Road to Europe. Speech to the German Bundestag, 28 April 2004', <http://ec.europa.eu/enlargement/archives/ear/publications/main/pub-speech_berlin_20040428.htm> (last accessed 28 Februrary 2014).

Paul, D. W. (1983), 'Introduction: Film Art and Social Commitment', in D. W. Paul (ed.), *Politics, Art, and Commitment in the East European Cinema*, New York: St Martin's Press, pp. 1–22.

Petrova, V. (2006), 'Migrating Minds and Bodies: The Transnational Subject and the Cinematic Synecdoches of "Glocalisation"', <http://www.kinokultura.com/specials/5/petrova-violetta.shtml> (last accessed 24 February 2014).

Petrowskaja, K. (2009), *Interview with Cynthia Beatts*, viewed 6 September 2013, <http://www.invisible-frame.com/en/the-film/interview/> (last accessed 18 March 2014).

Plenzdorf, Ulrich (1973), *Die neue Leiden des jungen W*, Rostock: VEB Hinstorff Verlag.

Powrie, Phil (2001), '*Marius et Jeannette*: nostalgia and utopia', in L. Mazdon (ed.), *France on Film: Reflections on Popular French Cinema*, London: Wallflower, pp. 133–44.

Rancière, Jacques (1999), *Disagreement. Politics and Philosophy* (trans. J. Rose), Minneapolis: University of Minnesota Press.

Rascaroli, L. (2013), 'On the Eve of the Journey: Tangier, Tbilisi, Calais', in M. Gott and T. Schilt (eds), *Open Roads, Closed Borders: The Contemporary French-Language Road Movie*, Bristol: Intellect, pp. 29–38.

Reimann, Brigitte (1961), *Ankunft im Alltag*, Berlin: Neues Leben.

Reinecke, S. (1998), 'Monströse Vergrößerung: Gespräch mit Thomas Heise über seinen Porträtfilm "Barluschke". Sein Held, Ex-Agent und Familientyrann, trägt schon professionell Masken', in *taz*, p. 15.

Reizen, O. (1993), 'Black humor in Soviet cinema', in A. Horton (ed.), *Inside Soviet film satire: laughter with a lash*, Cambridge: Cambridge University Press, pp. 94–7.

Rezková, H. (2009) 'Interview with B. Konopka, P. Rosolowski and A. Wydra', Institute of Documentary Film, 27 Oktober 2009, viewed 11 August 2013, <http://dokweb.net/cz/get_file.php?filename=../.../rabbitalaberlin_press_kit> (last accessed 18 March 2014).

Riegg, Natalya (2009), 'Revision of the Visions: Feminism and Empowerment in Post-Transitional Societies', in D. Budryte, L. M. Vaughn, and N. T. Riegg (eds), *Feminist Conversations: Women, Trauma, and Empowerment in Post-Transitional Societies*, Lanham, MD: University Press of America.

Rivi, Luisa (2007), *European Cinema after 1989: Cultural Identity and Transnational Production*, New York and Basingstoke: Palgrave Macmillan.

Robinson, Chris (2004), *Estonian Animation: Between Genius & Utter Illiteracy*, Eastleigh: John Libbey Publishing.

Roddick, N. (2007), 'Eastern Promise', *Sight and Sound* (October).

Roman, M. and Andren, D. (2011), 'The Case of Romania', 4th IZA Workshop

on EU Enlargement and the Labor Markets: Migration, Crisis and Adjustment in an Enlarged E(M)U, <http://www.iza.org/conference_files/EUenla2011/roman_m7097.pdf> (last accessed 22 February 2014).
Romney, J. (2006), 'Through the Looking Glass', *The Double Life of Véronique: A Film By Krzysztof Kieslowski*, The Criterion Collection, 10–15.
Romney, Jonathan (1993), 'Krzysztof Kieslowski – interview for *Three Colours Blue*', *The Guardian*, 9 November 2011, <http://www.theguardian.com/film/2011/nov/09/three-colours-blue-interview> (last accessed 14 March 2014).
Rose, J. (1988), 'Paranoia and the Film System', in Constance Penley (Ed.), *Feminism and Film Theory*, New York: Routledge, pp. 141–58.
Rose, S. (2011), '*Attenberg, Dogtooth* and the Weird Wave of Greek Cinema', *The Guardian*, 26 August, <http://www.theguardian.com/film/2011/aug/27/attenberg-dogtooth-greece-cinema> (last accessed 15 March 2014).
Rosello, M. (2007), 'Introduction I: "We ... Europe"'. *Culture, Theory & Critique* 48: 1, 1–9.
Rosenstone, Robert A. (1995), *Visions of the Past: The Challenge of Film to Our Idea of History*, Cambridge, MA: Harvard University Press.
Rothöhler, Simon (2011), *Amateur der Weltgeschichte: Historiographische Praktiken im Kino der Gegenwart*, Zurich: diaphanes.
Ruus, J. (2000), 'Film and finance in Estonia', *Eesti film/Estonian Film 1991–1999*, Tallinn: Eesti Filmi Sihtasutus, pp. 10–21.
Ruus, J. (2010), 'Jäine kunstmuinasjutt', *Eesti Ekspress*, 4 March, 40.
Rydzewska, J. (2012), 'Ambiguity and Change: Post-2004 Polish Migration to the UK in Contemporary British Cinema', *Journal of Contemporary European Studies*, 2, 215–27.
Said, Edward (1978), *Orientalism*, New York: Pantheon Books.
Said, E. (1985), 'Orientalism Reconsidered', *Cultural Critique*, 1 (September), 89–107.
Sailer, M. (1997), 'Bild dir deine Phantasie: In Leipzig ging gestern die 40. Dokfilmwoche zu Ende', *Junge Welt*, p. 12.
Sandu, D. (2000), 'Circulatory Migration as Life Strategy', Romanian Sociology, Sociologie Românesc/Romanian Sociology, Annual English Electronic Edition, Issue 2, 65–79.
Sandu, D. (2010) 'Modernising Romanian Society through Temporary Work Abroad', in R. Black, G. Engbersen, M. Okólski, and C. Panţiru, (eds), *A Continent Moving West? EU Enlargement and Labour Migration from Central and Eastern Europe*, Amsterdam: Amsterdam University Press, pp. 271–88.
Sandu, D. (2013) 'Mapping out social worlds by states of mind', Central European Labour Institute (CELSI) Discussion paper no. 10, June 2013, <http://www.celsi.sk/en/publication/paper-details/16/mapping-out-social-worlds-by-states-of-mind-in-europe/> (last accessed 22 February 2014).
Sathe, N. (2011), 'Trapped behind the "Golden Curtain": Labouring Relationships in Barbara Gräftner's *Mein Russland* and Ruth Mader's *Struggle*', *Seminar* 47: 4, 371–90.

Savage, Mike, Bagnall, Gaynor and Longhurst, Brian (2005), *Globalization & Belonging*, London: Sage.
Schenk, R. (1997), 'Vom doppelten zum demütigen Leben. Ein Stasimann in den USA, Ches Utopie in Deutschland und eine alte schwedische Nordpol-Expedition: Das 40. Leipziger Dokumentarfilmfestival', *Berliner Zeitung*, p. 9.
Schenk, R. (1998), 'Barluschke', *film-dienst* 51: 6, 23.
Schimmelfennig, F. (2001), 'The Community Trap: Liberal Norms, Rhetorical Action, and the Eastern Enlargement of the European Union', *International Organization* 55: 1, 47–80.
Schmitt, Carl (2003), *The Nomos of the Earth in the International Law of the Jus Publicum Europaeum*, New York: Telos Press.
Sciarini, P., Hug, S. and Dupont, C. (2000), 'Example, Exception or Both? Swiss National Identity in Perspective', in Lars-Edrik Cederman (ed.), *Constructing Europe's Identity: The External Dimension*, Boulder: Lynne Rienner, 57–88.
Scott, A. O. (2008), 'In film, the Romanian New Wave has arrived', *The New York Times*, 19 January.
Sebald, W. G. (2002), *The Rings of Saturn*, (trans. M. Hulse), London: Vintage.
Sellar, C., Staddon, C and Young, C. (2009), 'Introduction: Twenty years after the Wall: geographical imaginaries of "Europe" during European Union enlargement', *Journal of Cultural Geography*, 26: 3, 253–58.
Şerban, A. L. (2010), 'Romanian Cinema: From Modernity to Neo-Realism', *Film Criticism* 34: 2/3, 2–21.
Siani-Davies, Peter, (2005), *The Romanian Revolution of December 1989*, Ithaca: Cornell University Press.
Siefert, M. (2012a), 'Co-producing Cold War culture: East–West film-making and cultural diplomacy', in P. Romijn et al. (eds), *Divided Dreamworlds? The Cultural Cold War in East and West*, Amsterdam: Amsterdam University Press, pp. 73–94.
Siefert, M. (2012b), 'East European Cold War culture(s): Alterities, commonalities, and film industries', in A. Vowinckel et al. (eds), *Cold War Cultures: Perspectives on Eastern and Western European Societies*, New York and Oxford: Berghahn Books, pp. 23–54.
Sieg, Katrin (2008), *Choreographing the Global in European Cinema and Theater*, New York: Palgrave Macmillan.
Skrodzka, Aga (2012), *Magic Realist Cinema in East Central Europe*, Edinburgh: Edinburgh University Press.
Skrodzka-Bates, A. (2011), 'Clandestine human and cinematic passages in the United Europe: The Polish Plumber and Kieslowski's hairdresser', *Studies in Eastern European Cinema* 2: 1, 75–90.
Spector, J., Atayan, R., Rihtman, C. and Conway Morris, R. (2007), 'Grove Music Online: Saz'. *Oxford Music Online*. <http://www.oxfordmusiconline.com/subscriber/article/grove/music/47032?q=saz&search=quick&pos=1&_start=1#firsthit> (last accessed 18 October 2010).

Squires, M. (1973) 'Adam Bede and the Locus Amoenus', *Studies in English Literature, 1500–1900*, 13: 4 (autumn), 670–76.
Stan, L. and Zaharia, R. (2012), 'Romania', in D. Beacháin, V. Sheridan and S. Stan (eds), *Life in Post-Communist Eastern Europe after EU Membership: Happy ever after?*, New York: Routledge, pp. 185–204.
Stanciu, M. and David, I. (2006), 'Cătălin Mitulescu, Corneliu Porumboiu şi Radu Muntean despre filmele lor din 2006', <http://atelier.liternet.ro/articol/4114/Magdalena-Stanciu-Iulia-David-Catalin-Mitulescu-Corneliu-Porumboiu-Radu-Muntean/Catalin-Mitulescu-Corneliu-Porumboiu-si-Radu-Muntean-despre-filmele-lor-din-2006.html> (last accessed 14 February 2014).
Sterneborg, A. (2006), 'The Red Cockatoo', *epd-film* (2), <http://www.epd-film.de/33178_39817.php> (Last accessed 10 September 2013).
Stojanova, C. (2005), 'Fragmented Discourses: Young Cinema From Central and Eastern Europe', in A. Imre (ed.), *East European Cinemas*, New York and London: Routledge, pp. 213–27.
Suchsland, Rüdiger (2006), 'Der Historikerstreit bricht im Kino aus', *artechock filmmagazin*, <http://www.artechock.de/film/text/special/2006/berlinale/0210_berlinale_interview_graf.htm> (Last accessed 10 September 2013).
Talasi, F. (2014), 'Benedek Fliegauf', *GoEast: Festival of Central and Eastern European Film*, <http://www.filmfestival-goeast.de/index.php?article_id=394&clang=1> (last accessed 18 March 2014).
Taruste, T. (2013), 'Eesti filmitööstus januneb ärilise mõtteviisi järele', *Äirileht*, 18 August, <http://arileht.delfi.ee/news/uudised/eesti-filmitoostus-januneb-arilise-motteviisi-jarele.d?id=66602727> (last accessed 18 March 2014).
Tasker, Y. (2003), 'Office Politics: Masculinity, Femininity and the Workplace in *Disclosure*', in A. Beck (ed.), *Cultural Work: Understanding the Cultural Industries*, London: Routledge, pp. 169–80.
Terdiman, R. (2008), 'Taking Time: Temporal Representation and Cultural Politics', in T. Miller (ed.) *Given Time and World: Temporalities in Context*, New York: Central European University Press, pp. 131–44.
Thom, R. and Broph, P. (2000), 'Randy Thom In Conversation: Designing a Movie for Sound', in Philip Brophy (ed.), *Cinesonic*, Marrickville, NSW: Southwood Press, pp. 1–28.
Tismăneanu, Vladimir (2003), *Stalinism for All Seasons*, Berkeley: University of California Press.
Todorov, V. (1999–2013), 'The Bulgarian Cinema: Constants and Variables', <http://stason.org/TULARC/travel/bulgaria/12-1-Bulgarian-Cinema.html#.Ubmv1aB-WfR#ixzz2W5zZfGne> (last accessed 21 August 2013).
Todorova, M. N. (1994), 'The Balkans: From Discovery to Invention', *Slavic Review* 54: 2, 453–82.
Todorova, Maria (2004), *Balkan Identities: Nation and Memory*, New York: New York University Press.
Tomberg, D. (2006), '*Jukebox*'i ja tšello kohtumine', *Teater. Muusika. Kino*, 4, 97–100.

Tonkiss, F. (2003), 'Aural Postcards: Sound, Memory and the City', in M. Bull and L. Back (eds), *The Auditory Culture Reader*, Oxford and New York: Berg, pp. 303–9.
Tõnson, M. (2006), 'Konnatiigist avamerele', *Eesti Ekspress: Areen*, 9 November, B7.
Tõnson, M. (2010), 'Külm võttis ära', *Teater. Muusika. Kino*, 5, 100–6.
Tortajada, M. (2008), 'Comment échapper au paysage? Déconstruction d'un stéréotype identitaire', in A. Boillat, P. Brunner and B. Flückiger (eds.), *KINO CH/CINÉMA CH. Rezeption, Ästhetik, Geschichte. Réception, esthétique, histoire*, Marburg: Schüren Verlag, 115–26.
Trojanowska, T. (2011), 'Introduction', in T. Trojanowska et al. (eds), *New Perspectives on Polish Culture: personal encounters, public affairs*, New York: PIASA Books, pp. 1–10.
Trumpener, K. (2001), 'a Guerre est fini: New Waves, Historical Contingency, and the GDR "Rabbit Film"', in M. Geyer (ed.), *The Power of Intellectuals in Contemporary Germany*, Chicago: University of Chicago Press, pp. 113–37.
Uricaru, I. (2012), 'Follow the Money: Financing Contemporary Cinema in Romania', in A. Imre (ed.), *A Companion to Eastern European Cinemas*, Chichester: Wiley-Blackwell, pp. 427–52.
Vachon, Michael (1993–4), 'Bucharest: The House of the People', *World Policy Journal* 10: 4, 59–63.
Van Heuckelom, K. (2011), 'Polish (Im)Potence: Shifting Representations of Polish Labour Migration in Contemporary European Cinema', in J. Rostek and D. Uffelmann (eds), *Contemporary Polish Migrant Culture in Germany, Ireland, and the UK*, Frankfurt am Main: Peter Lang, pp. 277–98.
Van Heuckelom, K. (2013), 'Londoners and Outlanders. Polish Labour Migration Through the European Lens', *The Slavonic and East European Review*, XCI: II, 210–34.
Vattimo, Gianni (1991), *The End of Modernity: Nihilism and Hermeneutics in Postmodern Culture*, Baltimore: The Johns Hopkins University Press.
Verseck, K. (2013), 'Stimmungsmache gegen Zuwanderung: CSU-Kampagne irritiert Rumänen und Bulgaren', <http://www.spiegel.de/politik/ausl and/csu-zuwanderungsdebatte-migrationsangst-irritiert-rumaenen-bulgaren-a-941295.html> (last accessed 5 February 2014).
Verstraete, Ginette (2010), *Tracking Europe: Mobility, Diaspora, and the Politics of Location*, Durham: Duke University Press.
Vertovec, Steven (2009), *Transnationalism*, London and New York: Routledge.
Vinea, Ana (2003), (ed.) *LXXX. Mărturii orale: anii '80 și bucureștenii*, Bucharest: Editura Paideia.
Wang, Yiyan (2005), *Narrating China: Jia Pingwa and His Fictional World*, London and New York: Routledge.
Westphahl, A. (2009), 'An Approach to the Wall', *Berliner Zeitung*, 7 November, <http://www.invisible-frame.com/en/the-film/reviews/> (last accessed 18 March 2014).

Wheatley, C. (2011), 'Naked Women, Slaughtered Animals: Ulrich Seidl and the Limits of the Real', in T. Horeck and T. Kendall (eds), *The New Extremism In Cinema: From France To Europe*, Edinburgh: Edinburgh University Press, pp. 93–101.

White, Hayden (1987), *The Content of the Form: Narrative Discourse and Historical Representation*, Baltimore: The Johns Hopkins University Press.

Wolf, Naomi (1993), *Fire with Fire: The New Female Power and How it Will Change the 21st Century*, London: Chatto & Windus.

Wolff, Larry (1994), *Inventing Eastern Europe: The Map of Civilization on the Mind of the Enlightenment*, Stanford: Stanford University Press.

Wróblewski, J. (2010), 'Polish cinema success stories', in M. Werner (ed.), *Polish cinema now!: focus on contemporary Polish cinema*, London: John Libbey Publishing, pp. 170–92.

Xavier, I. (2004), 'Historical Allegory', in T. Miller and R. Stam (eds), *A Companion to Film Theory*, Malden: Blackwell, pp. 333–62.

Yıldız, Yasemin (2012), *Beyond the Mother Tongue: The Postmonolingual Condition*, New York: Fordham University Press.

Yuval-Davis, N. (1999), 'The "Multi-Layered Citizen"', *International Feminist Journal of Politics* 1: 1, 119–36.

Žižek, S. (1993), 'Why are the NSK and Laibach Not Fascists?', *M'ARS*, 3/4: 4.

Žižek, Slavoj (2004), *The Metastases of Enjoyment: Six Essays on Women and Causality*, London and New York: Verso.

Žižek, S. (2006), 'The Forced Choice of Freedom', *The Double Life of Véronique: A Film by Krzysztof Kieslowski*, The Criterion Collection, 16–25.

Zorba the Greek, ballet, composed and conducted by Mikis Theodorakis. Italy: Verona Arena, 1988.

Zorba the Greek, film, directed by Michael Cacoyannis. US: Twentieth Century-Fox, 1964.

Żurawiecki. B. (2004), 'Marek Koterski – Nie tym tonem, Miauczyński!'/'Marek Koterski – That's Not the Right Tone, Miauczyński!', in G. Stachówna and J. Wojnicka (eds), *Autorzy Kina Polskiego/Polish Cinema Auteurs*, Krakow: Rabid, pp. 125–34.

Zutavern, J. (2009), '"Es ist alles nur ein Film". Gedächtnissimulation und Erinnerungspolitik in *Barluschke – Psychogramm eines Spions*', in T. Ebbrecht, H. Hoffmann and J. Schweinitz (eds), *DDR – Erinnern, Vergessen: Das visuelle Gedächtnis des Dokumentarfilms*, Marburg: Schüren, pp. 38–55.

Index

2 Sunny Days, 9
4 luni, 3 săptămâni și 2 zile, 150; see also *4 Months, 3 Weeks and 2 days*
4 Months, 3 Weeks and 2 days, 150; see also *4 luni, 3 săptămâni și 2 zile*
5 Day Scam, 187–8; see also *5 dienų avantiūra*
5 dienų avantiūra, 187–8; see also *5 Day Scam*

A Lady in Paris, 8–9; see also *Une Estonienne à Paris*
A Long Winter without Fire, 5; see also *Tout un hiver sans feu*
Abbas, Acbar, 177
Adventurers, 4; see also *Kalandorok*
Agustín, Laura, 119–20
Ahadi, Ali Samadi, 11, 94–108
Ahmed, Sara, 115, 123–4
Akhmatova, Anna, 28
Ajlawju, 224
American frontier myth, 38–45
American western genre, 98
Angelopoulos, Theo, 159
Anna Karenina, 112
Antonioni, Michaelangelo, 161–2
Apele tac, 148, 151–2; see also *Silent River*
Arendt, Hannah, 32
Armenia, 4, 6, 17, 19, 279–92
Armenia, 17, 279–92; see also *Le Voyage en Arménie*
Artimos šviesos, 180, 182, 184, 185, 187; see also *Low Lights*
Aš esi tu, 180, 183–4; see also *You am I*
Asphalt Tango, 148, 151, 153
Atonement, 112
Auf der anderen Seite, 79–80, 86; see also *On the Edge of Heaven*

Austria, 6, 7, 10–11, 66–8, 73–5, 102, 140–1
Austrian cinema, 11, 65, 66–8, 78

Badiou, Alain, 3, 35, 281–4
Baier, Lionel, 36
Balibar, Étienne, 3, 7, 26, 35, 135–6
Balkans, 4, 13, 15, 18, 86, 159–60, 173, 205–18
Baltic cinema, 15, 18
Baltics, 2–3, 13, 14–15
Barbara, 16, 238, 244–51
Barluschke: Psychogramm eines Spions, 16, 252–66
Bartas, Šarūnas, 13, 176–8, 179, 186–9
Bauman, Zygmunt, 109–10, 155, 176, 180–2, 184
Beatts, Cynthia, 10, 26–7
Before the Rain, 25, 208–10, 210–11, 215–16; see also *Pred doždot*
Berdahl, Daphne, 31
Berghahn, Daniela, 4, 11
Berlin, 10, 23, 24–7, 81, 88, 245–6, 267, 282
  West Berlin, 138–9, 243
Berlin Ecke Schönhauser, 243; see also *Berlin Schönhauser Corner*
Berlin Schönhauser Corner, 243; see also *Berlin Ecke Schönhauser*
Berlin Wall, 1, 3, 4, 6, 10, 23–36, 98, 205, 232, 236, 239, 241, 279
Bessette, Christopher, 120
Bibliothèque Pascal, 109, 117, 118–24
Blanc, 50, 232–3; see also *White*
blaxploitation, 111–12
Blumenberg, Hans-Christoph, 106
Boillat, Alain, 42
Bolse vita, 7–8

INDEX

Bordwell, David, 166–7, 250–1
Britain, 5, 144, 146, 160, 163–4, 196–7, 216
Brothers Grimm, 109, 111–12
Brown, Keith, 209
Brown, William, 248
Buchowski, 205
Bulgaria, 6, 7, 14, 81–2, 89–91, 127–46, 173
Bulgarian cinema, 127–46
Bulgarian Lovers, 5; see also *Los novios búlgaros*
Burns, Rob, 90
Byg, Barton, 34–5

California Dreamin', 148, 151, 153
capitalism, 2–3, 8, 47, 96, 103–4, 105–6, 110, 117–18, 133, 134–5, 143, 195–7, 222
    Lithuanian, 176–9
    neo-capitalism, 195–7
    neo-liberal capitalism, 191, 193–4
    Romanian, 153–8
Catholicism, 2, 236
Ceaușescu, Nicolae, 17, 150, 268, 270–5
Ceaușescu, Elena, 150
Cendrars, Blaise, 39, 42, 45
Central Europe, 1–6, 11–12, 18, 66, 84, 112–13, 118, 176, 205–8
Children of the Decree, 151; see also *Decrețeii*
Clark, J. R., 226–7
Coates, Paul, 175
Code inconnu, 9, 52–3, 60–2; see also *Code Unknown*
Code Unknown, 9, 52–3, 60–2; see also *Code inconnu*
Cold War, 2, 3, 10, 16–17, 19, 23, 25, 37, 114, 116, 189, 204–6, 210, 215, 218, 251, 254–5, 291–2
    Romania, 267–77
Collectress, 180, 182–3; see also *Kolekcionierė*
Comme des voleurs (à l'est), 11, 37–50; see also *Stealth*
communism, 15, 18, 47, 99, 109, 129–30, 133, 137–8, 142, 147, 150–1, 206–7, 212, 222–3, 229, 231, 241, 244, 249, 268–74, 285
    post-communism, 27–8
Cum mi-am petrecut sfârșitul lumii, 17, 148, 151, 267–9, 269–70; see also *The Way I Spent the End of the World*
Cycling the Frame, 10, 23–30

Czech Republic, 18, 44, 54–5, 67, 175–6
Czechoslovakia, 266

Dabashi, Hamid, 179
Dacia, dragostea mea, 151, 154; see also *My Beautiful Dacia*
Dardenne, Jean-Pierre and Luc, 5, 92, 111
Das Fräulein, 5
Das Kaninchen bin ich, 34, 243; see also *The Rabbit is Me*
Das Leben der Anderen, 237, 244–5, 247, 248; see also *The Lives of Others*
Das Versprechen, 16, 250; see also *The Promise*
Decrețeii, 151; see also *Children of the Decree*
Delanty, Gerard, 79
Deleuze, Gilles, 186, 189, 246, 248
Deltcheva, Roumiana, 175
democracy, 3, 222, 227
Der Geteilte Himmel, 16, 250; see also *Divided Heaven*
Der rote Kakadu, 16, 238–48; see also *The Red Cockatoo*
Die Wende, 27; see also German Reunification
Divided Heaven, 16, 250; see also *Der Geteilte Himmel*
Dog Days, 68; see also *Hundstage*
Dogtooth, 159, 163; see also *Kynodontas*
Dragojević, Srđan, 205, 210–15
Druxes, Helga, 72, 77
Dual, 9; see also *Dvojina*
Dvojina, 9; see also *Dual*
Dyer, Richard, 113–14
Dzień świra, 221–36; see also *The Day of the Wacko*

E pericoloso sporgersi, 148, 151–3; see also *Sundays on Leave*
East-Central Europe, 112–13, 118, 175, 176, 205, 206–7
East Germany, 16, 33, 94, 102, 105–6, 236–51, 256
East–West, 5, 11, 13–14, 15, 16, 18–19, 37, 41, 45, 65, 66, 79, 198–9, 253–66
    cinema, 9
    divide, 2, 3, 4, 10, 15, 37, 40, 49, 80, 95, 114, 215–18, 277
    migration, 12
Eastern Drift, 188, 190; see also *Indigène d'Eurasie*
Eastern Europe, 1–6, 11, 12, 15–16, 18–19, 40, 63, 65, 66–9, 69–71, 81–2, 83–4,

90, 92–3, 102, 123, 131, 175–6, 206–7, 221–3, 227, 235, 268–9
Eastern Plays, 134, 141; see also *Iztochni piesi*
economic crisis, 1, 3, 5
Eder, Klaus, 6, 49
Elsaesser, Thomas, 134
emigration, 100–1, 132–5, 137–8, 140, 142, 143, 146, 148, 149, 154–5, 185–6
Eu când vreau să fluier, fluier, 147, 154–5, 157; see also *When I want to whistle, I whistle*
European cinema, 1–19, 41, 52, 130, 159–62, 163, 166–7, 267
Eastern European cinema, 175, 179
post-1989, 41, 128, 189
European Parliament's Cinema Lux Prize, 79–80
European Union, 1, 2–3, 4, 19, 37, 49, 52–3, 66, 79–80, 92–3, 101, 149, 160, 175–6, 179–80, 185–6, 206–7, 217, 269, 276, 282–3
Ezra, Elizabeth, 202

Fekete, Ibolya, 7–8
Felicia înainte de toate, 148, 151; see also *First of all, Felicia*
Ferguson, James, 90–1
Fire with Fire, 117; see also Wolf, Naomi
First of all, Felicia, 148, 151; see also *Felicia înainte de toate*
Footsteps in the Sand, 138, 140; see also *Stapki v pyasaka*
Foucault, Michel, 121, 177, 182
Foxes, 5; see also *Lištičky*
France, 4–5, 6, 9, 10–11, 13–14, 17, 51–63, 150–1, 153, 160, 162–4, 166–7, 188, 196–7, 261, 267, 280–3, 285–7, 289–91
Francesca, 148, 151, 155
Freud, Sigmund, 172
Friedman, Victor, 209
Friedrich, Caspar David, 246, 249
Frodon, Jean-Michel, 291
Fulbrook, Mary, 241–2

Galt, Rosalind, 161
Gegen die Wand, 80, 86; see also *Head On*
German reunification, 27; see also *Die Wende*
Germany, 4, 6–7, 10–11, 16, 33, 44, 48, 85, 89–93, 101, 103, 105–6, 116–17, 133, 141, 155, 157, 177, 187, 196–9, 239–40, 241, 242, 244, 256, 265
Gilda, 114
Global South, 3–5, 66
Godard, 161–2, 166–7
Goldberg, Andreas, 89–90
Gondry, Michel, 107
Goskino, 178, 192
Gott, Michael, 46, 284
Graf, Dominik, 16, 238–9, 239–44, 244–5, 250–1
Gräftner, Barbara, 66
Greece, 6, 14, 18, 155, 158
Greek national cinema, 162–3, 168, 170
Greek national identity, 164–7
Greek 'weird wave', 14, 159–60, 169–70
Grønstad, Asbjørn, 68–9
Guattari, Félix, 186
Guédiguian, Robert, 17, 279–92
Gueneli, Berna, 8, 11
Gupta, Aghil, 90–1

Hajdu, Szabolcs, 109–24
Hall, Stuart, 146, 179
Hands in the Air, 5; see also *Les mains en l'air*
Haneke, Michael, 11, 51–63, 93
Hanna, 109–24
Harvey, David, 194
Head On, 80, 86; see also *Gegen die Wand*
Heart over Head, 42; see also *Herz im Kopf*
Heidegger, Martin, 127–8
Heimat, 95–6, 105, 107, 133, 146, 246
Heine, Matthias, 68
Heise, Thomas, 252–66
Helvetia, 42–3
Herz im Kopf, 42; see also *Heart over Head*
Higson, Andrew, 146, 162
Holocaust, 44–5, 48–9
Hundstage, 68; see also *Dog Days*
Hungarian–Romanian borderlands, 8–9, 82
Hungary, 6–7, 10–11, 18, 87, 89, 175–6

Il Deserto Rosso, 161; see also *Red Desert*
Im Juli, 8; see also *In July*
immigration, 4, 13–14, 43, 53, 111, 128, 131–7, 149, 154–5, 185–6
Import/Export, 11, 65–78, 111
Imre, Aniko, 18
In July, 8; see also *Im July*
Indigène d'Eurasie, 188, 190; see also *Eastern Drift*

Indignados, 4
Investigation, 134–5; *see also Razsledvane*
Iordanova, Dina, 179, 207–10, 175, 213, 216
Iraq, 4
Ireland, 185–6, 215
Iron Curtain, 2, 37, 153, 205–7
Italiencele, 148, 154; *see also The Italian Girls*
Italy, 4–5, 92, 154–7, 273, 276
Iztochni piesi, 134, 141; *see also Eastern Plays*

Jedliki, Jerzy, 211, 213
Jeunet, Jean-Pierre, 107
Jonsson, Stefan, 213

Kalandorok, 4; *see also Adventurers*
Kaplan, Ann, 120–1
Karalis, Vrasidas, 163
Kieslośki, Krzysztof, 51–63
Kolekcioniere, 180, 182–3; *see also Collectress*
Kopp, Kristin, 41
Koterski, Marek, 16, 221–36
Kristensen, Lars, 25–7
Kudelski, Stefan, 43
Kumar, Niven, 53
Kusturica, Emir, 122, 205, 210–15, 216, 218
Kuus, Merje, 207
Kynodontas, 159, 163; *see also Dogtooth*

L'or, 39, 42, 45; *see also Sutter's Gold*
La Double vie de Véronique, 51–6, 60; *see also The Double Life of Véronique*
La promesse, 5; *see also The Promise*
Lampedusa, 4
Landscape in the Mist, 159; *see also Topio stin omichli*
Lanthimos, Yorgos, 159–60, 163, 165
Last Resort, 111
Le Silence de Lorna, 111; *see also Lorna's Silence*
Le Voyage en Arménie, 17, 279–92; *see also Armenia*
Lefebvre, Henri, 184
Lepa sela, lepo gore, 205, 210–15; *see also Pretty Village, Pretty Flame*
Les mains en l'air, 5; *see also Hands in the Air*
Les Grandes Ondes (à l'ouest), 49–50; *see also Longwave*

Lévi-Strauss, Claude, 172
Lišticky, 5; *see also Foxes*
Lithuania, 6, 13, 14–15, 195–6, 174–90
Lithuanian national cinema, 174–90
Livanios, Dmitris, 206
Long distance Call, 148, 153; *see also Telefon în străinătate*
Longwave, 49–50; *see also Les Grandes Ondes (à l'ouest)*
Lorna's Silence, 111; *see also Le Silence de Lorna*
Los novios búlgaros, 5; *see also Bulgarian Lovers*
Loss is to be Expected, 67; *see also Mit Verlust ist zu rechnen*
Low Lights, 180, 182, 184, 185, 187; *see also Artimos šviesos*
Ludewig, Alexandra, 11–12

Macaitis, Saulius, 178
MacCabe, Colin, 52
Mannin, Ethel, 124
mapping, 1–19, 205
marginalisation, 160, 163, 164, 179
Marsden, John, 31
Marussia, 8
Massey, Doreen, 80, 81, 87–8
Massumi, Brian, 167–8, 171–2, 173
Material, 262
Mätzig, Kurt, 34
Mazierska, Ewa, 9, 12, 16, 91–2, 109, 149–50, 175, 185, 221, 226, 229
Mazower, Mark, 18
Mein Russland, 66; *see also My Russia*
migration, 1, 4–5, 6–7, 9, 11–12, 14, 16–17, 37–8, 89, 100–1, 109, 119–21, 128, 131–7, 146, 151, 154–5, 176, 179–80, 181, 185–9, 276
Mirek n'est pas parti, 8
Misiya London, 138, 143–4; *see also Mission London*
Mission London, 138, 143–4; *see also Misiya London*
Mit Verlust ist zu rechnen, 67; *see also Loss is to be Expected*
Mitchell, W. J. T., 32
mobility, 9, 12–13, 17, 34, 46, 77, 117, 118, 119, 123, 126, 146, 149, 156, 180, 185, 226, 241
female mobility, 12, 109–24
transnational mobility, 12, 37, 109
Morgen, 8 , 148, 151–2, 164, 156–7
Morzeck, Maria, 243

INDEX

My Beautiful Dacia, 151, 154; see also, *Dacia, dragostea mea*
My Russia, 66; see also *Mein Russland*
Naficy, Hamid, 91

national cinema, 6, 9–10, 14, 127–8, 146, 160–1, 162–7, 191–2, 194, 204
   international cinema, 161
   national identity, 4, 9, 128, 129–46, 148, 175–6, 178, 195, 222, 279–81, 281–4, 288–92
   supranational identity, 130
   transnational cinema, 111, 130, 202
   transnational identity, 149–50, 157
Nava, Mica and Mike Savage et al., 85
Navasaitis, Valdas, 177–8, 179–80, 182
Nazism, 109, 222
   Lebensborn project, 116
   neo-Nazism, 101
negative voyage, 37, 42
Neregiu žemė, 177–8; see also *The Earth of the Blind*
New Europe, 2, 4, 6–10, 11–12, 18, 79–93, 109, 112, 117, 121, 128, 130, 149–50, 167, 175, 189, 197–200, 205, 217–18, 225–30, 235, 236
New Greek wave, 3, 159–61, 164
New Romanian Cinema, 14, 16–17, 146–58, 267–77
Nietzsche, Friedrich, 127–8, 238
Nora, Pierre, 241
Nowhere Promised Land, 4; see also *Nulle part terre promise*
Nulle part terre promise, 4; see also *Nowhere Promised Land*
Nunta lui Oli, 148, 151; see also *Oli's Wedding*
Nuomos sutartis, 180, 182, 183, 184; see also *The Lease*

O'Brien, Mary Elisabeth, 27
O'Shaughnessy, Martin, 279
Oberschall, Anthony, 211
Occident, 148, 151, 152–3, 238
Oli's Wedding, 148, 151; see also *Nunta lui Oli*
orientalism, 15, 205–6, 208
   auto-orientalism, 208
   Balkan orientalism, 216
   Western orientalism, 208–9, 211
Orthodoxy, 2, 129, 209
Ostalgie, 16–17, 105, 239–40, 244, 267–77
Outbound, 147–8, 155; see also *Periferic*

Oxigen, 148, 151, 155; see also *Oxygen*
Oxygen, 148, 151, 155; see also *Oxigen*

Panossian, Razmik, 280, 288, 290
Paris, 52, 88, 257, 266
Parvulescu, Anca, 77–8, 123, 124
Patten, Chris, 206
Paul, David, 227
Periferic, 147–8, 155; see also *Outbound*
periphery, 18–19, 40, 47–8, 121–2, 159, 207–8
Perpetuum Mobile, 180–2, 183, 187, 190
Petzold, Christian, 16, 238–9, 244–9, 250–1
Pintilie, Lucian, 150–1
Podzemlje, 205, 210–14; see also *Underground*
Poland, 4–5, 10–11, 16, 18, 39–40, 44–6, 46–50, 51–61, 95, 98, 112–13, 175–6, 222–35, 266
Polish Plumber, 1
Portugal, 4
positive voyage, 37, 46
Post-wall German cinema and National History, 27
Pöttering, Hans Gert, 79
Prag, 9; see also *Prague*
Prague, 9; see also *Prag*
Pred doždot, 205, 208–10, 210–11, 215–16; see also *Before the Rain*
Pretty Village, Pretty Flame, 205, 210–14; see also *Lepa sela, lepo gore*
Pride and Prejudice, 112
primitivism, 18, 46
Puipa, Algimantas, 179, 186, 187

queering, 11

Rääk, Kaie-Ene, 201, 203
Raat, Marko, 191, 200–3
Rabbit à la Berlin, 10, 23–36
Rascaroli, Laura, 9, 12, 91–2, 109, 149–50, 185
Razsledvane, 134–5; see also *Investigation*
Red Desert, 161; see also *Il Deserto Rosso*
Redirected, 176, 187–8, 190; see also *Už Lietuvą!*
Reizen, Olga, 224–6
return road movie, 44, 284
Rezervni deli, 4; see also *Spare Parts*
Richter, Gerhard, 246, 249
road movie, 36, 44–6, 80, 82, 109, 153, 185, 198, 284–6

'road to Europe,' 10, 12
Romania 5, 6, 8–9, 13–14, 15–19, 52–3, 61–2, 63, 82–4, 110, 119, 121, 146–58, 267–77
Romney, Jonathan, 51–2
Rosello, Mirielle, 5–6
Rosenstone, Robert, 243
Rowden, Terry, 202

Salami Aleikum, 11–12, 95–108
Schengen Zone, 1, 187
Schilt, Thibaut, 46
Schmitt, Carl, 32
Schoonover, Karl, 161
Sebald, W. G., 249
Seidl, Ulrich, 11–12, 65–78, 111
Sepp, Edith, 195
Sieg, Katrin, 92
Silberman, 32
Silent River, 148, 151–2; see also *Apele tac*
Simm, Peeter, 191, 197–200, 203
Slovakia, 44, 67, 70–1, 175–6
Solina, 90
Some Secrets, 4; see also *Výlet*
Soul Kitchen, 80, 93
Soviet Union, 18, 47, 174, 186–8, 189, 192–4, 195–6
    USSR, 8, 18, 192, 196
Spain, 4–5, 19, 147–8, 154–5, 185, 253
Spare Parts, 4; see also *Rezervni deli*
Spiegelman, Art, 31
Squires, Michael, 83
Stapki v pyasaka, 138, 140; see also *Footsteps in the Sand*
Stealth, 11, 37–50; see also *Comme des voleurs (à l'est)*
Sundays on Leave, 148, 151–3; see also *E pericoloso sporgersi*
Sutter's Gold, 39, 42, 45; see also *L'or*
Sutter, Johann August, 39
Sutter, John, 42–6
Svetat e golyam i spasenie debne otvsyakade, 7, 9, 132, 133; see also *The World is Big and Salvation Lurks Around the Corner*
Swiatek, Lucyna, 53
Swinton, Tilda, 26–36
Swiss Confederation, 49
Switzerland, 5, 6, 10–11, 38, 39, 42–3, 45–6, 48–9, 50, 79, 93, 203, 265

Talasi, Flora, 118
Talvik, Artur, 199–200

Telefon în străinătate, 148, 153; see also *Long distance Call*
Terdiman, Richard, 29
The Day of the Wacko, 221–36; see also *Dzień świra*
The Double Life of Véronique, 51–6, 60; see also *La Double vie de Véronique*
The Earth of the Blind, 177–8; see also *Neregiu žemė*
The Edge of Heaven, 79–80, 86; see also *Auf der Anderen Seite*
The Idiots, 143
The Invisible Frame, 10, 23–36
The Island, 137–45
The Italian Girls, 148, 154; see also *Italiencele*
The Lease, 180, 182, 183, 184; see also *Nuomos sutartis*
The Lives of Others, 237, 244–5, 247, 248; see also *Das Leben der Anderen*
The Promise, 5; see also *La Promesse*
The Promise, 16, 250; see also *Das Versprechen*
The Rabbit is Me, 34, 243; see also *Das Kaninchen bin ich*
The Red Cockatoo, 16, 238–48; see also *Der rote Kakadu*
The Way I Spent the End of the World, 17, 148, 151, 267–9, 269–70; see also *Cum mi-am petrecut sfârșitul lumii*
The World is Big and Salvation Lurks Around the Corner, 7, 9, 132, 133; see also *Svetat e golyam i spasenie debne otvsyakade*
Three Colours, 52, 233; see also *Trois couleurs*
Three Days, 177, 186; see also *Trys dienos*
To vlemma tou Odyssea, 159; see also *Ulysses' Gaze*
Todorova, Maria, 207–8
Topio stin omichli, 159; see also *Landscape in the Mist*
Tout un hiver sans feu, 5; see also *A Long Winter without Fire*
trafficking, 12, 149
transnationalism, 154–5, 188
Transylvania, 9
travel, 12–14, 17, 37, 44–6, 53, 80–3, 84, 87, 89, 90, 91, 92, 102, 109–10, 121, 140, 149–50, 152–3, 155–9, 159, 187, 273, 275–6
travel games, 184–5
Trifonova, Temenuga, 14

Trois couleurs, 52, 233; *see also* *Three Colours*
Trojanowska, Tamara, 222
Trys dienos, 177, 186; *see also* *Three Days*
Tsangari, Athina Rachel, 159–74
Turkey, 4, 18–19, 79–80, 89–90, 92–3, 280, 282–3, 288–90

Ukraine, 5–6, 67, 73, 195–6
Ulysses' Gaze, 159; *see also* *To vlemma tou Odyssea*
Underground, 205, 210–14; *see also* *Podzemlje*
Une Estonienne à Paris, 8–9; *see also* *A Lady in Paris*
Urbla, Peeter, 196–7
Už Lietuvą!, 176, 187–8, 190; *see also* *Redirected*

Vélyvis, Emilis, 176, 179, 187–8
Vidor, Charles, 114
Vildžiūnas, Kristijonas, 179–80, 183
Voice-Over, 138, 139, 140; *see also* *Zad kadar*
von Trier, Lars, 143, 202
Výlet, 4; *see also* *Some Secrets*

Wajda, Adrzej, 221, 232–3, 236
Wang, Ban, 120–1

Warsaw Pact, 18
Welcome to Sarajevo, 205, 215–18
Wenders, Wim, 91
We're All Christs, 221–36; *see also* *Wszyscy jesteśmy Chrystusami*
Western Europe, 1–6, 8, 10–11, 14–15, 17–18, 38, 63, 66, 69–73, 80, 91–2, 122, 160–1, 167–9, 189, 205–6, 207–8, 210, 215–18, 268
Westphal, Anke, 25
When I want to whistle, I whistle, 147, 154–5, 157; *see also* *Eu când vreau să fluier, fluier*
White, 50, 232–3; *see also* *Blanc*
Wilhelm Tell, 42–6
Winterbottom, Michael, 205, 216–18
Wolf, Naomi, 117; *see also* *Fire with Fire*
Wright, Joe, 109–124
Wszyscy jesteśmy Chrystusami, 221–36; *see also* *We're All Christs*

You am I, 180, 183–4; *see also* *Aš esi tu*
Yugoslavia, 1, 5, 6, 8, 15, 18, 86 151–2, 207–8, 209, 210–14, 225, 272–3

Zad kadar, 138, 139, 140; *see also* *Voice-Over*
Zero II, 187–8, 190
Žižek, Slavoj, 209, 211–12

EU representative:
Easy Access System Europe
Mustamäe tee 50, 10621 Tallinn, Estonia
Gpsr.requests@easproject.com